INFLUENCING HUMAN BEHAVIOR

Theory and Applications in Recreation, Tourism, and Natural Resources Management

Michael J. Manfredo, Editor

SAGAMORE PUBLISHING INC.
Champaign, Illinois

BF
637
. P4
I54
1992

©1992 Sagamore Publishing Co., Inc.

All rights reserved. No part of this book may be reproduced in any form or by any means without written permission from the publisher.

Book design: Brian J. Moore
Cover design: Michelle R. Dressen
Copyeditor: Peter T. Tomaras
Proofreader: Phyllis L. Bannon

Printed in the United States of America

Library of Congress Catalog Card Number: 91-67445
ISBN: 0-915611-35-x

LONGWOOD COLLEGE LIBRARY
FARMVILLE, VIRGINIA 23901

Contents

- **Acknowledgments** _____ vii
- **Preface** _____ viii

1 **Persuasive Communication Theory in Social Psychology:**
A Historical Perspective
Icek Ajzen _____ 1

2 **A Theory of Behavior Change**
Martin Fishbein and Michael J. Manfredo _____ 29

3 **Attitude Accessibility and Its Consequences**
for Judgment and Behavior
Mark A. Vincent, Russell H. Fazio _____ 51

4 **The Elaboration Likelihood Model of Persuasion:**
Applications in Recreation and Tourism
Richard E. Petty, Stacey McMichael, Laura Brannon _____ 77

5 **Behavioral Systems Framework for Media-Based**
Behavior Change Strategies
Richard E. Winett _____ 103

6 **Mass Communication Research:**
Lessons for Persuasive Communication
Michael D. Slater _____ 127

7 **Use of Persuasion to Reduce Resource**
Impacts and Visitor Conflicts
Joseph W. Roggenbuck _____ 149

8 **A Multidisciplinary Model for Managing Vandalism**
and Depreciative Behavior in Recreation Settings
Richard C. Knopf, Daniel L. Dustin _____ 209

9 **Persuasive Communication and the Pricing**
of Public Leisure Services
Ronald E. McCarville, B.L. Driver, John L. Crompton ___ 263

10 **Persuasive Messages and Safety Hazards**
in Dispersed and Natural Recreation Settings
Stephen F. McCool, Amy M. Braithwaite _____ 293

11 **Research in Tourism Advertising**
. Manfredo, Alan D. Bright, Glenn E. Haas ____ 327

LONGWOOD LIBRARY

1000287670

Chapter Authors

1   Icek Ajzen is professor in the Department of Psychology, University of Massachusetts.

2   Martin Fishbein is professor in the Department of Psychology, University of Illinois. Michael J. Manfredo is an associate professor in the Department of Recreation Resources and Landscape Architecture, Colorado State University.

3   Mark A. Vincent is a graduate student in psychology at Indiana University. Russell H. Fazio is professor of psychology at Indiana University.

4   Richard E. Petty is professor of psychology at the Ohio State University. Stacey McMichael and Laura Brannon are doctoral students in the social psychology program at the same university.

5   Richard A. Winett is with the Center for Research in Health Behavior, Department of Psychology, Virginia Polytechnic Institute and State University.

6   Michael D. Slater is an assistant professor in the Department of Technical Journalism, Colorado State University.

7   Joseph W. Roggenbuck is an associate professor in the Department of Forestry, Virginia Polytechnic Institute and State University.

8   Richard C. Knopf is professor and coordinator in the Leisure Studies Program, Arizona State University. Daniel L. Dustin is professor in the Department of Recreation, San Diego State University.

9   Ronald E. McCarville is with the Department of Recreation and Leisure Studies, University of Waterloo, Canada. B.L. Driver is with the Rocky Mountain Forest and Range Experiment Station, USDA Forest Service. John L. Crompton is with the Department of Recreation and Parks, Texas A&M University.

10 Stephen F. McCool and Amy M. Braithwaite are with the School of Forestry, University of Montana.

11 Michael J. Manfredo, associate professor, Alan D. Bright, research assistant, and Glenn E. Haas, department chair, are all with the Department of Recreation Resources and Landscape Architecture at Colorado State University.

Acknowledgments

There are a number of people who have assisted in bringing this book to publication. The book would have remained just an idea if it were not for Dr. Robert Lucas's commitment to the effort. Upon Bob's retirement from the U.S. Forest Service, Alan Watson assisted in steering me to final completion of the effort. I am also indebted to Dr. Martin Fishbein, University of Illinois, who helped me in the initial stages of securing authors, and to Dr. Don Zimmerman, Colorado State University, who provided guidance in seeking authors and in locating a very fine editor, Robin Tabor.

Thanks also goes to Arch Woodside, Tulane University; Perry Brown, Oregon State University; Jim Fazio, University of Idaho and Maureen McDonough, Michigan State University for help in the review process.

The research for this book was supported in part by funds provided by the USDA Forest Service, Intermountain Research Station.

Michael J. Manfredo
Editor

Preface

In the fields of recreation, natural resource management, and tourism, we often hear that the solution to a management problem is communication or education. If we could instill a stronger environmental ethic, we would have fewer problems with vandalism, litter, and resource impacts. If we could explain the biological consequences of a controlled burn fire policy, we would, in the long run, have a healthier, more naturally functioning ecosystem. If we could show people that our town is an interesting destination for them to visit, our tourism industry would grow and we would realize a host of economic and social benefits. If we could make people understand wildlife biology, we'd have better support for the hunting programs we introduce.

Unfortunately, persuasive attempts to influence the public often meet with only modest success or fail entirely. There are any number of reasons a program might fail, not the least of which is that the realm of persuasion is highly competitive. A more basic reason is that we often embark upon our programs of influence with only weak understanding of the persuasion process. It is particularly true in public recreation and land management agencies that our egocentric view of the profession drives our attempts to persuade. In contrast to what persuasion theory would suggest, we provide information on a topic in *our* own language, with arguments that *we* accept, in a mode that *we* would typically attend to.

This reflects strongly on the teaching and research emphasis in the natural resources, recreation and tourism disciplines. It is interesting that, although professionals have reported using information and education prominently as a management tool, and the need for more research in the area of communication is often cited, a strong program of persuasion research is absent from the recreation, tourism and natural resources literature. Most of our communication research tends to be evaluative in nature and because it is not linked to broader concepts of persuasion or communication theory, the results are severely limited. Without the superordinate structure of theory, how do we determine the predictable and controllable influences as opposed to the unique, situational ones?

We embarked upon this book recognizing the need for more emphasis on persuasion theory in the recreation, natural resources and tourism disciplines. Consequently, one goal of the book was to overview the prominent theories of persuasion. To accomplish that goal, we turned to the persuasion theorists in social psychology. Social psychology is the basic behavioral science from which many of the applied fields such as advertising, marketing, political science, health, and journalism, obtain conceptual grounding in the persuasion area.

In the first chapter, Icek Ajzen reviews the development of persuasion theory in psychology. His review describes the early approaches to persuasion, through the long standing Hovland tradition, to the more recent developments of Theory of Reasoned Action and Elaboration Likelihood Model of Persuasion. The next two chapters deal with theories that model the relationship between attitudes and behavior. The validity of the attitude-causes-behavior explanation is key to theories of persuasion since a preponderance of these theories focus on attitude change as the route to influencing behavior. Whether or not attitudes cause behavior was a serious issue of debate during the late 1960s and early 1970s. It was the framework offered in Fishbein and Ajzen's Theory of Reasoned Action that marked a dramatic renewal of credibility for the attitude concept. In Chapter 2, Martin Fishbein and Mike Manfredo review the Theory of Reasoned Action and discuss its implications for behavioral prediction and persuasion in our applied disciplines.

Psychologists no longer question whether or not attitudes cause behavior, but they do recognize that there are times when attitudes don't influence behavior. One line of inquiry in this vein has focused on the process by which attitudes influence behavior. The most prominent theory in this area is Fazio's Process Model of Attitudes, which is described in Chapter 3 by Mark Vincent and Russell Fazio. These authors suggest that there are times when attitudes are not retrieved from memory and at these times situational and normative influences will dominate.

Chapter 4, by Richard Petty, Stacy McMichael and Laura Brannon introduces the reader to the Elaboration Likelihood Model of Persuasion (ELM). This theory has attained prominence among contemporary theories of persuasion. This theory proposes two routes to persuasion, a central route and a peripheral route. The central route involves the deliberative processing of the arguments within an appeal and the peripheral route focuses on persuasion that occurs due to factors tangential to the message. Recognition of this distinction has tremendous implications for researchers and for the management community, some of which are detailed in later chapters in the book.

In Chapter 5, Richard Winett overviews a behavior systems framework for media based behavior change strategies, developed largely through his work in the public health area. Winett illustrates how the framework might apply to a recreation management case. This approach is important because it incorporates a number of different theoretical traditions that have emerged in psychology. It is an attempt to provide a holistic model that is applicable in a variety of disciplines.

Finally, Michael Slater overviews advancements that have occurred in the area of mass communication theory. This chapter provides a highly readable overview of a very diverse field. The chapter describes media functions, media organizations, media as language, use of media and its effects, and segmenting audience for message design and channel selection.

The second goal of this book was to focus on several distinct areas in our applied disciplines, reviewing the existing literature and making suggestions for new theoretical directions in these areas. In Chapter 7, Joe Roggenbuck provides an extensive review of literature that has addressed the use of persuasion to reduce resource impacts and visitor conflicts. The effectiveness of persuasion for a variety of different management objectives is addressed. It also suggests the applicability of theories that distinguish high versus low information processing (such as ELM) for the use of persuasion when dealing with impact and conflict problems.

In Chapter 8, Rick Knopf and Dan Dustin focus on the topic of vandalism and depreciative behavior. These authors suggest that one of the main problems in managing this behavior is that we have failed to define the problem. Their approach advocates that we attempt to understand the goal of vandalistic behavior. They advocate a multidisciplinary model for examining vandalism and depreciative behavior.

Ron McCarville, Bev Driver and John Crompton look at the use of persuasion in influencing people's attitude toward paying for public recreation facilities. These authors present a thoughtful model of persuasion that would be applicable not only to the pricing issues but to a host of other problem areas. The model is particularly useful in how it integrates notions introduced by other authors in the book.

Steve McCool and Amy Braithwaite, in Chapter 10, examine the area of visitor safety and hazards. After defining what should be considered hazards in recreation settings, this chapter reviews theoretical approaches to hazard research found in psychology, geography, consumer behavior, and health. Building from Fishbein and Ajzen's Theory of Reasoned Action, these authors present a model of persuasive communication for hazards research.

Mike Manfredo, Alan Bright and Glenn Haas look at research in the area of tourism advertising. Their review determined that a significant focus of prior research has been on conversion studies that are plagued with a number of methodological problems. These researchers suggest that tourism advertising become more fully integrated with the methods and theory of consumer psychology. In a review of the consumer psychology area, they suggest that research focus on three areas; high versus low routes to persuasion, affective responses to advertising and verbal versus nonverbal effects in advertising.

In a recent speech to Regional Foresters of the Forest Service, Assistant Secretary of Agriculture James R. Mosley noted, "I have learned that what we need is a little more talking, more listening, more communication between forestry and society." I believe that most natural resources, recreation, and tourism professionals would agree with the main point of this statement as it might apply to their respective disciplines. We hope that some of the ideas presented in this book can assist in meeting the challenge of communication in recreation, tourism and natural resources.

Persuasive Communication Theory in Social Psychology: A Historical Perspective

Icek Ajzen

Few social psychology subjects have attracted as much attention as persuasive communication. One of the first topics to be systematically investigated, persuasion has been the focus of intense study throughout much of social psychology's brief scientific history. Researchers have conducted countless experiments to unravel the intricate web of factors that ostensibly influence the effectiveness of a persuasive message. Their efforts have revealed a degree of complexity that seems to defy explanation and to impede theory construction.

Recent research, however, has produced important progress at the theoretical level, and a resurgence of empirical work has invigorated the field and expanded understanding of the fundamental psychological processes underlying persuasion. To appreciate the significance of these developments, we must compare the emerging ideas and findings with those from earlier efforts.

Although social psychologists have rarely tested their ideas within the context of recreation and tourism, solving problems encountered in this field often involves persuasion in one form or another. As later chapters illustrate, recreationists must be persuaded to observe rules of safety, to avoid conflicts with other visitors, and to minimize their impact on the environment. The findings and conclusions presented in this chapter have clear implications for any attempts to influence beliefs, attitudes, and behavior in this domain.

The chapter's thrust is to provide the required historical perspective, reviewing developments in our understanding of the persuasion process, placing emphasis on ideas and theories rather than on methodological or practical concerns. When needed to make a point of theoretical significance, empirical research findings are summarized only in broad outline.

THE NATURE OF PERSUASION

Persuasive communication involves the use of verbal messages to influence attitudes and behavior. Although context must be considered, the verbal message designed to sway the hearts and minds of the receivers is at the core of persuasive communication. Through a process of reasoning, the message exerts its influence by force of its contained arguments.

Structure of a Message

As a general rule, a message consists of three parts: an advocated position, a set of general arguments in support of the advocated position, and specific factual evidence designed to bolster the general arguments (Fishbein and Ajzen, 1981). The advocated position may be a stand on a particular issue (e.g., support for a tax increase) or a recommended action (e.g., donating blood). The general arguments will typically supply reasons for adopting the advocated position, and factual evidence provides justification for the arguments.

Consider the question of instituting a senior comprehensive examination for undergraduate college students. Petty and Cacioppo (1986, pp. 54-59) published examples of general arguments and supportive evidence they have used in their research program. Among major arguments contained in Petty and Cacioppo's messages were claims that instituting a comprehensive exam raises students' grade point averages and improves the quality of undergraduate teaching. The factual evidence supporting the first argument was formulated as follows (pp. 54-55):

> The National Scholarship Achievement Board recently revealed the results of a five-year study conducted on the effectiveness of comprehensive exams at Duke University. The results of the study showed that since the comprehensive exam has been introduced at Duke, the grade point average of undergraduates has increased by 31%. At

comparable schools without the exams, grades increased by only 8% over the same period. The prospect of a comprehensive exam clearly seems to be effective in challenging students to work harder and faculty to teach more effectively. It is likely that the benefits observed at Duke University could also be observed at other universities that adopt the exam policy.

The factual evidence, if acceptable as valid, should result in acceptance of the argument for instituting a senior comprehensive exam; acceptance of the argument in turn should increase the likelihood that receivers will endorse the position in favor of instituting the exam, as advocated in the message. There is, of course, no assurance that receivers of the message will in fact accept the argument and its supporting evidence. Identifying the factors and conditions that produce acceptance of information contained in a message is the major purpose of persuasion theory and research.

Alternative Influence Strategies

Contrasting persuasion with a few alternative strategies develops a better understanding of the nature of persuasion. While far from exhaustive, the review presented here highlights some critical aspects of persuasive communication.

Coercive Persuasion

Offering a sizeable reward for compliance or threatening severe punishment for noncompliance can induce people to behave in a prescribed way. This strategy of change can be very effective in producing the desired behavior, but its effectiveness is contingent on supervision (French and Raven, 1959) and has few lasting effects on beliefs or attitudes.

Enduring attitude change through coercion is more likely in the context of total institutions such as prisons, mental hospitals, or prisoner-of-war camps. Such situations enable control over many aspects of an individual's life for extended periods. Even here, however, enduring attitude change is difficult to obtain and often fades after release from the institution (Schein, 1961).

Hypnosis and Subliminal Perception

Instead of trying to overcome resistance to change by coercion, one can attempt to circumvent conscious opposition by hypnosis or by presentation of subliminal messages. Posthypnotic induction can be used to instruct individuals to engage, upon awakening, in specified behaviors, or to hold new attitudes (Rosenberg, 1956). However, some researchers question whether hypnosis actually represents an altered state of consciousness that can be used to circumvent people's usual resistance to manipulation of their beliefs and actions (Barber, 1965; Wagstaff, 1981).

Effecting change through subliminal perception is similarly problematic. Its efficacy depends on presentation of information at an intensity level too low for conscious perception, yet high enough for it to enter unconscious or subconscious awareness. Clearly, such a fine balance demands careful calibration and, given individual differences in perceptual acuity, may not be achievable in a mass communication context. In any event, the effects of demonstrated subliminal perception on attitudes and behavior tend to be rather small (Erdelyi, 1974).

Conditioning and Affect Transfer

Another way of trying to avoid resistance to change involves the use of conditioning procedures. Researchers have argued that classical conditioning can change attitudes (Staats and Staats, 1958), and that the systematic use of reinforcements in an instrumental conditional paradigm can influence behavior (Krasner, 1958). Since the advantage of conditioning over direct persuasion rests on the assumed ability of conditioning to operate without awareness of the influence attempt, the extent to which individuals submitted to conditioning form hypotheses about systematic associations created in the conditioning paradigm is of crucial importance. Contrary to earlier claims, there now appears to be no convincing evidence that adult humans can be conditioned without awareness (Brewer, 1974).

An idea related to classical conditioning has emerged in recent marketing literature, where it has been proposed (Batra and Ray, 1986; Mitchell and Olson, 1981) that positive or negative affect elicited by one stimulus (the advertising) can transfer automatically to an associated stimulus (the advertised brand). This affect transfer, however, is assumed to occur only when individuals have no other, more informed basis for evaluating the brand in question (Shimp, 1981). Moreover, given the results of research on conditioning in human beings, it can be assumed that affect transfer, if it occurs at all, occurs only in the presence of awareness of the contingencies involved.

Subterfuge

Where previously discussed strategies all (in one way or another) try to prevent or neutralize awareness of, and thus resistance to, the influence attempt, subterfuge strategies subtly manipulate the situation in order to promote a psychological state that leads people to engage voluntarily in the desired behavior. The foot-in-the-door technique (Freedman and Fraser, 1966) and other sales ploys are good examples of this approach.

In the foot-in-the-door technique, a small request acceded to by most people is followed by a much larger request. Due presumably to the commitment produced by agreeing to the small request, conformity with the larger request tends to increase.

An alternative strategy involves first confronting a person with an unreasonably large request and then appearing to compromise by offering compliance with a smaller request. In a highly readable book, Cialdini (1988) describes ways in which subterfuge of this kind can elicit behaviors that otherwise might not be performed. Subterfuge strategies take advantage of people's various needs to reciprocate favors received, to be liked, to be consistent, and so forth. Compliance is secured without benefit of discussing the merits or costs of the requested action.

Heuristics

We have stated that most change via persuasive communication is based on careful deliberation of the pros and cons associated with an advocated position or action. In subsequent sections, however, we shall note that receivers of a message sometimes make judgments about the advocated position without going through an elaborate reasoning process. Instead, they may rely on heuristics or rules of thumb to arrive at a conclusion (Chaiken, 1980, 1987).

The most obvious heuristic in a persuasion context has to do with the communicator's credibility. The receiver may accept a position advocated in a message if the message comes from a highly credible source, but may reject it if the source is perceived to lack credibility. When using this rule of thumb, receivers accept or reject the advocated position without considering the merits of the arguments contained in the message.

Conclusions

We have shown that social influence can operate in a variety of ways, and that various strategies are available to take advantage of the different possibilities. Nevertheless, persuasive communication occupies a unique position in the matrix of social influence. It is the only one of all the available strategies that appeals to reason, attempting to effect change and compliance by convincing the receiver of the validity or legitimacy of the advocated position. This tactic can be much more difficult than, say, coercion, but it has important advantages. Besides being more compatible with democratic and humanistic values, persuasive communication can produce profound and lasting change, a goal not easily attained by other means.

THE PERSUASION CONTEXT

No message appears in a vacuum. At a minimum, we can usually identify the source of a message: a newspaper editorialist, a lawyer pleading a case before a jury, or a movie star soliciting charitable donations. The communication's source, however, is only one of many factors constituting the context of persuasive communication. Classical analysis (Lasswell, 1948) divides communication into distinct aspects that we can summarize as who says what, how, and to whom. More formally, these aspects are known as source, message, channel, and receiver factors; taken together, they constitute the context of persuasion.

Source Factors

Source factors are observed or inferred characteristics of the communicator. They include biological attributes such as age, race, height, and gender; behavioral features such as facial expressions, mannerisms, hand and body movements, and dress; social properties such as income, power, and social status; and personality traits such as self-confidence and extraversion.

The most frequently studied source factors, however, are the communicator's credibility and attractiveness. We earlier noted that persuasion is generally assumed to increase with credibility, which refers to the perceived expertise and trustworthiness of the communicator. In other words, does the communicator have the knowledge to provide an informed opinion on the issue in question and, if so, can he or she be trusted to present all relevant information without bias?

Researchers similarly propose that the source's attractiveness or likability influences the amount of change, whether attractiveness is defined in terms of physical features or psychological and behavioral characteristics.

Receiver Factors

On the opposite end of the communication context, parallel to source factors, are characteristics of the receiver or audience to whom the message is addressed. These characteristics include the receiver's personality traits, sex, social status, intelligence, involvement, and so on. Any attribute or combination of attributes of the receiver may provide a context contributing to the effectiveness of the message.

Channel Factors

We also define the context of the message by the means used to communicate it. Information can be communicated face-to-face, in writing, or by audio or video tape. Note that while the message content (the general arguments and factual evidence) may be held constant across channels, different communication modes often vary in terms of some context factors. For instance, the audience obtains more information about physical and behavioral characteristics of the source from face-to-face or video messages than from information presented orally or in writing. This makes it difficult in some instances to determine whether differences in persuasion stem from variations in the communication channel or from associated contextual differences that may confound the observed effect.

Message Factors

Message factors concern the ways in which information is communicated to the audience, and can produce potential confounding of a more serious kind because variations in message features are often accompanied by differences in content. Among factors considered are the order in which arguments are presented, one- versus two-sided presentations, and emotional versus non-emotional appeals (e.g., humorous or fear-arousing messages versus neutral ones).

To see why variations in message characteristics are often confounded with differences in message content, consider the case of one- versus two-sided communications. Clearly, to present both sides of an issue, an effective message must contain information and arguments not contained in a message supporting only the advocated position. In a two-sided message, the communicator mentions arguments that could be used to support the opposite side, then refutes those arguments. In addition, of course, the communicator also discusses the arguments in favor of the position his message advocates. Only the latter part is the same as or similar to the one-sided message.

With emotional versus neutral appeals, problems of confounding occur because humorous or fear-arousing communications generally contain information and arguments specifically designed to generate these emotions. This makes it difficult to separate the effects of the emotion from the effects due to differences in the information contained in humorous versus nonhumorous messages or in high- versus low-fear messages.

Situational Factors

The persuasion context contains several situational variables that do not fit easily into the traditional framework of source, message, channel, and receiver factors. Among these variables are distraction and forewarning. Distraction can result from environmental noise, or can be internal as when a receiver is preoccupied with other concerns. Forewarning refers to the availability of information before exposure to the message, which warns the receiver either that an influence attempt is imminent, or that the communicator is planning to advocate a certain position. In either case, forewarning may prepare receivers to rally their defenses against the forthcoming message.

The Hovland Tradition

Scientific work on persuasive communication began in earnest during World War II with attempts to determine the effects of wartime propaganda (Hovland, Lumsdaine, and Sheffield, 1949). In the 1950s, Carl Hovland directed a period of intensive experimental research at Yale University (Hovland, Janis, and Kelley, 1953; Sherif and Hovland, 1961). Though extremely prolific and influential, the Hovland-initiated research program produced few generalizable conclusions, leading to widespread disappointment with this approach by the late 1960s (Eagly and Himmelfarb, 1974; Fishbein and Ajzen, 1975). We will review the major lines of work in the Hovland tradition and some of the reasons for their failure.

Theoretical Orientation

The empirical work of the Hovland group was guided by a loose theoretical analysis based on learning principles, and by a conceptual framework that incorporated context variables (source, message, channel, and receiver factors), target variables (immediate attitude change, retention, behavior change), and mediating processes (attention, comprehension, and acceptance) (see McGuire, 1969, 1985). Briefly, the theoretical analysis of the Hovland group was based on learning principles, and assumed that attitude change involves learning a new response to a given stimulus (the attitude object). Exposure to a persuasive message suggests the new response (the advocated position) and provides an opportunity to practice the response. The various contextual factors were assumed to facilitate learning by reinforcing and firmly embedding the new response in the receiver's response hierarchy.

Empirical Research

The conceptual framework of context, target, and mediating variables (attention, comprehension, and acceptance) served to organize thinking about the persuasion process. However, much of the empirical research in the Hovland tradition dealt primarily with the impact of contextual factors. Thus, in the 1950s and 1960s, hundreds of studies examined the effects of source credibility and attractiveness; receiver intelligence, self-esteem, and involvement; fear appeals and order of presentation; distraction and forewarning; and a multitude of other contextual variables (see McGuire, 1985 for a recent review).

Little attention was devoted to the dependent variable that serves as the target of the communication, although persistence of change over time was an early concern (Cook and Flay, 1978). Of the mediating variables, only attention and comprehension were directly assessed. Thus, many studies contained a recall or recognition test to measure the degree to which the message was "received" (McGuire, 1968); that is, the degree to which the message was attended to and comprehended. Generally speaking, the test purported to insure that reception did not vary across conditions of the experiment, and that whatever effects were observed could not be attributed to differences in reception. In other words, the goal was usually to rid the experiment of the mediating effect of reception, rather than to study reception in its own right.

Note also that the conceptual framework had little to say about the content of persuasive communication and its role in the persuasion process. Message content was treated largely as a given, while the questions addressed involved the effects of contextual factors on the amount of change produced by the message. We shall see that this approach to the study of persuasive communication was one of the major reasons for the failure of the Hovland tradition.

Effects of source factors. One of the first lines of research initiated by the Hovland group dealt with the effects of communicator credibility (Hovland and Weiss, 1951), and innumerable studies since have manipulated this variable. Of all the contextual factors studied in the Hovland tradition, variations in source credibility have produced the most consistent findings. By and large, communicators high in expertise and trustworthiness tend to be more persuasive than communicators with low standing on these factors. However, even here, some contradictory evidence has been reported. Source credibility does not always increase the amount of change, and in some situations can even have a negative effect (McGuire 1985, p. 263).

Other source characteristics are generally found to have no simple or easily predictable effects on persuasion. The communicator's attractiveness, education, intelligence, social status, and so on can serve as cues for inferring expertise and can thus affect persuasion. However, these indirect effects do not appear to be strong enough to produce consistent results across different investigations.

Effects of receiver factors. Age, gender, intelligence, self-esteem and other individual differences among receivers are rarely found to have strong effects on persuasion, and the results of different investigations are often inconsistent. Moreover, receiver factors are found to interact in complex ways with each other and with additional factors such as the complexity of the message, the type of arguments used, the credibility of the communicator, and so on.

Effects of channel factors. A rather discouraging picture also emerged with respect to the effects of the medium of communication. While visual messages tend to be better liked and attended to than spoken or written messages, recall is sometimes better for written material, and adding pictures to print can be distracting (McGuire, 1985, p. 283). In light of these contradictory effects, it is hardly surprising that empirical research on channel factors has produced largely inconsistent results.

Effects of message factors. Some of the most complex patterns of findings are associated with message factors such as emotional versus nonemotional appeals, message style, and ordering of message content. With respect to the latter, consider for example whether one should state the message's basic position at the outset or at the end. Stating it at the beginning may have the advantage of clarity, making the source appear more trustworthy, and of attracting the attention of receivers sympathetic to the advocated position. It can also have the disadvantage, however, of lowering interest and antagonizing receivers initially opposed to the advocated position (McGuire 1985).

Other message factors can have equally complicated effects. To illustrate, consider the degree to which the message arouses fear or concern. Contrary to expectations, initial research (Janis and Feshbach, 1953) showed a low-fear message to be more effective than a high-fear message in producing compliance with recommended dental practices. Later research, however, has often found the opposite effect, and many investigations have reported no differences between high- and low-fear messages (for reviews, see Boster and Mongeau, 1985 and Higbee, 1969). Similarly inconsistent findings have emerged with respect to the effects of humor in persuasive communication (see Markiewicz, 1974).

Retrospective

In light of largely inconsistent research findings concerning the effects of contextual variables, many investigators became discouraged with the Hovland approach. Thus, after editing a book on attitude change in 1974, Himmelfarb and Eagly reached the following pessimistic conclusions:

> After several decades of research, there are few simple and   direct empirical generalizations that can be made concerning how to change attitudes. In fact, one of the most salient features of recent research is the great number of studies demonstrating that the empirical generalizations of earlier research are not general, but contingent on conditions not originally apparent (Himmelfarb and Eagly, 1974, p. 594).

In fact, the complexity of the persuasion process noted by Himmelfarb and Eagly in their reference to contingencies has been a favorite explanation for the failure of the Hovland approach. This explanation holds that persuasion is influenced by so many different factors interacting with each other that only complicated, multidimensional research strategies can cope with the complexities. However, when investigators have studied higher-order interactions, no clear or replicable patterns have emerged. Indeed, there is serious doubt that the search for complicated interactions can ever be a viable strategy (cf. Cronbach, 1975; Nisbett, 1977).

The role of the receiver. Besides failing to advance our understanding of the persuasion process, the complexity explanation had the unfortunate effect of hiding the basic shortcomings of the Hovland tradition and thus delaying the search for alternatives. As is usually the case, realizing where this approach went wrong is much easier in retrospect than it was at the time. Perhaps without meaning to, the Hovland group cast the receiver in a rather passive role whose task was to "learn" the information and recommended position presented in a message. Attention and comprehension would assure that the information was absorbed, and persuasion would thus follow automatically.

This view of the receiver stands in clear contradiction to much that is known about information processing. People are far from passive receivers of information. Instead, they usually act on the information that is available, integrating it (Anderson, 1971), constructing interpretations of their own (Neisser, 1976), and going in many ways beyond the information given (Bruner, 1957). This is just as true in the domain of attitudes as it is in other areas of information processing. For example, research on impression formation has shown that people draw far-ranging inferences about the attributes of another person on the basis of very limited information (Asch, 1946; Fishbein and Ajzen, 1975; Wiggins, 1973). Such inferences are often said to rely on "implicit theories of personality" (Schneider, 1973) that might suggest, among other things, that if a person is said to be hostile, he is also likely to be rash, aggressive, and inconsiderate.

Several other lines of research demonstrate more directly the potential importance of inference processes in persuasive communication. Thus it has been shown that a persuasive communication designed to produce a change in one belief will also lead to changes in other, related, beliefs (McGuire, 1960a; Wyer and Goldberg, 1970). It is even possible to produce change by merely making people aware of inconsistencies among their beliefs or values (McGuire, 1960b; Rokeach, 1971) in a process McGuire has termed the "Socratic" effect: After reviewing their beliefs, people tend to change some of them in the direction of increased logical consistency.

In short, there is every reason to expect that receivers exposed to a persuasive communication may engage in an active process of deliberation that involves reviewing the information presented, accepting some arguments, rejecting others, and drawing inferences about issues addressed that go beyond what was mentioned in the original message. The image of the passive learner fostered in the Hovland tradition is thus highly misleading, and misses the most important aspect of persuasive communication: the receiver's capacity for reasoning and for being swayed by the merits of a well-presented argument.

Persuasion by the Peripheral Route

The passive-learner view of the receiver implicit in the Hovland approach quite naturally led to a focus on the persuasion context. If the communicator's task is to make sure that receivers learn and absorb the contents of the message, concern turns to a search for conditions that facilitate attention to the message and comprehension of its arguments, with a concomitant lessening of interest in what the receiver does with the information that is received. Ironically, recent theory and research have established the potential importance of contextual factors, at least under certain well-specified conditions. Once we realize what these conditions are, we can begin to understand the reasons for the inconsistent findings of research conducted within the Hovland paradigm. In the previous section we emphasized the active role of the receiver who may engage in an elaborate process of reasoning about the merits of the arguments presented in the message. This view assumes, first, that receivers are in fact sufficiently motivated to exert the required cognitive effort and, second, that they have the ability to carefully process the incoming information. It now appears that contextual factors influence persuasion only when one or both of these conditions are not met (Chaiken, 1980; Petty and Cacioppo, 1981, 1986).

Motivation to process the message and elaborate on it is largely a matter of the receiver's involvement. Different aspects of the self may be activated in a given situation, depending largely on the issue addressed, and as a result, different kinds of involvement can be generated. Specifically, the message may create involvement by dealing with receivers' enduring values, with receivers' ability to obtain desirable outcomes or avoid undesirable outcomes, or with the impression receivers make on others (Johnson and Eagly, 1989). However, when the message has few implications for enduring values, for important outcomes, or for self-presentation, it produces little motivation to carefully deliberate its contents.

Ability to process a message is related to factors internal to the receiver as well as to external factors. Among the internal factors are familiarity with the issues and cognitive ability and intelligence, factors that tend to increase capacity for information processing; and preoccupation with other matters and lack of time, which tend to reduce the ability to elaborate. External factors that increase the ability to process include message repetition and clarity of presentation, while external distraction and use of complicated language can reduce processing ability. Some of the contextual factors studied by the Hovland group can come into play when internal or external factors lower the receiver's ability to process the information presented in the message.

Empirical Research

When ability and motivation to process the message are low, receivers can use peripheral cues (Petty and Cacioppo, 1986) or cognitive heuristics (Chaiken, 1980) to form their opinions. Chaiken assumed that receivers of a message, even if they are not very greatly involved, nevertheless are motivated to hold a "correct" view on the issue. Since, under conditions of low motivation and ability, receivers are either incapable or unwilling to deal with the merits of the advocated position, they look for contextual or peripheral cues that might provide a basis for forming an opinion. Perhaps the most powerful such cue is the communicator's credibility, and it may be argued that this is the reason for the relatively consistent findings associated with communicator credibility. The heuristic strategy might in this case involve the following line of reasoning: "If this expert on the matter says so, it must be right." This heuristic appears quite reasonable in that it accepts the position advocated by a credible source, even if one has not carefully scrutinized the arguments presented.

Receivers can also use the source's attractiveness, or factors related to the message such as the number of arguments it contains, as peripheral cues. Thus, a message coming from a liked source might be viewed as more trustworthy, and one that contains many arguments (even if specious) might be seen as more reliable than a message that contains few arguments. Note, however, that these rules of thumb are far less convincing as a rational basis for accepting or rejecting an advocated position, and it is perhaps for this reason that factors of this kind often fail to have strong or consistent effects on persuasion. In any event, relying on heuristics obviates the need for careful message processing, and at the same time provides a basis for adoption of a position on the issue.

Recent empirical research tends to support this view of the peripheral route to persuasion, although some complications have recently been noted (Johnson and Eagly, in press). Since excellent reviews are available elsewhere (Chaiken, 1987; Petty and Cacioppo,1986), we limit our discussion here to an example concerning the effects of source characteristics. Recall that communicator attractiveness was one of the source characteristics studied in the Hovland paradigm that did not have a clear and consistent effect on persuasion. If treated as a peripheral cue used only when processing motivation or ability is low, more consistent findings tend to emerge. Attractiveness of the source has been varied by attributing the message to famous versus unknown individuals (Petty, Cacioppo, and Schumann, 1983) or to a likable versus an unlikable person (Chaiken, 1980). The investigators also manipulated the degree of involvement and found, as expected, that communicator attractiveness has a significantly greater effect on persuasion under low than under high involvement.

Conclusions

Work on the peripheral route to persuasion suggests that the source, message, channel, and receiver factors studied in the Hovland tradition can indeed influence the effectiveness of a message, but that this is likely to be the case only under conditions of low motivation or low ability to process the message. Such conditions can be obtained in the psychological laboratory that ensures some degree of attention by a captive audience even if the receivers have little interest in the topic or lack the ability to process the information presented (Hovland, 1959).

In more naturalistic field settings, receivers who lack the motivation or ability to process a message can usually leave the situation, while those who remain and are exposed to the message will tend to be sufficiently involved and able to process the information it contains. Persuasion by the peripheral route is clearly an inappropriate model for many realistic situations, and it is often inapplicable even in the artificial context of the laboratory.

REASONING AND PERSUASION

Even when it works, there is something distinctly unsatisfactory in the demonstration of change via the peripheral route, because the change brought about does not represent persuasion as we usually think of it. We noted at the beginning that it is the process of reasoning, the evaluation of the merits of arguments in favor and opposed to the advocated position, that is at the heart of persuasive communication. Persuasion involves more than simply going along with an expressed point of view because of the presence of some peripheral cue; it requires that the advocated position be accepted only after careful scrutiny of the message and after application of whatever other information the receiver can bring to bear.

Moreover, change produced by the peripheral route is generally of little practical significance. Petty and Cacioppo (1986) noted that peripheral attitude change tends to be short-lived, tends to be susceptible to counterpropaganda (McGuire, 1964), and tends to have little effect on actual behavior. Clearly then, from both a theoretical and a practical point of view it would be to our advantage to focus less on the context of persuasion and more on the central processes that occur when a person is exposed to a message.

Persuasion by the Central Route

In the remainder of this chapter we examine persuasion that occurs when the receiver of a message is sufficiently able and motivated to give at least some scrutiny to the contents of the communication and to evaluate the merits of the arguments it contains. This has been termed the central route to persuasion (Pettyand Cacioppo, 1981) and the deliberations receivers perform are known as systematic information processing (Chaiken, 1980). Instead of asking what makes a given message more effective, we must now ask how to construct an effective message. That is, what arguments, when systematically processed via the central route, will have the greatest impact on the receiver's attitudes and behavior? Before we can review what is known about this question, however, we must consider the role of the receiver in greater detail.

The Elaboration Likelihood Model

The peripheral route to persuasion discussed earlier is one of two tracks a receiver can take in Petty and Cacioppo's (1981, 1986) elaboration likelihood model (ELM). The second track is persuasion via the central route. According to the ELM, central route persuasion depends on and is determined by the degree to which receivers elaborate on the information presented in the message. Briefly, during exposure to a persuasive communication, receivers are assumed to generate arguments of their own, either in support of the advocated position (pro arguments) or opposed to it (con arguments). These cognitive responses determine the direction and degree of change in attitudes and behavior.

Increased motivation and ability to process the information in the message is, according to the model, associated with an increase in the number of cognitive responses (pro and con arguments) generated. To the extent that the number of arguments generated on the pro side exceeds the number of arguments on the con side, the receiver will change in the advocated direction. When elaboration leads to the production of more con than pro arguments, however, either no change or a "boomerang effect" (change in the opposite direction) may occur.

From the communicator's point of view, therefore, motivation and ability to elaborate on message content is a two-edged sword. If, on balance, the thoughts generated by the receiver favor the advocated position, then the central route to persuasion works to the communicator's advantage. On the other hand, if the receiver's cognitive responses consist predominantly of counterarguments, then elaboration on message content can be quite detrimental to the communicator's purpose.

A number of studies, summarized in Petty and Cacioppo (1986), have examined the role of cognitive responses in the persuasion process. In these studies, cognitive responses are elicited in a free-response format following exposure to the message. The thoughts listed by the receivers are coded as either in favor or opposed to the advocated position, and the number of responses of each type is determined. Results, by and large, support the idea that the production of cognitive responses increases with motivation and ability to elaborate. Moreover, it is also found that changes in attitudes and behavior are consistent with the pattern of cognitive responses that are generated: a balance of thoughts in favor of the advocated position tends to be associated with change in the desired direction.

Yielding and Impact

Consideration of cognitive responses generated by receivers in the course of exposure to the message is, however, not sufficient to account for observed changes in attitudes and behavior. For change to occur in the central mode, some of the receiver's fundamental beliefs and values must undergo modification. Elaboration on the message may in fact lead to changes in cognitive structure, but evidence for the production of pro- or counter-arguments does not, in itself, assure that such changes have indeed taken place.

Work on the elaboration likelihood model has focused primarily on cognitive responses to the message and has not dealt directly with changes in cognitive structure. The ideas discussed below are based on other recent work concerning persuasive communication via the central route (Fishbein and Ajzen, 1975, 1981). According to Fishbein and Ajzen, a message can bring about changes in a receiver's cognitive structure in one of two ways. First, in a process termed yielding, acceptance of arguments presented in the message can produce changes in corresponding beliefs held by the receiver. Consider, for example, a pregnant smoker who initially is not aware that cigarette smoking can adversely affect the health of her unborn baby. This woman is now exposed to a message containing an argument and supportive evidence that establish the link between smoking and adverse health effects on the fetus. To the extent that the argument is accepted, it produces yielding in the sense that the woman's cognitive structure now contains a new belief that corresponds directly to the argument in question. That is, she now believes, as stated in the message, that smoking may have ill effects on her unborn baby.

Changes in a receiver's primary beliefs, however, can extend far beyond the information directly contained in the message. Such changes that go beyond the information given are termed impact effects. To illustrate, the pregnant woman exposed to the message that smoking can have detrimental health effects on her fetus may infer that she would feel guilty if she did not stop smoking and that her doctor would want her to quit, even though neither argument was explicit in the message. It is also possible, however, for her to draw inferences that would work against the aims of the communicator. For example, the woman may unexpectedly form the belief that quitting would be even worse than continued smoking because it would result in overeating. These impact effects can, of course, play a major role in the woman's decision to quit or not to quit smoking. Evidence for the importance of considering yielding as well as impact effects can be found in a study on drinking reported in Ajzen and Fishbein (1980, pp. 218-242).

Persuasive Argumentation

The challenge facing a communicator trying to produce change via the central route is to create a message that will originate favorable responses, produce yielding to its arguments, and generate impact effects in accordance with the advocated change. Arguments contained in a message can be considered effective to the extent that they influence the receiver's cognitive structure. The essential question, therefore, is what makes an argument effective.

Considering that rhetoricians have written about argumentation for over 2,000 years, it is surprising how little empirical knowledge is available about the relative effectiveness of different types of arguments (McGuire, 1985). An analysis of this problem reveals at least three important aspects of an argument's effectiveness: novelty, strength, and relevance.

Argument Novelty

An argument contained in a message may well be accepted (i.e., believed to be true), but if the receiver already held the belief in question before exposure to the message, no change in belief structure would result (Fishbein and Ajzen, 1981). To be effective therefore, an argument contained in a message must not be part of the receiver's initial belief system. Some empirical evidence for this proposition can be found in research on group decision making (Vinokur and Burnstein, 1974). In the course of group discussions, members who offer novel arguments in support of a given decision alternative are found to be more influential than members who raise points that are well known to the rest of the group.

Argument Strength

Besides being novel, an argument must also be strong if it is to sway the receiver to adopt the advocated position. A strong argument is one that tends to produce agreement (positive thoughts) and does not generate many counterarguments (Petty and Cacioppo, 1986). Although it is not clear what makes a strong argument, its strength or weakness can be empirically established. Earlier in this chapter we gave an illustrative example of a persuasive argument taken from Petty and Cacioppo's (1986) research program. The argument asserted that instituting a senior comprehensive examination would raise grade point averages (see p. 2-3). This argument and the associated evidence make a strong case for the advocated position.

Compare this to the following argument, also designed to generate support for a comprehensive exam:

> The National Scholarship Achievement Board recently revealed the results of a study conducted on the effectiveness of comprehensive exams at Duke University.

One major finding was that student anxiety had increased by 31%. At comparable schools without the exam, anxiety increased by only 8%. The Board reasoned that anxiety over the exams, or fear of failure, would motivate students to study more in their courses while they were taking them. It is likely that this increase in anxiety observed at Duke University would also be observed and be of benefit at other universities that adopt the exam policy (Petty and Cacioppo, 1986, p. 57).

Although this argument is quite similar in structure to the strong argument presented earlier, it appears to present a much weaker case. In fact, this argument is typically found to generate many counterarguments. Clearly, in order to create an effective message, it is in the communicator's interest to select strong arguments and avoid including arguments that tend to elicit negative thoughts about the advocated position.

Argument Relevance
Related to the question of an argument's strength is its relevance to the advocated position. An argument may be strong in the sense that it generates few counterarguments and many pro arguments, but if it addresses an issue that is not directly relevant to the advocated position, it may fail to produce the desired effect. This point is often not sufficiently appreciated.

Suppose a communicator would like to convince students to attend an anti-apartheid demonstration in Washington, D.C., and thus exposes the students to a persuasive message against apartheid in South Africa. Although the arguments contained in the message may be strong in the sense that they are believable and generate few counterarguments, the message may not be very effective as a means of inducing students to go to Washington. To make the message more relevant in terms of this goal, one would have to include strong arguments that deal more directly with the advantages of attending the planned demonstration.

A relevant argument, then, is one that changes those primary beliefs of the receiver that are directly related to the target of the influence attempt, that is, to the attitude or behavior the communicator wishes to affect. Different target variables are based on different primary beliefs, and an effective message must be tailored to fit the target in question.

Target Variables
Although it is beyond the scope of this chapter to provide an in-depth review, discussions of different target variables and their respec-

tive foundations of primary beliefs can be found in Fishbein and Ajzen (1975, 1981) and in Fishbein and Manfredo (Chapter 2, this volume). Briefly, Fishbein and Ajzen distinguish among beliefs, attitudes, intentions, and behaviors as possible targets of a persuasive communication. To effect a change in any one of these target variables, the message arguments must be directed at the primary beliefs that provide the basis for the target in question. The first step in the construction of a message, therefore, requires a decision about the relevant primary beliefs, a process that cannot be left to intuition but must be guided by a model of the target's determinants.

Social psychologists have discussed a variety of approaches to understanding beliefs and attitudes and their relations to behavior, but perhaps the most popular models can be found within the framework of the Theory of Reasoned Action (Fishbein and Ajzen, 1975; Ajzen and Fishbein, 1980) and its recent extension, the theory of planned behavior (Ajzen, 1985, 1988). The discussion below considers each target variable in turn; however, a full understanding of the process is gained only by considering the relations among the different variables.

Changing behavior. According to the theory of reasoned action, many behaviors of interest to social psychologists are under volitional control and, hence, are in an immediate sense determined by the intention to perform the behavior in question. A successful persuasive communication designed to change a certain behavior must therefore contain arguments that will bring about a change in the antecedent intention. The theory of planned behavior goes beyond the question of intended action, taking into account the possibility that the behavior of interest may not be completely under volitional control. To be successful, the message may have to provide information that will enable the receiver to gain volitional control and overcome potential obstacles to performance of the behavior. A review of evidence in support of these propositions can be found in Ajzen (1988).

Changing intentions. The antecedents of behavioral intentions are, according to the theory of reasoned action, the person's attitude toward the behavior and his or her subjective norm. The attitude toward the behavior refers to the evaluation of the behavior as desirable or undesirable, and the subjective norm is the perceived social pressure to perform or not to perform the behavior in question. The theory of planned behavior again adds to this model a consideration of volitional control. When issues of control arise, intentions are influenced not only by attitudes and subjective norms but also by perceived behavioral control (Ajzen and Madden, 1986; Schifter and Ajzen, 1985). A persuasive communication designed to influence intentions (and thus also behavior) can be directed at one or more of the intention's three determinants: attitudes, subjective norms, and perceived behavioral control.

Changing attitudes. We arrive at the level of primary beliefs as we consider the determinants of a person's attitudes. According to the theory of reasoned action, attitudes are a function of salient beliefs about the attitude object (a person, group, institution, behavior or other event). Each salient belief links the object to an attribute or to an outcome in the case of a behavior. The attitude is determined by the strength of these beliefs and by the evaluations associated with the attributes (Fishbein, 1963; Ajzen and Fishbein, 1980). Beliefs about the attitude object that are salient prior to presentation of the message can be elicited in a free-response format. The message is then constructed such that it will either change some of the existing beliefs, either in their strength or their evaluations, or introduce new beliefs into the belief system.

Changing beliefs. To change a specific belief on an issue, the persuasive communication has to address some of the information on which the belief is based. Several probabilistic models that link prior information to a given belief have been proposed and validated (McGuire, 1960b; Wyer and Goldberg, 1970; for a review see Slovic, Fischhoff, and Lichtenstein, 1977). These models suggest that the information introduced by the persuasive communication must be information from which the belief in question can be probabilistically inferred.

Conclusions
The focus in recent years on the central route to persuasion holds great promise for a better understanding of persuasive communication. This route deals with the essence of the persuasion process, with changes in the fundamental beliefs on which the receivers' attitudes and actions are based. Although much remains to be done, social psychologists have gained considerable insight into some of the cognitive processes that are at work during and after exposure to a persuasive communication, and into the practical aspects of constructing an effective message.

SUMMARY

This chapter presented a brief historical perspective on persuasive communication theory in social psychology. No attempt was made to discuss all theoretical developments in detail as this task would require a book in itself. Instead, the focus was on a few dominant lines of theoretical development, from the beginnings of scientific research on persuasion in the 1940s to the present day.

The work initiated by Hovland and his associates tended to view the receivers of a persuasive communication as passively learning the information presented and then changing their beliefs and attitudes accordingly. This view led to a concern with contextual factors, and virtual neglect of the contents of the communication and its processing by the receiver. Few generalizable conclusions emerged from the research guided by this approach, and by the late 1960s the failure of the Hovland approach was widely acknowledged.

Progress was recorded when attention turned from contextual or peripheral factors to persuasion via the central route. Contextual factors were found to be important only under conditions of low involvement or low ability to process the message. It was discovered, however, that as a general rule, receivers of a message are far from passive, engaging in an active process of analyzing and elaborating on the information presented. It became clear that the effects of a persuasive communication could not be understood unless careful attention was given to these cognitive processes.

Theoretical and empirical developments of the past two decades have enabled us to consider receivers' cognitive responses during exposure to a message, yielding to the arguments contained in the message, and the message's impact on other beliefs not explicitly mentioned. These developments have also resulted in a much closer examination of the contents of persuasive communications, with an eye toward selecting arguments that will have the maximum effect on the target of the influence attempt. In this way, the theoretical developments of recent years have important implications for the practitioner who is concerned with constructing effective persuasive communications.

REFERENCES

Ajzen, I. 1985. From intentions to actions: A theory of planned behavior. In: J. Kuhl & J. Beckmann, (eds.) *Action-control: From cognition to behavior*. Heidelberg: Springer: 11-39.

Ajzen, I. 1988. *Attitudes, personality, and behavior*. Chicago: Dorsey Press.

Ajzen, I., & Fishbein, M. 1980. *Understanding attitudes and predicting social behavior*. Englewood-Cliffs, NJ: Prentice-Hall.

Ajzen, I., & Madden, T. J. 1986. Prediction of goal-directed behavior: Attitudes, intentions, and perceived behavioral control. *Journal of Experimental Social Psychology, 22*: 453-474.

Anderson, N. H. 1971. Integration theory and attitude change. *Psychological Review, 78*: 171-206.

Asch, S. E. 1946. Forming impressions of personality. *Journal of Abnormal and Social Psychology, 41*: 258-290.

Barber, T. X. 1965. Physiological effects of 'hypnotic suggestions': a critical review of recent research. *Psychological Bulletin, 4*: 201-222.

Batra, R., & Ray, M. L. 1986. Affective responses mediating acceptance of advertising. *Journal of Consumer Research, 13*: 234-249.

Boster, F. J., & Mongeau, P. 1985. Fear-arousing persuasive messages. In: R. N. Bostrom, (ed.) *Communication Yearbook, Vol. 8*. Beverly Hills, CA: Sage: 330-375.

Brewer, W. F. 1974. There is no convincing evidence for operant or classical conditioning in adult humans. In: W. B. Weimer & D. S. Palermo, (eds.) *Cognition and the symbolic processes*. Hillsdale, NJ: Erlbaum: 1-42.

Bruner, J. S. 1957. On going beyond the information given. In: H. E. Gruber, K. R. Hammond, & R. Jessor, (eds.) *Contemporary approaches to cognition*. Cambridge, MA: Harvard University Press: 41-69.

Chaiken, S. 1980. Heuristic versus systematic information processing and the use of source versus message cues in persuasion. *Journal of Personality and Social Psychology, 39*: 752-766.

Chaiken, S. 1987. The heuristic model of persuasion. In: M. P. Zanna, J. M. Olson, & C. P. Herman, (eds.) *Social Influence: The Ontario Symposium, Vol. 5*. Hillsdale, NJ: Erlbaum: 3-39. Cialdini, R. B. 1988. Influence: Science and practice, 2nd Ed. Glenview, IL: Scott, Foresman.

Cook, T. D., & Flay, B. R. 1978. The persistence of experimentally induced attitude change. In: L. Berkowitz, (ed.) *Advances in experimental social psychology, Vol. 11*. New York: Academic Press: 1-57.

Cronbach, L. J. 1975. Beyond the two disciplines of scientific psychology. *American Psychologist, 30:* 116-127.

Eagly, A. H., & Himmelfarb, S. 1974. Current trends in attitude theory and research. In: S. Himmelfarb & E. H. Eagly, (eds.) *Readings in attitude change*. New York: Wiley: 594-610.

Erdelyi, M. H. 1974. A new look at the new look: perceptual defense and vigilance. *Psychological Review, 81*: 1-25.

Fishbein, M. 1963. An investigation of the relationships between beliefs about an object and the attitude toward that object. *Human Relations, 16*: 233-240.

Fishbein, M., & Ajzen, I. 1975. *Belief, attitude, intention, and behavior: An introduction to theory and research.* Reading, MA: Addison-Wesley.

Fishbein, M., & Ajzen, I. 1981. Acceptance, yielding, and impact: Cognitive processes in persuasion. In: R. E. Petty, T. M. Ostrom, & T. C. Brock, (eds.) *Cognitive responses in persuasion.* Hillsdale, NJ: Erlbaum: 339-359.

French, J. R. P., & Raven, B. H. 1959. The bases of social power. In: D. Cartwright (ed.), *Studies in social power.* Ann Arbor: University of Michigan Press: 118-149.

Freedman, J. L., & Fraser, S. C. 1966. Compliance without pressure: The foot-in-the-door technique. *Journal of Personality and Social Psychology, 4*: 195-203.

Higbee, K. L. 1969. Fifteen years of fear arousal: Research on threat appeals: 1953-1968. *Psychological Bulletin, 72*: 426-444.

Himmelfarb, S., & Eagly, A. H., (eds.) 1974. *Readings in attitude change.* New York: Wiley.

Hovland, C. I. 1959. Reconciling conflicting results derived from experimental and survey studies of attitude change. *American Psychologist, 14*: 8-17.

Hovland, C. I., Janis, I. L., & Kelley, H. H. 1953. *Communication and persuasion.* New Haven: Yale University Press.

Hovland, C. I., Lumsdaine, A. A., & Sheffield, F. D. 1949. *Experiments on mass communication.* Princeton, NJ: Princeton University Press.

Hovland, C. I., & Weiss, W. 1951. The influence of source credibility on communication effectiveness. *Public Opinion Quarterly, 15*: 635-650.

Janis, I. L., & Feshbach, S. 1953. Effects of fear-arousing communications. *Journal of Abnormal and Social Psychology, 48*: 78-92.

Johnson, B. T., & Eagly, A. H. 1989. The effect of involvement on persuasion: A meta-analysis. *Psychological Bulletin, 106*: 290-314.

Krasner, L. 1958. Studies of the conditioning of verbal behavior. *Psychological Bulletin, 55*: 148-170.

Lasswell, H. D. 1948. The structure and function of communication in society. In: L. Bryson (Ed.), *Communication of ideas.* New York: Harper.

Markiewicz, D. 1974. Effects of humor on persuasion. *Sociometry, 37*: 407-422.

McGuire, W. J. 1960a. Cognitive consistency and attitude change. *Journal of Abnormal and Social Psychology, 60*: 345-353.

McGuire, W. J. 1960b. A syllogistic analysis of cognitive relationships. In: C. I. Hovland & M. J. Rosenberg, (eds.) *Attitude organization and change.* New Haven, CT: Yale University Press: 65-111.

McGuire, W. J. 1964. Inducing resistance to persuasion: Some contemporary approaches. In: L. Berkowitz, (ed.) *Advances in experimental social psychology, Vol. 1.* New York: Academic Press: 191-229.

McGuire, W. J. 1968. *Personality and susceptibility to social book of personality theory and research.* Chicago: Rand McNally: 1130-1187.

McGuire, W. J. 1969. The nature of attitudes and attitude change. In: G. Lindzey & E. Aronson, (eds.) *The handbook of social psychology, 2nd Ed.,* Vol. 3. Reading, MA: Addison-Wesley: 136-314.

McGuire, W. J. 1985. Attitudes and attitude change. In: G. Lindzey & E. Aronson, (eds.) *The handbook of social psychology, 3rd Ed.,* Vol. 2. New York: Random House: 233-346.

Mitchell, A. A., & Olson, J. C. 1981. Are product attribute beliefs the only mediator of advertising effects on brand attitude? *Journal of Marketing Research, 18*: 318-332.

Neisser, U. 1976. *Cognition and reality: Principles and implications of cognitive psychology.* San Francisco: Freeman.

Nisbett, R. E. 1977. Interaction versus main effects as goals of personality research. In: D. Magnusson & N. S. Endler, (eds.) *Personality at the crossroads: Current issues in interactional psychology.* New York: Wiley: 235-241.

Petty, R. E., & Cacioppo, J. T. 1981. *Attitudes and persuasion: Classic and contemporary approaches.* Dubuque, Iowa: Wm. C. Brown.

Petty, R. E., & Cacioppo, J. T. 1986. *Communication and persuasion.* New York: Springer Verlag.

Petty, R. E., Cacioppo, J. T., & Schumann, D. 1983. Central and peripheral routes to advertising effects: The moderating role of involvement. *Journal of Consumer Research, 10*: 134-148.

Rokeach, M. 1971. Long-range experimental modification of values, attitudes, and behavior. *American Psychologist, 26*: 453-459.

Rosenberg, M. J. 1965. Inconsistency arousal and reduction in attitude change. In: I. D. Steiner & M. Fishbein, (eds.) *Current studies in social psychology.* New York: Holt, Rinehart, & Winston: 121-134.

Schein, E. H. 1961. *Coercive Persuasion.* New York: Norton.

Schifter, D. B., & Ajzen, I. 1985. Intention, perceived control, and weight loss: An application of the theory of planned behavior. *Journal of Personality and Social Psychology, 49*: 843-851.

Schneider, D. J. 1973. Implicit personality theory: A review. *Psychological Bulletin, 79*: 294-309.

Sherif, M., & Hovland, C. I. 1961. *Social judgment: Assimilation and contrast effects in communication and attitude change.* New Haven, CT: Yale University Press.

Shimp, T. A. 1981. Attitude toward the ad as a mediator of consumer brand choice. *Journal of Advertising, 10*: 9-16.

Slovic, P., Fischhoff, B., & Lichtenstein, S. 1977. Behavioral decision theory. *Annual Review of Psychology, 27*: 1-39.

Staats, A. W., & Staats, C. K. 1958. Attitudes established by classical conditioning. *Journal of Personality and Social Psychology, 57*: 37-40.

Vinokur, A., & Burnstein, E. 1974. The effects of partially shared persuasive arguments on group induced shifts: A group problem solving approach. *Journal of Personality and Social Psychology, 29*: 305-315.

Wagstaff, G. 1981. *Hypnosis, compliance, and belief.* New York: St. Martin's Press.

Wiggins, J. S. 1973. *Personality and prediction: Principles of personality assessment.* Reading, MA: Addison-Wesley.

Wyer, R. S., Jr., & Goldberg, L. 1970. A probabilistic analysis of relationships among beliefs and attitudes. *Psychological Review, 77*: 100-120.

2

A Theory of Behavior Change

Martin Fishbein
Michael J. Manfredo

Traditionally, public land management has been thought to be a job focused on administering natural resources. Academic credentials of land management professionals have been rooted in disciplines such as fisheries, wildlife, forestry, and range science. Over the past two decades, however, as land management professionals have become increasingly concerned with influencing public action or thought, managing humans has emerged as a significant component.

For example, introducing new policy or plans necessitates informing and educating the public; attracting recreation and tourism to a destination involves advertising and promotion; minimizing depreciative behavior and vandalism requires targeting both culprits and victims. To minimize resource and social impacts we must redirect recreationists' uses of an area; and enhancing recreational enjoyment of an area can involve directing attention through interpretation.

The more land managers know about the factors influencing a decision to perform or not perform a given behavior (e.g. wearing a life vest), a class of behaviors (practicing water safety), or the factors underlying public support for or opposition to policies or issues (public support for new water safety rules), the more likely their ability to develop effective messages or other types of interventions to influence these decisions or positions. Accordingly, we need to examine theoretical approaches that increase our understanding of why a person does or does not engage in a given action.

This chapter focuses on the relevance of one particular social psychological theory for understanding a wide range of resource management and tourist-related behaviors. Specifically, it presents certain implications of the Theory of Reasoned Action for understanding recreation-related behaviors, and for developing educational or other types of interventions to change or maintain these behaviors.

The Theory of Reasoned Action

First introduced in 1967, the Theory of Reasoned Action (Fishbein, 1967, 1973, 1980; Fishbein & Ajzen, 1975; Ajzen & Fishbein, 1980) is a general theory of human behavior that deals with the relationships among beliefs, attitudes, intentions and behavior. The theory has been used to predict and to explain why people have or have not engaged in a wide variety of behaviors, including smoking (e.g. Fishbein, 1980; Chassin et al., 1981), drinking (e.g. Budd & Spencer, 1985; Schlegel et al., 1977), signing up for a treatment program (Fishbein et al., 1980), using contraceptives (e.g. Fisher, 1984; Jaccard & Davidson, 1972), dieting (e.g. Saltzer, 1978; Sejwacz et al., 1980), wearing seat belts or safety helmets (e.g. Allegrante et al., 1980; Budd et al., 1984; Fishbein et al.., 1988) exercising regularly (e.g. Godin & Shephard, 1986), voting (e.g. Bowman & Fishbein, 1978; Shepherd, 1987), taking medication (e.g. Miller et al., 1985), breast feeding (e.g. Manstead et al., 1983), buying various goods and services (e.g. Ryan, 1982), and choosing a career (e.g. Greenstein et al., 1979).

Since it is thoroughly described in several of the references cited, we will provide only a brief overview of the Theory of Reasoned Action as it is presently formulated. [For a complete presentation of the theoretical constructs, the procedures to measure these constructs, and illustrations of the theory's applicability in various content domains, the reader is referred to Ajzen and Fishbein (1980).]

The Theory of Reasoned Action rests on the assumption that humans are reasoning animals who systematically utilize or process the information available to them (Fishbein, 1980; Ajzen & Fishbein, 1980). In some respects, this theory is best seen as a series of hypotheses linking (1) behavior to intentions, (2) intentions to a weighted combination of attitudes and subjective norms, and (3) attitudes and subjective norms to behavioral and normative beliefs.

These hypotheses are represented in Figure 1 by the arrows between adjoining columns. If one accepts the causal chain illustrated in Figure 1, it follows that behavior is ultimately determined by one's underlying beliefs. In the final analysis, then, changing behavior is viewed primarily as a matter of changing the underlying cognitive structure.

The Behavioral Criterion

To apply the Theory of Reasoned Action in a substantive area, one first identifies the behavior(s) of interest. Full identification of any behavior requires consideration of the four elements of action, target, context, and time. That is, every action occurs with respect to some target, within a given context, and at a given point in time. Although one may arrive at more general behavioral criteria by generalizing across one or more of these elements, a change in any one of the four elements redefines the behavior of interest.

For example, visiting Yellowstone is a different behavior than camping at Yellowstone (a change in action), and visiting Yellowstone is a different behavior than visiting Yosemite (a change in target). Similarly, visiting Yellowstone with family is a different behavior than visiting Yellowstone with friends (a change in context), and visiting Yellowstone in August is a different behavior than visiting Yellowstone in December (a change in time).

More importantly, as the behavior changes, so do its determinants, and as the determinants change, the most effective intervention may also change.

Any given content domain encompasses many different behaviors that could be considered, and each behavior may require a different intervention strategy. For example, the information necessary to increase the likelihood that one will visit Yellowstone with family may be very different from that required to increase the likelihood that one will visit Yellowstone with friends. Similarly, the information necessary to increase the likelihood that one will visit Yellowstone in winter may differ significantly from that required to increase the likelihood that one will visit in summer. In the land management, recreation and tourism arena, we may wish to consider many different behaviors, and it is important to clearly specify the behavior(s) one wishes to change or maintain.

Figure1

A Theory of Reasoned Action: factors determining a person's behavior. From Ajzen, I. and Fishbein, M. (1980) *Understanding Attitudes and Predicting Social Behavior.* **Prentice Hall, New Jersey, p. 8.** **Arrows indicate the direction of influence within hypothesized relationships**

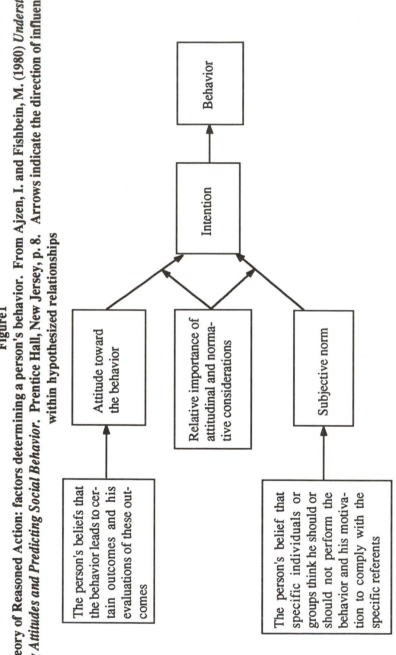

Predicting Behavior from Intentions

Once a behavior is identified, the Theory of Reasoned Action assumes that the behavior can be predicted from the intention that corresponds directly (i.e., in terms of action, target, context and time) to that behavior. That is, this theory assumes that most socially relevant human behaviors are under volitional control and, therefore, that the most immediate determinant of any given behavior is the *intention* to perform or not perform that behavior.

For example, in trying to predict whether people will use a life vest the next time they go boating, the best predictor will be each person's intention to "use a life vest the next time I go boating" rather than the intention to "practice water safety" or to "use a life vest" (in general). Considerable research demonstrates that, when properly measured, correspondent intentions are very accurate predictors of most social behaviors. Given this strong relationship between behavioral intentions and behaviors, the Theory of Reasoned Action is primarily concerned with identifying the factors underlying the formation and change of intentions.

It is important to recognize however, that not all intentions are behavioral intentions. People also intend to reach certain goals (e.g., "I intend to catch enough fish for dinner", or "I intend not to have a boating accident") and to engage in classes of behavior (e.g., "I intend to practice water safety"). Unfortunately, unlike intentions to engage in specific behaviors, intentions to reach goals or engage in classes of behaviors do not necessarily lead to accurate predictions. Because goal attainment is usually not causally linked to the performance of a single behavior and because it often involves factors beyond an individual's control, intentions to reach goals are often very poor predictors of actual goal attainment or of the particular behavior(s) people might perform in their attempts to attain that goal.

Similarly, knowing that one intends to engage in a class of behaviors does not mean that the person intends to engage in any given behavior within that class. In fact, since different people may define a behavioral category in different ways, a given behavior may not be included in an individual's definition of the category. More important, that person may be unaware of, or incorrectly informed about, the behaviors that other persons (e.g., a physician or a resource manager) would include in a given behavioral category (e.g., water safety).

Despite the low predictive validity of intentions to reach goals or engage in categories of behavior, these intentions do influence or guide an individual's behavior choices. Therefore, it is often important to understand *why* people intend to reach certain goals or engage in a given class of behaviors. The Theory of Reasoned Action applies to understanding the determinants of goal intentions, and the intentions to engage in behavioral categories, as well as to understanding the determinants of behavioral intentions.

Predicting Intentions from Attitudes and Subjective Norms

For ease of presentation, the following analysis focuses on intentions to perform a given behavior. It should be clear, however, that once a goal or behavioral category is defined, the analysis of the determinants of that intention is virtually identical to an analysis of the determinants of a behavioral intention. More specifically, according to the theory, a person's intention—whether an intention to reach a goal, to engage in some category of behavior, or to perform a given behavior—is a function of two basic determinants, one personal in nature and the other reflecting social influence.

The personal factor is the individual's positive or negative feelings about performing the behavior in question; this factor is termed "attitude toward the behavior." The second determinant of intention is the individual's perceptions of the social pressures to perform or not to perform the behavior. Since this factor deals with perceived proscriptions, it is termed the "subjective norm."

Generally, individuals will intend to perform a behavior when they have a positive attitude toward the behavior and when they believe their "significant others" think they should perform it. Note that the attitude and the subjective norm specified by the Theory of Reasoned Action is the individuals' attitude toward their own performance of the behavior in question. That is, like the intention, the attitude and the norm must correspond to the behavior in terms of the four elements of action, target, context and time.

Implication. Correspondence of attitude to behavior intention and behavior is important because it helps explain why many educational programs and interventions have been unsuccessful. Many educational programs or other types of interventions have focused on broad attitudes or issues rather than focusing directly upon the attitude(s) and/or subjective norm(s) that correspond directly to the behavior(s) one wishes to change. For example, although I may have a positive attitude toward boating safety and a positive attitude toward wearing a life vest (i.e., feel that for most people wearing a life vest would be good), I may nevertheless feel quite negatively about *my* wearing a life vest. Similarly, although I believe, in general, that going camping or hiking is a good thing, I may feel quite negative toward *my* going camping or hiking next week. According to the Theory of Reasoned Action, one is most likely to be successful in producing a change in a given intention if one first changes the attitudes and/or norms that directly correspond in terms of action, target, context and time to that intention.

Although attitudes and subjective norms both may influence the formation of any given intention, the relative importance of these two factors often varies from behavior to behavior and from individual to individual. Thus, for some behaviors and intentions, attitudinal considerations may be more important than normative ones, while for other behaviors and intentions, normative considerations may predominate. Similarly, the intention to perform a given behavior may be primarily under attitudinal control for some individuals or segments of the population, and predominantly under normative control for other individuals or groups.

The discussion to this point is summarized in equation 1,

$$B{\sim}I = f[w_1 Ab + w_2 SN]$$

where B is the behavior of interest (e.g. "Did you visit Yellowstone National Park during the past 12 months?"); I is the intention to perform that behavior (i.e. "I intend to visit Yellowstone National Park during the next 12 months"); Ab is the attitude toward performing that behavior (i.e., the attitude toward "my visiting Yellowstone National Park during the next 12 months"); SN is the subjective norm concerning this behavior (i.e., the belief that "most of my significant others think I should/should not visit Yellowstone National Park during the next 12 months"); and w_1 and w_2 are the weights or relative importance of the attitudinal and normative components, respectively.

To illustrate how the Theory of Reasoned Action can be applied in the recreation domain, consider Young and Kent's (1985) study of camping behavior. Specifically, these investigators wished to predict and explain why some residents of a small midwestern community went camping during the summer while others did not. As part of face-to-face interviews conducted in the spring of 1984, respondents were asked to indicate their intentions to "go camping this summer" as well as to indicate their attitudes and subjective norms with respect to this behavior. In the fall, respondents were recontacted and asked whether they had gone camping during the summer. Consistent with expectations, Young and Kent (1985) found a high correlation between people's intentions to go camping during the summer and their self-reports of whether they did or did not go camping (r=0.77, p<0.01).

Table 1
Scales used by Young and Kent (1985) to measure intentions, attitudes, and subjective norms with respect to "going camping this summer."

INTENTION: I intend to camp this summer
    likely ___:___:___:___:___:___:___ unlikely

ATTITUDE: Going camping this summer
    favorable___:___:___:___:___:___:___ unfavorable

SUBJECTIVE NORM: Most people who are important to me think I should go camping this summer
    likely ___:___:___:___:___:___:___ unlikely

Table 2
Multiple correlation (R) and standardized regression coefficients (Beta Weights) for prediction of camping intention from attitudes and subjective norms for males, females, and the total sample (Young and Kent, 1985).

Groups	R	Beta Attitude	Beta Norm
Males (N=39)	0.76	0.51	0.36
Females (N=60)	0.74	0.41	0.46
Total (N=100)	0.74	0.45	0.41

NOTE: All correlations and regression coefficients are statistically significant, p <0.01

Intention = Attitude + Subjective Norm

Table 1 shows the scales used to measure respondents' intentions, attitudes, and subjective norms with respect to "going camping this summer," while Table 2 shows how well the theory predicted the respondents' intentions from their attitudes and subjective norms. More specifically, Table 2 shows the multiple correlation (R) of attitude and norm with intention, as well as the standardized regression coefficients (or Beta weights) for the attitudinal and normative components. These regression weights indicate the relative importance of the two components as determinants of the intention.

Note that the model leads to quite accurate predictions of intentions for both males and females as well as for the sample as a whole (R=0.76, 0.74 and 0.74 for males, females and the total sample, respectively). There are however, some very important differences between the men and women: while the men's intentions to go camping are primarily under attitudinal control, the women's intentions are influenced slightly more by normative than by attitudinal considerations. These findings demonstrate that different strategies will be necessary to maintain or change men's and women's intentions to go camping.

Implication. As indicated above, if one wants to change or reinforce a given intention, one must change or strengthen the attitude toward performing that behavior and/or change or strengthen the subjective norm with respect to that behavior. Whether one should change the attitude or the subjective norm depends upon the relative importance of these two components as determinants of a specific intention in that population. If a behavior is primarily under attitudinal control, attempts to change that behavior through the use of normative pressure will not be very successful. Similarly, if the members of some group perform a given behavior because their significant others think they should perform the behavior, little will be accomplished by trying to change member attitudes toward performing that behavior.

Unfortunately, these kinds of theoretical considerations are rarely taken into account in determining intervention programs or developing messages. Instead, most messages and interventions are constructed somewhat arbitrarily based on intuition and on what too often turn out to be false assumptions about the determinants of the behavior one wishes to change.

The Underlying Cognitive Structure

Although the above provides initial insight into why people behave the way they do, a more complete understanding of intentions requires an explanation of why people hold given attitudes or subjective norms. The Theory of Reasoned Action also attempts to answer these questions. Since the theory views behavior change as ultimately being a matter of changing the cognitive structure underlying that behavior, the key to developing a successful intervention is identifying and examining the cognitive structure of behavioral beliefs and evaluations underlying specific attitudes, as well as identifying and examining the cognitive structure of normative beliefs and motivations to comply, which determine the subjective norm. The next two sections examine this premise in more depth.

Attitude and Behavioral Beliefs

A person's attitude toward performing a given behavior is a function of the person's salient ("top of the mind") beliefs that performing the behavior will lead to certain outcomes, and of the person's evaluation of these outcomes. The more one believes performing the behavior will lead to positive outcomes or prevent negative outcomes, the more favorable the person's attitude.

Conversely, the more one believes that performing the behavior will lead to negative consequences or prevent positive outcomes, the more negative the attitude.

This expectancy-value relationship between attitude and behavioral beliefs is summarized symbolically by Equation 2,

$$Ab = f\left(\sum_{i=1}^{n} b_i e_i\right)$$

where Ab is the attitude toward one's own performance of the behavior in question (e.g., "My visiting Yellowstone National Park in the next 12 months"); b_i is the belief that one's performance of the behavior will lead to a given outcome, "i" (e.g. the likelihood that "my visiting Yellowstone National Park in the next 12 months will allow me to see the effects of the 1988 fire."); e_i is the person's evaluation of outcome "i" (e.g. how good or bad is "seeing the effects of the 1988 fire"); and a belief times evaluation crossproduct is formed for each of n salient outcomes. Note that not all of the possible outcomes of performing a behavior are seen as determinants of the attitude toward that behavior.

The determinants of a given attitude in a given population are only those behavioral beliefs that are salient in the population under examination. Furthermore, one's attitude toward a behavior is determined by the evaluative implications of the total set of salient beliefs one holds; attitudes are not determined by any single belief.

Subjective Norm and Normative Beliefs

A person's subjective norm with respect to a given behavior is a function of his or her normative beliefs that particular salient individuals or groups think he or she should or should not perform the behavior, plus the person's motivation to comply with those individuals or groups. Generally, if a person is motivated to comply with referents and believes the referents would approve of a behavior, the person will perceive social pressure to perform it. Conversely, a person who believes that most referents with whom he or she is motivated to comply think he or she should not perform the behavior will have a subjective norm that puts perceived pressure on him or her to avoid performing the behavior.

The relation between a subjective norm and normative beliefs is expressed mathematically in Equation 3,

$$SN=f(\sum_{i=1}^{n}b_j m_j)$$

where SN is the subjective norm, (e.g., the person's belief that "most people who are important to me think I should/should not" visit Yellowstone National Park in the next 12 months); b_j is a normative belief that referent "j" thinks I should/should not perform the behavior (e.g. the person's belief that "My parents think I should visit Yellowstone National Park in the next twelve months"); m_j is the person's motivation to comply with referent "j" (e.g. the belief that "Generally, I want to do what my parents think I should do") and a normative crossproduct is formed for each of n salient referents. Again, note that the theory designates that subjective norms are determined by the normative implications of a set of salient normative beliefs rather than by the perceived normative pressure being exerted by any one referent.

Implication. In order to change or reinforce attitudes toward performing a given behavior, one must change or reinforce salient behavioral beliefs and/or their evaluative aspects. Similarly, in order to change or reinforce a subjective norm with respect to a given behavior, one must change or reinforce salient normative beliefs and/or motivations to comply. At this level of analysis, four main points should be considered in developing educational messages or other types of interventions.

(1) Salience. Just as one must determine whether a given behavior in a given population is under attitudinal or normative control, one must also identify the behavioral and normative beliefs that underlie the attitude or subjective norm. That is, in order to develop effective interventions, one should first determine the outcomes and referents that are salient for the behavior in the population under consideration. Salient outcomes and referents vary from behavior to behavior and, perhaps more importantly, from population to population.

For example, the "top of the mind" consequences one thinks about when one considers visiting Yellowstone may be very different from those that are salient when one considers visiting Yosemite or Craters of the Moon. And the outcomes and referents that are salient vis-a-vis either of these behaviors are quite likely to differ depending upon the gender and socioeconomic status of the population of interest. Thus, in applying the Theory of Reasoned Action to a new behavior or with a different population, it is imperative to conduct an elicitation survey (See Ajzen and Fishbein, 1980, for a description of how an elicitation survey is conducted.) to determine the salient outcomes and referents. Unfortunately, very few practitioners identify the behavioral and/or normative beliefs that are salient in a population *prior* to developing a behavior change campaign.

(2) Selecting Target Beliefs. Once one has identified salient outcomes and referents, one must then decide which of these behavioral or normative beliefs to target in an intervention. As stated previously, this decision should be guided by the relative weights of the attitudinal and normative components. In addition, with respect to either component, it is important to identify those beliefs that discriminate between people who do and do not intend to perform the behavior in question.

For example, consider a belief such as "my visiting Yellowstone in the next twelve months will be an educational experience." One must determine whether all members of the population are homogeneous with respect to this belief (i.e. do they all believe or do they all disbelieve that "my visiting Yellowstone in the next twelve months will be an educational experience"?). Or, perhaps more important, does this belief discriminate between those who do and do not intend to visit Yellowstone in the next twelve months (i.e do those who intend to visit Yellowstone believe it will be an educational experience while those who do not intend to visit Yellowstone believe that visiting Yellowstone will not be an educational experience?).

One of the main reasons written communications and other forms of behavioral intervention fail is that often they do not address appropriate beliefs. For example, many messages provide people with information they already have or try to convince them of something they already believe. If most members of a group already believe that performing some behavior will lead to a certain consequence or outcome (e.g. that "visiting Yellowstone will allow them to observe Old Faithful"), little will be accomplished by a persuasive communication focusing on that information. Similarly, if most members of a group or some segment of the population are aware that their parents are strongly in favor of their visiting Yellowstone, little will be accomplished by basing one's intervention on parental pressure.

(3) Multiple Determinants. Since both attitudes and subjective norms are based on sets of beliefs, a change in any one behavioral or normative belief may not be sufficient to produce a change in an attitude or subjective norm. However, changing one belief may impact upon another belief and, depending upon the direction of this effect, the impact may facilitate or inhibit change. For a successful intervention, one must change the evaluative or normative implication of the underlying cognitive structure. That is, one must change the value of the attitudinal [Σbe] or normative [Σbm] crossproducts.

(4) The Rule of Correspondence. Just as an intention must correspond to the behavior one wishes to predict, change or understand, so too must attitudes, subjective norms, behavioral beliefs and normative beliefs correspond to the intention. Thus, if one wants to change a person's intention to visit Yellowstone with family members this coming summer, one must change the person's attitude or subjective norm with respect to "my visiting Yellowstone with my family this coming summer." To change the attitude or subjective norm one must change the person's beliefs about visiting Yellowstone this summer with family, or the beliefs that one or more specific referents think he should visit Yellowstone with family this summer. In sum, behavior change is brought about by producing changes in the correspondent intention, which is in turn created by changing the corresponding attitudes and/or subjective norm, which change is, in the final analysis, produced by altering a set of correspondent beliefs.

To illustrate these four points, consider a study by Manfredo et. al. (1990) that was directed at understanding why people support or oppose a controlled burn fire policy. Note that "supporting a controlled burn policy" refers to a behavioral category rather than a single behavior. Recall that, according to the Theory of Reasoned Action, knowing someone's intention to support a controlled burn policy may tell very little about whether the person will or will not perform any given supportive behavior (e.g., calling a congressman, writing a letter to the editor, or voting for a controlled burn proposition in a referendum election). Nevertheless, the stronger one's intention to support a controlled burn policy, the greater the likelihood that one will perform one or more supportive behaviors.

And just as one can examine the factors underlying one's intention to perform or not perform a given behavior, one can examine the factors underlying the intention to engage in a behavioral category. According to the Theory of Reasoned Action, a person's intention to "support a controlled burn policy" should be predicted from his or her attitude toward "my supporting a controlled burn policy" and/or his or her subjective norm with respect to this behavioral category (i.e., the perception that "most of my important others think I should/should not support a controlled burn policy). Consistent with this, Manfredo et al. (1990) obtained a multiple correlation of 0.87 between the intention to support a controlled burn policy and the two components of the model, with attitudes being much more important determinants of this intention (Beta = 0.76, p<.001) than subjective norms (Beta = 0.14, p<0.05).

To better understand the basis of support for a controlled burn policy, it is necessary to understand the determinants of the respondents' attitudes toward this behavioral category. To accomplish this, Manfredo et al. (1990) assessed their respondents' beliefs about the advantages and disadvantages of following a controlled burn policy. As part of a pilot study, two groups of 40 forestry students each (one group at the University of Illinois and one at the University of Montana) were asked to list what they believed to be the advantages and disadvantages of "following a controlled burn policy."

Table 3 shows the most frequently mentioned outcomes. Each of these "salient" outcomes was then used to construct two questionnaire items, one item to assess the degree to which a respondent felt that the outcome was good or bad (i.e., a measure of the evaluative aspect of the belief) and the other to assess the likelihood that following a controlled burn policy would lead to the outcome in question (i.e., the strength of the belief). These items were included as part of a larger interview administered by phone to a national sample of 910 respondents. In addition, the respondents were asked to indicate their attitudes toward "following a controlled burn policy" on three semantic differential scales (i.e. good - bad; wise - foolish; beneficial - harmful — the attitude

Table 3

Mean beliefs and evaluations for those supporting (y) and opposing (n) a controlled burn policy—total national sample (Manfredo, et al, 1990)

| | BELIEF | | EVALUATION | |
	Y (N=501)	N (N=409)	Y (N=501)	N (N=409)
Improves conditions	1.06	-1.11	1.85	1.34
Destroys nat. settings	0.12	1.71	-1.10	-2.01
Allows nat. events	1.29	0.54	1.59	0.50
Fires out of control	0.22	1.95	-2.11	-2.71
Saves money	0.46	-0.59	-0.31	-1.82
Affects private prop	0.34	1.33	-2.19	-2.53
Removes dead vegetation	1.93	1.47	1.34	0.44
Destroys scenery	0.95	2.30	-1.53	2.50
Animals lose homes	0.82	2.34	-2.04	-2.61
Threats to human life	-0.53	1.35	-2.70	-2.82

Note: All differences between supporters and opposers are significant

was computed by summing the responses to the three scales). Table 3 shows the mean evaluations and belief strengths for respondents who do (Y) and who do not (N) intend to support a controlled burn policy.

Consider the kinds of beliefs that are salient vis-a-vis this behavioral category. Not surprisingly, when people consider a controlled burn policy they worry about whether the fire will get out of control, threaten human lives or damage private property. They also worry about the effect of the policy on wildlife — will it destroy habitat or improve conditions for wildlife? Other salient beliefs concern the environment (effect on scenery, natural settings, and so on), ecology (fire allows natural events to occur or fire removes dead vegetation), and financial issues (will it save money?).

According to the Theory of Reasoned Action, knowledge of how strongly the population holds each of these beliefs and their evaluations of the outcomes should permit accurate predictions of public attitudes toward a controlled burn policy. The correlation between the belief-based estimate of attitude [Σbe] and the direct (semantic differential) measure of attitude is 0.67 (p<0.001) supporting the prediction. Thus we know these beliefs account for much of the variation in the public's attitudes toward following a controlled burn policy.

The next step in this analysis is to see which of these beliefs distinguish between those people who support and those who oppose a controlled burn policy. Not surprisingly, those who are favorable and those who are unfavorable toward following a controlled burn policy evaluate most outcomes quite similarly. [Because of the larger sample size (n=910), almost all differences between supporters and opponents of the controlled burn policy are statistically significant. For the purpose of the present analysis, we will focus on substantive (qualitative) differences rather than upon quantitative differences.] That is, almost everybody feels that burning natural settings and scenery, letting fires get out of control, threatening human life, and causing animals to lose their homes are "bad," while improving conditions for wildlife, removing dead vegetation and allowing natural events to occur are "good."

In marked contrast to this evaluative agreement, those favoring and opposing "following a controlled burn policy" have very different beliefs. Before turning to these differences however, it is important to recognize that the two groups do hold some beliefs in common. Whether one is "for" or "against" a controlled burn policy, one is likely to believe that following this policy will allow natural events to occur, remove dead vegetation, destroy scenery, and cause animals to lose their homes. However, the stronger one's beliefs about the first two outcomes and the weaker one's beliefs about the latter two outcomes, the more favorable the attitude toward following the policy.

Bigger attitude differences occur with respect to beliefs about whether or not following the policy will affect private property, allow fires to get out of control, or destroy natural settings.

The more one believes these negative consequences will result from following a controlled burn policy, the more one is likely to oppose such a policy. Interestingly, while opponents of the policy strongly believe these negative consequences will occur, supporters of the policy are essentially uncertain that the policy will lead to these outcomes.

The major differences between those people "for" and "against" following a controlled burn policy appear to focus upon three key beliefs. Specifically, those who believe that following a controlled burn policy (1) will not threaten human life, but (2) will improve conditions for wildlife and (3) will save money, are supporters of the controlled burn policy. In contrast, those who believe that this policy (1) threatens human life, (2) does not improve conditions for wildlife and (3) does not save money, are opposed to the policy.

Clearly, one of the first steps in gaining additional support for a controlled burn policy would be to try to demonstrate to opponents that the policy would not only save the taxpayers money, but more importantly, will improve conditions for wildlife without threatening human life. One could also try to weaken opponents' beliefs that following the policy will allow fires to get out of control and affect private property.

Conversely, if one were interested in increasing opposition to a controlled burn policy, one could try to convince supporters that such a policy neither saves money nor improves conditions for wildlife. One could also try to demonstrate to supporters that a controlled burn policy will allow fires to get out of control and, therefore, that following this policy will ultimately affect private property and threaten human life.

It is important to recognize, however, that, in their entirety, neither of these strategies would be ethical. For example, at the time we conducted our studies, whether or not a controlled burn policy saves money was unknown and thus it would have been inappropriate to focus a communication on this belief. Similarly, since evidence suggests that fires do improve conditions for wildlife, it would be unethical for policy opponents to argue the opposite.

Clearly, one cannot always develop messages that maximize the theoretical likelihood of producing the desired change. That is, one cannot always attack those beliefs that best discriminate between those who favor and oppose a given policy or who do and do not intend to perform a given behavior. Communicators, particularly those working in the public service sector, must ensure that information in a message is both accurate and ethical. For example, if one wished to reduce support for a controlled burn policy, one could focus upon issues of fire control and damage to private property instead of on costs or wildlife conditions.

Such a message opposing a controlled burn policy was sent to a sample of visitors to Yellowstone National Park with known positive attitudes toward the controlled burn policy in the summer of 1989. These visitors were asked to fill out a questionnaire similar to the one described above. Among other things, the respondents indicated their attitudes toward following a controlled burn policy as well as their beliefs and outcome evaluations with respect to this behavioral category. Intentions and subjective norms were also measured. Although a substantial minority (24 percent) of respondents were opposed to the controlled burn policy, the vast majority (66 percent) held favorable attitudes toward "following a controlled burn policy." The remaining 10 percent were neutral.

Of the 270 respondents with positive attitudes, 209 (77 percent) agreed to fill out a second questionnaire approximately 30 to 45 days later. Half received a questionnaire that was identical to the one they filled out "on site," while the remaining half received the same questionnaire with the following message:

> Some experts object to the controlled burn policy because they do not believe it is possible to control fires once they develop into a larger blaze. Yellowstone National Park was an example of this in the summer of 1988. Fires started in mid-June, but, because of the controlled burn policy, were not fought as wildfires until July. By that time, fires had grown beyond the control of firefighters and more than 40% of the park was burned. Furthermore, fires spread to privately owned land where they destroyed valuable timber and burned homes and businesses. Many people now believe that the controlled burn policy should be abandoned and all forest fires suppressed.

Note that this message attacks both normative and behavioral beliefs by saying "experts" and "many people" think the controlled burn policy should be abandoned. In addition, it directly addresses two of the discriminating beliefs: (1) that the controlled burn policy allows fires to get out of control, and (2) that the policy leads to the destruction of private property.

Table 4 shows the mean changes in these two behavioral beliefs, as well as the mean change in (1) the evaluative implications of the underlying cognitive structure (i.e. changes in $\sum_{i=1}^{10} b_i e_i$,); (2) the attitude toward "supporting a controlled burn policy;" (3) the subjective norm with respect to "supporting a controlled burn policy;" and (4) the intention to support the controlled burn policy for those receiving and not receiving the message. The study results in Table 4, consistent with expectation, show that changes in all these variables were greater in the message group than in the group receiving no message. Unfortunately,

Table 4

Mean change in direction advocated in targeted beliefs, $\sum_{i=1}^{10}b_ie_i$, attitude, norm and intention for those who did and did not receive the message

Dependent Variant	Message	No Message
Belief (control)	0.51	0.06
Belief (private property)	0.62	0.06
$\sum_{i=1}^{10}b_ie_i$	0.76	-0.02
Attitude	0.55	0.23
Subjective Norm	0.62	0.32
Intention	0.55	0.25

although all the differences between conditions are in the positive direction, none are statistically significant.

These results suggest that some, but not all, of the respondents who were exposed to the message changed at least one of the two behavioral beliefs addressed in the message. A more detailed analysis revealed that in comparison to those who did not yield to the contents of the message, those who changed at least one of the two targeted behavioral beliefs were significantly more likely to change both their attitudes ($X^2 = 7.88$, df=2, P <0.02) and their intentions ($x^2 = 14.0$, df = 2, p<0.001).

Thus, if the message changed at least one of the two behavioral beliefs addressed, it started a causal chain reaction that ultimately decreased the receivers' intentions to support a controlled burn policy. More specifically, considering the sample as whole, the greater the change in the two targeted behavioral beliefs, the greater the change in $\sum be$ (n=0.40); the greater the change in $\sum b$, the greater the change in attitude (r=0.61); and the greater the change in attitude, the greater the change in intentions (r=0.86).

SUMMARY AND CONCLUSIONS

In this chapter we showed how the Theory of Reasoned Action can be used to identify the determinants of a given intention. After outlining the theory, we showed how it has been applied in a study of why people do or do not intend to go camping, as well as in a study of intentions to support (or not support) a controlled burn fire policy.

Generally, this chapter showed intentions to be a function of attitudes and subjective norms; attitudes and subjective norms were in turn shown to be functions of underlying behavioral and normative beliefs, respectively.

More importantly, we demonstrated how information about these underlying behavioral and normative beliefs can be used to develop mass media communications designed to reinforce or change intentions. We argued that messages should be designed to attack specific beliefs underlying the targeted intention. To illustrate these points, a fire control message was developed and sent to a sample of visitors to Yellowstone National Park. Consistent with the Theory of Reasoned Action, respondents who yielded to the message (i.e. those who changed one or more of the targeted beliefs) also changed their attitudes and intentions.

We propose that natural resource managers will more effectively manage the public as they obtain a better understanding of social science theory and practice, and as sound social research in the land management arena becomes more available. The Theory of Reasoned Action offers an explanation of human behavior that gives direction to both managers and researchers in achieving those ends.

REFERENCES

Ajzen, I.; Fishbein, M. 1980. *Understanding Attitudes and Predicting Social Behavior*. Englewood Cliffs, N.J.: Prentice Hall, Inc.

Allegrante, J. P.; Mortimer, R. G. and O'Rourke, T. W. 1980. Social-psychological factors in motorcycle safety helmet use: Implications for public policy. *Journal of Safety Research: 12*(3): 115-126.

Bowman, C. H.; Fishbein, M. 1978. Understanding public reactions to energy proposals: An application of the Fishbein model. *Journal of Applied Social Psychology: 8*: 319-340.

Budd, R. J.; North, D.; Spencer, C. P. 1984. Understanding seat-belt use: A test of Bentler and Speckart's extension of the theory of reasoned action. *European Journal of Social Psychology: 14*: 69-78.

Budd, R. J.; Spencer, C. P. 1985. Exploring the role of personal normative beliefs in the theory of reasoned action: The problem of discriminating between alternative path models. *European Journal of Social Psychology: 15*: 299-313.

Chassin, L.; Presson, C. C.; Bensenburg, M., et al.. 1981. Predicting adolescents' intentions to smoke cigarettes. *Journal of Health and Social Behavior: 22*: 445-455.

Fishbein, M. 1967. Attitude and the prediction of behavior. In: Fishbein, M., (Ed.) *Readings in Attitude Theory and Measurement*. New York: John Wiley, 477-492.

Fishbein, M. 1973. The prediction of behavior from attitudinal variables. In: Mortensen C. D.; Serano, K. K., (Eds.) *Advances in Communication Research*. New York: Harper & Row, 3-31.

Fishbein, M. 1980. A theory of reasoned action: Some applications and implications. In: Howe, H. E.; Page, M. M., (Eds.) *Nebraska Symposium on Motivation, 1979*. Lincoln: University of Nebraska Press, 65-116.

Fishbein, M.; Ajzen, I. 1975. *Belief, Attitude, Intention and Behavior: An Introduction to Theory and Research*. Reading, Mass: Addison-Wesley.

Fishbein, M.; Ajzen, I.; McArdle, J. 1980. Changing the behavior of alcoholics: Effects of persuasive communication. Chapter 15 In: Ajzen, I.; Fishbein M. *Understanding Attitudes and Social Behavior*. Englewood Cliffs, N.J.: Prentice Hall, Inc.

Fishbein, M.; Salazar, J. M.; Rodriguez, P. R.; et al.. 1988. Predicting Venezuelan students' use of seat belts: An application of the theory of reasoned action in Latin America. *Revista de Psicologia Social y Personalidad*. 4(2): 19-41.

Fisher, W. A. 1984. Predicting contraceptive behavior among university men: The role of emotions and behavioral intentions. *Journal of Applied Social Psychology*. 14(2): 104-123.

Godin, G.; Shephard, R. J. 1986. Psychosocial factors influencing intentions to exercise of young students from grades 7 to 9. *Research Quarterly for Exercise and Sport*. 57(1): 41-52.

Greenstein, M.; Miller, R. H.; Weldon, D. E. 1979. Attitudinal and normative beliefs as antecedents of female occupational choice. *Personality and Social Psychology Bulletin*. 5(3): 356-362.

Jaccard, J. J.; Davidson, A. R. 1972. Toward an understanding of family planning behaviors: An initial investigation. *Journal of Applied Social Psychology*. 2(3): 228-235.

Manfredo, M. J.; Fishbein, M.; Haas, G.; Watson, A. 1990. Attitudes toward prescribed fire policies. *Journal of Forestry*. 88(9): 19-23.

Manstead, A. S. R.; Proffitt, C.; Smart, J. L. 1983. Predicting and understanding mothers infant-feeding intentions and behaviors: Testing the theory of reasoned action. *Journal of Personality and Social Psychology*. 44(4): 657-671.

Miller, P.; Wickoff, R. L.; McMahon, M.; et al.. 1985. Indicators of medical regimen adherence for myocardial infarction patients. *Nursing Research*. 34: 268-272.

Ryan, M. J. 1982. Behavioral intention formation: The interdependency of attitudinal and social influence variables. *Journal of Consumer Research*. 9: 263-278.

Saltzer, E. B. 1978. Locus of control and the intention to lose weight. *Health Education Monographs.* 6(2): 118-128.

Schlegel, R. P.; Crawford, C. A.; Sanborn, M. D. 1977. Correspondence and mediation properties of the Fishbein model: An application to adolescent alcohol use. *Journal of Experimental Social Psychology. 13*: 421-430.

Sejwacz, R.; Ajzen, I.; Fishbein, M. 1980. Predicting and understanding weight loss: Intentions, behaviors and outcomes. Chapter 9 In : Ajzen, I.; Fishbein, M. *Understanding Attitudes and Predicting Social Behavior.* Englewood Cliffs, N.J.: Prentice Hall, Inc.

Shepherd, G. J. 1987. Individual differences in the relationship between attitudinal and normative determinants of behavioral intent. *Communication Monographs. 54*: 221-231.

Young, R. A.; Kent, A. T. 1985. Using the theory of reasoned action to improve the understanding of recreation behavior. *Journal of Leisure Research. 17*(2): 90-106.

3

Attitude Accessibility and Its Consequences for Judgment and Behavior

Mark A. Vincent
Russell H. Fazio

Countless fires are started each year in federally-owned parks, many by individuals who would profess positive attitudes toward fire prevention and negative attitudes toward destructive behavior in public areas. Furthermore, we assume that people visit such areas because they have positive attitudes toward parks. Why, then, do they engage in costly and dangerous behaviors, such as carelessly discarding cigarette butts in wooded areas or leaving campfires unattended? If most park visitors claim to have positive attitudes toward park preservation and safety guidelines, how can we explain the repeated display of discrepant behaviors? Perhaps more importantly, how do these individuals differ from individuals who have similar attitudes, yet act in a manner consistent with their attitudes, carefully avoiding dangerous behaviors and situations? Can we identify those who are likely to act correspondence with their attitudes, and those who are not?

Prior to the mid-1960s, most treatments of attitudes included an implicit assumption that a one-to-one correspondence existed between an individual's attitude and relevant behavior. We now know that there are myriad situations in everyday life when our behavior does not correspond to our attitudes. What determines when we will act according to our attitudes, and when we will not? Prior to the mid-1980s, the answer to that question would have been a catalog of variables that are known to affect attitude-behavior consistency. This chapter introduces a model proposed by Fazio and his colleagues (Fazio, Powell and Herr 1983, Fazio 1986) that seeks to explain the actual process by which attitudes influence or fail to influence behavior.

Fazio's model contends that the major determinant of the attitude-behavior relation is the likelihood that one's attitude will be spontaneously accessed from memory upon encountering the object. Such spontaneous activation will lead the individual to view the object in question in evaluative terms (i.e., to include one's appraisal of the object in thoughts about the object). This model makes important predictions concerning situations in which attitudes that traditional measurement techniques would consider equivalent can be expected to differ dramatically in their ability to guide behavior. As a result, the model has much to say about efforts to alter established behaviors, as well as efforts aimed at establishing new behaviors.

PREVIOUS RESEARCH ON THE
ATTITUDE-BEHAVIOR RELATION

Although social psychologists describe the domain of attitudes as cornerstone of their field, little empirical research in the first half of this century addressed the attitude-behavior relationship. As early as the 1920s and 1930s, social psychologists showed interest in the study of attitudes. However, they were interested primarily in how attitudes should properly be defined and measured. These researchers, one may reasonably infer, found such an enterprise useful because a direct correspondence existed between the attitudes they were measuring and relevant behavior. One might, for example, measure attitudes toward fire safety guidelines in order to predict the likelihood of following these guidelines. In fact, several early definitions of the attitude concept included behavioral correspondence as an essential element of the definition—implying that if such a correspondence did not exist, one really did not have an attitude (Allport 1935, Doob 1947). There were, of course, exceptions to this rule, such as studies by Corey (1937) and LaPierre (1943), both of which found reason to doubt the assumed relationship between stated attitudes and subsequent behavior. Yet the view that attitudes constituted a useful predictor of behavior remained dominant.

Beginning in the late 1960s, attitude researchers increasingly questioned the notion of attitude-behavior correspondence. In probably the most noted and extreme version of this new skepticism, Wicker (1969) reviewed the attitude literature and found 31 studies reporting weak or nonexistent correlations between attitudes and related behaviors. He later went so far as to suggest that the attitude concept be abandoned, since it apparently had little or no connection with behavior (Wicker 1971).

Although Wicker's conclusions proved to be clearly overstated, they succeeded in generating a great deal of research on attitude-behavior consistency. A number of studies found weak attitude-behavior correlations, while other studies reported finding sizable relationships (Kelley and Mirer 1974). In fact, recent reviews have portrayed the state of the attitude-behavior relationship in a much more optimistic light (Fazio and Zanna 1981, Schuman and Johnson 1976, Zanna and Fazio 1982).

Variables Affecting the Attitude-Behavior Relation

Is there a relationship between attitudes and behavior? The answer to that question seems to fall somewhere between the overconfident assumptions of early theorists and the skepticism of Wicker and others. Numerous studies conducted during the last two decades have contributed to an expanding catalog of variables that play a significant role in moderating the attitude-behavior relation. These variables include normative constraints and expectations (Ajzen and Fishbein 1973), the existence of a vested interest in the attitude object (Sivacek and Crano 1982), and personality factors such as levels of moral reasoning (Rholes and Bailey 1983) and self-monitoring (Kardes et al. 1984, Snyder and Swann 1976, Zanna, Olson and Fazio 1980).

In addition, factors related to the attitudes themselves, such as manner of attitude formation (Fazio and Zanna 1981), were also found to be an important consideration in gauging the attitude-behavior relationship. By the early 1980s the answer had become a little clearer: some attitudes guide some behaviors in some circumstances.

Yet, although research had demonstrated the usefulness of the attitude construct by the early 1980s, it had still failed to shed much light on the process by which this ever-growing list of important attitudinal, situational and personality variables exert their influence. Clearly, a model was needed to identify important steps in the attitude-to-behavior process. What follows is a description of Fazio's model of the attitude-to-behavior process. This model details the process by which attitudes guide information processing and subsequent behavior, thereby providing an explanation for at least some of the variables mentioned above that have been shown to affect the attitude-behavior relationship.

The Process Model

Behavior is a Function of Perceptions

The process model begins by assuming that an individual's behavior toward an object is a function of his or her interpretation of the situation in which the attitude object is encountered. Most social interactions engender many possible interpretations of events and situations, and social stimuli, such as the actions or intentions of others, often lend themselves to multiple meanings. For example, two observers might witness the same park visitor abandoning a smoldering campfire, but perceive the event quite differently. Observer A might make note of the fire, recognize this as a dangerous situation, and approach the camper about his behavior. Observer B, on the other hand, might see the campfire without recognizing the behavior as dangerous. Observer B would thus not approach the man about his dangerous behavior, even though, if asked, Observer B would profess concern about campsite safety.

Although both observers saw the same man leaving the fire unattended, the two witnesses arrived at different interpretations of the same event. Most importantly, how an observer would behave in this situation (e.g., whether she would approach the visitor about his carelessness) would depend on her interpretation of the event. Such disparate interpretations are part of everyday life, and obviously have important implications with regard to subsequent behavior. Indeed, research by Latane and Darley (1970) has demonstrated the impact that differing definitions of events can have on behaviors such as bystander intervention in the event of a fire. Subjects in their experiment who did not interpret smoke-like vapors as evidence of a fire were not inclined to summon help or report the vapors to the experimenter.

Attitudes Can Guide Perceptions

This step of interpreting events is crucial in the attitude-to-behavior process. The impact of attitudes on the defining of events is posited to guide behaviors.

The idea that attitudes can guide perceptions is not new. In fact, a great deal of research conducted during the last 50 years suggests that attitudes do in fact determine perceptions of objects. An example of this literature is the research on the use of the adjectives "warm" and "cold" in describing others, first initiated by Asch (1946). In a test of the implications of the use of these terms, Kelley (1950) found that students who were led to believe that an instructor was "warm" tended to participate more in a class discussion than did students who were led to believe that the instructor was "cold." Perceptions of the instructor influenced behaviors toward that person.

Figure 1
Attitude-to-Behavior Process

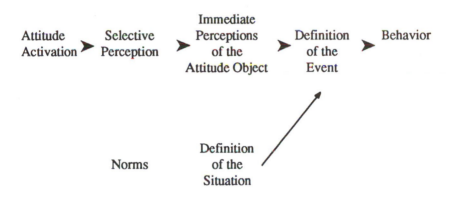

The notion that attitudes guide perceptions was heavily emphasized in the "New Look" movement among social psychologists during the 1940s and 1950s, a movement that emphasized the effects of existing knowledge structures on perceptions. Bruner (1957) and his colleagues saw the structuring of one's perceptual experiences as one of the most important functions of attitudes. Attitudes were said to provide a "ready aid in 'sizing up' objects and events in the environment" (Smith et al. 1956). Allport (1935), in a classic paper on attitudes, stated the case succinctly:

> Without guiding attitudes the individual is confused and baffled. Some kind of preparation is essential before he can make a satisfactory observation, pass suitable judgment, or make any but the most primitive reflex type of response. Attitudes determine for each

individual what he will see and hear, what he will think and what he will do. To borrow a phrase from William James, they "engender meaning upon the world;" they draw lines about and segregate an otherwise chaotic environment; they are our methods for finding our way about in an ambiguous universe (p. 806).

This idea of attitudes being used to categorize objects and organize perceptions is known as the object appraisal or knowledge function of attitudes. Several researchers in the New Look tradition were able to demonstrate that attitudes do in fact alter perceptions. Most of these studies dealt with the value of an object to an individual and perceptions of the objects' physical attributes, such as children's estimates of the size of coins (Bruner and Goodman 1947). Attitudes were also shown to bias interpretations of ambiguous pictures (Proshansky 1943), and perceptions of infractions in a college football game (Hastorf and Cantril 1954).

More recently, Lord et al. (1979) have demonstrated that individuals' attitudes toward capital punishment can strongly affect their evaluations of relevant empirical evidence. Similar processes have been shown to play a role in the interpretation of and behavioral reactions to the behaviors of others (Darley and Fazio 1980). To return to our campfire example, an observer with a well-established negative attitude about careless campfire behaviors is likely to notice this behavior and interpret the event in terms of fire safety, leading her to approach the visitor about the situation.

Behavior is Also Guided by Other Factors

In light of these findings, it would appear that attitudes do in fact bias perceptions. Why, then, have so many studies found a lack of covariation between attitudes and subsequent behaviors if behavior is truly a function of such perceptions? Attitudes certainly have the potential to affect behaviors via altered perception in a manner the Fazio model would predict. There are two plausible explanations for this apparent discrepancy: (1) some attitudes may not be considered at all in interactions involving the attitude object, and 2) even in situations where attitudes are in fact activated from memory, other forces compete to influence behavior within a situation.

Normative guidelines. With regard to the latter explanation, notice that in the model diagram in Figure 1, attitudes are only one determinant of the definition of an event. How one defines the surrounding situation also affects the definition of an event. In any given situation, several knowledge structures are potentially applicable. One particularly important kind of information that may affect an individual's definition of the situation is knowledge of relevant norms. Knowledge about the behaviors that are normative for a given situation or class of situations can exert tremendous influence upon both one's definition of a situation and one's subsequent behaviors. Milgram's (1963) obedience study, in which individuals were led to administer what they thought were potentially fatal levels of electric shock to others as part of an experiment, serves as a powerful reminder of the influence that norms can exert on behavior. Subjects in that experiment were apparently driven by normative considerations of their status vis-a-vis the experimenter to commit acts that were clearly disturbing to them.

In our campsite example, an observer would be less likely to act on his observation of the fire if the camper leaving the smoldering fire was wearing the uniform of a conservation officer, since norms indicate that conservation officers are authorities about fire safety in parks.

Consideration of relevant attitudes. While norms are certainly an important situational influence on behavior, consideration of relevant norms cannot explain all of the failures of attitudes to guide behaviors. People experience dozens of situations that do not have strong normative guidelines, in which they fail to act according to their attitudes toward the objects involved. In many of these situations, it is likely that attitudes toward the objects in question simply are not accessed from memory. To initiate the process depicted in Fazio's model, one's attitude must first be activated from memory. The importance of accessing relevant attitudes is illustrated by two studies conducted by Snyder and his colleagues.

Snyder and Swann (1976) asked subjects to make judgments in simulated court cases involving sex discrimination. These researchers found that subjects' judgments correlated to a much higher degree with subjects' attitudes toward affirmative action when subjects were asked to take some time to consider their attitudes *before* reading the case. In terms of the process model, these subjects were being asked to access their relevant attitudes, thus initiating the sequence of selective perception depicted by the model.

In another demonstration of the importance of accessing an attitude, Snyder and Kendzierski (1982) engineered a situation in which a contextual cue served to prompt subjects to consider their attitudes toward participating in psychology experiments. The term "cue" as used here refers to any stimulus that specifically prompts consideration of an attitude. These researchers exposed subjects who had previously indicated favorable attitudes toward psychological research to a notice posted in a waiting room. The notice was a request for volunteers to participate in a psychology experiment, and every subject was exposed to the sign.

However, half of the subjects were also exposed to a conversation among confederates of the experimenters that prompted activation of the subjects' own favorable attitudes toward psychology experiments (a cue): "[It's] really a question of how worthwhile you think experiments are." The other subjects were not exposed to this particular cue. Snyder and Kendzierski found that subjects exposed to the verbal prompt acted upon their attitudes more often than those who were not exposed to that cue. Thus, some cues do prompt attitude activation.

Our safety-minded Observer B might have passed the smoldering campfire without ever considering her attitude; she might have been busy thinking about the beautiful oak trees around her or the rare bird she had just spotted. However, a sign at the campsite encouraging fire safety might have prompted her to consider her attitude, leading her to notice the dangerous campsite behavior and act accordingly.

However, not all situations provide such cues. Whether attitudes exert any influence in such situations would appear to depend upon the chronic accessibility of the attitude from memory (i.e., the likelihood of spontaneous activation of the attitude upon merely being presented with or encountering the object). That is, some attitudes must be activated without contextual cues or explicit demands for activation such as those used in Snyder's experiments. But what determines whether an attitude is chronically accessible?

Determinants of Automatic Activation

The issues of what makes an attitude chronically accessible and how such chronically accessible attitudes affect behavior have been a major focus of research on Fazio's model. One important determinant of accessibility follows readily from our definition of attitude.

Our working definition of attitude. Researchers have defined "attitudes" in many different ways (Greenwald 1968, McGuire 1969). These definitions have variously included elements of affect or emotion toward the target object, behaviors toward the object, and cognitions or thoughts about the object. We have chosen to use the simplest common denominator of previous definitions to define attitudes simply as the association in memory between an object and an evaluation (e.g., Fazio, Chen, McDonel and Sherman 1982). That is, the one thing that all attitude definitions have in common is the notion that having an attitude toward an object connotes having categorized an item along an evaluative dimension. This definition involves the affective component of attitudes. To have an attitude toward cockroaches is to have an evaluation (e.g., "extreme dislike") associated with cockroaches. Furthermore, representation of both the object (cockroach) and evaluation (extreme dislike) are assumed to be stored in long-term memory.

In general, research has demonstrated that the strength of association between items in memory can vary (e.g., the more often and consistently two items are experienced as pairs, the stronger the association between them), and this strength of association can have important information processing consequences. In the research to be discussed later in this chapter, Fazio and his associates have found that the strength of the association between the representations of the object in memory and its accompanying evaluation largely determines the accessibility of the attitude (Fazio, Chen, McDonel and Sherman 1982).

When presented with the name of an object (e.g., "cockroach") and asked to indicate one's attitude toward it as quickly as possible, the speed with which one can respond indicates how accessible or easily recalled one's attitude is from memory. Attitude accessibility may be thought of as determining an attitude/nonattitude continuum (Figure 2). At the nonattitude end of the continuum is the case of an individual having no *a priori* judgment stored with regard to the attitude object; thus, an attitude is not available in memory. As one moves along the continuum, an evaluation is available in memory and the strength of association between the object and evaluation increases. Toward the opposite end of the continuum are evaluations that are sufficiently strong to automatically activate the evaluation in memory upon mere observation of the object.

The accessibility of an attitude plays the crucial role in the attitude-behavior process model. More specifically, attitudes that are so accessible as to be activated or called to mind automatically upon encountering an object may guide perceptions of the object, and in so doing, exert their influence upon subsequent behavior toward the object. When an individual possesses an attitude that is not automatically accessible, the individual may encounter the attitude object without ever viewing it in evaluative terms, and therefore may not act in a manner consistent with his attitude. In such cases, the individual interactions with the object may in fact be guided by momentarily salient, situational influences.

Determinants of accessibility: repeated expression. Early research on Fazio's process model concerned the strength of association between an object and its evaluation in memory as a determinant of attitude accessibility. Because of the definition of attitude as an association in memory, it follows that one might be able to apply well-established principles of associative learning in order to strengthen an

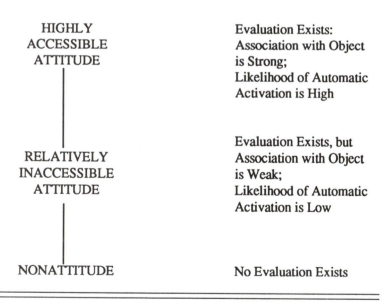

Figure 2
Attitude-Nonattitude Continuum

HIGHLY ACCESSIBLE ATTITUDE	Evaluation Exists: Association with Object is Strong; Likelihood of Automatic Activation is High
RELATIVELY INACCESSIBLE ATTITUDE	Evaluation Exists, but Association with Object is Weak; Likelihood of Automatic Activation is Low
NONATTITUDE	No Evaluation Exists

attitude. As stated above, one manner in which associations can be strengthened is through repeated pairing; that is, the more often the word "bacon" is paired with "eggs," the greater the strength of association between them. The strength of association between two items in memory has been found to have specific consequences. One such consequence is that the greater the strength of association in memory, the more likely it becomes that one word will be brought to mind, or "activated," when the other is encountered (e.g., presentation of "nurse" should facilitate recognition of the word "doctor"). Thus, repeatedly and consistently pairing an object with a given evaluation should increase the accessibility of that evaluation upon presentation of the attitude object. This is exactly what Fazio and his colleagues (Fazio, Chen, McDonel and Sherman 1982, exp. 3, Powell and Fazio 1984) have found in a number of studies. Subjects who repeatedly express their attitudes toward objects can respond to direct inquiries concerning these attitudes relatively quickly.

As an example, consider the experimental situations created by Fazio, Chen, McDonel and Sherman (1982). Subjects were shown a videotape of an individual working with five novel experimental puzzles. All subjects indicated how interesting they found these puzzles. The experimenter then asked half of the subjects to copy their ratings on two additional forms in order to provide both a data entry person and the experimenter's professor with a copy of the results. Each form placed the five puzzles in a different order, and was of a different format. Thus, the subjects in this condition were induced to repeatedly note and express their attitudes toward each puzzle.

Accessibility of attitudes toward these puzzles was then measured by presenting the subjects with slides of the names of the puzzles coupled with an evaluative adjective (e.g., "Letter Series: Interesting?"), and asking subjects to respond as quickly as possible by pressing keys labelled "Yes" or "No." The speed with which these judgments were made, or latency of response, was then measured to the nearest millisecond. Subjects who had expressed their judgments of the puzzles repeatedly on the two forms responded significantly faster in this task than did those subjects who had expressed their attitudes only once.

In a later study, a similar procedure was followed to determine whether this finding could be generalized to less trivial attitudes. Powell and Fazio (1984) used a lengthy questionnaire to manipulate the number of times subjects expressed their attitudes regarding several different issues (e.g., capital punishment) by varying the number of semantic differential items that were relevant to a given attitude issue. In this fashion subjects were thus induced to express their attitudes toward a given issue zero, one, three or six times. In a subsequent judgment task, the subjects were presented with each attitude issue and asked to make a good/bad judgment as fast as possible by pressing the appropriately labelled key. The attitude issue was displayed on a computer screen and the computer measured the time elapsed between the display of the issue and the subject's response. Response latency related positively to the number of attitudinal expressions: the greater the number of expressions, the faster the latency of the response.

Determinants of accessibility: direct experience. Repeated expression is not the only process that leads to increased accessibility of a construct. Any variable that increases the strength of the object-evaluation association in memory should accomplish the same thing. Fazio, Chen, McDonel and Sherman (1982) examined the link between attitude accessibility and the manner of attitude formation. Specifically, they were interested in whether attitudes based on direct experience with the attitude object would be characterized by greater accessibility. An important tenet of self-perception theory (Bem 1972) is that behavior toward an object affords more attitudinally-reflective information. Self-perception theory views attitudes as summaries of one's past behaviors. The theory predicts that actual interaction with an object provides more reflective information about how a subject feels about the object than does indirect, nonbehavioral experience such as listening to a description of the object. Furthermore, several studies have found that attitudes based on direct experience are more likely to lead to attitude-consistent behavior (see Fazio and Zanna 1981, for a review). Fazio, Chen, McDonel and Sherman (1982) theorize that such attitudes have a greater influence upon behavior as a consequence of producing attitudes characterized by higher levels of accessibility.

Subjects were asked to make judgments of intellectual puzzles either after playing with samples of each puzzle type (direct experience) or after hearing descriptions of and seeing each sample (indirect experience). The subjects were then asked to respond as quickly as possible to inquiries regarding their judgments of the puzzles. Subjects with the direct experience reliably responded more quickly than those who based their attitudes upon descriptions. It thus appears that the manner of attitude formation also has an effect on attitude accessibility: direct experience attitudes are more accessible than indirect-experience attitudes (see Fazio 1987, and Fazio, Herr and Olney 1984, for further evidence and discussion of the accessibility of attitudes that are inferred from behavior). These findings support the view of attitudes as object-evaluation associations, and support the notion that the strength of such associations determines attitude accessibility. The accessibility of an attitude can be affected by the manner of attitude formation, as well as by repeated expression.

Confirming Automatic Activation of Accessible Attitudes

An important element of Fazio's model is that attitudes that are very accessible can be activated automatically from memory upon mere presentation of the object, without prompting from any sort of cues. The distinction between automatic versus controlled processes has received a good deal of attention in psychological literature. In general, an automatic process is defined as any process that leads to the activation of some concept or response "whenever a given set of external initiating stimuli are presented, regardless of a subject's attempt to ignore or bypass the distraction (Shiffrin and Dumais 1981)."

In order to test whether attitudes can be automatically activated when a subject is presented with an object, Fazio, Sanbonmatsu, Powell and Kardes (1986) used a research paradigm known as *priming*. Past research has demonstrated that the activation of one construct in memory can facilitate or prime judgments, such as identification, of subsequently presented items, and that such facilitation is a function of the association among the items. Fazio, Sanbonmatsu, Powell and Kardes (1986) reasoned that such priming effects might extend to evaluations associated in memory with a target object. That is, priming with a negative adjective might facilitate responses to other negative adjectives by virtue of the objects' evaluative similarity. If so, the mere presentation of objects characterized by automatically accessible attitudes should facilitate similar evaluative judgments. For example, the word "disgusting" should facilitate responses to an evaluatively similar word such as "awful." Because the words "disgusting" and "awful" are strongly linked in memory, presentation of the former should facilitate responses to the latter. In this case, one negative evaluative adjective would be priming another evaluative adjective.

If this is true, then an object with a very accessible negative attitude (e.g., "cockroaches") might also facilitate responses to words like "awful." In the case described above, the word "disgusting" is given to subjects, and facilitation of the responses to "awful" is measured. In the second case, no adjective is presented as a prime. Only an attitude object toward which the experimenters can assume subjects have a strongly associated evaluative response is presented. The important point here is that if some attitudes automatically bring to mind associated evaluations, then one should be able to present the attitude objects as evaluative primes.

Fazio, Sanbonmatsu, Powell and Kardes (1986) asked subjects to make a simple identification of the positive or negative connotations of the target adjectives. Thus, subjects might see "cockroach" displayed on their computer terminal, followed by the word "disgusting." Subjects were instructed to press an appropriately labelled key when they knew whether the adjective had positive or negative connotations. Highly accessible attitudes should prime associated evaluations, and thus ought to facilitate judgments of consistent valence (e.g., "cockroach" should facilitate the response that "disgusting" has a negative connotation).

Such facilitation was observed in a series of experiments (Fazio, Sanbonmatsu, Powell and Kardes 1986), provided that the object-evaluation association in memory was strong. In some experiments, such strong associations were identified by measuring the latency of responses to an attitudinal inquiry. Objects toward which the individual could indicate a relatively quick evaluation produced more facilitation (i.e., faster responses in identifying the evaluative connotation of target adjectives that followed) than did objects toward which the individual could indicate a relatively slow evaluation.

In a related experiment, strong associations among attitude objects and evaluations were created experimentally via repeated attitudinal expressions. Regardless of whether associative strength was measured or manipulated, objects involving strongly-associated positive evaluations facilitated responses to positive adjectives. Likewise, objects involving strongly-associated negative evaluations facilitated responses to negative adjectives. Objects characterized by weak associations did not facilitate responses to either positive or negative adjectives.

It is important to note that subjects were not asked during the word connotation task to consider their attitudes toward the primes. In fact, they were told that the prime was simply a memory word, and that their task was to judge the target words. This research provides evidence that some attitudes can be activated automatically.

Further Research on the Process Model

Thus far, we have presented the results of experiments indicating that attitudes may be considered as associations in memory between an object and an evaluation. We have also discussed research that indicates that the strength of such associations reliably affects the accessibility of the evaluation from memory upon encountering the object, and thus affects the likelihood that an attitude will be activated automatically upon presentation of the attitude object.

Attitude Accessibility and Information Processing

Fazio's research program has also sought to verify the effects of differential levels of accessibility on information processing. The process model predicts that highly accessible attitudes should initiate a process of selective perceptions of the attitude object, shaping one's definition of an event. Selective processing is thus hypothesized as the initial step in deriving consistent behaviors from highly accessible attitudes. Our research demonstrates that attitude accessibility does in fact have an effect on subsequent information processing.

Our first effort necessitates the description of a research paradigm that has been used to demonstrate how the priming of a construct can increase the likelihood that it will be used in the interpretation of ambiguous information (Higgins et al. 1977, Srull and Wyer 1979, 1980). Higgins et al. (1977) presented subjects with a Stroop color/word task, in which words were written in different colors. The subjects' task was to name the color in which the words were written. Some of the words were the names of colors (e.g., the word "brown" was written with red ink, and the subjects should have responded "red"). Other words that the subjects saw during this task were trait-related words, such as "adventurous."

In a second experiment which subjects were told was unrelated to the first, subjects were asked to judge target individuals who were described with behaviors that could be interpreted as the result of positive or negative traits (e.g., reckless or adventurous). When positive trait words had appeared in the Stroop task, subjects were more likely to evaluate the ambiguous behaviors as evidence of positive traits, and the reverse happened when negative trait words served as primes. For example, if the word "adventurous" was presented in the Stroop task, subjects were likely to view the act of driving a boat at high speed as more positive than if they had been exposed to the word "reckless." Thus, the appearance of trait words in the first task increased the likelihood that the traits would be used in judgments in the second task. The essential principle evident here is that activating a construct temporarily enhances the accessibility of the construct from memory, thus increasing the likelihood that the construct will be employed to interpret subsequently presented ambiguous information.

The priming conducted by Higgins et al. (1977) involved the use of trait words potentially related in meaning to the ambiguous behaviors described in the second part of their study. In a conceptual replication of Higgins et al. (1977), Fazio, Powell and Herr (1983) used evaluative adjectives as primes. Adjectives such as "pleasant," "exciting," "frustrating" and "tiresome" were used as primes in a Stroop task. A second task involved judging the motives of a person described in a short paragraph. Subjects were asked to decide whether the described person participated in an experimental task because of intrinsic interest in the experiment or because of situational factors such as monetary inducements. The evaluative adjectives did in fact affect these judgments. When the adjectives were positive and applicable to the judgment in the second task, more subjects rated the target as having acted on intrinsic interest. The opposite results were found when negative adjectives appeared in the Stroop task.

In a second experiment, Fazio, Powell and Herr (1983) used attitude objects about which subjects had highly accessible attitudes as primes instead of evaluative adjectives. The purpose of this experiment was to test the information processing consequences of highly accessible attitudes. If such attitudes automatically activated their associated evaluations, presentation of the attitude objects alone as primes should be sufficient to activate the associated evaluation from memory. Once activated, these evaluations should then affect subsequent judgments in a manner similar to that observed in the earlier experiment.

Subjects were introduced to and evaluated five intellectual puzzles. In the relevant conditions, half of the subjects were then asked to express their attitudes toward these puzzles repeatedly, thus increasing the accessibility of their attitudes. Subjects then went through the Higgins et al. (1977) paradigm, in which they were exposed to either the puzzle that they disliked or liked the most in the course of a "color perception" task. Following completion of this task, subjects read the ambiguous paragraph and judged the target person described. As predicted, the experimenters found that the puzzles about which subjects had accessible attitudes, via repeated expression, biased judgments in a manner similar to the use of evaluative adjectives in the first experiment. Those puzzles about which subjects did not have highly accessible attitudes did not bias subjects' judgments.

These findings indicate that biased information processing is likely to occur following activation of accessible attitudes. Such biased processing is predicted in Fazio's model to guide perceptions of further interactions with the attitude object.

This idea was tested in a more naturalistic context in a study by Fazio and Williams (1986). In this experiment, the experimenters tested the accessibility of attitudes toward the two participants in the 1984 presidential debates. Before the debates, the experimenters set up a booth in a shopping mall and local townspeople volunteered as subjects. Latency of response toward a variety of topics, including the candidates Walter Mondale and Ronald Reagan, was measured. Subjects were then mailed a questionnaire after the debates, asking the subjects to rate the performances of the candidates. Attitudes toward the candidates correlated significantly with perceptions of debate performances. However, this correlation was much stronger among those subjects with highly accessible attitudes. Thus, this study provides additional evidence that accessible attitudes do bias perceptions.

Research by Lord et al. (1979) demonstrated that attitudes toward a social policy issue affected subjects' perceptions of relevant empirical evidence. Lord et al. (1979) exposed subjects to summaries of one study that supported capital punishment, and one study that did not. Subjects were found to view the study that supported their own position as better conducted and more convincing than the one that disconfirmed their position. In terms of Fazio's model, one would expect this biased processing of evidence to be a function of the accessibility of one's attitude toward capital punishment.

To test this idea, Houston and Fazio (1989) manipulated the accessibility of attitudes toward the death penalty via repeated expression. This manipulation subsequently affected the degree of biased evidence processing. That is, subjects with very accessible attitudes exerted much greater influence upon perceptions of the evidence than the attitudes of subjects characterized by low accessibility. Thus, it appears that individuals with accessible attitudes are more likely to process information relevant to their attitudes in a biased fashion, than those with equivalent but less accessible attitudes.

Overall, it appears that attitudes do guide perceptions and affect judgments. However, this process appears to be much more pronounced for attitudes that are readily accessible from memory. Regardless of whether attitudes are simply measured, as in the presidential debate study, or manipulated, as in the capital punishment study, individuals with relatively accessible attitudes were more likely to engage in biased information processing than individuals with less accessible attitudes.

Attitude Accessibility and Behavior

The final element of Fazio's model that has received empirical scrutiny is the impact of attitude accessibility on subsequent behavior. Many of the studies discussed previously included a test of behavioral consequences. In the presidential debate study (Fazio and Williams 1986), subjects were contacted by telephone beginning one day after the election and asked if they voted and if so, for whom. Even though the initial attitude measures had taken place four months prior to the election, 80 percent of the variance in voting behavior was predicted by attitudes toward Reagan among subjects with highly accessible attitudes, compared with 44 percent among those subjects in the low accessibility group. The link between attitude accessibility and behavior in this study may have been moderated by biased processing of information about the candidates throughout their campaigns. The apparent result is that accessible attitudes are likely to persist over time. On the other hand, individuals with relatively inaccessible attitudes, and therefore lacking the influence of selective perception, were more likely to encounter information that altered their sentiments toward the candidates and, ultimately, altered their vote.

Fazio, Chen, McDonel and Sherman (1982, experiment 4) gave subjects a chance to examine and work on any of the five puzzle types after completing either the single or repeated expression manipulation described earlier. Repeated expression subjects exhibited greater attitude-behavior consistency than did single expression subjects. The average within-subject correlation between attitude scores toward the puzzles and the proportion of attempted problems of a given type was .474 for repeated expression subjects, and .218 for single expression subjects. Furthermore, the repeated expression subjects differed only in the accessibility of their attitudes; attitudes toward the puzzles were not significantly different between the groups.

Finally, the issue of accessible attitudes guiding behavior and influencing behavioral choices was tested in a recent study conducted by Fazio, Powell and Williams (1989). In this study, attitude accessibility was measured by having subjects indicate whether they liked or disliked each of 100 consumer products that were presented on a computer screen. Subjects also provided an attitude rating of each of the

100 products on a questionnaire scale of one (extremely bad) to seven (extremely good). The experimenters recorded both traditional attitude rating scores and accessibility.

Following completion of these scales, subjects were thanked for their participation and told that they could select five products from among ten that were displayed on a table (the items included candy bars, chewing gum, soda and so on, and the items were judged to be roughly equivalent in valence in pretesting. All ten items had previously appeared on the attitude measures. For each product, the subjects were divided into three groups of high, moderate and low attitude accessibility toward that product on the basis of response latencies. Averaged across the ten products, the correlations between attitude ratings and whether the subjects chose the product or not revealed a significant linear trend across the high, moderate and low accessibility groups. Attitude accessibility moderated the extent of the attitude-behavior relation. The more accessible a subject's attitude toward a given product, the more likely that product selection behavior was consistent with that attitude.

Limitations of the Model

The sequence of events that the process model seeks to describe is not the only way in which attitudes can guide behavior. The process model is intended to explain how attitudes might exert their influence on behaviors when the behavior in question is spontaneous in nature and stems from one's perceptions of the attitude object in the immediate situation. However, some decisions and behaviors are not spontaneous, but deliberate and even preplanned. The most frequently discussed model of the effect of attitudes on deliberate decisions and behaviors is Ajzen and Fishbein's (1980) Theory of Reasoned Action. Whereas the process model seeks to describe the influence of attitudes in situations where behavior occurs spontaneously, Ajzen and Fishbein describe the influence of attitudes when the process is deliberate in nature; hence the name "Theory of Reasoned Action." In this model, behavior follows from behavioral intention, which in turn is a function of one's attitude toward the specific behavior in question and toward subjective norms.

An interesting question arises concerning when individuals will engage in the deliberative processing described by the Ajzen and Fishbein model, and when they will engage in the spontaneous processing described by Fazio's model. Fazio (1990) has provided a possible answer to this question in what he has termed the MODE model (Motivation and Opportunity as DEterminants of which processing mode will likely operate in a given situation). The MODE model postulates that an individual must both be motivated to engage in deliberative processing and have the opportunity to do so. In situations that fulfill these requirements, attitudes do not need to be automatically accessible in order to guide behavior. However, when either motivation or opportunity are absent, accessibility becomes a crucial determinant of the degree to which behavior can be expected to follow from attitudes.

An example of the motivation factor is what Kruglanski (Kruglanski and Freund 1983) has termed the "fear of invalidity." When the perceived consequences of an incorrect judgment are high, individuals are more likely to process information carefully in making that judgment. Conversely, when an erroneous judgment is perceived to have little consequence, the individual is less likely to engage in careful information processing. An example of this factor would be asking subjects to make a judgment in an experiment, either with the expectation that they were going to have to justify their judgments in front of a group of fellow subjects, or that no further exchange concerning their judgments would take place. In the former situation, high fear of invalidity would likely motivate subjects to carefully process information; the latter situation provides no such motivation. The issue of opportunity concerns limitations on human processing capacity. If an individual does not have the opportunity to process information, even given the motivation to do so, he obviously will not.

Thus, Fazio's MODE model predicts that in situations in which individuals do not have both the motivation and opportunity to engage in deliberative processing, the process model described in this chapter is likely to describe the attitude-behavior relationship. When motivation and opportunity are both present, however, one could expect a more deliberative process, such as that described in Ajzen and Fishbein's model, to predominate.

Implications of the Fazio Process Model
for Social Influence Strategies

The process model described above and its accompanying body of evidence may provide managers or others interested in initiating attitude change and/or attitude formation programs with some concrete goals. While specific applications of the model in a persuasion context have not been addressed to date, several predictions and recommendations can be made with current knowledge.

The single most important implication that the Fazio model offers, with regard to persuasion, stems from the model's central tenet that attitudes that seem to be equivalent by traditional standards (i.e., equivalent as measured on a Likert scale) may still differ markedly with respect to associative strength in memory and, hence, differ in accessibility from memory. If the purpose of a social influence program is to modify behavior, then it will not be sufficient to simply modify attitudes in the desired direction. These newly modified attitudes must themselves be made accessible from memory if they are to have much likelihood of affecting behavior.

In situations where both motivation and opportunity to deliberate on the attitude can be expected or encouraged, efforts to alter attitude accessibility may not be necessary. One may assume that efforts to encourage motivation and opportunity would be a logical first step in any such social influence program. The aim would be to induce people to consciously deliberate about their actions rather than engage in undesired spontaneous behavior.

In the long run, however, one cannot assume that desired behaviors will always be the product of careful and deliberate processing, since the vast majority of daily behaviors are not performed deliberately, and prompts to encourage deliberation will not be present in every relevant situation. Thus, those interested in altering behaviors via a persuasion program should include attitude accessibility as a criterion both in designing and measuring the effectiveness of such attempts.

Attempts aimed at establishing new attitudes or strengthening existing attitudes may also benefit from two principles that emerge from the research on the process model. First, attitudes based upon direct experience tend to be more accessible, and thus exert a much greater influence on subsequent behavior than those attitudes based on indirect experience. Programs aimed at bringing about voluntary participation in desirable behaviors are likely to be especially effective, since attitude accessibility can be expected to increase with direct experience. An example would be demonstrations of fire safety that maximize participation by the intended persuasion recipients. Second, attitudes that are rendered accessible via repeated expression are also more likely to guide behavior. For example, social influence campaigns that encourage people to repeatedly associate a given evaluation with a particular issue may prove more effective in modifying behavior.

These suggestions are meant only as a starting point for the application of attitude accessibility in a persuasion context. Again, the important implication of Fazio's process model is that the enhancement of the accessibility of the desired attitude should be included as a major goal in social influence programs. Obviously, these ideas must be conceptualized and tested empirically. We hope, however, that they can provide some theoretical guidance for subsequent social influence research.

Preparation of this chapter was supported by Research Scientist Development Award MH00452 and Grant MH38832 from the National Institute of Mental Health to Russell H. Fazio.

REFERENCES

Ajzen, I.; Fishbein, M. 1973. Attitudinal and normative variables as predictors of specific behaviors. *Journal of Personality and Social Psychology.* 27: 41-57.

Ajzen, I.; Fishbein, M. 1980. *Understanding attitudes and predicting social behavior.* Englewood Cliffs, NJ: Prentice Hall.

Allport, G. W. 1935. Attitudes. In: Murchison, C., (ed.) *Handbook of social psychology. 6:* 1-62. New York, NY: Academic Press.

Asch, S. E. 1946. Forming impressions of personality. *Journal of Abnormal and Social Psychology. 41:* 258-290.

Bem, D. J. 1972. Self-perception theory. In: Berkowitz, L., (ed.) *Advances in experimental social psychology. 6:* 1-62. New York, NY: Academic Press.

Bruner, J. S. 1957. On perceptual readiness. *Psychological Review. 64:* 123-152.

Bruner, J. S.; Goodman, C. C. 1947. Value and need as organizing factors in perception. *Journal of Abnormal and Social Psychology. 42:* 33-44.

Corey, S. M. 1937. Professed attitudes and actual behavior. *Journal of Educational Psychology. 37:* 1364-1376.

Darley, J. M.; Fazio, R. H. 1980. Expectancy confirmation processes arising in the social interaction sequence. *American Psychologist. 35:* 867-881.

Doob, L. W. 1947. The behavior of attitudes. *Psychological Review. 54:* 135-156.

Fazio, R. H. 1986. How do attitudes guide behavior? In: Sorrentino, R. M.; Higgins, E. T., (eds.) *The handbook of motivation and cognition: Foundations of social behavior.* New York, NY: Guilford Press: 204-243.

Fazio, R. H. 1987. Self-perception theory: A current perspective. In: Zanna, M. P.; Olson, J. M.; Herman, C. P., (eds.) *Social influence: The Ontario symposium.* *5*: 129-150. Hillsdale, NJ: Erlbaum.

Fazio, R. H. 1989. On the power and functionality of attitudes: The role of attitude accessibility. In Pratkanis, A. R.; Breckler, S. J.; Greenwald, A. G., (eds.) *Attitude structure and function.* Hillsdale, NJ: Erlbaum: 153-177.

Fazio, R. H. 1990. Multiple processes by which attitudes guide behavior: the MODE model as an integrative framework. In: Zanna, M. P., (ed.) *Advances in Experimental Social Psychology.* New York, NY: Academic Press: 75-108.

Fazio, R. H.; Chen, J.; McDonel, E. C.; Sherman, S. J. 1982. Attitude accessibility, attitude-behavior consistency, and the strength of the object-evaluation association. *Journal of Experimental Social Psychology.* *18*: 339-357.

Fazio, R. H.; Herr, P. M.; Olney, T. J. 1984. Attitude accessibility following a self-perception process. *Journal of Personality and Social Psychology.* *47*: 277-286.

Fazio, R. H.; Powell, M. C.; Herr, P. M. 1983. Toward a process model of the attitude-behavior relation: Accessing one's attitude upon mere observation of the attitude object. *Journal of Personality and Social Psychology.* *44*: 723-735.

Fazio, R. H.; Powell, M. C.; Williams, C. J. 1989. The role of attitude accessibility in the attitude-to-behavior process. *Journal of Consumer Research.* *16*: 280-288.

Fazio, R. H.; Sanbonmatsu, D. M.; Powell, M.C.; Kardes, F.R. 1986. On the automatic activation of attitudes. *Journal of Personality and Social Psychology.* *50*: 229-238.

Fazio, R. H.; Williams, C. J. 1986. Attitude accessibility as a moderator of the attitude-perception and attitude-behavior relations: An investigation of the 1984 presidential election. *Journal of Personality and Social Psychology.* *51*: 505-514.

Fazio, R. H.; Zanna, M. P. 1981. Direct experience and attitude-behavior consistency. In: Berkowitz, L., (ed.) *Advances in experimental social psychology.* *14*: 162-202. New York, NY: Academic Press.

Greenwald, A. G. 1968. On defining attitude and attitude theory. In: Greenwald, A.G.; Brock, T.C.; Ostrom, T.M., (eds.) *Psychological foundations of attitudes.* New York, NY: Academic Press: 361-388.

Hastorf, A. H.; Cantril, H. 1954. They saw a game: A case study. *Journal of Abnormal and Social Psychology.* *49*: 129-134.

Higgins, E. T.; Rholes, W. S.; Jones, C. R. 1977. Category accessibility and impression formation. *Journal of Experimental Social Psychology.* *13*: 141-154.

Houston, D. A.; Fazio, R. H. 1989. Biased processing as a function of attitude accessibility. *Social Cognition. 7*: 51-66.

Kardes, F. R.; Sanbonmatsu, D. M.; Voss, R.; Fazio, R. H. 1984. Self-monitoring and attitude accessibility. *Personality and Social Psychology Bulletin. 12*: 468-474.

Kelley, H. H. 1950. The warm-cold variable in first impressions of persons. *Journal of Personality. 18*: 431-439.

Kelley, S.; Mirer, T. W. 1974. The simple act of voting. *American Political Science Review. 68*: 572-591.

Kruglanski, A. W.; Freund, T. 1983. The freezing and unfreezing of lay-inferences: Effects of impressional primacy, ethnic stereotyping, and numerical anchoring. *Journal of Experimental Social Psychology. 19*: 448-468.

LaPierre, R. T. 1943. Attitudes vs. actions. *Social Forces. 13*: 230-237.

Latane, B.; Darley, J. M. 1970. *The unresponsive bystander: Why doesn't he help?* New York, NY: Appleton-Century-Crofts.

Lord, C. G.; Ross, L.; Lepper, M. R. 1979. Biased assimilation and attitude polarization: the effects of prior theories on subsequently considered evidence. *Journal of Personality and Social Psychology. 37*: 2098-2109.

McGuire, W. J. 1969. The nature of attitudes and attitude change. In: Lindzey, G.; Aronson, E., (eds.) *Handbook of social psychology. 2nd ed. 3*: 136-314. Reading, MA: Addison-Wesley.

Milgram, S. 1963. Behavioral study of obedience. *Journal of Abnormal and Social Psychology. 67*: 371-378.

Powell, M. C.; Fazio, R. H. 1984. Attitude accessibility as a function of repeated attitudinal expression. *Personality and Social Psychology Bulletin. 10*: 139-148.

Proshansky, H. M. 1943. A projective method for the study of attitudes. *Journal of Abnormal and Social Psychology. 38*: 393-395.

Rholes, W. S.; Bailey, S. 1983. The effects of level of moral reasoning on consistency between moral attitudes and related behaviors. *Social Cognition. 2:* 32-48.

Schuman, H.; Johnson, M. P. 1976. Attitudes and behavior. *Annual Review of Sociology. 2*: 161-207.

Shiffrin, R. M.; Dumais, S. T. 1981. The development of automatism. In Anderson, J. R., (ed.) *Cognitive skills and their acquisition.* Hilldale, NJ: Erlbaum: 111-140.

Sivacek, J.; Crano, W. D. 1982. Vested interest as a moderator of attitude-behavior consistency. *Journal of Personality and Social Psychology. 43*: 210-211.

Smith, M. B.; Bruner, J. S.; White, R. W. 1956. *Opinions and Personality.* New York, NY: John Wiley and Sons.

Snyder, M.; Kendzierski, D. 1982. Acting on one's attitude: procedures for linking attitude and behavior. *Journal of Experimental Social Psychology. 18*: 165-183.

Snyder, M.; Swann, W. B. 1976. When actions reflect attitudes: the politics of impression management. *Journal of Personality and Social Psychology. 34:* 1024-1032.

Srull, T. K. and Wyer, R. S. 1979. The role of category accessibility in the interpretation of information about persons: Some determinants and implications. *Journal of Personality and Social Psychology. 37*: 1660-1672.

Srull, T. K.; Wyer, R. S. 1980. Category accessibility and social perception: Some implications for the study of person memory and interpersonal judgments. *Journal of Personality and Social Psychology. 38*: 841-856.

Wicker, A. W. 1969. Attitudes versus actions: The relationship of verbal and overt behavioral responses to attitude objects. *Journal of Social Issues. 25*: 41-78.

Wicker, A. W. 1971. An examination of the "other variable" explanation of attitude-behavior inconsistency. *Journal of Personality and Social Psychology. 19*: 18-30.

Zanna, M. P.; Fazio, R. H. 1982. The attitude-behavior relation: Moving toward a third generation of research. In: Zanna, M. P.; Higgins, E. T.; Herman, C. P., (eds.) *Consistency in social behavior: The Ontario symposium. 2*: 283-301. Hillsdale, NJ: Erlbaum.

Zanna, M. P.; Olson, J. M.; Fazio, R. H. 1980. Attitude-behavior consistency: An individual difference perspective. *Journal of Personality and Social Psychology. 38*: 432-440.

4

The Elaboration Likelihood Model of Persuasion: Applications in Recreation and Tourism

———————————————— **Richard E. Petty**
———————————————— **Stacey McMichael**
———————————————— **Laura A. Brannon**

Millions of dollars are spent each year in attempts to persuade people to visit recreation and tourist attractions in the United States. Once the visitors arrive, more money is spent to persuade them to take care of the environment, follow rules and engage in safe, nondestructive behaviors. These persuasion attempts typically involve providing people with information via the mass media, mailed or on-site brochures and pamphlets, signs or face-to-face contact. The success of such informational efforts depends in part on: (a) whether the attitudes of the recipients are modified in the desired direction (e.g., do people become more favorable toward visiting the scenic rivers of West Virginia and less favorable toward littering in state parks?), and (b) whether these attitudes in turn influence peoples' behaviors (e.g., do people actually visit West Virginia's rivers and dispose of their trash properly?).

Our goal in this chapter is to present an overview of psychological approaches to social influence, and to outline in some detail a general framework for understanding the processes responsible for attitude change. This framework is called the Elaboration Likelihood Model of persuasion (Petty and Cacioppo 1981, 1986b).

BEHAVIORAL INFLUENCE VIA
PERSUASIVE COMMUNICATION

As the chapters in this volume document, many recreation and tourism studies have investigated the effect of providing information on changes in recipients' knowledge, attitudes and behaviors. Yet relatively few studies have focused on the processes responsible for these changes. Understanding the causal links among knowledge, attitudes and behaviors, and familiarity with the basic mechanisms by which change is achieved should increase the likelihood of selecting appropriate persuasion strategies.

Overview of Approaches to Persuasion

Social scientists concerned with the study of human influence have focused on the concept of "attitudes," or peoples' general predispositions to evaluate other people, objects and issues favorably or unfavorably. Among the attitudes relevant to the field of recreation and tourism are those toward: (a) oneself (e.g., low self-esteem may contribute to vandalism); (b) authority figures (e.g., are park rangers seen as credible and helpful facilitators or as strict disciplinarians?); (c) peers (e.g., are fellow campers respected or denigrated?); (d) different environments (e.g., are nature areas seen as worth preserving for future generations?); and (e) wildlife (e.g., are bears seen as dangerous?). Any of these attitudes might be appropriate targets for change.

The attitude construct has achieved its preeminent position in social influence research because of the assumption that a person's attitude is an important mediating variable between the acquisition of new knowledge, on the one hand, and behavioral change, on the other. For example, an educational intervention might be based on the idea that giving people information about the habits of bears will lead them to infer that bears are dangerous and take safety precautions.

Over the past 50 years, researchers have developed numerous theories of attitude change and models of knowledge-attitude-behavior relationships (see reviews by Chaiken and Stangor 1987, Cooper and Croyle 1984, Petty, Unnava and Strathman 1991). One of the earliest assumptions in theories of attitude change was that effective influence required a sequence of steps (e.g., McGuire 1985, Strong 1925). For example, typical models of influence contend that a person first needs to be *exposed* to some new information. Secondly, the person must *attend* to the information presented. Just because a person is handed a brochure doesn't mean that the person will be motivated to read it. Or, a person driving past a 100-word sign at 50 m.p.h. may be unable to attend to the information it presents. A third issue concerns *reception*, or what part of the information presented enters long-term memory. Just because a person is consciously aware of an informational presentation, there is no guarantee that any aspect of what is seen and heard will create more than a fleeting impression.

Nevertheless, when some new information *is* learned as a result of an educational intervention, will this new knowledge lead to attitude or behavior change? Current research strongly indicates that attitude change depends upon the manner in which a persuasive message is idiosyncratically evaluated and *interpreted* so that it makes some psychological sense to the person. Received information may trigger thoughts, images and ideas that are favorable, unfavorable or neutral, or the information may not produce any cognitive or affective responses. The more favorable the cognitive or affective responses to the information, the more likely that attitudes will change in a positive direction, and the more negative the cognitive or affective responses elicited, the more likely that attitudes will not change or will change in a direction opposite to that intended (Greenwald 1968, Petty, Ostrom and Brock 1981).

Once the information received has elicited thoughts and/or feelings, these must be *integrated* into an overall impression or evaluation that is then stored in memory (Anderson 1981). The integration process may be very simple if few thoughts are triggered, but in other circumstances may involve a complex weighting of information. In any case, only after some overall evaluation or attitude is formed is it capable of guiding subsequent *action,* which is the ultimate stage in the influence sequence (Petty and Cacioppo 1984b).

Variants of this general information processing model were often interpreted in theory and in practice as suggesting that a change early in the sequence would inevitably lead to a change later in the sequence. One problem with this reasoning is that the likelihood that a message will evoke each of the steps in the sequence may be viewed as a conditional probability. Thus, even if the likelihood of achieving each step in a campaign was 60 percent, the probability of achieving all six steps (exposure, attention, reception, interpretation, integration and action), would be $.6^6$ or only five percent (McGuire 1981).

A second factor is that some steps in the sequence may be independent of each other. For example, although a person's ability to learn and recall information (e.g., facts about a tourist destination) was often thought to be an important causal determinant of and prerequisite to attitude and behavior change (e.g., liking and visiting the destination), little empirical evidence supports this view (McGuire 1985, Petty and Cacioppo 1981). Rather, existing evidence shows that message learning can occur in the absence of attitude change, and that a person's attitudes may change without learning the specific information in the communication.

That is, a person may be able to learn all of the intended information perfectly, but not be persuaded because the information is either counterargued or deemed personally irrelevant. On the other hand, a person may get the information all wrong (scoring zero on a knowledge test), but think about it in a manner that produces the intended change. This analysis may help to explain why previous research on recreation and tourism has sometimes found that knowledge changes occur in the absence of attitude change and vice-versa (see other chapters in this volume). Verbatim recall of a message is most likely to be related to attitudes when the initial message is not elaborated and no initial attitude is formed, but an attitude is subsequently formed on the basis of the unelaborated message information that can be retrieved from memory (Mackie and Asuncion 1990, Petty, Unnava and Strathman 1991).

The Elaboration Likelihood Model of Persuasion [ELM]

Current psychological theories of influence focus on how and why various features of a persuasion situation (i.e., aspects of the source, message, channel, context and recipient) affect each of the steps in the communication sequence (e.g., how does the *credibility* of the source affect attention to the message?). By far the most research, however, focuses on how variables affect the interpretation stage of information processing. This stage is sometimes viewed as the most critical one, since it is during interpretation that the message achieves some meaning, is evaluated favorably or unfavorably, and is accepted or rejected (i.e., at this stage the person yields to or resists the message).

According to the Elaboration Likelihood Model of persuasion (ELM), the processes that occur during the interpretation stage are seen as emphasizing one of two distinct "routes to persuasion" (Petty and

Cacioppo 1981, 1986a). These routes are depicted in Figure 1. The "central route" involves effortful cognitive activity whereby the person draws upon prior experience and knowledge to scrutinize and evaluate the issue-relevant arguments presented in the communication. For this to occur, the person must be both motivated and able to process the perceived merits of the information provided. The result of this processing is an attitude that is well articulated and integrated into the person's belief structure. Attitudes changed by this route have been found to be relatively accessible, persistent over time, predictive of behavior, and resistant to change until they are challenged by cogent contrary information (see Petty and Cacioppo 1986a). People engaged in this effortful cognitive activity have been characterized as engaging

Figure 1
Schematic depiction of The Elaboration Likelihood Model of Persuasion. The figure shows the possible endpoints after exposure to a persuasive communication for people following central and peripheral routes to attitude change (from Petty & Cacioppo 1986a).

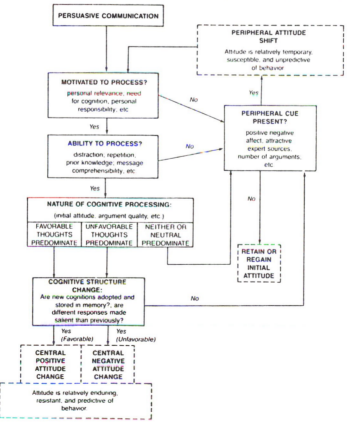

in "systematic" (Chaiken 1987) or "mindful" (Palmerino et al. 1984) processing.

In stark contrast to the central route to persuasion, the ELM holds that attitude change does not always require effortful evaluation of the message arguments. Instead, when a person's motivation or ability to process the issue-relevant arguments is low, persuasion may occur by a "peripheral route" in which simple cues in the persuasion context influence attitudes. For example, cues may elicit an affective state (e.g., happiness) that becomes associated with the advocated position (as in classical conditioning, Staats and Staats 1958), or trigger a relatively simple inference (e.g., "I bought it, so I must like it," Bem 1972) or heuristic (e.g., "experts are correct," Chaiken 1987) by which a person can judge the message. Public service announcements employ this strategy when they rely on a well-liked celebrity to induce attitude change rather than focusing on the merits of the arguments presented.

Peripheral approaches can be quite effective in the short term. The problem is that over time, peoples' feelings about celebrities may change, and the sources may become dissociated from the message. These factors would then undermine the basis of the attitude. Laboratory research has shown that attitude changes based on peripheral cues tend to be less accessible, persistent and resistant to subsequent attacking messages than attitudes based on careful processing of message arguments (Petty and Cacioppo 1986a). Thus, people who hold positive environmental attitudes based solely on trendy celebrity endorsements may be less likely to resist situational pressures to engage in anti-environmental acts than are people who have developed positive attitudes toward the environment after careful reflection upon and understanding of the consequences of various anti-environmental behaviors.

In sum, attitudes changed via the central route tend to be based on active thought processes resulting in a well-integrated cognitive structure, but attitudes changed via the peripheral route are based on more passive acceptance or rejection of simple cues and have a less well-articulated cognitive foundation.

Persuasion Processes in the Elaboration Likelihood Model

Discussing the central and peripheral routes to persuasion has highlighted two basic processes of attitude change, but the depiction of the ELM in Figure 1 outlines more specific roles that variables may play in persuasion situations. Some variables affect a person's general motivation to process a message. For example, people are more interested in thinking about messages that are perceived to have some direct personal relevance. In one study (Petty and Cacioppo 1979b), for example, undergraduates were told that their university (high personal involvement), or a distant university (low personal involvement), was considering implementing a policy requiring all seniors to pass an exam in their major as a prerequisite to graduation. The students were presented with either strong or weak arguments in favor of the exam policy. As predicted by the ELM, when the speaker advocated that the exams should be instituted at the students' own university, the quality of the arguments in the message had a greater impact on attitudes than when the speaker advocated that the exams should be instituted at a distant campus. That is, as the personal relevance of the message increased, strong arguments were more persuasive, but weak arguments were less persuasive than in the low relevance conditions (see left panel of Figure 2).

In addition, an analysis of the thoughts students listed after the message suggested that the more extreme attitudes were accompanied by more extreme thoughts. When the arguments were strong, students exposed to the high relevance message produced more than twice as many favorable thoughts as low relevance subjects, and when the arguments were weak, high relevance subjects generated almost twice as many unfavorable thoughts as students exposed to the low relevance version.

In an interesting extension of this work, a recent study has found that simply changing the pronouns in a message from the third person (e.g., "one" or "he and she") to the second person (i.e., "you") was sufficient to increase personal involvement and processing of the message arguments (Burnkrant and Unnava 1989, see right panel of Figure 2). That is, when the messages contained relevant pronouns, strong arguments were more persuasive and weak arguments were less persuasive than when third person pronouns were used.

Although increasing the perceived personal relevance of a message is an important way to increase thinking (see also Brickner et al. 1986, Leippe and Elkin 1987), it is not the only one. For example, several recent studies have shown that when a person is normally not motivated to think about the message arguments, more thinking can be provoked by summarizing the major arguments as questions rather than as assertions (Howard 1990, Petty, Cacioppo and Heesacker 1981, Swasy and Munch 1985). Thus, following an argument in a radio

Figure 2

Self-relevance increases message processing. In each panel, as self-relevance (involvement) increases, argument quality becomes a more important determinant of the attitudes expressed after exposure to a persuasive message. Data in the left panel are from an experiment by Petty and Cacioppo (1979b). Data in the right panel are from an experiment by Burnkrant and Unnava (1989). In each panel, higher numbers indicate more favorable attitudes toward the position taken in the persuasive message.

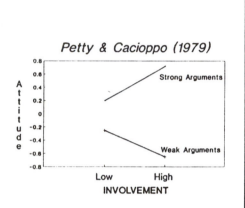

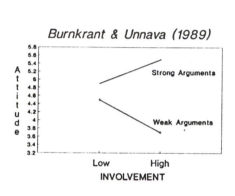

commercial by a question ("Wouldn't this help to prevent forest fires?") rather than by an assertion ("This would help to prevent forest fires"), would result in greater processing of the argument. Of course, this processing will aid persuasion if the argument preceding the question is cogent, but it will be detrimental to persuasion if the argument is specious.

As outlined in Figure 1, having the necessary motivation to process a message is not sufficient to trigger the central route to persuasion. People must also have the ability to process a message. For example, a complex or long message may require more than one exposure for maximal processing, even if the recipient is highly motivated to think about it. The increased processing with multiple exposures should lead to more favorable thoughts and attitudes if the arguments are strong, but to more counterarguments and less favorable attitudes if the arguments are weak (Cacioppo and Petty 1989).

Message repetition, of course, is just one variable that influences a person's ability to think about a message. For example, if a message is accompanied by distraction (Petty, Wells and Brock 1976) or if the speaker talks too fast (Smith and Shaffer, in press), thinking about the message will be disrupted. When strong arguments are presented, disrupting thinking should diminish persuasion, but when weak arguments are presented, disrupting thinking should enhance persuasion by reducing counterarguing (see Petty and Brock 1981).

In addition to affecting a person's motivation or ability to process a message, Figure 1 indicates that variables can also affect persuasion by influencing the *nature* of the thoughts elicited. That is, some features of the persuasion situation increase the likelihood of favorable thoughts being elicited, but others increase the likelihood of unfavorable thoughts coming to mind. Although the subjective cogency of the arguments employed in a message is a prime determinant of whether favorable or unfavorable thoughts are elicited, other variables can also be influential in determining whether favorable or unfavorable thoughts predominate (Petty and Cacioppo 1990). For example, instilling "reactance" in message recipients by telling them that they have no choice but to be persuaded on an important issue motivates counterarguing even when the arguments used are strong (Brehm 1966, Petty and Cacioppo 1979a). Similarly, people who possess considerable attitude-congruent knowledge are better able to defend their attitudes than those who have little information supporting their views (Wood 1982).

Next, as shown in Figure 1, features of the persuasion situation may influence the extent to which thoughts elicited by a message are consolidated and stored in long term memory. For example, arguments that match a person's attitude schema are more easily incorporated into the existing cognitive structure than arguments that do not match (Cacioppo, Petty and Sidera 1982).

Finally, Figure 1 indicates that variables may serve as simple peripheral cues, allowing favorable or unfavorable attitude formation in the absence of diligent consideration of the true merits of the object or issue. Among the variables that can serve as simple cues when motivation or ability to process arguments is low are the credibility of the message source (Petty, Cacioppo and Goldman 1981), how likable or attractive the source is (Chaiken 1980, Petty, Cacioppo and Schumann 1983), the mere number of arguments in the message (Alba and

Marmorstein 1987, Petty and Cacioppo 1984a), the length of the arguments (Wood et al. 1985), the number of other people thought to endorse the position (Axsom et al. 1987), and others.

The ELM holds that as the likelihood of elaboration is increased, whether or not thinking about the arguments proceeds in a relatively objective or a more biased fashion, the perceived quality of the issue-relevant arguments presented becomes a more important determinant of persuasion. As the elaboration likelihood is decreased, however, peripheral cues become more important. In short, when the elaboration likelihood is high, the central route to persuasion dominates, but when the elaboration likelihood is low, the peripheral route takes precedence.

As we have noted, the accumulated research on persuasion points to many variables that can be employed to either increase or decrease the amount of thinking about a persuasive message. Although we have focused on motivational and ability variables that can be modified by external means (e.g., including rhetorical questions in a message enhances motivation to think about the arguments), other determinants of motivation and ability to process a message are dispositional (e.g., "people high in 'need for cognition' tend to chronically engage in and enjoy thinking," Cacioppo and Petty 1982).

Multiple Roles for Variables in the Elaboration Likelihood Model

One of the most important features of the ELM is its premise that any one variable can affect persuasion by serving in different roles in different situations. That is, a variable can serve as a peripheral cue in some contexts, affect the motivation or ability to think about the message in other situations, and influence the nature of the thoughts that come to mind in still other domains. For example, in separate studies, the attractiveness of a message source has (a) served as a simple peripheral cue when it was irrelevant to evaluating the merits of an attitude object and subjects were not motivated to process the issue-relevant arguments; (b) served as a message argument when it was relevant to evaluating the merits of the attitude object and the elaboration likelihood was high; and (c) affected the extent of thinking about the message arguments presented when the elaboration likelihood was moderate (see Petty, Kasmer, Haugtvedt and Cacioppo 1987, for discussion).

If any one variable can influence persuasion by several means, it becomes critical to identify the general conditions under which the variable acts in each of the different roles. The ELM holds that when the elaboration likelihood is high (such as when perceived personal relevance and knowledge are high, the message is easy to understand, no distractions are present, and so on), people typically know that they want and are able to evaluate the merits of the arguments presented, and they do so. Variables in the persuasion setting are likely to have little direct impact on evaluations by serving as simple peripheral cues in these situations. Instead, when the elaboration likelihood is high, a variable may serve as an argument if it is relevant to the merits of the issue, or the variable may determine the nature of the ongoing information processing activity (i.e., is the processing relatively objective or biased?).

On the other hand, when the elaboration likelihood is low (e.g., low personal relevance or knowledge, complex message, many distractions, and so on), people know that they do not want or are not able to evaluate the merits of the arguments presented, or they do not even consider exerting effort to process the message. If any evaluation is formed under these conditions, it is likely to result from relatively simple associations or inferences based on salient cues.

When the elaboration likelihood is moderate (e.g., uncertain personal relevance, moderate knowledge, moderate complexity, and so on), people may be uncertain as to whether or not the message warrants or needs scrutiny and whether or not they are capable of providing this analysis. In these situations they may examine the persuasion context for indications (e.g., is the source credible?) of whether or not they are interested in or should process the message. A few examples should help to clarify the multiple roles that a variable can have in different situations.

Multiple roles for source factors. First, consider the multiple processes by which source factors (e.g., expertise, attractiveness) can have an impact on persuasion (see Petty and Cacioppo 1984c). Some research has found that when the elaboration likelihood was low, source factors such as expertise and attractiveness served as simple positive cues, enhancing attitudes regardless of argument quality. However, when the elaboration likelihood was high, source factors did not serve as simple cues. Instead, attitudes were determined primarily by the nature of the arguments presented (Chaiken 1980, Petty, Cacioppo and Goldman 1981). Finally, in two separate experiments in which the elaboration likelihood was not manipulated but was held constant at a moderate level, the source factors of expertise and attractiveness determined how much thinking subjects did about the arguments presented (Heesacker et al., 1983, Puckett et al. 1983). That is, attractive and expert sources led to more persuasion when the arguments were strong, but to less persuasion when the arguments were weak.

Interestingly, the self-monitoring scale (see Snyder 1987) has been used recently to distinguish people who tend to think more about what experts have to say (i.e., low self-monitors) from those who are more interested in what attractive sources have to say (i.e., high self-monitors; DeBono and Harnish 1988, DeBono and Telesca 1990). In any case, the accumulated research has shown clearly that source factors are capable of serving in different roles.

Only one study to date has examined the effects of a source factor across three distinct levels of elaboration likelihood. This study (Moore et al. 1986, Experiment 3) provided support for the ELM contention that variables can serve in different roles in different situations. Specifically, Moore et al. manipulated the likelihood of message elaboration by varying the speed of a radio advertisement for a product. In addition to the speed of the announcement, the credibility of the product endorsers and the quality of the arguments for the product were also varied. This experiment revealed that when the advertisement was presented at a very rapid pace so that it was difficult to process (i.e., low elaboration likelihood), people were greatly influenced by the credibility of the product endorser, but the quality of the arguments for the product had little effect. When the message was presented at a normal pace and was easy to process (i.e., high elaboration likelihood), the quality of the arguments in the ad made a difference, but the credibility of the endorser was reduced in importance compared to the fast message conditions. Finally, when the message was presented at a moderately fast pace and processing was possible but challenging, the expertise of the endorser determined how much message processing occurred—the expert source induced more thinking than the nonexpert (see Petty, Kasmer, Haugtvedt and Cacioppo 1987, for further discussion).

Multiple roles for message factors. Message factors have also been shown to serve in multiple roles in different situations. For example, in a recent study the effect of a direct advertisement for an unknown product was contrasted with an advertisement that compared the new product to a well-established one (Pechman and Estaban 1990). Unlike a direct message that simply provides support for its position (e.g., You should visit Wicwac park because...), an upward comparison message suggests that the critical issue or product is similar to one that is already seen as desirable (e.g., You should visit Wicwac park, similar to Yellowstone, because...). In order to examine the multiple roles for this message variable, direct and upward comparison ads containing either strong or weak arguments were presented following instructions and procedures designed to elicit either a relatively low motivation to process the critical ad (the target ad was embedded in a magazine format and subjects were instructed to read the magazine as they normally would), or moderate motivation to process (the target ad was embedded in a magazine format, but subjects were instructed to pay special attention to the critical ad), or high motivation to think (subjects were simply handed the target ad and were told to read it carefully). Effectiveness of the ads was assessed by asking subjects to rate their intentions to purchase the product.

When the low motivation procedure was used, the upward comparison ad produced more favorable intentions than the direct ad, but strong arguments did not produce more favorable intentions than weak ones. That is, under the low elaboration likelihood conditions, the comparison with the well known product served as a simple peripheral cue, and argument processing was minimal. When the high motivation to process conditions were examined, the opposite resulted. That is, under the high elaboration likelihood conditions, the strong arguments produced more favorable intentions than the weak ones, but the upward comparison was completely ineffective as a cue for producing more favorable intentions. Finally, when the moderate motivation conditions were analyzed, the use of an upward comparison ad was found to enhance processing of the message arguments. That is, when the upward comparison ad employed strong arguments, it led to more persuasion than the direct ad, but when the upward comparison ad used weak arguments, it produced less persuasion than the direct ad.

The results of the Pechman and Estaban (1990) study are comparable to the effects observed by Moore et al. (1986) who employed very different experimental operations. When motivation or ability to process the message arguments was low, source credibility and upward comparison claims served as simple cues. When motivation and ability to think about the arguments were high, credibility and upward comparison were unimportant as simple cues. Instead, whether the arguments were strong or weak was the primary determinant of persuasion. Finally, when motivation and ability to process were moderate, people evaluated the arguments only when it seemed worthwhile to do so—

when the source was credible or when the unknown product was linked to a desirable one.

Multiple roles for recipient factors. Finally, consider how an individual's mood, a recipient factor, might serve in multiple roles in different situations. If the elaboration likelihood is very low, a pleasant mood should be capable of serving as a simple cue, rendering people more positive toward whatever view is presented. What should happen if the elaboration likelihood is very high and people are clearly motivated and able to think about the arguments presented? Since pleasant moods have been shown to increase the accessibility of positive thoughts and ideas (see Bower 1981, Clark and Isen 1982), a pleasant mood under high elaboration conditions should introduce a positive bias to the thoughts generated. Finally, if the elaboration likelihood conditions are moderate, such as when a message is of uncertain relevance and people must decide whether or not to devote effort to thinking about the message, their current mood state may determine whether they engage in effortful cognitive activity (Bless et al. 1990, Mackie and Worth 1989, see Petty, Gleicher and Baker, 1991, for further discussion).

In a partial examination of the multiple ways in which a person's mood can influence attitudes, subjects were exposed to an advertisement for a product in the context of a relatively pleasant television program (an episode of a popular situation comedy) or a more neutral program (a segment from a documentary; Petty, Schumann, Richman and Strathman 1991).

The likelihood of thinking about the critical ad was varied by telling some subjects that they would be allowed to select a free gift at the end of the experiment from a variety of brands of the target product (high involvement), or that they would be allowed to select a free gift from another product category (low involvement). Following exposure to the ad subjects reported on their mood, rated their attitude toward the product, and listed the thoughts they had during the message.

The results of this study revealed that the pleasant program led to a more positive mood and more positive evaluations of the product under both high and low elaboration conditions. Importantly, and consistent with the notion that a pleasant mood produces positive attitudes by different processes under high and low elaboration conditions, was the finding that a pleasant mood was associated with more positive thoughts about the product under high but not low elaboration conditions.

Figure 3
**Direct and indirect effects of positive mood on attitudes under high and
low involvement conditions. Data in the left panel show that when
involvement is low and people are not motivated to process the message, mood has a direct effect on attitudes. Data in the right panel show
that when involvement is high and people are motivated to process the
message, the effect of mood on attitudes is mediated by the generation
of positive thoughts
(Figure adapted from Petty, Gleicher and Baker 1991).**

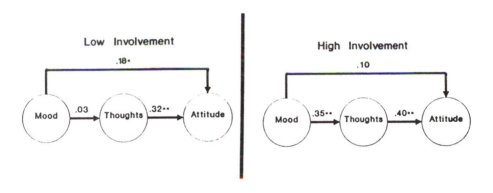

Figure 3 presents the results from causal path analyses that
simultaneously estimated the three paths between (a) self-reported
mood and attitude toward the product, (b) self-reported mood and
proportion of positive thoughts generated, and (c) proportion of positive
thoughts and attitude toward the product. Under low elaboration
conditions, mood had a direct effect on attitudes, but did not influence
thoughts (see left panel). In contrast, under high elaboration conditions,
mood had no direct effect on attitudes. Instead, mood influenced the
production of positive thoughts which in turn had an impact on attitudes
(see right panel).

Consequences of multiple roles. Because any one variable can produce persuasion in multiple ways, it is important to understand the process by which the variable has influenced a person's attitude. For example, our discussion of the two routes to persuasion suggests that if a good mood has produced persuasion by serving as a simple cue under low elaboration conditions, the attitude induced will be less accessible, less persistent, less resistant, and less predictive of behavior than if a good mood produced the same amount of persuasion, but worked by increasing positive thoughts to the message arguments under high elaboration conditions. Empirical research on recreation and tourism has examined many source, message, recipient and contextual variables but, as noted above, has paid little attention to the processes by which these variables work. The ELM holds that source, message, recipient and contextual factors can work by different processes in different situations, and that the process, central or peripheral, by which the variable induces change is critical for understanding the consequences of the new attitude (see Figure 1).

ATTITUDE-BEHAVIOR LINKS

Once a person's attitude changes (e.g., moves from anti- to pro-environment), it is important that the new attitude rather than old habits guide behavior. Considerable research has addressed the links between attitudes and behavior, and a number of situational and dispositional factors have been shown to enhance attitude-behavior consistency. For example, attitudes have a greater impact on behavior when: (a) the attitudes in question are consistent with underlying beliefs; (b) the attitudes are based on high rather than low amounts of issue-relevant information and/or personal experience; (c) the attitudes were formed as a result of considerable issue-relevant thinking; and (d) cues in the situation indicate that the person's attitude is relevant to the behavior (see Ajzen 1988, for a comprehensive review).

Reasoned Action Versus Spontaneous Action

Two general models of the process by which attitudes guide behavior have achieved widespread acceptance. One type is exemplified by Ajzen and Fishbein's (1980) Theory of Reasoned Action, which assumes that "people consider the implications of their actions before they decide to engage or not engage in a given behavior" (p. 5). In this model, people are hypothesized to form intentions to perform or not perform behaviors, and these intentions are based on the person's attitude toward the behavior as well as perceptions of the opinions of significant others (norms). The model focuses on the relatively thoughtful processing involved in considering the personal costs and benefits of engaging in a behavior, in particular on the perceived likelihood that certain benefits will be obtained or costs avoided, and on the desirability or aversiveness of those benefits or costs.

In contrast to the Theory of Reasoned Action, Fazio (1990) has proposed that much behavior is rather spontaneous and that attitudes guide behavior by a relatively automatic process. Fazio notes that motivational and ability factors will be important in determining whether the reasoned action or the automatic activation process occurs. That is, for behavioral decisions that are high in perceived personal consequences, attitudes are likely to guide behavior by a deliberate reflection process; but when perceived consequences are low, spontaneous attitude activation should be more important. Similarly, as the time allowed for a decision is reduced, the importance of spontaneous attitude activation processes should increase over more deliberative processes. When there is sufficient motivation and ability to think about one's behavior, a person may reflect upon the costs and benefits of the anticipated action. When motivation and ability to reflect are low, people's actions are determined by which attitudes are the most accessible.

Since attitudes formed by the central route tend to be more accessible than attitudes formed by the peripheral route, peripheral cues are likely to have an impact on immediate behavior only when the likelihood of reflection in the current environment is low and there are no accessible attitudes to guide behavior. For example, a person exploring a new park may need to make a quick decision about which trail to follow. If motivation and ability to think about the alternative paths are low or the information provided on a park sign is not useful, and no previous attitude or intention is available to guide action, simple cues in the immediate environment are likely to guide behavior (e.g., which trail seems more well traveled).

Social-Cognitive Learning Model of Behavior

In some domains an accessible attitude translates easily into behavior (e.g., I like candidate X, I will vote for this candidate). In other domains, however, translating new attitudes into new behaviors is complex even if the person has the desire to act on the attitude. In some recreation and tourism situations attitudes change, though an important first step, may still be insufficient to produce the desired behavioral responses. People may also need to acquire new skills and self-perceptions that allow newly acquired attitudes and intentions to be translated into action. Furthermore, once an attitude has yielded new behavior, this new behavior may not persist in the absence of incentives. Bandura's (1977, 1986) social-cognitive theory provides a framework to understand these processes.

Like the central route to persuasion and Theory of Reasoned Action described above, the social-cognitive theory perspective views voluntary behavior as determined in part by the personal consequences that a person anticipates from various courses of action. These consequences (rewards and punishments) may be anticipated because of prior personal experience or the observed experiences of others, or they may be expected simply as a result of cognitive reasoning processes.

According to Bandura, producing behavior change may require that a person learns new actions or skills or new sequences of already acquired actions. Learning of new skills may occur via direct experience or by observing the behavior patterns of others (modeling). The most effective models are those people who are most similar to the target of influence or people with whom the target identifies or admires. An important aspect of Bandura's framework is the idea that people do not always behave optimally, even though they know the "correct" behaviors and have positive attitudes about these behaviors. That is, people are not always motivated to translate their acquired skills into action.

One particularly important cognitive determinant of whether people's skills are put into action concerns people's assessments of their own capabilities or their judgments of self-efficacy or competence (Bandura 1982). Judgments of self-efficacy are important because abundant research indicates that the higher the level of perceived efficacy, the more likely people are to persist in a new behavior that has been learned. Of the various ways to influence self-efficacy, providing guided practice and specific skills training are particularly powerful techniques.

IMPLICATIONS OF SOCIAL INFLUENCE MODELS

Although considerable work has shown that it is possible to change people's knowledge, we have argued that knowledge acquisition does not invariably result in attitude and behavior change. Our brief review of basic theory and research on persuasion emphasizes that information will succeed in producing enduring changes in attitudes and behavior only if people are motivated and able to process the information, and if this processing results in favorable cognitive and/or affective reactions. Furthermore, once attitudes have changed, implementing changes in behavior may require learning new skills and perceptions of self-efficacy. Thus, current work on attitude and behavior change may help account for some unsuccessful translations of knowledge and/or attitudes into behaviors. First, the knowledge acquired may have appeared irrelevant to the recipients, or may have led to unfavorable rather than favorable reactions. Second, even if appropriate attitude changes were induced, the changes may have been based on simple peripheral cues rather than on elaborative processing of the message. Third, even if attitude changes occurred via the central route, the people influenced may have lacked the necessary skills or self-confidence to translate their new attitudes into action.

Perhaps the three most important issues raised in our review are: (1) although some attitudes are based on a careful reasoning process in which externally provided information is related to oneself and integrated into a coherent belief structure (central route), other attitudes are formed as a result of relatively simple cues in the persuasion environment (peripheral route); (2) any one variable (e.g., source credibility) may be capable of inducing persuasion by either the central or the peripheral route in different situations; and (3) although both central and peripheral route processes can lead to attitudes similar in their valence (how favorable or unfavorable they are), the manner of attitude change bears important consequences.

If the goal of a persuasion-based program is to produce long lasting changes in attitudes with behavioral consequences (e.g., attitudes about fire safety in parks), the central route to persuasion appears to be the preferred influence strategy. If the goal is immediate on-site formation of a new attitude, even if it is ephemeral (e.g., attitudes toward one park trail over another), the peripheral route may prove acceptable.

Influence via the central route requires that the recipient of the new information have the motivation and ability to process it. As noted previously, one of the most important determinants of motivation to think about a message is the perceived personal relevance of that message. When personal relevance is high, people are motivated to scrutinize the information presented and integrate it with their existing beliefs, but when perceived relevance is low, messages may be ignored or processed primarily for peripheral cues. Many people in the population may feel that the messages generated by recreation and tourism strategists are not relevant to them or have few consequences for them. An important goal of any persuasion strategy aimed at enduring change will be to increase people's motivation to think about the messages by increasing the perceived personal relevance of the communications or employing other techniques to enhance processing (e.g., ending arguments with questions rather than statements).

Even if people are motivated to attend to and think about the messages, it is also critical that they respond to these messages with favorable cognitive and/or affective reactions. It is likely that different types of information will evoke favorable responses from different segments of the population. For example, people scoring high on the self-monitoring scale respond favorably to "image" and "status" arguments, whereas low self-monitors respond favorably to "quality" arguments (Snyder and DeBono 1985, see also Manfredo, Bright and Haas this volume). Much research is needed on the level of complexity to present to different audiences, and on the type of information that, when presented, will elicit favorable thoughts and implications.

Finally, even if the appropriate attitudes are changed, a new attitude cannot influence behavior if it does not come to mind prior to the opportunity for behavior, or if people lack the skills or confidence necessary to implement their new attitudes. People need to be encouraged to think before they act so that their *new* attitudes, rather than old habits or salient situational cues, are accessed. Alternatively, a person may form an appropriate new attitude, but if the person's personal experiences contradict the attitude (e.g., a message convinces a person that some behavior is harmful and bad, but prior or subsequent experience suggests that it is exciting and fun), two contrary attitudes are formed: "this behavior is supposed to be bad" and "this behavior is fun." Since beliefs and attitudes based on direct experience come to mind more readily than attitudes based solely on externally provided information, the effectiveness of the new attitude is at a competitive disadvantage (Fazio and Zanna 1981). To the extent that these effects are anticipated, educational programs can incorporate role-playing and other direct experiences in which people receive appropriate practice exercises.

Research on social influence has come a long way from the early notion that providing information alone was sufficient to influence behavior. Social influence is a complex, though explicable process. We now know that the extent and nature of a person's cognitive responses to external information may be more important than the information itself. We know that attitudes can be changed in different ways, such as central versus peripheral routes, and that some attitude changes are more accessible, stable, resistant and predictive of behavior than others. We also know that even apparently simple variables such as a likable source or a person's mood can produce persuasion by very different processes in different situations. We hope this overview of current thinking about attitude change processes may be useful in developing and evaluating persuasive communications that are relevant to recreation and tourism.

This chapter was supported in part by NSF grant BNS 90-21647.

REFERENCES

Ajzen, I. 1988. *Attitudes, personality, and behavior*. Chicago: Dorsey Press.

Ajzen, I.; Fishbein, M. 1980. *Understanding attitudes and predicting social behavior*. Englewood-Cliffs, NJ: Prentice-Hall.

Alba, J. W.; Marmorstein, H. 1987. The effects of frequency knowledge on consumer decision making. *Journal of Consumer Research, 13*: 411-454.

Anderson, N. H. 1981. Integration theory applied to cognitive responses and attitudes. In R. Petty et al, (ed), *Cognitive responses in persuasion*. Hillsdale, NJ: Erlbaum.

Axsom, D.; Yates, S.; Chaiken, S. 1987. Audience response as a heuristic cue in persuasion. *Journal of Personality and Social Psychology, 53*: 30-40.

Bandura, A. 1977. *Social learning theory*. Englewood Cliffs, NJ: Prentice-Hall.

Bandura, A. 1982. Self-efficacy mechanism in human agency. *American Psychologist, 37*: 122-147.

Bandura, A. 1986. *Social foundations of thought and action*. Englewood Cliffs, NJ: Prentice-Hall.

Bem, D. J. 1972. Self-perception theory. In L. Berkowitz (ed.). *Advances in experimental social psychology (Vol. 6)*. New York: Academic Press.

Bless, H.; Bohner, G.; Schwarz, N.; Strack, F. 1990. Mood and persuasion: A cognitive response analysis. *Personality and Social Psychology Bulletin, 17*: 332-346.

Bogart, L. 1967. *Strategy in advertising*. New York: Harcourt.

Bower, G. 1981. Mood and memory. *American Psychologist, 36*: 441-446.

Brehm, J. W. 1966. *A theory of psychological reactance*. New York: Academic Press.

Brickner, M. A.; Harkins, S. G.; Ostrom, T. M. 1986. Effects of personal involvement: Thought provoking implications for social loafing. *Journal of Personality and Social Psychology, 51*: 763-769.

Burnkrant, R.; Unnava, R. 1989. Self-referencing: A strategy for increasing processing of message content. *Personality and Social Psychology Bulletin, 15*: 628-638.

Cacioppo, J. T.; Petty, R. E. 1982. The need for cognition. *Journal of Personality and Social Psychology, 42*: 116-131.

Cacioppo, J. T.; Petty, R. E. 1989. Effects of message repetition on argument processing, recall, and persuasion. *Basic and Applied Social Psychology, 10*: 3-12.

Cacioppo, J. T.; Petty, R. E.; Sidera, J. 1982. The effects of a salient self-schema on the evaluation of proattitudinal editorials: Top down versus bottom-up message processing. *Journal of Experimental Social Psychology, 18*: 324-338.

Chaiken, S. 1980. Heuristic versus systematic information processing and the use of source versus message cues in persuasion. *Journal of Personality and Social Psychology, 39*: 752-756.

Chaiken, S. 1987. The heuristic model of persuasion. In M. P. Zanna, J. Olson, & C. Herman (eds.), *Social influence: The Ontario symposium*. Hillsdale, NJ: Erlbaum.

Chaiken, S.; Stangor, C. 1987. Attitude and attitude change. *Annual Review of Psychology, 38*: 575-630.

Clark, M. S.; Isen, A. 1982. Toward understanding the relationship between feeling states and social behavior. In A. Hastorf and A. Isen (eds.), *Cognitive social psychology*. New York: Elsevier North-Holland.

Cooper, J.; Croyle, R. 1984. Attitude and attitude change. *Annual Review of Psychology, 35*: 395-426.

DeBono, K.; Harnish, R. 1988. Source expertise, source attractiveness, and the processing of persuasive information: A functional approach. *Journal of Personality and Social Psychology, 55*:541-546.

DeBono, K.; Telesca, C. In press. The influence of source physical attractiveness on advertising effectiveness. *Journal of Applied Social Psychology*.

Fazio, R. H. 1990. Multiple processes by which attitudes guide behavior: The MODE model as an integrative framework. In M. Zanna (ed.), *Advances in experimental social psychology*. New York: Academic Press.

Fazio, R. H.; Zanna, M. P. 1981. Direct experience and attitude-behavior consistency. In L. Berkowitz (ed.), *Advances in experimental social psychology* (Vol. 14, pp. 161-202). New York: Academic Press.

Greenwald, A. G. 1968. Cognitive learning, cognitive response to persuasion, and attitude change. In A. Greenwald, T. Brock, & T. Ostrom (eds.), *Psychological foundations of attitudes*. New York: Academic Press.

Heesacker, M.; Petty, R. E.; Cacioppo, J. T. 1983. Field dependence and attitude change: Source credibility can alter persuasion by affecting message-relevant thinking. *Journal of Personality, 51*:653-666.

Howard, D. J. 1990. Rhetorical question effects on message processing and persuasion: The role of information availability and the elicitation of judgment. *Journal of Experimental Social Psychology, 26*: 217-239.

Leippe, M. R.; Elkin, R. A. 1987. When motives clash: Issue involvement and response involvement as determinants of persuasion. *Journal of Personality and Social Psychology, 52*: 269-278.

Mackie, D. M.; Asuncion, A. 1990. On-line and memory-based modification of attitudes: Determinants of message recall-attitude change correspondence. *Journal of Personality and Social Psychology, 59*:5-16

Mackie, D. M.; Worth, L. 1989. Processing deficits and the mediation of positive affect in persuasion. *Journal of Personality and Social Psychology, 57*: 27-40.

McGuire, W. J. 1981. Theoretical foundations of campaigns. In R. Rice & W. Paisley (eds.), *Public communication campaigns*. Beverly Hills, CA: Sage.

McGuire, W. J. 1985. Attitudes and attitude change. In G. Lindzey & E. Aronson (eds.), *Handbook of social psychology* (Vol 2, 3rd ed.). New York: Random House.

Moore, D. L.; Hausknecht, D.; Thamodaran, K. 1986. Time pressure, response opportunity, and persuasion. *Journal of Consumer Research,13*: 85-99.

Palmerino, M.; Langer, E.; McGillis, D. 1984. Attitudes and attitude change: Mindlessness-mindfulness perspective. In J. R. Eiser (ed.), *Attitudinal judgment*. New York: Springer-Verlag.

Pechman, C.; Estaban, G., 1990. How comparative claims affect the route to persuasion. Working paper, Graduate School of Management, University of California, Irvine, CA.

Petty, R. E.; Brock, T. C. 1981. Thought disruption and persuasion: Assessing the validity of attitude change experiments. In R. Petty, T. Ostrom, & T. Brock (eds.), *Cognitive responses in persuasion* (pp. 55-79). Hillsdale, NJ: Erlbaum.

Petty, R. E.; Cacioppo, J. T. 1979a. Effects of forewarning of persuasive intent on cognitive responses and persuasion. *Personality and Social Psychology Bulletin, 5* : 173-176.

Petty, R. E.; Cacioppo, J. T. 1979b. Issue-involvement can increase or decrease persuasion by enhancing message-relevant cognitive responses. *Journal of Personality and Social Psychology, 37*: 1915-1926.

Petty, R. E; Cacioppo, J. T. 1981. *Attitudes and persuasion: Classic and contemporary approaches*. Dubuque: Wm. C. Brown.

Petty, R. E.; Cacioppo, J. T. 1984a. The effects of involvement on responses to argument quantity and quality: Central and peripheral routes to persuasion. *Journal of Personality and Social Psychology, 46*: 69-81.

Petty, R. E.; Cacioppo, J. T. 1984b. Motivational factors in consumer response to advertisements. In W. Beatty, R. Geen, & R. Arkin (eds.), *Human motivation*. New York: Allyn & Bacon.

Petty, R. E.; Cacioppo, J. T. 1984c. Source factors and the elaboration likelihood model of persuasion. *Advances in Consumer Research, 11*: 668-672.

Petty, R. E.; Cacioppo, J. T. 1986a. *Communication and persuasion: Central and peripheral routes to attitude change*. New York: Springer/Verlag.

Petty, R. E.; Cacioppo, J. T. 1986b. The Elaboration Likelihood Model of persuasion. In L. Berkowitz (ed.), *Advances in experimental social psychology* (Vol. 19, pp. 123-205) New York: Academic Press.

Petty, R. E.; Cacioppo, J. T. 1990. Involvement and persuasion: Tradition versus integration. *Psychological Bulletin, 107*: 367-374.

Petty, R. E.; Cacioppo, J. T.; Goldman, R. 1981. Personal involvement as a determinant of argument-based persuasion. *Journal of Personality and Social Psychology, 41*: 847-855.

Petty, R. E.; Cacioppo, J. T.; Heesacker, M. 1981. The use of rhetorical questions in persuasion: A cognitive response analysis. *Journal of Personality and Social Psychology, 40*: 432-440.

Petty, R. E.; Cacioppo, J. T.; Schumann, D. 1983. Central and peripheral routes to advertising effectiveness: The moderating role of involvement. *Journal of Consumer Research, 10*: 134-148.

Petty, R. E.; Gleicher, F.; Baker, S. M. 1991. Multiple roles for affect in persuasion. In J. Forgas (ed.), *Affect and judgment*. London: Pergamon.

Petty, R. E.; Kasmer, J.; Haugtvedt, C.; & Cacioppo, J. T. 1987. Source and message factors in persuasion: A reply to Stiff's critique of the Elaboration Likelihood Model. *Communication Monographs, 54*: 233-249.

Petty, R. E.; Ostrom, T. M.; Brock, T. C. (eds.) 1981. *Cognitive responses in persuasion*. Hillsdale, NJ: Erlbaum.

Petty, R. E.; Schumann, D.; Richman, S.; Strathman, A. 1990. Positive mood and persuasion: Central and peripheral routes to attitude change. Unpublished manuscript, Ohio State University, Columbus, OH.

Petty, R. E.; Unnava, R.; Strathman, A. 1991. Theories of attitude change. In H. Kassarjian & T. Robertson (eds.). *Handbook of consumer theory and research*. Englewood Cliffs, NJ: Prentice-Hall.

Petty, R. E.; Wells, G. L.; Brock, T. C. 1976. Distraction can enhance or reduce yielding to propaganda. *Journal of Personality and Social Psychology, 34:* 874-884.

Puckett, J.; Petty, R. E.; Cacioppo, J. T.; Fisher, D. 1983. The relative impact of age and attractiveness stereotypes on persuasion. *Journal of Gerontology, 38*: 340-343.

Smith, S.; Shaffer, D. In press. Celebrity and cajolery: Rapid speech may promote or inhibit persuasion via its impact on message elaboration. *Personality and Social Psychology Bulletin.*

Snyder, M. 1987. *Public appearances, private realities: The psychology of self-monitoring.* New York: Freeman.

Snyder, M.; DeBono, K. 1985. Appeals to image and claims about quality: Understanding the psychology of advertising. *Journal of Personality and Social Psychology, 49*: 586-597.

Staats, A. W.; Staats, C. 1958. Attitudes established by classical conditioning. *Journal of Abnormal and Social Psychology, 67*: 159-167.

Strong, E. K. 1925. *The psychology of selling and advertising.* New York: McGraw Hill.

Swasy, J. L.; Munch, J. M. 1985. Examining the target of receiver elaborations: Rhetorical question effects on source processing and persuasion. *Journal of Consumer Research, 11*: 877-886.

Wood, W. 1982. Retrieval of attitude relevant information from memory: Effects on susceptibility to persuasion and on intrinsic motivation. *Journal of Personality and Social Psychology, 42*: 798-810.

Wood, W.; Kallgren, C; Priesler, R. 1985. Access to attitude relevant information in memory as a determinant of persuasion. *Journal of Experimental Social Psychology, 21*: 73-85.

5

Behavioral Systems Framework for Media-Based Behavior Change Strategies

— Richard A. Winett

BEHAVIORAL MANAGEMENT OF RECREATIONAL AND LEISURE SETTINGS

At first blush, recreation, tourism and general leisure time pursuits suggest relatively free-spirited, nonconstrained behaviors. The notion that recreational and leisure time settings need to be managed to effectively influence behaviors seems incompatible with the multipurpose uses of such settings, including enjoyment, social interaction, relaxation, physical exercise, challenge, discovery and solitude. However, more considered observations argue that the diverse goals of recreation will not be achieved unless settings and behaviors are professionally managed.

Crowded "wilderness" areas, littered campgrounds, boisterous and drunken boaters, unsafe and irresponsible hunters, and defacements of museums, zoos and historical sites are examples of how poorly-managed settings and behaviors ruin recreation and leisure pursuits for many participants. Such inappropriate uses of settings also increase costs for the public in federally or state operated areas, and reduce business at commercially operated sites.

Clearly, we need effective behavioral management strategies so that recreational and leisure settings can continue to enhance our lives.

However, management strategies need to be compatible with the purposes and mores of the settings in which they are implemented. For example, it would be incompatible with quiet wilderness areas to have them patrolled by well-armed rangers who issue stiff fines to litterers at gun point. While it might "work" in the short term, this strategy would destroy the atmosphere of the setting in the long term.

Strategies to manage behaviors in leisure and recreational settings need to be more subtle. In fact, it is more reasonable to use the term "behavior influence" strategies (Krasner and Ullman 1973) to indicate that strategies should only direct and guide people, that is, facilitate some degree of appropriate change, and not manipulate and control people. Importantly, behavior influence is not only more compatible with the goals of recreation and leisure, but is also more reflective of how psychological and communication strategies work and more indicative of their relative potencies (Bandura 1986).

Informational "media-based" strategies appear most compatible with the purposes of the users of recreational and leisure settings. Additionally, informational strategies can educate users about appropriate behaviors in different settings. Such education can continue to influence behavior in subsequent visits to areas, and the knowledge and appropriate behaviors can be conveyed to others both within and outside the setting. Effective informational strategies can also enhance relationships among management agencies and businesses and the publics they serve.

Unfortunately, despite compelling arguments for implementing media-based approaches, the conceptual and strategic foundations for their implementation appear less definitive. This chapter's purpose is to couple these compelling arguments for media-based approaches with a behavioral system framework that offers a template for the design, development, implementation and evaluation of media-based, behavior-influencing strategies.

The first section discusses some of the pivotal historical debates in the general area of communication and behavior and concludes that there is reasonable evidence for using media (but not just any media or approach) for influencing behavior. The second section overviews the conceptual and strategic foundations of an effective framework for media-based behavior-influence programs. This section also includes a complete review and extended discussion of an evolving framework that has been used in a number of large-scale behavior-influence projects. The final section provides a detailed illustration of how the framework can be used for a specific management problem in recreation, leisure and tourism.

HISTORICAL PERSPECTIVE:
UNRAVELING THE PARADOX

As detailed in Winett (1986), the history of communication and behavior influence has involved highly contrasting models of media effects. In the 1930s and early 1940s, a period of radio expansion and the rise of totalitarian states, it is not surprising that a dominant model was the "hypodermic needle" model. As the name suggests, the audience was perceived as passive recipients of information through the media, which people acted upon in relatively predictable ways. People were viewed as automotons, a depiction reinforced, for example, by mass reactions to a Hitler spectacle, radio broadcast, or newsreel (Shirer 1960), an Orson Wells radio broadcast about invaders from Mars (Manchester 1974), or even a fireside chat from Franklin D. Roosevelt (Lash 1971).

In less controlled, contrived or unusual situations, the hypodermic needle model proved to be inappropriate. People do not simply receive and then act upon information. This is particularly the case when there are competing sources of information, when some information is not well crafted, or when some of the information may be difficult to act upon.

As studies in the 1940s and 1950s failed to support the hypodermic needle model, the opposing "weak effects" model gained ascendence. Media, at best, were seen as capable of informing and marginally changing attitudes, but not of modifying behavior. From a conceptual standpoint this model was wanting, because in many ways such blanket statements are intellectually vacuous. It is utterly simplistic to generalize about a range of stimuli, strategies and target behaviors, claiming that no behaviors will be influenced by any media format and presentation (see Bandura 1986). Moreover, by way of self-fulfilling prophecies, studies investigating the weak effects model often appeared to develop ostensively ill-designed media and to test for media effects with vaguely defined behaviors (see Winett 1986). Not surprisingly, no effects were found, providing confirming evidence for the weak effects model.

A mid-way model that followed the diffusion of innovation research (Rogers and Shoemaker 1971) became prominent in the 1950s and is still prominent today. Diffusion of innovation models study how ideas, new behaviors and products become incorporated into society. Traditionally, this model has rested on interpersonal processes. This approach has been called a "two-step" model in which opinion leaders and gatekeepers were influenced by media. That is, these higher status individuals gain knowledge and adopt new attitudes and behaviors based on their exposure to media. Through personal contact and social influence processes, their new information, attitudes and behaviors are conveyed to others.

Although facets of this "two-step"model make sense and have been incorporated into campaigns (e.g., Maccoby and Altman 1988), several points make the overall model less viable. I will shortly cite evidence indicating that many people are influenced by media. A key process in behavior influence is behavioral modeling. This involves actual, detailed depictions of appropriate behaviors and skills, which are then tried, modified and adopted by the observer. Modeling can occur through interpersonal or media-based observation. Diffusion of innovation is, therefore, a specific example of interpersonal and media-based modeling (Bandura 1986). Further, in a review of analyses from the diffusion of innovation studies purportedly showing the primacy of interpersonal influence (Rogers and Kincaid 1981), Winett (1986) showed that exposure to appropriate media was actually the major influence on decisions to adopt an innovation (birth control). I will return to the notion of examining more conceptually-sound, specific and efficacious aspects of media that influence behavior.

However, an interesting and revealing anomaly existed in media research at the same time that the weak-effects and two-step models were prominent. While some behavioral scientists were proclaiming the minimal potency or even inability of media to influence behavior, other behavioral scientists were decrying the omnipresent influence of media, specifically television, on specific behaviors, such as aggressive behaviors in children (Liebert et al. 1982). More than 30 years after the first scientific concerns were voiced, the debate about television's content, and its impact on children in particular, continues. Most behavioral scientists would agree with the conservative conclusion that graphic violence on television tends to increase the aggressive behavior of some children, perhaps those children prone to aggression through preexisting individual, family or other social factors (Rubenstein 1983). Some behavioral scientists clearly believe that specific media formats and content can significantly influence specific behaviors.

The apparent anomaly between the weak-effects model and the research on televised violence and aggressive behavior is easily solved when a number of key points discussed by Winett (1986) are delineated, including:

- Weak-effects studies, as noted, often used poorer quality media and vague dependent measures.

- A number of well-known studies in the weak-effects era were done before the widespread availability of television, generally a more potent behavior-influence medium.

- The television programs depicting violence most often use excellent production qualities and formative features designed to hold attention.

- The dose and duration of violent behaviors on television via numerous programs and depictions is very high.

- Particular programs are often targeted to specific audiences.

These points are similar to ones made in Mendelsohn's (1973) classic article that was a counterpoint to many previous articles about why media campaigns failed. His article, "Some Reasons Why Information Campaigns Can Succeed," can be seen as opening a new era. Mendelsohn indicated that campaigns can be successful if middle range and reasonable goals are chosen and if a social marketing approach is used. Basically, social marketing (touched on again later in this chapter) is the transposition of marketing concepts and strategies from the commercial sphere to the health-promotion, prosocial behavior spheres. A central part of social marketing involves targeting specific communications and programs to specific audiences, based on formative research about particular audiences.

Mendelsohn noted that many failed information campaigns incorporated little from communication or marketing research, concluding in 1973:

> … very little of our mass communications research has really tested the effectiveness of the application of empirically grounded mass communications principles simply because most communications practitioners do not consciously utilize these practices (p. 51).

Unfortunately, almost 20 years later, similar points may be made about some recent campaigns for alcohol and drug abuse (Winett 1986) and AIDS prevention (Winett et al. 1990).

Research in diverse areas supports the premise that media, particularly television and other graphic media, are potent forces for promoting both healthful and unhealthful behaviors. For example, Albright et al. (1988) discussed and documented the targeting of graphic cigarette ads in magazines for women and teenagers. It is difficult to understand, much less defend, the manufacturers' arguments that the ads have minimal impact on overall consumption because they are designed to promote brand switching, not to develop new nicotine addicts. However, it has been pointed out that the manufacturers depend on the ads to enlist new recruits to replace adults who have stopped smoking or have died (Warner 1986). Thus, graphic, well-placed and targeted cigarette ads do activate "appropriate behaviors." Can anyone believe that manufacturers would spend millions of dollars each year for ineffective ads?

On a more positive note, diverse instructional television programs have shown documented effectiveness in helping viewers *stop* smoking (Flay 1987). Indeed, when such programs are sustained and offer specific smoking cessation and maintenance strategies, they may be as effective as many interpersonal group smoking cessation programs (Jason et al. 1987).

Winett (1986, 1987) also has shown that a number of prosocial television programs using specific formats, communication strategies and psychological principles showed documented behavioral change in areas pertinent to health, education and social interactions. Importantly, the commonalities between the programs were apparent and fit the first behavioral systems framework. Thus, while we cannot assert that any and all media can and will influence behavior, it is becoming apparent that when media use certain guiding principles, formats and delivery systems, the probability of influencing designated behaviors is markedly increased.

The next section describes in detail a conceptual and strategic framework for designing, developing, implementing and evaluating media-based, behavior-influence interventions.

BEHAVIORAL SYSTEMS FRAMEWORK

Figure 1 shows the "second generation" of the behavioral systems framework. The notion of "generation" means that this is an evolving framework; it is not offered as final or definitive. The framework also borrows freely from similar frameworks in health education (Green and

Anderson 1986), social marketing (Manoff 1985), and one developed for integrating health psychology and public health (Winett et al. 1989).

Figure 1
Behavioral Systems Framework

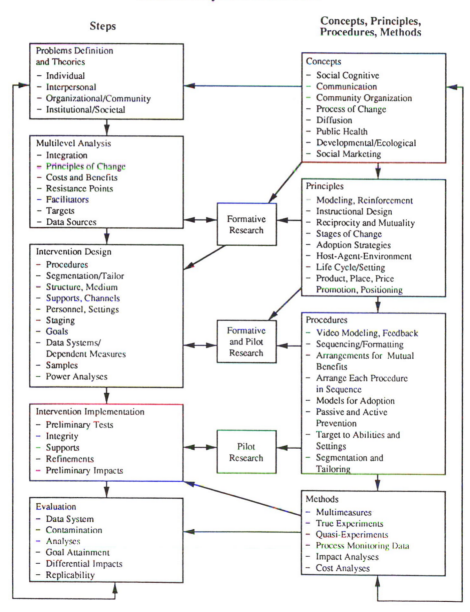

Basically, the behavioral systems framework delineates a series of steps involving:
- •conceptualization
- •formative and pilot research
- •procedural design and development
- •overall intervention design
- •implementation of an intervention
- •process, outcome and cost analyses.

Since Figure 1 shows so many steps and concepts, procedures and other inputs into each step, at first glance the framework may appear overwhelming.

My goal is to articulate each step and show that the many steps and procedures are often followed when planning, designing, implementing and evaluating information interventions. However, I contend that these steps are less frequently done systematically with a major emphasis on influencing specific behaviors.

Concepts

Any intervention rests on its conceptual underpinnings. Theories and models provide the boundaries to define problems, as well as the grounds for the principles and procedures of an intervention.

The concepts box in the framework (Fig. 1) indicates that a number of theories and models can be melded to form a basis for an information intervention. As previously noted, social cognitive theory (Bandura 1986) is now an integrative theory in contemporary psychology. In an elegant fashion, the theory integrates much of what has been studied in psychology and other disciplines with regard to cognitive and affective processes, behavioral processes and environmental influences. All these processes and influences are interactive, leading to the notion that any event such as a behavior change is determined by multiple influences, and that the event, in turn, influences other events (e.g., retrieving litter from a campground can lead to more proenvironmental beliefs and feelings of the retrievers; the cleaner campground influences subsequent campers to reduce or eliminate littering). Although events are multiply determined and influence is seen as reciprocal (e.g., behavior influences environment, and vice versa), people are regarded as highly engaged, active processors and architects of their own behaviors and environments.

Most importantly, for more than 20 years social cognitive theory has proven to be a highly fertile ground for the design of effective interventions. Its concepts about behavioral influence lead directly to specific procedures. For example, as active observers of behavior and environments, people learn directly about appropriate behaviors and context from observing others in a modeling process. Not surprisingly, one of the most effective behavioral influence strategies involves behavioral modeling either *in vivo* or through media. When behavioral modeling is combined with social psychological considerations (e.g., characteristics of the model) and principles of behavior change (e.g., step-by-step modeling with reinforcement, that is, shaping and successive approximation), a highly effective procedure can result if a number of other factors have been considered.

The other theories and models in the box augment social cognitive theory in a number of ways that will be only briefly noted here. Communication principles (Solomon and Maccoby 1984), an amalgamation of ideas from a number of fields, are essential for properly framing, formatting and presenting informational interventions. At times, an information intervention will be effective only if there is an organization in the community to make the topic of the intervention a salient item on the public agenda, so that the information gains access to and appropriate time on media, and so that procedures and settings to support particular behaviors called for by the information intervention are in place. Perhaps the best examples of combining informational and community organizational approaches are found in a number of large-scale community health promotion projects (Maccoby and Altman 1988).

Other prime conceptual inputs involve:

• Various stages of change schemas that rate persons as to "readiness" for change, with different programs and approaches aimed at different levels of readiness (see Brownell et al. 1986); and those schemas that attend more to the serial staging of procedures in a behavior-influence intervention (Winett et al. 1989, 1990).

• Diffusion theory, which may be subsumed under social cognitive theory (see Bandura 1986, Chapter 4), but which in its own right alerts us to focus more on interpersonal aspects of behavioral influence (Rogers 1983).

• The public health model, that in particular stresses understanding population characteristics and environmental influences, and using this knowledge to formulate preventive interventions (Hanlon and Pickett 1984).

• A developmental/ecological perspective that calls attention to assessing the abilities, perceptions and characteristics of persons at different stages of development, environments that are more important at certain stages, and designing interventions cognizant of these stages and environments (e.g., anti-littering campaigns for children and adults would use different themes and language, be directed toward behaviors in different settings, and be delivered in different ways).

• Social marketing, which provides an interactive framework and key variables (price, promotion, place, product and positioning) for designing and delivering interventions to targeted audiences.

Table 1 reviews and delineates the concepts, principles and procedures from the framework discussed to this point. The table also includes examples directly derived from the conceptual and procedural inputs for the framework. Of course, in many cases, the examples are overlapping or complementary.

Dependent upon the nature of the problem and the resources, all or most of these theories and models would presumably be used to define problems (see "Steps" in Fig. 1) and elucidate the principles (Fig. 1) on which the intervention will be based. And, as suggested by Table 1, concepts, principles and procedures can be meshed in logical and creative ways to solve particular problems.

Problems Definition and Multilevel Analysis

The theories, concepts and principles briefly discussed in the prior section provide a means to define problems. For the sake of brevity, note that the concepts and theories differ mainly in the relative primacy given to individual, interpersonal and environmental influence. For example, communication theory and stages-of-change schemas tend to focus on individual factors. Community organization and public health approaches emphasize the environment. Social cognitive theory, while stressing multiple and reciprocal influences, tends to emphasize individual and interpersonal influences, given its psychological foundations.

Problems in recreation and leisure can be conceptualized in a number of ways. For example, defacement of settings can be construed as representing faulty beliefs and personal irresponsibility (i.e., misinformation, ill-managed personal behaviors), inappropriate social norms (defacement is an acceptable behavior), or environmental mismanagement (e.g., inadequate surveillance and funds to regularly upgrade

Table 1

Delineation of the Concepts, Principles, and Procedures from the Behavioral Systems Framework

Concepts	Principles	Procedures	Example
Social Cognitive Theory – an encompassing, theory concerning the reciprocal influence of cognitive, behavioral, and environmental influences	Reciprocity of influence; specific change strategies such as modeling, goal-setting, feedback, and reinforcement	Use of any medium (video, interpersonal) which can encapsulate appropriate procedures	Demonstrating (modeling) appropriate behaviors via brief video programs
Communication Theory – an amalgamation of diverse theories and frameworks from psychology, education, and instructional design concerning effective information development, delivery, and reception	Social psychological, instructional design, learning theory, information processing	Use of any medium with properly, presented material (i.e., optimally formatted and sequenced)	Teaching appropriate safety behaviors to campers via an interactive video program that uses credible sources and brief learning sequences
Community Organization – a range of theories, perspectives, and frameworks on how to organize support in communities for specific programs and other changes	Wide variety of principles aimed toward the development and use of power, agenda-setting, orchestrating community actions, and setting-up mutually reinforcing interventions	Use a wide variety of tactics to achieve aims noted in principles	Designing a litter campaign so that campers, rangers, and a commercial concern all benefit
Process of Change – a number of different frameworks that examine stages of "readiness" for change and for different procedures and processes of change	Behavior change represents a sequence of person and environmental events; different interventions are required at different stages of change	Delineation of change steps and targeting different interventions to each step	Using an intensive intervention with goal-setting and frequent feedback for the initial stages of behavior change
Diffusion – primarily sociological theory about how innovations (broadly defined) are adopted by groups and individuals)	Diffusion often represents stages involving media representations of an innovation, adoption by key opinion leaders in social networks, and adoption by network members through modeling and other interpersonal processes	Identification of social network stars; network analyses	Training high status campers to routinely perform safety behaviors, which then will be modelled by others
Public Health – an overall discipline (composed of many subdisciplines) that uses epidemiological methods, examines interactive elements as they relate to mortality and morbidity data, and emphasizes prevention	Epidemiological methodologies; disease as a result of host (person), agent (contagion) and environmental factors	Besides epidemiological inquiries, diverse methods to achieve preventive objectives	The assessment that most injuries occurred at certain trail sites, leads to reconstruction of those sites to promote safer hiking
Development/Ecological – a perspective that human development entails stages and interactions with different environmental settings and demands	Life-span development; stages of cognitive or moral development; ecological principles of reciprocity, interaction, succession	Assessments of the fit of environmental demands and stage of development of individuals; modify setting to enhance individual abilities	Designing instructional materials and some of campground facilities to meet abilities of younger children
Social Marketing – a framework derived from commercial marketing for designing and targeting social, behavioral interventions	The delineation of the product, and its price , place (distribution), promotion, and positioning; segmentation and targeting	A range of assessment and formative research strategies for interventions design and pretesting	Designing somewhat different safety programs for different sets of campers, with each program based on the interests, skills, and objectives of discernible camper segments

settings). These different conceptualizations correspond to the levels noted in the problems definition box in Figure 1.

How a problem is construed frequently determines the kind of intervention used. For example, individual and interpersonal causality lend themselves to informational interventions, perhaps, without an environmental component. Environmental causality emphasizes organizational and community intervention strategies with or without an informational component.

Most problems, however, are caused by multiple factors at different levels of analysis, as the "multilevel analysis" box suggests. The processes here involve not only using the conceptual and problem definition inputs, but also integrating these inputs in a practical way. For example, the different inputs suggest different principles and programs of change that can be implemented in a number of ways. However, there are practical constraints to any intervention that involve resources, social and political acceptability, and fitting interventions to settings. Each type of intervention that may have parts representing different levels of intervention (e.g., an informational and an environmental component) has its unique set of "costs and benefits" in the larger sense of that term (i.e., not just monetary, but also effort and social psychological costs). These relative costs and benefits of different interventions need to be considered *a priori*; how each intervention may fit into a setting with regard to key resistance points (e.g., vacationers do not want an intrusive intervention) or facilitators of change (e.g., rangers have frequent social contact with campers) needs to be assessed; specific targets for intervention must be defined (e.g., presence or absence of orange vests for hunters); and relevant data sources must be enumerated (e.g., actual counts of properly and improperly attired hunters, number of accidents).

Note that the steps within "problems definition" and "multilevel analysis" are a combination of conceptualization, reviews of relevant prior work, intuition and integration, and consideration of practical constraints. When these steps are completed, the next steps delineating appropriate principles of change—intervention design and formative research—can begin.

Principles, Intervention Design and Formative Research

The "concepts," "problems definition and theories" and "multilevel analysis" steps narrow the focus both conceptually and strategically. With these steps completed, there should be a relatively clear understanding about what concepts are appropriate for a problem that is defined in a particular way, and particular ways of ameliorating the problem are stressed. The next set of steps, and those that follow, begin the "nuts and bolts" parts of the framework (Fig. 1).

As the principles box shows, each particular concept or theory has particular principles that guide change efforts. Note that each entry in the concepts box has an entry in the same order in the principles box. For example, social cognitive theory emphasizes behavioral modeling, feedback and reinforcement principles. A public health approach draws attention to host-agent-environment relationships not only to understand a problem, but also to intervene. Marketing rests on a multiple, interdependent variable model (Table 1).

Once relevant principles are gleaned, formative research can begin that is guided by the foregoing more conceptual analyses (concepts, problems definition, multilevel analysis), specific principles, and tentative plans for an intervention design. For example, consider the development of an information campaign that combines social cognitive and social marketing concepts, principles and procedures in order to decrease littering and other inappropriate disposal of waste in a recreational area. Surveys, focus groups and direct observations would be used in a formative research step to answer these questions:

- What types of information about litter and waste disposal are needed for which types of individuals using different recreational sites in different ways?

- What types of models, feedback strategies and reinforcers may be appropriate for differently defined segments?

- Can different segments be differentially approached, based on their "readiness" (stages of change) for change?

- How can a program be best defined (product), distributed (place), implemented (i.e., monetary, social and effort costs), delivered (promoted) and differentiated from other interventions (positioning)?

Note especially that these types of questions flow from the principles box and directly pertain to questions about intervention design. Any intervention involves certain procedures, encapsulated within a particular delivery system (e.g., freely distributed brochures, a cable TV program, personal instruction) in certain settings, targeted to certain population segments. Likewise, interventions are often "rolled-out" step by step and, hopefully, have definable goals (e.g., decreasing litter in specific recreational settings by 50%), with particular reliable sources to monitor goal attainment or nonattainment. As shown in the intervention design box, the range of concerns at this point also includes those that will be germane to evaluation, such as selection of dependent measures and samples, and the performance of power analyses to *a priori* determine the number of participants, sites and observations necessary for a sensitive evaluation design (see West 1985).

Procedures, Intervention Design, Formative and Pilot Research

The repetition of "intervention design" in the next series of steps indicates that the entire series of steps in the framework is more interactive than suggested by the presentation to this point. A realistic portrayal of the steps entails, for example, principles guiding ideas for an intervention, which are assessed in formative research, with the formative research pointing toward the use of particular procedures (see procedure box), with procedures and strategies also pointing toward a particular type of intervention. The preliminary ideas for an intervention can be assessed in formative research, but the process does not stop at that point.

The formative research should lead to a simple prototype of the intervention that is tried out in a pilot study, or actually, a "prepilot" or trial run (Winett et al. 1989, Winett and Moore 1990b). To be useful, the trial run must contain virtually all the elements of the planned intervention and evaluation, i.e., the same procedures, delivery system and dependent measures. It is a small low-cost study that forms the principles, procedures and intervention design steps, plus all steps prior to and after these steps. For example, the trial run should provide data on the viability of concepts and principles as well as how to better implement and evaluate an intervention. This simple trial run and a subsequent pilot test are invaluable, yet infrequently done, to the detriment of the entire enterprise.

Although the point may seem obvious, the timing of trial runs and pilot studies is critical. That is, too often a trial run and/or a pilot study are conducted at a time that provides little possibility for revising the overall intervention design. The intervention design and measures are virtual "givens." If that is the case, why do the trial run or pilot, except to trouble-shoot at the last minute?

Within the behavioral systems framework, trial runs and pilot tests are done because they may lead to reexamination of all prior and subsequent steps. A trial run that yields minimal or no behavior change may indicate the need to fortify procedures or even change the theory and principles that will guide the intervention design. For example, an information-only trial-run campaign for decreasing alcohol abuse among boaters may fail to show any observable decrease in drinking behaviors and reported accidents. Clearly, such results force careful reconsideration of the premises and procedures of an intervention.

Public health and other models would seriously suggest the addition of environmental components to the alcohol abuse campaign. These components could include personal contact procedures at docks and restriction of alcoholic beverage sales in the vicinity of the docks. Marketing theory, principles and procedures would also suggest ways to assess audience characteristics, target different audience segments and position a program for more positive perception.

The initial unsuccessful trial run should lead not only to "arm chair" reanalyses, but also to the redesign of another trial run. If that second or third trial run is successful, then the next step should begin. This step is the full-fledged pilot study.

Because of the expense of enacting large-scale campaigns and evaluations, the pilot study is essential. It usually will be the last chance to modify an intervention and the evaluation system so that optimal results are obtainable and documentable. In many ways the full-fledged pilot study is simply a miniaturized version of the overall large-scale intervention. Accordingly, it should have the same procedures, settings, personnel, target groups and measures as the large-scale campaign, but perhaps should have fewer sites, be conducted for a shorter time period, or involve fewer people.

The aim of the pilot study is to point out last-minute adjustments that need to be made in the intervention and evaluation measures. Importantly and sometimes painfully, if appropriate impacts are not discernible, the intervention plan probably should be abandoned. Careful and timely monitoring of trial runs and pilot studies should inform the intervention designers about possible problems.

For example, in our own work on media-based behavior change interventions, trial runs and pilot studies involve unobtrusive observations and process and outcome assessments (Winett and Moore 1990a, 1990b). In that way, we know how a redesigned program or system component is operating. These assessments are labor intensive, yet save time and money because problems can be discerned and fixed. The "fixing" may involve minor program refinements but, as suggested above, can entail a fresh redesign of a program.

Intervention Implementation, Evaluation and Methods

If all the foregoing steps are followed, presumably there should be relatively few surprises or disappointments in the larger-scale effort. That is, it should "work" and the effects should be observable. Some of the concerns in these final steps are therefore different from those of earlier steps. Concerns noted in the intervention implementation, evaluation and methods boxes include:

- What is the integrity of the intervention? That is, is the intervention followed and used the way is is intended? If not, how does process monitoring of an intervention suggest it has been perceived, acted upon and used? What other factors may be contributing to the effects that have been seen?
- What kinds of institutional and community supports may be necessary to maintain the intervention? That is, the goal of many interventions is long-term change that requires continual support, effort and monitoring.
- How can the intervention be refined not only to improve its less efficacious parts but also to keep the intervention up to date and vital?
- Is the evaluation design sufficiently rigorous so that the preliminary impacts observed can be attributed to the intervention? Are there reasonable assurances that contamination is nil or limited (e.g., between control and experimental recreational areas)? Parenthetically, it can be asked, if many resources and much care have been put into the design of the intervention, why have not more resources and more care been given to the evaluation design and tasks?
- If the impacts are discernible and the evaluation design rigorous, how do the impacts compare to specified goals? That is, a 30 percent drop in litter may be discernible, but if the goal was 90 percent, then goal attainment only is one third. Does the intervention show differential impact across different measures of outcome (e.g., reported accidents decrease, but treated injuries remain the same)? If this is the case, what do the differential impacts imply about the focus and viability of the intervention?
- How much is it costing for the effects obtained? Although sophisticated cost analyses can be done (Levin 1983), at a minimum the

cost for each relevant unit of change (e.g., each avoided accident, each percent of litter reduction) should be obtained.

- What can be said, given the integrity of the intervention, the evaluation design, and the impacts and associated costs, about the replicability of the intervention under similar and different circumstances? That is, most of the points noted here and in prior sections have emphasized internal validity. The rigor of the implementation and evaluation plan should assure a high degree of internal validity. Additionally, however even at the early stages of a demonstration/ research project, data pertinent to external validity can be collected (e.g., user acceptance, institutional and community support, impacts on diverse individuals; see West 1985 for a discussion of these points).

A final point on Figure 1 —The Behavioral Systems Framework—is the arrows on the last steps in the framework leading back to the first steps. This is because a well conceived and executed intervention should provide conceptual and strategic insights and guides for subsequent efforts.

ILLUSTRATION

The illustration in this section is an ambitious one. It attempts to focus on several critical behaviors in recreational areas by primarily using information strategies backed by limited personal contact and environmental change procedures. The problems to be addressed by the intervention for an extensive camping area surrounding a large lake include:

- decreasing littering and increasing appropriate litter disposal in receptacles placed around the camping areas;
- decreasing defacement of the natural environment, i.e., trees, shrubs and streams;
- decreasing public intoxication, boating while intoxicated, and boating accidents and injuries; and
- decreasing overall accidents and injuries.

Figure 2 is a depiction of many of the processes and steps that would be involved in this intervention, using the behavioral systems framework as the guide for its conceptualization, planning, pretesting, implementation and evaluation. For the sake of brevity and clarity, several assumptions have been made *a priori* about the intervention.

Figure 2
Outline of an Information Campaign with Interpersonal and Environmental Components for Cleaner, Safer Camping and Recreation

Steps	Concepts, Principles, Procedues, Methods
Problem Definition/Theories - Individual - Beliefs, Knowledge, Particular Behavior - Interpersonal - Family and Group Norms, Expectations - Organizational/Community - Environmental Design - Institutional/Societal - Legal Control of Behavior	**Concepts/Principles** - Social Cognitive - Modeling, Interpersonal Feedback - Communication - Specific Prescriptions - Community Organization - Acceptability to Most Campers - Process of Change - Less Important Diffusion - Respected Peers - Depicted in System Developmental/Ecological - - Specific Age Group; Delivery in Proper Settings Public Health - Environmental, - Legal Aspect Social Marketing - Tailoring - to Different Campers
Multilevel Analysis - Overcome Individual Beliefs about "Unrestrained" Behavior Provide Individual, Interpersonal, and Environmental - Components Ranger Facilitators - Multidimensional Evaluation (e.g., Litter, Defacements, - Accidents, Injuries)	
Intervention Design - Interactive Information System with Behavioral Prescriptions - Specific Scenes, Characters and Prescriptions Based on Age, Setting, Interests - Surveillance and Positive Feedback by Rangers - Deposit, Fines, Removal Strategies - Specific Goals for Litter, Defacement, Accident, Injury Reduction - Specific Measure for Each Goal - Formative Research, Initial Pilot Testing	**Procedures** - Modeling and Instruction via Interactive System; Use Valued Peer Images - Prescriptive - Step-by-Step Approach - Benefits for Campers - Specifically Design and Target Different Segments for Different Ages, Behaviors - Models for Adoption - Surveillance and Positive Feedback Fines, Removal
Intervention Implementation - Pilot Testing - Optimal Population and Setting for First Project - Integrity (e.g., Documented Use of System) - Continual Data Feedback and Refinements	
Evaluation - Checks for Contaminations between Campground - Outcomes on Each Measure compared to Goals and Control Setting - Impacts Across Measures - Plan of Replication Series with Refinements - Cost per Unit of Change	**Methods** - True Experiment - Random Assignment of Campgrounds - Multiple Measure for Major Goals - Monitoring of Parts of Intervention Used - Cost Figures

That is, for this example, we are not trying to discover the intervention strategies. These assumptions are:

- all users of the grounds must register at a central location;

- as one part of their registration, they must use an interactive information system that explicitly states why "unrestrained" camping and recreation is harmful to all, quickly shows appropriate campground behaviors, reviews particular situations, delineates enforcement strategies, provides special information for different kinds of campers and for children, clearly states and shows benefits to campers for following appropriate behaviors and has a review and brief quiz for each segment;

- noticeable but not overly obtrusive signs with pictures are placed throughout the grounds to prompt appropriate behaviors;

- rangers provide limited surveillance, but make personal contact with campers and provide positive verbal feedback on any appropriate behaviors they observe; and

- alcoholic beverages are prohibited at all times. Campers found with alcohol will lose a $50 security deposit collected at registration and must leave the campgrounds.

While the focus and components of the intervention have been decided *a priori*, it should be understood that the various facets of the intervention would typically be derived from the conceptual and formative research steps in the framework. Additionally, the rationale and procedures for the more particular steps involved in this intervention, and more generally in other interventions, are beyond the scope of this paper and Figure 2. These procedures may include how to present ideas that may be controversial in an influential way (e.g., a two-sided communication can help to convince campers that "unrestrained" recreational behaviors are inappropriate); how to discern (from formative research) the benefits people want and then clearly depict those benefits if certain behaviors are followed; how to fit a particular information delivery system into an environment where the system must seem appropriate to the setting; and how to decide on acceptable but effective fines (formative and pilot research).

Likewise, another assumption made in Figure 2 is that experimentation is desirable, that at least one setting could be an experimental one and a comparable one a control setting (or the overall intervention could be in place in one setting during different time periods, Kazdin

1984), and that replications of the effective intervention would proceed in a conservative way, i.e., the first project is in an optimal setting and the first replication is in a similar setting.

There are two final qualifications about the proposed information campaign. First, as noted previously, the intervention must be designed to fit into the setting. Overly instrusive or punitive surveillance will quickly negate whatever benefits this campaign might accrue. More-over, in the long run, it will be more efficacious if rangers give friendly, positive, verbal feedback for following the rules of the camping area. Second, it is essential that the interactive video program not only highlight the "please do nots," but also underscore the "please dos." Further, the alternative behaviors (e.g., carefully and regularly cleaning a campsite) must be clearly depicted in the program along with the natural positive consequences of following those behaviors (e.g., less trash and litter means fewer bugs). Thus, a classic dictum of behavior change strategy must be followed: when attempting to decrease negative behavior, reinforce alternative, incompatible, positive behav-iors (Kazdin 1984).

Conclusion and Caveat

The behavioral systems framework provides a series of concep-tual and strategic steps for planning, designing, implementing and evaluating interventions, where interventions have at their core an informational format and a media-based delivery system. Completion of the steps is laborious. The framework is a conservative and perhaps even plodding way to go about solving problems.

However, the framework also provides a contrast to the earlier days of media-based interventions. Frequently, these interventions seemed to be hatched overnight and were implemented with little or no formative or pilot research. Not surprisingly, they often failed.

The danger in closely following the behavioral systems frame-work may be that the framework appears to offer a guarantee of success. Unfortunately, this is not the case. At best, any approach can only modestly increase the probability of success (the extent of impacts). However, if all steps in the framework are followed, the probability and degree of impact should be known prior to the final decision to launch a large-scale effort.

The framework's development and research reported in this chapter were supported by grants from the National Science Foundation, the National Cancer Institute and the National Institute of Mental Health. Parts of this chapter also are based on an article by Winett, R. A., King, A. C. and Altman, D. G. 1990. Conceptual and strategic foundations for effective media campaigns for preventing the spread of HIV infection, *Evaluation and Program Planning.*

REFERENCES

Albright, C. L.; Altman, D. G.; Slater, M. D.; Maccoby, N. 1988. Cigarette advertisements in magazines: Evidence for a differential focus on women's and youth magazines. *Health Education Quarterly. 15*: 225-233.

Bandura, A. 1986. *Social foundations of thought and action: A social cognitive theory.* Englewood Cliffs, NJ: Prentice Hall. 526 p.

Brownell, K. D.; Marlatt, A.;Lichtenstein, E.; Wilson, G. T. 1986. Understanding and preventing relapse. *American Psychologist. 41*: 765-782.

Flay, B. R. 1987. Mass media and smoking cessation: A critical review. *American Journal of Public Health. 77*: 153-160.

Green, L. W.; Anderson, C. L. 1986 . *Community health.* St. Louis, MO: Mosby.

Hanlon, J.J.; Pickett, G. E. 1984. *Public health: Administration and practice.* 8th ed. St. Louis, MO: Mosby. 850 p.

Jason, L. A.; Gruder, L. L.; Martina, S.; Flay, B. R.; Warnecke, R.; Thomas, N. 1987. Worksite groups meetings and the effectiveness of a televised smoking cessation intervention. *American Journal of Community Psychology. 15*: 57-70.

Kazdin, A. E. 1984. *Behavior modification in applied settings.* 3rd ed. Homewood, IL: Dorsey. 187 p.

Krasner, L.; Ullman, L. P. 1973. *Personality and behavior influence: The social matrix of human interaction.* New York, NY: Holt, Rinehart, & Winston. 621 p.

Lash, L. P. 1971. *Eleanor and Franklin.* New York, NY: W.W. Norton & Co. 659 p.

Levin, H. M. 1983. *Cost effectiveness: A primer.* Beverly Hills, CA: Sage. 143 p.

Liebert, R. M.; Sprafkin, I. N.; Davidson, E. S. 1982. *The early window: Effects of television on children and youth.* 2nd ed. Elmsford, NY: Pergamon Press. 476 p.

Maccoby, N.; Altman, D. G. 1988. Disease prevention in communities: The Stanford Heart Disease Prevention Program. In: Price, R.; Cowen, E.; Lorian, R. ; Ramos-McKay, J., (eds.) *14 ounces of prevention.* Washington, DC: American Psychological Association. 165-174.

Manchester, W. 1974. *The glory and the dream.* Toronto: Bantam Books. 716 p.

Manoff, R. K. 1985. *Social marketing: Imperative for public health.* New York, NY: Praeger. 380 p.

Mendelsohn, H. 1973. Some reasons why information campaigns can succeed. *Public Opinion Quarterly. 37:* 50-60.

Rogers, E. M. 1983. *Diffusion of innovation.* 3rd ed. New York, NY: Free Press. 432 p.

Rogers, E. M.; Kincaid, D. C. 1981. *Communication networks: Toward a new paradigm for research.* New York, NY: Free Press. 412 p.

Rogers, E. M.; Shoemaker, F. 1971. *Communication of innovation.* New York, NY: Free Press. 506 p.

Rubenstein, E. A. 1983. Television and behavior: Research conclusions of the 1982 NIMH report. *American Psychologist. 38:* 820-825.

Shirer, W. L. 1960. *The rise and fall the the Third Reich.* New York, NY: Simon & Schuster. 937 p.

Solomon, D. S.; Maccoby, N. 1984. Communication as a model for health enhancement. In: Matarazzo, J.D.; Weiss, S.M.; Herd, J.A.; Miller, N.E.; Weiss, S.M., (eds.) *Behavioral health: A handbook for health enhancement.* New York, NY: Wiley. 209-221.

Warner, K. E. 1986. Selling smoking: Cigarette advertising and public health. Washington, DC: *American Public Health Association.* 231 p.

West, S. G. 1985. Beyond the laboratory experiment: Experimental and quasi-experimental designs for interventions in naturalistic settings. In: Karoly, P., (ed.) *Measurement strategies in health psychology.* New York, NY: Wiley. 183-233.

Winett, R. A. 1986. *Information and behavior: Systems of influence.* Hillsdale, NJ: Lawrence Erlbaum Associates. 247 p.

Winett, R. A. 1987. Prosocial television for community problems: Framework, effective methods, and regulatory barriers. In: Jason, L.A.; Felner, R.D.; Hess, R.; Moritsugu, J.N., (eds.) *Communities: Contributions from allied disciplines.* New York, NY: Haworth Press. 117-160.

Winett, R. A.; Altman, D. G.; King, A. C. 1990. Effective media campaigns to prevent the spread of HIV infection. *Evaluation and Program Planning. 13:* 91-104.

Winett, R. A.; King, A. C.; Altman, D. G. 1989. *Health psychology and public health: An integrative approach.* Elmsford, NY: Pergamon Press. 456 p.

Winett, R. A.; Moore, J. F. 1990a. *Family-media approach to AIDS prevention.* Ongoing National Institute of Mental Health Project, Virginia Polytechnic Institute & State University, Blacksburg, VA 24061.

Winett, R. A.; Moore, J. F. 1990b. *Feedback-video systems to promote nutritious purchases.* Ongoing National Cancer Institute Project, Virginia Polytechnic Institute and State University, Blacksburg, VA.

6

Mass Communication Research: Lessons for Persuasive Communication

Michael D. Slater

INTRODUCTION

Media in the form of advertisements, public service announcements, press releases, direct mail, posters, or flyers stuck under a windshield wiper are a mainstay of most public communication efforts. This chapter provides an overview of the many forms, uses and limitations of media, especially the mass media, as identified through several decades of theory-building and research in mass communication.

Mass communication theory addresses issues ranging from the information seeking and processing behavior of individuals, to the institutional behavior of media organizations and the social impact of media content. As a field of empirical social science inquiry, mass communication often has an applied focus, as well.

Interest in mass communication research developed following the first World War from fears concerning the power of propaganda and the possible social harm caused by massive exposure to popular media such as movies. More recently, campaigns have developed in the area of public communication, typically on behalf of governmental or non-profit agencies, to influence diet and exercise habits, crime prevention awareness, environmental conservation, and use of drugs and alcohol.

Mass communication research in these applied contexts is highly synthetic. Theorists and researchers attempt to integrate developments in psychology, marketing, and sociology with insights from the field of mass communication. Many relevant developments have been described in earlier chapters. In a sense, then, this chapter connects the fundamental social science theory from preceding chapters with the specific applications to follow. Additionally, the chapter suggests some general principles and guidelines, derived from several theoretical perspectives, that concern the use of media in communication campaigns.

MASS COMMUNICATION THEORY AND PERSUASION: AN OVERVIEW

Mass communication, like business and education, is less a single discipline than a meeting place of disciplines. Fields such as psychology and sociology tend to focus on a single level of analysis. Psychology studies the individual, and sociology studies groups, communities and social systems. Interdisciplinary fields such as mass communication study some aspect of society (in this case, media) across each of these levels of analysis (Berger and Chaffee 1987, Paisley 1984).

This section, therefore, groups theories by level of analysis, moving from the macroscopic to the more microscopic perspectives. These groupings include: a) functions for media in society (i.e., the influence of the media on public opinion and socialization); b) media organizations (i.e., structural issues that mediate the flow of persuasive communication); c) media as language (i. e., use of media to convey powerful symbolic language); d) media and the media audience (i.e., the relationship of media and interpersonal communication in influencing people); e) use of media by the audience (i.e., understanding how different types of people use media); and f) segmenting and understanding audiences for message design and channel selection. This review is not comprehensive, but highlights theories of particular relevance to public education and public behavior change.

Functions of Media in Society

Functional Approaches
Lasswell (1948) described three functions of mass communication : a) surveillance of the environment (providing information and

data about events to individuals and organizations); b) correlation of the parts of society responding to the environment (providing information concerning relations of social groups and individuals, making possible some community discourse), and; c) transmission of social heritage (education and socializing people concerning values of society). Wright (1960) extended Lasswell's conceptualization, adding a fourth function—entertainment.

In and of themselves, lists of mass communication functions may have only descriptive value. However, important theoretical developments, described below, have sprung from each of these functional categories.

Media and Public Opinion

Agenda-setting. Lasswell's (1948) concept of the surveillance function of the mass media has evolved into one of the single most influential concepts concerning the function of the mass media: agenda-setting. The agenda-setting concept (e.g., Shaw and McCombs 1977) proposes that the media determine what issues will be important to the public. This proposition is summarized in an oft-quoted phrase: "It [the mass media] may not be successful much of the time in telling people what to think, but it is stunningly successful in telling its readers what to think *about*" (Cohen 1963:#13, author's emphasis).

Critics of agenda-setting research have pointed out that, in fact, media often pick up cues on what to cover from their audiences, so the agenda-setting function is interactive rather than unidirectional (see Severin and Tankard 1988 for a review). Zucker (1978) pointed out that agenda-setting would most likely occur for unobtrusive or initially obscure issues. This suggestion is reflected in a related research tradition that examines media's role in forming community public opinion. A series of studies (e.g., Olien et al. 1984) suggested that media, especially local print media , have an important role to play in establishing what issues become subject to public concern and debate.

Poll-taking and Media Influence on Public Opinion. More recent theory has explored the role of mass media in shaping public opinion. Price and Roberts (1987) introduced a concept called poll-taking. Poll-taking is closely akin to Lasswell's(1948) notion of correlation. Price and Roberts suggest that a principal function of the media is to provide both political activists and various other segments of the public with ongoing information about how everyone else is reacting. As they point out, public opinion is largely a consequence of how people and groups form coalitions and allegiances. A prerequisite to intelligent formation of coalitions is knowing where both one's friends and enemies stand on an issue.

Van Leuven and Slater (1991) develop this model further, exploring how organizations and professional communicators seek to influence the public opinion process. They describe how organizations and communicators can use the media to mobilize publics and constituencies, and conversely use these publics to influence media coverage.

Implications

The literature on media and public opinion is worth careful study if one is engaged with a public opinion problem. For example, managers of national, state and local forests and parks are often at the center of potential public controversy concerning competing alternatives for land use, facility expansion and funding. The concept of agenda-setting also underscores a fundamental point about mass media. As we will develop in some detail later, perhaps the most productive use of mass media by professional communicators is simply to gain attention and to build awareness and involvement in an issue, product or service. This awareness and involvement may be prerequisite to achievement of communication objectives.

Media and Socialization

Another important research theme in mass communication concerns Lasswell's third function, socialization (see Greenberg 1982 for a review). Cultivation theory is the best known theoretical approach to understanding this function (e.g., Gerbner et al. 1986). Cultivation theory addresses the socializing function of mass media presentations, especially entertainment television. Cultivation theorists propose that mass media create homogeneous and often inaccurate impressions of social environments throughout our society. Other research efforts have explored the effect of television on violent behavior (see Pearl et al. 1982) and of pornography on perceptions of women (e.g., Linz et al. 1984).

Implications

Socialization research emphasizes how media can influence beliefs, attitudes and behavior without an obvious persuasive intent. It is useful here to recall Bandura's (1986) social learning theory, reviewed by Winett in chapter five. Attitudes, skills, and behaviors can be modeled in the course of media programming (e.g., Flora et al. 1989, Singhal and Rogers 1989). By presenting such models, it may be possible to avoid counterarguing and other cognitive responses that inhibit the influence of a communication (Petty et al., Chapter 4), because the persuasive intent may be less apparent. It also may be possible to directly influence perceptions of social norms and expectations, which are significant determinants of behavior (Ajzen, Chapter 1, Bandura 1986).

Media Organizations

Considerable research has examined media from an organizational point of view, examining how decisions are made and how professional roles are defined. Much of this research has a management focus; however, understanding newsroom decision-making and professional roles is important for persuasive communicators.

Gatekeeping

One fundamental concept in news decision-making is that of the gatekeeper, a term coined by White (1950). A basic fact of journalistic life is that far more information is available than can be accommodated in the "news hole," or news content of a newspaper, magazine or television broadcast. Daily, journalists at major news outlets are typically confronted with dozens of news alerts, press releases and press kits. Only a fraction of these find their way into the public eye.

Journalists are gatekeepers in that they have to make many daily decisions about what will be communicated and what will not, information that may then become part of public awareness and discourse—the public agenda. Editors, including managing editors, assignment editors, and desk editors such as city desk and health and lifestyles editors, are primarily responsible for making such decisions in print publications. On many publications, the reporter covering a particular news "beat" may serve a similar role. Broadcast news directors and assistant news directors serve the same gatekeeping role as newspaper editors (see Gans 1979). Talk shows and other feature coverage opportunities are more often managed by producers and assistant producers, who will determine which guests appear and what features are covered (Klepper 1984).

Gatekeepers' criteria for the value of a story include timeliness, community impact, and reader interest (see Brooks et al. 1988). It is important to note that these criteria may sometimes be mutually exclusive. An important ongoing situation may not be well covered because it is not "breaking news": that is, nothing specific and concrete is taking place that lends itself to news coverage. Similarly, human interest feature coverage may not be especially timely or important, but may simply make a good story.

Professional Role and Identity

Another fundamental reality of newsroom life concerns professional roles or self-perceptions among journalists. Journalism is a notoriously underpaid profession. Job satisfaction stems largely from the feeling of social importance and public service as well as from the visibility, access and influence of journalists in most communities (e.g., Cross 1953, Goodwin 1983). Journalists build their careers by regularly getting good stories—stories that merit prominent exposure on the front pages and bylines.

Therefore, although journalists seldom admit the possibility, journalistic self-interest and the public interest can sometimes collide. To maximize newsworthiness, the unusual, striking or dramatic aspect of a story is often emphasized at the expense of a balanced, rational presentation of an event or issue. As Lippmann (1922:226) put it, "News and truth are not the same thing."

Implications

The persuasive communicator and the journalist have both a symbiotic and an adversarial relationship. The journalist is heavily dependent on the persuasive communicator for access to information sources and story ideas (Turk 1986). The persuasive communicator is dependent on the journalist for access to the mass media other than through paid advertising. Persuasive communicators promote a point of view; journalists purport to be objective. Persuasive communicators often promote "good news" about a product, service, location or facility; however, bad news in the form of problems, scandals or confrontations are usually more newsworthy (see Cutlip et al. 1985 for a good introductory discussion of this ambivalent relationship).

To work successfully with mass media, the persuasive communicator must try to interpret his or her message in terms that are attractive to the gatekeeper or reporter. Avenues include importance to public interest: stories ranging from vandalism prevention to new facilities permitting handicapped access may fall in this category. Special interest to a given audience is the most typical route: information about special activities, programs, classes or even schedules are bread-and-butter to reporters covering life styles and leisure. A human interest angle, such as a long-time employee beloved by children of the community or a handicapped climber or swimmer, may also provide opportunities for exposure.

Media as Language

A number of scholars have developed more esoteric approaches to understanding the functions and effects of mass media, with Marshall McLuhan (1964) being the best-known among them. For the most part, these approaches are not directly pertinent to the present discussion on persuasion. However, one such approach—semiotics—does provide some provocative insights.

Semiotics refers to the study of how the meanings of events, situations and messages are interpreted (see Fry and Fry 1986). The central tenet of semiotic approaches, greatly simplified, is that words, events and images all have a wealth of implications and meanings beyond their literal meanings. The persuasive impact of a powerful slogan or dramatic image is not well accounted for by theories of persuasion or social influence. Yet millions of advertising dollars are spent posing political candidates with the American flag or a loving family, with virtually no persuasive message other than the image itself.

Implications

Most persuasive communication can be conceptualized by using various theories of persuasion, consumer psychology and social influence, either separately or in combination. Based on anecdotal and historical experience, however, images and events that capture and symbolize a host of emotional commitments and values seem to have a powerful persuasive impact. These images are not easily analyzed through social scientific methods, but advertisers and other persuasive communicators regularly attempt to capitalize on such imagery.

Media and the Media Audience

For the persuasive communicator, perhaps the most directly applicable set of mass communication research questions concern the relationship between mass media and the individuals who comprise the media audience. Some of these questions concern mass media effects: how exactly does the media influence individual attitudes and behaviors? Other questions address mediating circumstances: under what circumstances are mass media most likely to be effective? What outcomes can mass media achieve most reliably? Does outcome success depend on the types of people in the audience, the types of media or the type of message?

This section summarizes principal research directions and findings concerning these questions.

Media and Interpersonal Influence

Two-step Flow. A key study from the early 1950s (Katz and Lazarsfeld 1955) argued that media were primarily effective in influencing key individuals within a community. These individuals, called opinion leaders, tended both to follow the mas media and to have considerable influence on the opinions of their less well-informed peers. Opinion leadership can be found among union members, housewives and teenagers, as well as among politically active and civic-minded citizens. The identity of opinion leaders also varies: a respected authority on fishing and trout streams may not be regarded with similar deference on the topics of family campground or golf facilities. The influence of the media on a community, according to Katz and Lazarsfeld (1955), is due to its effects on opinion leaders, who then help mold the views of their peers. Katz and Lazarsfeld referred to this process as two-step flow.

Multi-step Flow/Diffusion Research

The two-step flow hypothesis has been criticized frequently. Some studies, for example, have found that major news stories reach most of the public directly, not through an intervening opinion leader (Westley 1971). Other commentators have pointed out that opinion leaders themselves vary in how actively they seek information from the media (Rogers and Shoemaker 1971; see also Chaffee 1972 for an excellent conceptual discussion and Severin and Tankard 1988: 202-203 for a summary of criticism).

Subsequent interest has shifted to the more complex diffusion model. Diffusion research is based on early work in rural sociology (e.g., Ryan and Gross 1943) that examined how innovations were adopted over time in a community. Rogers (1983) distinguishes five types of people, in the order in which they tend to adopt a new technology or behavior: innovators, early adopters, early majority, and laggards or traditionals. While innovators may most closely follow the media, they tend to be less central socially and thus less influential as opinion leaders than early adopters.

Diffusion research emphasizes the importance of a combination of mass media, used primarily to inform and build awareness, and interpersonal communication used to actually achieve persuasion and attitude change (Rogers 1983, Rogers and Kincaid 1981). Other commentators differ, pointing out that some attitudes and behaviors seem more readily influenced by the media than are the important economic decisions such as choice of food crops typically addressed in diffusion research (Chaffee 1972), and that the diffusion model does not take into account the possible direct impact of modeling behaviors via media (Winett, Chapter 5).

Implications

Clearly, diffusion research emphasizes the importance of identifying and reaching opinion leaders, innovators and early adopters via the media. We will develop this strategy further in a later discussion of segmenting and targeting audiences. In addition, the two-step flow and diffusion models suggest that the principal importance of mass media is in building awareness, and that persuasion and behavior change is best accomplished interpersonally.

Use of the Media by Audiences

Persuasion-oriented approaches emphasize how media may act upon the media audience. This audience, however, is not a captive audience. Armed with a remote control device, television viewers can flip through 40 or more channels if served by a cable franchise—or may even turn the appliance off. Only the most diehard newspaper readers read the entire contents of their favorite daily or weekly paper; most readers scan the paper as suits their fancy. A number of mass communication researchers have focused on how people actively peruse their information environment.

Demographic Factors and the Knowledge Gap

The easiest way of distinguishing patterns of media use is demographically. For example, television is most heavily watched by older people, poorer people, less educated people and women (Comstock et al. 1978, Frank and Greenberg 1980). Conversely, newspaper readers tend to be more affluent, better educated and male (American Newspaper Publishers Association 1979).

Knowledge gaps (Tichenor et al. 1970), an important phenomenon in communication campaigns, may largely be a consequence of demographic differences in the type of media used, and the amount of attention with which information is processed. Knowledge gaps refer to the tendency for better-educated, more affluent audiences to learn relatively more from communication efforts than less educated, less affluent audiences. The educated and affluent learn more for several reasons: they are heavier users of print media, which contain more information than broadcast media; and being better educated, they are better skilled in assimilating new information. In other words, as a result of communication campaigns, the information-rich get richer relative to the information-poor. The information-poor, however, nonetheless often show some knowledge gains.

Of course, each individual television program or publication has its "demographics," or profile of people who comprise its audience. These audiences are usually well-documented (see the publications of Simmons Market Research Bureau, Inc., available in most business libraries) for the sake of the advertisers seeking the appropriate vehicle for their messages.

Audience Selectivity and Information-seeking

Demographics alone provide only general insights into how people use media and information. People may actively seek information that interests them, or avoid information that is either uninteresting or threatening. For example, one study conducted as part of a health promotion effort found that high-risk males, though they tended to be heavy newspaper readers, nonetheless did not read the health information conveyed in newspapers (Slater and Flora, 1990).

Theory and research on information-seeking (Atkin 1973, Donohew and Tipton 1973) emphasize several factors that predict how actively people will look for relevant information. First, there is instrumental utility: do audience members need the information in order to make decisions or take action, to vote for a candidate or choose a vacation spot? Second, there is uncertainty: the less committed audience members are to their candidate or vacation destination, the more likely they are to seek relevant information (Atkin 1973). The concept of utility is much expanded and explored by researchers in the uses and gratifications tradition (Blumler and Katz 1974, Palmgreen 1984), who distinguish a wide range of reasons for media use.

Donohew and Tipton (1973) discuss cognitive factors that predict whether information will be processed or avoided. In particular, information that is consistent with existing beliefs or frames of reference will tend to be processed, and information which is discrepant will not be processed. This latter issue of how people deal with discrepant or consistent information is at the heart of the problem of selectivity. Seeking consistent or avoiding discrepant information is commonly referred to as selective exposure (see Sears and Freedman 1967 for a classic critical discussion).

There are also other kinds of selectivity. Selective perception refers to the tendency to reinterpret messages according to one's existing beliefs. In the well-known Mr. Biggott study (Cooper and Jahoda 1947), prejudiced respondents interpreted a cartoon mocking racism as in fact endorsing it; similar studies on the television program "All in the Family" showed that both prejudiced and unprejudiced viewers interpreted the program as endorsing their values (Vidmar and Rokeach 1974). Selective attention refers to a tendency to attend to information in a given message that is consistent with existing beliefs, and selective retention refers to a tendency to better recall consistent information. However, as the Ajzen, Petty et al., and Winett chapters in this volume indicate, the processes triggered by counterattitudinal messages are in fact quite complex.

The four forms of selectivity, nonetheless, provide useful cautions to persuasive communicators: because a message is communicated via the media, it won't necessarily be seen; if seen, not necessarily attended to; if attended to, not necessarily remembered (see also McGuire 1989).

Sense-making and Convergence Models

On a similar theme, other scholars have pointed out that audiences often have a rather different set of concerns and definitions regarding the topic of an information campaign than do communicators, described by Dervin (1989) as sense-making. Communicators need to cast communication in the frame of reference of their audiences, rather than in terms of institutional values and assumptions. From this point of view, common understanding, or convergence (Rogers and Kincaid 1981), is a prerequisite to influence. The process of research, understanding and targeting communication is discussed below in the context of segmenting audiences.

Implications

The implications of audience-centered approaches should be largely self-evident. Message content must be responsive to the needs, concerns and frameworks of diverse audiences. These messages must then be delivered via media used by the people one wishes to reach. The next section explores these message design and channel selection problems.

Segmenting and Understanding Audiences
for Message Design and Channel Selection

If there is a fundamental rule for effective persuasive communication, it is to know one's audience and to design one's arguments accordingly. In mass communication, the audience is typically highly diverse. To communicate effectively, then, one must divide the audience into smaller, more homogeneous subgroups, a process called audience segmentation (Levitt 1986, Smith 1956).

Audience segmentation is heuristic: there is no one right way to segment an audience. However, if it is to be useful, audience segmentation should meet several criteria. Audience segments should differ on some characteristic that will indicate to the communicator that either somewhat different messages or different message delivery strategies are needed. These differentiating characteristics may be demographic, or based on awareness, attitudinal or behavioral differences.

This section reviews some typical strategies from the mass communication and marketing literature for identifying such distinguishing characteristics and for segmenting audiences.

Audience Involvement and the Hierarchy of Effects

Theoretical approaches such as McGuire's message-yielding approach (McGuire 1989), the elaboration likelihood model (Petty et al. Chapter 4), and expectancy-value theory (Ajzen, Chapter 1) convincingly portray the inherent difficulties in persuasion. Why, then, do some forms of persuasive communication such as advertising seem so effective?

Krugman (1965) offered an influential explanation. Perhaps when people really have very little personal investment in a topic, behaviors are influenced in a very different way than when people have some interest or involvement. When involvement is low, Krugman suggested, perhaps simple awareness or accessibility of information influences behavior such as purchasing some product or service. Once a purchase was made, one would then tend to develop positive attitudes about that product or service if only to rationalize one's choice.

Ray and his associates (Ray 1973) more formally developed and tested this concept in a study of what they called the hierarchy of effects. Ray pointed out that conventional persuasion models presumed, logically enough, that knowledge precedes attitudes, which precede behavior. However, Krugman's argument implies that behavior precedes attitudes when one's audience is not very involved with the message topic. In other words, people may select a product or service because of a familiar name or brand and then develop positive attitudes consistent with that behavior. This proposition was supported in a variety of empirical tests (see Ray 1973 for a review).

Situational Theory

Involvement has been incorporated as an important mediating variable in other theoretical approaches as well, including the elaboration likelihood model (Petty et al. Chapter 4) and situational theory (Grunig and Hunt 1984). Since the elaboration likelihood model has been presented in detail, this discussion focuses on situational theory.

Situational theory is concerned with understanding and prediction of two selectivity variables: the extent of information-seeking, and the amount of attention given to relevant messages if received, which Grunig calls information processing (Grunig and Hunt 1984). Grunig proposes three predictors of both information-seeking and information processing: awareness or recognition of the problem or issue, and constraint recognition (the perceived ability or inability to do anything about the problem or issue).

Depending on the various permutations of high versus low involvement, problem recognition, and constraint recognition, Grunig has distinguished four types of publics. These include *active publics*, high in involvement and problem recognition and low in constraint recognition, who tend to be heavy media consumers and responsive to many issues; *aware publics*, also heavy media users who tend to be more restricted in their political/civic activity; *latent publics*, who are less heavy users of the media but who may be mobilized if an issue or topic is sufficiently relevant; and *inactive publics*, who have minimal concern with most issues and pay relatively little attention to the media for information gathering (Grunig and Hunt 1984).

Implications

Grunig's typology of publics is useful primarily in campaigns directed at controversial issues, and less useful as a marketing tool. Also, as Grunig (1989) points out, his typology identifies types of publics. Further segmentation is required to target specific publics within each type. However, situational theory does suggest some basic guidelines for persuasive communicators.

First, it is essential to have some sense of the level of problem recognition or awareness of your various publics. If awareness or problem recognition is lacking among some key publics, the communication emphasis should be on the widest possible visibility of your message, conveyed in a rather simple fashion. If constraint recognition is high, communication will have to emphasize empowerment: identifying and providing the necessary information and skills required to take action. Modeling techniques are especially appropriate here (see Bandura 1986, Flora et al. 1989, Winett, Chapter 5).

Both the situational theory and the hierarchy of effects approaches highlight involvement as a determinant of message effects on attitude and behavior. Highly involved publics should be approached with sophisticated messages responsive to existing knowledge and attitudes. Fortunately, such publics are heavy media consumers, and can usually be targeted through specialized publications and other print media. With less involved publics, sometimes simply gaining a sufficiently high level of awareness may be enough to trigger behavior and attitude change. Message design for less involved audiences should focus on memorability, vividness, and ease of comprehension, not on sophistication. Channels should primarily be those that reach the largest possible relevant audience (Van Leuven and Slater 1991).

These problems will be explored in more detail at the close of this chapter. First, however, it may be useful to review some strategies and procedures for identifying specific publics.

Strategies for Identifying Specific Publics

There are a variety of specific techniques for breaking one's audience into segments or subgroups (see Grunig 1989 for a conceptual overview). The crudest and cheapest method is simply to make demographic distinctions among one's publics according to age, gender, race ethnicity, etc. In contemporary society, however, demographics are an increasingly weak predictor of attitudes and behavior: the middle-income white 35-year old female with a college degree may be an environmentally-conscious but somewhat sedentary housewife, or a conservative single woman active primarily in skiing.

Psychographics and lifestyle segmentation, in contrast, involves creation of typologies based on typical patterns of values and behaviors. The best known of these typologies is VALS—values and lifestyles (Mitchell 1983). The VALS typology is often used to predict consumer behavior. Another version of this approach is geodemographics, which combines consumer typologies with zip-code analyses to provide a rough summary of consumer patterns in given locales (Winkelman 1987).

A problem and advantage with each of these approaches is that they are not tailored to different domains of attitude and behavior. The advantage is that using these typologies minimizes the required research effort. When the communication problem is primarily one of marketing, these typologies may be quite useful. When communication is intended to modify more complex attitudes and behaviors, such as efforts to reduce destructive or unsafe behaviors by users of recreational facilities and areas, these typologies may be inadequate.

To effectively use research to segment audiences with reference to these more complex problems, one must first identify the probable determinants of relevant attitudes and behaviors. These determinants typically include beliefs, values and knowledge; social clues, models and pressures; and situational/environmental constraints (Slater and Flora, in press). A survey instrument incorporating measures for these determinants can then be used to create lifestyle typologies tailored to the relevant domain of activity. Distinctive message and channel delivery strategies can be tailored to relevant audience segments (see Slater and Flora 1991 and Flora et al. 1990 for a detailed example in the domain of health communication).

Alternatively, one can simply cross-tabulate demographics with measures of media use in order to provide some basic insights. If survey techniques are not possible due to time or budget constraints, various other exploratory research techniques such as focus groups or in-depth interviews may suffice. Ideally, both exploratory and quantitative research should be conducted (see Atkin and Freimuth 1989 regarding formative evaluation techniques).

CAPABILITIES AND LIMITATIONS OF MASS MEDIA
IN PERSUASIVE COMMUNICATION

How effective, then, are the mass media as a means of influencing people? The answer, of course, is "it depends." More usefully, media effectiveness depends on several factors: the desired impact, the tractability of the targeted attitude or behavior, and predispositional factors among the target audience.

Desired impacts may be divided into three types: to inform (increase knowledge or awareness); to persuade (create or change attitudes); and to initiate or change behavior (Rogers and Storey 1987). Communication efforts may be directed at one of these outcomes or at a combination of several outcomes.

The appropriate outcome is sometimes inherent in the particular communication campaign. For example, in the context of recreation and tourism, interpretation and education are primarily concerned with informing publics. Other types of communication efforts are more complex.

Tourism promotion and advertising (Manfredo et al., Chapter 11 for example), may be focused on one, two or all three levels of outcome. Promotion of a little-known attraction, of course, will probably have to focus on awareness and name recognition before the attraction can even be considered by the public as a vacation option. Awareness may also be a principle objective under another set of circumstances: when recreational users or tourists do not distinguish carefully between alternative destinations, and choose a destination based on name recognition. Mass media, of course, is an ideal way to build awareness, at least at the level of name recognition (e.g., Krugman 1965). Subject to the public's willingness to process media information (Grunig 1989; Petty et al., Chapter 4), mass media media promotion also can be an effective educational strategy.

Promotion of a better-known tourist destination in a competitive market may focus on attitudinal impact, attempting implicitly or explicitly to foster the perception of the destination as a superior choice among alternatives. To the extent that attitudes are based on relevant beliefs, such as the quality of the climate or facilities, mass media may be a very effective way to make the appropriate claims or to make the relevant attitudes more salient (Vincent and Fazio, Chapter 3). The main challenges are to identify the relevant beliefs and attitudes, address these effectively in the message, and select media channels appropriate to the targeted audiences. The problem of attitude change—Seattle is not really so rainy, Hawaii is not so terribly expensive—is, of course, a more difficult proposition than making existing attitudes more salient or creating attitudes where none previously exist (see Petty et al., Chapter 4).

If the tourist attraction is already perceived as highly attractive, promotional efforts may focus on motivation-specific behaviors such as making the travel agent contact or calling for reservations. Again, simply being reminded of the behavior may be enough to cue action, if the timing is appropriate. Media may also be used to model the desired behavior (Winett, Chapter 5). For example, an ad showing a consumer telephoning in a reservation might be especially effective during the months when people are planning their summer or winter vacations.

Behavior modification, such as reducing destructive or unsafe behaviors at a recreational site, often poses the greatest challenge to communicators. To the extent that a consistency exists between knowledge, attitude, and behaviors, communication efforts must be directed at all three (Ajzen, Chapter 1; see also Ray 1973). As Ajzen suggests, it is crucial to identify and address those beliefs and attitudes that in fact determine a particular behavior (see also Slater and Flora, in press). For example, vandals know that vandalism is fun, from an adolescent's point of view. Increased knowledge concerning legal consequences facing the vandal may make some difference; so might knowledge about the unintended consequences of vandalism that endanger people or wildlife. More likely, communication attempts might emphasize trying to mobilize peers or role models of potential vandals to discourage vandalism. Messages may focus on exhortations from role models or behavioral modeling. In any case, extensive formative research used to understand the determinants of relatively intractable behaviors is a prerequisite to effective campaign design. Media efforts alone are likely to achieve limited success at best. Intervention programs should include the involvement of community organizations such as schools and workplace, as well as direct individual contact if possible (Flora et al. 1989).

Some behaviors (Roggenbuck, Chapter 7), however, are more amenable to media influence. For example, littering and, to some extent, fire safety involve behaviors of minimal consequence to the perpetrating individual. Very little of an individual's economic well-being or social identity is invested in whether a cigarette butt is stubbed out in an ashtray or flicked out of a car window. Yet, the potential consequences to recreation resources are immense. Similarly, proper disposal of waste requires only a slight investment in time and plastic bags.

In such cases, media campaigns can be quite effective (see Cialdini 1989 and Rice 1989 for relevant case descriptions). Such media campaigns may serve to increase individual involvement with an issue, which in turn serves to increase the consistency of relevant behaviors with knowledge and attitudes (Chaffee and Roser, 1986; Grunig 1989). In other words, people do not litter and flick cigarette butts because they believe in the rightness of the behavior. Media campaigns can focus attention on this inconsistency, and make the relevant beliefs and attitudes more salient (Vincent and Fazio, Chapter 3).

The research on media campaigns, attitude, and behavior change, then, can be summarized in a few basic propositions (see Rogers and Storey 1987 for a similar but more extensive discussion). First, mass media is a powerful way to build awareness when employing media used heavily by desired audiences. Such media may also be effective at building knowledge, if targeted audiences are sufficiently interested and involved to attend to the messages. If such involvement is initially absent, a media campaign can increase interest and involvement, stimulate interpersonal discussion, and improve the likelihood of later campaign success in influencing attitudes and behavior. Also, some behaviors are not associated with much personal or social commitment. In such cases, simple awareness may be enough to prompt appropriate behaviors.

However, when substantive behavior change (rather than behavior choice) is desired, such as the abandonment of gratifying but risky or destructive behaviors (rather than the selection of a vacation site or use of an ashtray), the potential impact of mass media is usually less. Media can increase involvement and knowledge-attitude-behavior consistency, which may then facilitate changing less-entrenched behaviors. When behaviors are largely determined by social factors, including peer pressure or ethnic traditions such as hunting in public lands, the leverage provided by media is limited. Messages come from "them," not "us." Media can sometimes be used, through judicious selection of people and situations, to model behavior change or to provide potentially influential information. However, in such cases media can often best be used to support organizational or interpersonal interventions.

When resources permit, use of multiple message delivery strategies is usually more productive than using a single type of media.

Effective communication strategies often involve maximizing exposure to different versions of a message through complementary channels, including broadcast and print media, flyers and brochures, and organizational and interpersonal contact.

Using mass media effectively requires determining the kind of impact needed, tailoring messages to specific, segmented audiences, finding the channels attended to by those audiences, and providing maximum message exposure to targeted audiences.

REFERENCES

American Newspaper Publishers Association. 1979. *Facts about newspapers.* Washington, D.C. 26 p.

Atkin, C.K.; Freimuth, V.1989. Formative evaluations research in campaign design. In: Rice, R.E.; Atkin, C.K. (eds.) *Public communication campaigns.* 2nd ed. Newbury Park, CA: Sage:131-150.

Atkin, C.K. 1973. Instrumental utilities and information seeking. In: Clarke, P. (ed.) *New models for mass communication research.* Newbury Park, CA: 202-242.

Bandura, A. 1986. *Social foundations of thought and action.* Englewood Cliffs, NJ: Prentice-Hall, Inc. 617 p.

Berger, C.R.; Chaffee, S.H. 1987. The study of communication as a science. In: Berger, C.R.; Chaffee, S.H. (eds.) *Handbook of communication science.* Newbury Park, CA: Sage: 15-19.

Blumler, J.; Katz, E.1974. *The uses of mass communication.* Newbury Park, CA: Sage. 318 p.

Brooks, B.S.; Kennedy G.; Moen, D.R.; Ranly D. 1988. *News reporting and writing.* 3rd ed. New York, NY: St. Martins. 571 p.

Chaffee, S.H.; Roser, C.1986. Involvement and the consistency of knowledge, attitudes and behaviors. *Communication Research. 13*(3); 373-399.

Chaffee, S.H. 1972. The interpersonal context of mass communication. In: Kline, G.; Tichenor, D. (eds.) *Current perspectives in mass communication research.* Newbury Park, CA: Sage: 95-120.

Cialdini, R.B. 1989. Littering: When every litter bit hurts. In: Rice, R.E.; Atkin, C.K. (eds.) *Public communication campaigns.* 2nd ed. Newbury park, CA: Sage 221-223.

Cohen, B.C. 1963. *The press and foreign policy.* Princeton, NJ: Princeton University Press. 285 p.

Comstock, G.; Chaffee, S.H.; Katzman, N.; McCombs, M.E.; Roberts D.F. 1978. *Television and human behavior.* New York, NY: Columbia University Press. 581 p.

Cooper, E.; Jahoda, M. 1947. The evasion of propaganda: How prejudiced people respond to anti-prejudice propaganda. *Journal of Psychology. 23*:15-25.

Cross, H.L. 1953. *The people's right to know.* New York, NY: Columbia University Press. 36 p.

Cutlip, S.M.; Center, A.H.; Broom, G.M. 1985. *Effective public relations.* 6th ed. Englewood Cliffs, NJ: Prentice-Hall. 670 p.

Dervin, B. 1989. Audience as listener and learner, teacher and confidante: The sense-making approach. In: Rice, R.E.; Atkin, C.K. (eds.) *Public communication campaigns.* 2nd ed. Newbury Park, CA: Sage: 67-86.

Donohew, L.; Tipton, L. 1973. A conceptual model of information seeking, avoiding and processing. In: Clarke, P. (ed.) *New models for mass communication research.* Newbury Park, CA: Sage: 243-268.

Flora, J.A.; Maccoby, N.; Farquhar, J.W. 1989. Communication campaigns to prevent cardiovascular disease: The Stanford community studies. In: Rice, R.E.; Atkin, C.K. (eds.) *Public communication campaigns.* 2nd ed. Newbury Park, CA: Sage: 233-252.

Flora, J.A.; Maibach,E.; Slater, M.D. 1990. The relationship between health lifestyle, media use, and interpersonal communication. Manuscript under review.

Frank, R.E.; Greenberg, M.G. 1980. *The public's use of television.* Newbury Park, CA: Sage: 463-482.

Fry, D.L.; Fry, V.H. 1986. A semiotic model for the study of mass communication. In: McLaughlin, M. (ed.) *Communication Yearbook 9.* Newbury Park, CA: Sage: 463-482.

Gans, H.J. 1979. *Deciding what's news.* New York, NY: Pantheon. 393 p.

Gerbner, G.; Gross, L.; Morgan, M.; Signorielli, N. 1986. In: Jennings, B.; Zillman, D. (eds.) *Perspectives on media effects.* Hillsdale, NJ: Erlbaum: 17-40.

Goodwin, H.E. 1983. *Groping for ethics in journalism.* Iowa City, IA: Iowa University Press. 335 p.

Greenberg, B.S. 1982. Television and role socialization: an overview. In: Pearl, D.; Bouthilet, L.; Lazar. J. (eds.) *Television and behavior. Vol. 2.* Rockville, MD: National Inst. of Mental Health: 179-190.

Grunig, J.E.; Hunt, T. 1984. *Managing public relations.* New York: Holt, Rinehart and Winston. 550 p.

Grunig, J.E. 1989. Publics, audiences, and market segments: Segmentation principles for campaigns. In: Salmon, C.K. (ed.), *Information campaigns: Balancing social values and social change.* Newbury Park, CA: Sage: 199-228.

Katz, E.; Lazarsfeld, P.F. 1955. *Personal influence: The part played by people in the flow of mass communications.* New York, NY: Free Press. 400 p.

Klepper, M..M. 1984. *Getting your message out: How to get, use, and survive radio and television airtime.* Englewood Cliffs, NJ: Prentice-Hall. 174 p.

Krugman, H.E. 1965. The impact of television advertising: Learning without involvement. *Public Opinion Quarterly. 29*: 349-356.

Lasswell, H.D. 1948. The structure and function of communication in society. In: Bryson, L. (ed.) *The communication of ideas*. New York, NY: Institute for Religious and Social Studies: 37-52.

Levitt, T. 1986. *The marketing imagination*. New York,NY: Free Press. 238 p.

Linz, D.; Donnerstein, E.; Penrod, S. 1984. The effects of multiple exposure to filmed violence against women. *Journal of Communication. 34*(3): 130-147.

Lippmann, W. 1922. *Public opinion*. New York, NY: Macmillan. 427 p.

McGuire, W.J. 1989. Theoretical foundations of campaigns. In: Rice, R.E.; Atkin, C.K. eds. *Public communication campaigns*. 2nd ed. Newbury Park, CA: Sage: 43-66.

McLuhan, M. 1964. *Understanding media*. New York,NY: McGraw-Hill. 365 p.

Mitchell, A. 1983. *The nine American lifestyles*. New York,NY: Warner Books. 302 p.

Olien, C.N.; Donohue, G.A.; Tichenor, P.J. 1984. Media and stages of social conflicts. *Journalism Monographs. 90*:1-31.

Paisley, W.J. 1984. Communication in the sciences. In: Dervin, B.; Voight, M. eds. *Progress in the communication sciences*. Vol. V. Norwood, NJ: Ablex, 1-4.

Palmgreen, P. 1984. Uses and gratifications: A theoretical perspective. In: Bostrom, R.N. (ed.), *Communication yearbook 8*. Newbury Park, CA: Sage: 20-55.

Pearl, D.; Bouthilet, L.; Lazar, J. (eds.) 1982. *Television and behavior. Vol. 2.* Rockville, MD: National Institute of Mental Health. 362 p.

Price, V.; Roberts, D.F. 1987. Public opinion processes. In: Berger, C.R.; Chaffee, S.H. (eds.) *Handbook of communication science*. Newbury Park, CA: Sage: 781-816.

Ray, M.L. 1973. Marketing communication and the hierarchy of effects. In: Clarke, P. (ed.) *New models for mass communication research.* Newbury Park, CA: Sage: 147-176.

Rice, R.E. 1989. Smokey Bear. In: Rice, R.E.; Atkin, C.K. (eds.) *Public communication campaigns*. 2nd ed. Newbury Park, CA: Sage: 215-217.

Rogers, E.M. 1983. *The diffusion of innovations*. NY: Free Press. 453 p.

Rogers, E.M.; Kincaid, D.L. 1981. *Communication networks*. New York: Free Press. 476 p.

Rogers, E.M.; Storey, J.D. 1987. *Communication campaigns*. In: Berger, C.R.; Chaffee, S.H. eds. *Handbook of communication science*. Newbury Park, CA: Sage: 817-846.

Ryan, B.; Gross, N. 1943. The diffusion of hybrid seed corn in town Iowa communities. *Rural Sociology. 8*: 15-24.

Sears, D.O.; Freedman, J.L. 1967. Selective exposure to information: A critical review. *Public Opinion Quarterly. 31*:194-213.

Severin, W.J.; Tankard, J.W. 1988. *Communication theories.* 2nd ed. New York, NY: Longman. 351 p.

Shaw, D.L; McCombs, M.E. 1977. *The emergence of American political issues.* St. Paul; West Publishing. 221 p.

Singhal, A.; Rogers, E.M. 1989. Prosocial television for development in India. In: Rice, R.E.; Atkin, C.K. (eds.) *Public communication campaigns.* 2nd ed. Newbury Park, CA: Sage: 331-350.

Slater, M.D.; Flora, J.A. 1990. Is health behavior consumer behavior? Health behavior determinants, audience, segmentation and designing health promotion campaigns. In: Clark, E.; Stewart, D.; Brock, T. (eds.) *Advertising and consumer psychology.* Hillsdale, NJ: Erlbaum.

Slater M.D.; Flora, J.A. 1991. Health lifestyles: Audience segmentation analysis for public health interventions. *Health Education Quarterly.*

Smith, W.R. 1956. Product differentiation and market segmentation as alternative marketing strategies. In: Walters, C.J.; Robins, D.P. (eds.) *Classics in marketing.* Santa Monica, CA: Goodyear: 443-439.

Tichenor, P.J.; Donohue, G. A.; Olien, C.N. 1970. Mass media flow and differential growth in knowledge. *Public Opinion Quarterly. 34*:159-170.

Turk, S.V. 1986. Information subsidies and media content. *Journalism Monographs. 100*:1-29.

Van Leuven, J.K.; Slater, M.D. 1991. Publics, organizations, and the media: How changing relationships shape the public opinion process. In: Grunig, J.; Grunig, L. (eds). *Public Relations Review Annual (Vol. 3).* Hillsdale, NJ: Erlbaum.

Vidmar, N.; Rokeach, M. 1974. Archie Bunker's bigotry: a study in selective perception and exposure. *Journal of Communication. 24* (1): 36-47.

Westley, B. 1971. Communication and social change. *American Behavioral Scientist. 14*: 719-742.

White, D. M. 1950. The "Gate-keeper": A case study in the selection of news. *Journalism Quarterly. 27*: 383-390.

Winkleman, M. 1987. Their aim is true. *Public Relations Journal. 43* (August): 18-19, 22-23, 39.

Wright, C. R. 1960. Functional analysis and mass communication. *Public Opinion Quarterly. 24*: 605-620.

Zucker, H. G. 1978. The variable nature of news media influence. In: Ruben, B. D. (ed.), *Communication yearbook 2.* New Brunswick, NJ: Transaction: 225-240.

7

Use of Persuasion to Reduce Resource Impacts and Visitor Conflicts

Joseph W. Roggenbuck

INTRODUCTION

This chapter reviews the use of persuasive communication as a management tool to reduce resource impacts and visitor conflicts in recreation settings. Specifically, the chapter provides: (1) a review of the nature, amount, causes and trends of impacts and conflicts in recreation settings; (2) a classification of impact behaviors and identification of those behaviors that seem amenable to reduction through persuasion; (3) a classification of conceptual routes to persuasion; (4) an evaluation of the appropriateness and feasibility of persuasive communication in recreation settings, and (5) a review of empirical studies on the effectiveness of persuasive communication in reducing impacts and conflicts in park settings. The influence of key elements in the communication process such as message source, content, channel, timing and audience characteristics on the success of persuasion is also examined.

RECREATION IMPACTS AND CONFLICTS

Impacts on the Natural Environment

Recreational use inevitably causes changes in the natural resource base, including changes in vegetation, soil, wildlife and water quality. Whether the impact is unacceptable depends upon the legally mandated purposes of the area, managerial goals, and visitor perceptions and preferences. Most recreation managers and visitors are concerned about resource impacts, particularly at parks at or near the primitive or natural end of the outdoor recreation opportunity spectrum. These concerns result from possible losses in the natural condition; from recreation areas becoming less attractive, desirable or functional; from increases in maintenance costs; and from increases in on-site activity causing off-site impacts (Cole 1986).

Most studies on resource impacts have focused on campsites, where human trampling or depreciative behavior has negatively affected both vegetation and soils (e.g., see Hammitt and Cole 1987, Cole and Marion 1986). Campsite use often reduces the abundance, reproductive capacity, height and vigor of vegetation, changes species composition, and destroys tree seedlings (Cole 1986, Frissell and Duncan 1965). The area of barren ground (i.e., devoid of vegetation) at the campsite's core gradually expands with continued use (Cole and Marion 1986). Tree trunks become scarred by recreational carving or vehicular contact, and tree limbs are sometimes removed for firewood.

Human movement around campsites scuffs and abrades the protective organic layer and leaf litter on the ground surface, exposing mineral soil. The mineral soil then becomes compacted, reducing water and air infiltration, increasing both puddling and runoff, causing erosion and exposing tree roots (Hammitt and Cole 1987). Erosion is also a problem on trails and in off-road vehicle areas (Webb and Wilshire 1983).

The wildlife literature contains increasingly common references to the impact of human disturbances on wildlife populations including mountain lions (Van Dyke et al. 1986), deer (Freddy et al. 1986, Nixon et al. 1988), mountain sheep (MacArthur et al. 1982), bears (McLellan and Shackleton 1989), raptors (Fraser et al. 1985, Knight and Skagen 1986), waterfowl (Bartelt 1987, Belanger and Bedard 1989, Morton et al. 1989), seabirds (Anderson 1988, Anderson and Keith 1980, Hand 1980) and other avifauna (Erwin 1989, Kaiser and Fritzell 1984). Wildlife responses to recreationists vary. Sometimes a population benefits, as when deer use snowmobile tracks to avoid deep snow in searching for food. At other times recreationists have a devastating effect. For example, the removal of shrubs and dead snags for firewood likely reduces the number and diversity of avian species. The invasion of recreationists into critical wildlife habitat such as birthing grounds or desert watering holes can displace animals, causing stress and even death. Recreationist littering may attract raccoons and bears, causing nutrition and habituation problems for the animals, as well as conflicts and even injury to park visitors (Hammitt and Cole 1987). Finally, wildlife species sometimes seem to ignore recreationists, but may actually have negative reactions not easily observed by researchers. For example, MacArthur et al. (1982) found that mountain sheep had elevated heart rates when disturbed by aircraft, despite showing no outward evidence of response.

Although few studies have carefully evaluated the specific causes of negative wildlife responses to recreationists, the adaptive characteristics of wildlife, the recreationists' behavior and the context of the disturbance all seem to be important. Individual wildlife species react differently to human intrusion. For example, approaching humans elicited alarm calls from golden plovers at approximately 187 meters, but dunlins failed to respond at distances greater than 20 meters (Yalden and Yalden 1989). Colonial seabirds reacted to approaching humans at distances three times that of distances for colonial waders (Erwin 1989).

Individuals and specific populations within a species may also react differently to human disturbances. For example, Stalmaster and Newman (1978) found that older bald eagles tended to be more sensitive to human activity. Cooke (1980) noted that passerines in rural areas flushed sooner in response to an approaching human than did their counterparts in suburban areas. Belanger and Bedard (1989) observed that the flight response of a goose flock to disturbance was largely determined by the individual behavior of the flock's most nervous members.

The frequency, magnitude, duration, type and timing of recreationists' behaviors all seem to be important in understanding wildlife responses. Freddy et al. (1986) found that mule deer reacted more strongly to humans on foot than on snowmobiles. Hammitt and Cole (1987) speculated that the frequency and timing of recreationists' instrusion into the habitats of sensitive animals such as bighorn sheep may be more obtrusive than the size of the recreationists' group or duration of the visit.

Contextual influences upon the degree of disturbance are numerous. Wildlife react differently to humans during the times of nesting, birthing and raising young. Belanger and Bedard (1989) found that snow geese staging in the spring resumed feeding much sooner after a disturbance than did geese staging in the fall. Fraser et al. (1985)

reported that bald eagle flush distances were partially explained by the time of day and season of the year. Wildlife behavior at the time of disturbance can also affect response. For example, bald eagles on the ground almost always flew when approached and generally flew a much greater distance from humans than did eagles in trees (Knight and Knight 1984). Finally, flight responses of wintering bald eagles to approaching humans varied in different habitats (Stalmaster and Newman 1978).

Most studies on the potential recreational impacts on water quality have found little cause for concern. For example, few water quality impacts from vacation home development (Ponce and Gary 1979), swimming (Nelson and Hansen 1984), campground use (Auckerman and Springer 1976) or dispersed recreational uses (Werner et al. 1985) have been discovered. However, some recreation-caused bacterial contamination has been found near campsites in the Boundary Waters Canoe Area (King and Mace 1974). Taylor and Erman (1979) also reported physical, biological and chemical changes in mountain lakes in Kings Canyon National Park, California.

Cole (1986) identified four primary factors that influence the amount of environmental impact caused by recreation: the *amount* of use, *type* of use, *season* of use, and the *environmental conditions* of the *site* being used.

A noteworthy finding about the relationship between the *amount* of use and the extent of impacts is that most vegetation and soil impacts occur even under conditions of light use (Cole 1982, Cole and Fichtler 1983, Frissell and Duncan 1965, Marion and Merriam 1985). Much ground-level vegetation, including tree seedlings, shrubs and herbaceous vegetation, is quickly lost, and species composition changes rapidly when a site is opened to recreational use. Then after a few years vegetation stabilizes at low cover levels (Cole and Marion 1986). The only impacts that appear to continue beyond the initiation period of recreational use are site expansion (i.e., the disturbed campsite area continues to increase in size with time and continued use) and loss of organic matter on the soil surface.

Type of use, although little studied, almost certainly has a substantial effect on the degree of impact. Recreational impacts increase in magnitude from human to recreational stock to motorized vehicular use of an area (Cole 1986). Large parties have a significantly larger impact than the same total number of people divided into smaller groups, particularly increasing the area of disturbed zones in campsites. Length of stay presumably influences the degree of site impact, but the exact relationship is unknown. Longer stays at a campsite may have greater impacts because of an increased tendency by individual campers to modify the site. Impacts may also vary according to the type of camping equipment; for example, Roggenbuck et al. (1982a) noted that tent campers damaged more trees than did campers in tent trailers or recreational vehicles.

The *time* of use, especially the season of the year, has a substantial effect on the extent of impacts. Snow cover protects vegetation, soil and water from impact, even that from snowmobiles, but winter is likely to be a high-impact season for wildlife (Cole 1986). Spring may be the most vulnerable time because park trails and campsites are water-saturated, plants are sprouting tender shoots, and animals are both recovering from winter and giving birth. Wet conditions in any season increase the likelihood of trail impact, because use causes greater compaction, erosion and increased trail width as recreationists try to avoid the mud.

Site durability is an important moderating variable in the relationship between recreational use and impacts. Indeed, trail deterioration problems are probably more closely related to soil characteristics, vegetation types, landforms and design features than to the amount of use (Cole 1983a). Impacts on camp and picnic sites vary with factors such as overstory canopy cover and vegetation type (Cole 1983b). Meadow variations in vegetation composition, elevation and wetness affect their ability to tolerate use.

A fifth variable, the actual behavior (including improper behavior) of recreationists, strongly influences impact on the natural environment. For problems such as litter and tree defacement, appropriate behavior could permit high levels of use without any impacts. Knowing when, where and how to build a campfire greatly reduces impacts on soil, vegetation and site aesthetics. Appropriate backcountry behavior can reduce wildlife harassment and also wildlife habituation to human presence. Finally, knowing how to select a durable site for camping, whether to select a previously used or unused site for a backcountry camp, and where to place the tent in the campsite can all reduce the level of environmental impact.

Few systematic studies have been conducted on the extent and trends of recreational impacts on the natural environment. Most existing studies address conditions in wilderness or natural areas, and are often managers' perceptions of impacts, not scientific measures of actual changes in the environment. For example, in a survey by Washburne and Cole (1983), 71 percent of all the managers of areas contained in the National Wilderness Preservation System indicated unacceptable campsite vegetation impacts in their wildernesses, 61 percent noted soil impacts on trails, 33 percent considered wildlife disturbance a problem, and 18 percent were concerned about water pollution. Roggenbuck (1988) surveyed wilderness managers in the southern region of the Forest Service in 1981 and again in 1985 to determine their perceptions of the impact problem. The most frequently mentioned problems in 1981 were people conflicts/crowding, vandalism/law enforcement, off-road vehicle intrusion, trail maintenance, lack of adequate budgets and manpower, and site impacts. By 1985, people conflicts/crowding, vandalism/law enforcement and trail maintenance were lower on the list of serious problems; but off-road vehicle intrusion, lack of adequate budgets and manpower, uncontrollable access points and site impacts remained at the top of the list.

Managers' perceptions do not always reflect reality, but trends in their judgments do seem to reflect changes in the type and amount of use in wilderness. In the late 1970s and 1980s wilderness use levelled off, and in many areas use levels have actually dropped (Roggenbuck and Watson 1989). Also, limited trend information suggests that there is currently a lower concentration of total use at high-use times and places. There also seem to be somewhat smaller proportions of horse use and hunters in wilderness, activities which tend to cause higher than normal impacts and conflicts (Lucas 1985). These changing use patterns might explain the drop in managerial concerns about people conflicts/crowding.

Still, concern about site impacts remains high. As mentioned, most site impacts such as tree injury, loss of tree seedlings and vegetative ground cover, soil compaction, and pronounced changes in soil pH, organic matter and nutrients occur under conditions of light use. Many past managers have inadvertanly increased the areal extent of impacts by dispersing use in order to increase opportunities for solitude or to reduce site disturbance. Finally, site recovery from impacts is very slow, even when sites have been closed and use reduced to virtually zero. In some fragile and harsh environments, such as alpine sites with short growing seasons and thin soils, site recovery is projected to take hundreds of years.

Visitor Conflicts and Impacts

A primary purpose of virtually all recreation areas is to provide a high quality leisure experience for people. When managers have attempted to identify threats to enjoyable visitor experiences, they have traditionally focused on three types of problems: visitor perceptions of crowding, feelings of incompatibility and animosity among user groups, and visitor perceptions of unacceptable environmental conditions. In each of these areas of concern, the perceptions of the recreationists are paramount, and recreationists frequently do not perceive and evaluate reality in the way that managers do (Clark et al. 1971).

Crowding

Crowding and its counterpart, social carrying capacity, are probably the most studied issues in the outdoor recreation literature. For example, Manning (1986) recently summarized 14 major studies that assessed density-perceived crowding-satisfaction relationships. Vaske et al. (1986) described ten studies that used social norm theory to understand perceptions of crowding in recreation settings. Most often this research has been conducted among wilderness or whitewater river users, and often a majority or significant minority of recreationists felt they saw too many people during their visits. The density of use in an area is often (but not always) related to the number of encounters between visitor groups. Density of use is often not related to perceptions of crowding, but the number of encounters usually has a low but significant positive relationship with perceived crowding. Finally, density of use, number of encounters and perceived crowding are almost never related to overall trip satisfaction.

Crowding is a normative concept based on a personal judgment of what is appropriate in a particular setting; it is a function of more than just the number of other users encountered. Instead, motivations for participation, preferences and expectations held by visitors, visitor attitudes, experience levels of visitors, type of areas and location of encounters all influence perceptions of crowding (Manning 1986, Stankey and Manning 1986). For example, Schreyer and Roggenbuck (1978) found that river floaters who scored high on stress release/ solitude or self-awareness measures reacted much more negatively to encounters with other groups on the river than did individuals with low scores on these motives. In the same study, individuals with attitudes highly congruent with values expressed in the 1964 Wilderness Act registered a higher level of perceived crowding at each level of encounter than did those who were less supportive of wilderness values.

Several studies have shown that weak relationships between actual encounters and perceived crowding can be increased by adding expectations and preferences for encounters to the predictive model. For example, Womble and Studebaker (1981) studied campers at Katmai National Monument, and the density of use explained only nine percent of the variation in perceived crowding; however, expectations and preferences for density explained 20 and 37 percent, respectively, of the variations in perceived crowding. Shelby et al. (1983) and Vaske et al. (1982) found that by adding expectations and preferences for contacts to actual encounters across several studies, the amount of explained variance in perceived crowding increased from five to 19 percent. Expectations about contacts with other groups tended to have a more consistent effect on perceptions of crowding than did preferences for such contacts.

Experience level has been related to crowding in some studies (e.g., Vaske et al. 1980, Ditton et al. 1983), but not in others (West 1981, Stankey 1980, Absher and Lee 1981). There is some evidence to suggest that first-time users have little or no expectations of the activity, but they then begin to evaluate future engagements against past experience (Schreyer et al. 1976). Vaske et al. (1980) found this to be the case among visitors to Apostle Islands National Lakeshore in Lake Superior. Boaters who first experienced the islands years ago when use levels were low felt much more crowded at current use levels than did users who only recently began to visit the area. Heberlein and Dunwiddie (1979), using a behavioral measure of crowding, observed that more experienced campers tended to select campsites in the Bridger Wilderness farther from other campers.

The type of area and the location of an encounter within an area affect perceptions of crowding. The type of area probably influences expectations, and these expectations in turn shape perceptions of crowding. For example, McConnell (1977) found different relationships between use density and visitor evaluations of the area as he moved from a natural beach to a highly developed "singles" beach. Manning and Ciali (1981) reported different desired use densities as they moved from primitive to urban river settings. One of the most consistent findings across studies of wilderness and backcountry areas is the tendency for visitors to rate contacts with other parties at the campsite (e.g., camping within sight or sound of another party) much more negatively than if the encounter occurs on the trails (Stankey 1973, 1980; Lucas 1980, Roggenbuck et al. 1982b). In addition, Stankey (1973) reports that wilderness users are much more sensitive to encounters with other groups in the interior of the area compared to contacts near the wilderness boundary.

Conflict

Crowding in recreation settings represents a type of conflict, but conflict also encompasses a larger array of conditions and situations that depreciate high quality recreational experiences. Conflict occurs when the behavior of an individual or group is incompatible with the social, psychological or physical goals of another person or group (Jacob and Schreyer 1980, Gramann and Burdge 1981). Given this conceptualization, two elements are critical to an understanding of recreation conflict. The first element is the assumption that recreation behavior is goal-oriented, i.e., people seek to obtain certain outcomes when they engage in recreational activities. Considerable conceptual and empirical evidence supports this assumption (Driver and Knopf 1976, Driver and Tocher 1970, Driver et al. 1987, Hawes 1978, Pierce 1980, Tinsley and Kass 1978, Tinsley et al. 1977).

Second, while goal interference may be physical, as when the presence of four people on a tennis court prevents a fifth person from participating, the more common conflict is psychological. Psychological conflict exists when values about appropriate definitions and uses of recreational settings clash. Differences in values are usually attributed to another person when that individual's behavior is unlike our own, as when radios are played in a wilderness campsite or when a tourist climbs on the walls of Anasazi ruins. Such behaviors violate norms of appropriate behavior, causing feelings of anger and stress and sometimes resulting in confrontation. These clashes of values are often asymmetrical; for example, canoeists may be bothered by motorboats in the Boundary Waters Canoe Area Wilderness, but motorboaters often enjoy the sense of wilderness engendered by canoeists (Lucas 1964). Sometimes feelings of conflict are reinforced by membership in social groups (Stankey and Schreyer 1987). For example, a recreationist of his own volition may not oppose hunting in wilderness areas, but he might feel pressure to do so from his friends who are members of an animal rights organization.

Perceived differences in type and size of groups, method of travel, activities, and behavior are all specific causes of conflict. Stankey

(1973) found that seeing one large party of hikers during a day in wilderness caused more negative evaluations than seeing several small parties. Stankey and Schreyer (1987) have suggested that experienced and inexperienced participants, sensitive and tolerant users, and solitude seekers versus thrill seekers are examples of recreational user groups that conflict with each other.

Differences in modes of travel have often influenced perceptions of conflict. In one of the earliest studies of recreation behavior in wildland settings, Lucas (1964) found that canoeists were quite tolerant of seeing other paddling canoeists in the Boundary Waters Canoe Area, somewhat less tolerant of encountering motor canoeists, and very intolerant of motorboats. Stankey (1973, 1980) found less tolerance among hikers for meeting horseback riders in the backcountry than for meeting other hiking parties. These conflicts are likely attributable partly to perceptions of "unlikeness" among the groups involved, but probably have more to do with actual physical interference by the offending party. Hikers must leave the trail to permit horses to pass, and must watch their step to avoid manure on the trails. Canoeists must alter their paddling to avoid the noise and wakes of motorboats. In contrast, motorboaters have less negative feelings about seeing canoeists, who pose no physical threat.

The type of activity engaged in can also be a source of conflict. Driver and Bassett (1975) reported conflicts between fisherman and canoeists, Knopp and Tyger (1973) found conflicts between snowmobiles and cross-country skiers, and Noe et al. (1981) reported conflicts between pedestrian and off-road-vehicle beach users. Vaske et al. (1986) found that canoeists on Wisconsin's Brule River tolerated more contacts with fishermen than with other canoeists, but accepted far more canoeists than tubers. As with the mode of travel, actual disruption of the recreational activity, either by noise or by physical interference, seems to explain the degree of conflict more than perceptions of differences.

A final and powerful predictor of conflict is behavior (Manning 1986). In the Driver and Bassett (1975) study, streamside residents and fishermen reacted negatively to seeing canoeists, but the primary reason given for the conflict was the yelling and shouting by the canoeists. West (1982) found that among national forest hikers who were bothered by other users, more than half were upset with the behavior of the recreationists, less than a third by too many others on the site, and only a few percent by different types of users. Titre and Mills (1982) found that the number of disruptive encounters with others was the best predictor of crowding perceptions among floaters on the Guadalupe River in Texas, exceeding the explanatory power of both the density of use and the total number of contacts.

Perceptions of Environmental Degradation

Recreation managers and researchers are concerned about the loss of experience quality attributable to recreationists' perceptions of degraded or unacceptable resource conditions in park settings. While studies are relatively few, park visitors usually respond in one of three ways to known environmental deterioration: (1) they fail to notice it, (2) they notice it, but it doesn't bother them, and (3) they notice the deterioration and it does cause negative reactions.

By far the most common visitor response to environmental deterioration in recreation settings is a failure to even notice the deterioration (Cole and Benedict 1983, Lucas 1979, Manning 1986). For example, Merriam and Smith (1974) found no correlation between visitor ratings of campsite physical condition in the Boundary Waters Canoe Area and expert ratings of the severity of environmental impacts at the sites. Helgath (1975) found hikers to be well satisfied with trail conditions in the Selway-Bitterroot Wilderness, even though many trails there were severely eroded. Hansen (1975) reported that only one percent of the canoeists on Michigan's Pine River were concerned about the prominent streambank erosion, and four percent listed viewing and enjoying the steep, eroded banks as a high point of the trip.

Knudson and Curry (1981) studied visitor perceptions of environmental impacts at three Indiana state park campgrounds. Most respondents rated ground cover conditions as satisfactory to excellent, even in areas where over three-fourths of the campsite was bare or heavily disturbed. Also, more than two-thirds of the respondents failed to report damaged trees or shrubs in the campgrounds, even though damage was extensive (Manning 1986). Finally, Hammitt and McDonald (1983) related users' experience levels to perceptions of five environmental impacts on southeastern rivers. Hammitt and McDonald found a small positive correlation, but a majority of even the most experienced floaters failed to notice or report any of the five impacts studied.

A few studies have demonstrated that park visitors sometimes notice environmental impacts, but that these impacts do not cause a loss in enjoyable experiences (Graefe et al. 1984, Lucas 1979). In the Knudson and Curry (1981) study noted above, even those few visitors who rated campsite ground cover vegetation as poor said that this situation did not adversely affect their experience. Apparently, some environmental attributes are relatively unimportant to the overall recreational experience.

Finally, several studies have noted that certain kinds of environmental impacts, especially those that are evidence of thoughtless or careless acts by humans, do cause negative reactions by park visitors. Of all impacts of this type, litter is the primary culprit. For canoeists on the Pine River study by Solomon and Hanson (1972), litter was by far the most objectionable environmental condition. Litter was the only impact mentioned by over 50 percent of visitors to roaded forest lands in the Pacific Northwest (Downing and Clark 1979). Roggenbuck et al. (1982b) found that about half of all Linville Gorge and Shining Rock wilderness users in North Carolina considered litter to be a moderate or big problem, and about a third were concerned about destruction of vegetation.

When recreationists do notice litter and other evidence of humans, they react more negatively to these impacts than to actual contacts with others (Lee 1975, Lucas 1980, Stankey 1973). Such impacts tend to increase the perception that the area is overused (Ditton et al. 1983), and is often a better predictor of perceived crowding than measures of use. For example, Vaske et al. (1982) found few visitors to the Dolly Sods Wilderness of West Virginia who found environmental conditions worse than expected, but among those who did, perception of environmental deterioration was a better predictor of perceived crowding than reported, preferred or expected contacts.

Trends
Because there have been virtually no studies of changes in perceptions of crowding, conflict and reactions to resource degradation in park settings across time, we can say little about trends of change. Some larger societal and recreational use and user trends do, however, permit educated guesses. The United States' population as a whole is getting older and better educated, and the growth rate is slowing. Social concern about environmental pollutants and degradation is broader. We also know that the rapid growth rates in recreation participation in the 1950s, 1960s and early 1970s have levelled off considerably. In most recreation settings and activities, we now find small annual increases in participation. In a few areas, however, such as wilderness use, participation has levelled off or even declined (Roggenbuck and Watson

1989). We expect that the population of recreationists is getting older, and we are sure that the recreation population is getting smarter. Indeed, high education levels have always been a characteristic of most outdoor recreation participants.

These general trends suggest conflicting conclusions about future crowding, recreationist conflicts, and perceptions of impact. On the positive side, slowing population growth rates and decreasing recreation participation rates might mean an easing of congestion in recreation settings. Indeed, this is almost certainly occurring in many wilderness areas. Also, Lucas (1985) has noted a shift toward lower-impact activities, smaller groups, greater visitor knowledge about minimizing impact, and a reduction in littering in some wilderness areas. Greater knowledge might also reduce perceptions of crowding and conflict. With better information the park visitor will have more realistic expectations, more knowledge of existing park conditions, more awareness of alternative recreation settings, and more knowledge and skill for avoiding or reducing conflicts.

On the negative side, we could expect perceptions of conflict and crowding to grow, because use in most settings and activities is increasing. We can expect a larger proportion of our visitors to be older and, at least for a time, to remember what use density was in the "good old days." This standard for comparison from the 1940s and 1950s will tend to produce harsh judgments of today's use conditions. We can also expect continued development of new technologies, often motorized, to permit easier and more frequent access to parklands, and these inventions are likely to conflict with traditional park uses. Finally, as the recreation population becomes more educated and more committed to environmental conservation, its demands for resource protection and managerial performance will increase. As more visitors begin to notice environmental degradation in parks, we can expect more conflict and outcries from and among recreation clientele groups.

Vandalism and Depreciative Behaviors

Vandalism (including destruction and defacement of public and private property) and depreciative behavior (littering, theft, poaching and violations of minimum impact hiking and camping ethics) are currently great concerns for both park managers and users (Christensen 1986). Park practitioners rate the need to "develop a package of methods to identify patterns of vandalism and a series of effective management techniques (and/or facility designs) to combat this behavior" as one of the top ten issues requiring research (Szwak 1984, U.S. Department of the Interior 1981). Recreation managers in the southern states recently rated vandalism, littering and other depreciative behaviors as their highest priority problem (Cordell 1982).

These deviant behaviors reduce visitor enjoyment, cause the loss of aesthetic values, destroy natural environments, damage public and private property, and substantially increase park maintenance costs. We know little about the people who vandalize or commit depreciative acts, or why they do so. Conflict control theory suggests that what is labelled as deviant or depreciative behavior depends in large measure upon the context of official values and policies (Christensen 1986). Thus, the park manager defines deviance and promulgates rules and regulations to guide behavior. If recreationists support these definitions, then conformity is likely. If, however, the law or official actions are seen as inappropriate or enforcement is ineffective, then violations can be expected. The subject of vandalism and depreciative behavior is examined in detail in the following chapter.

PERSUASION'S POTENTIAL TO REDUCE RESOURCE AND VISITOR IMPACTS

We have seen how many kinds of behavior cause many types of resource and visitor impacts within recreation settings, and that people have a variety of motives for their impacting behavior. The following section addresses the potential of persuasive communication to reduce or solve problems of impacts and conflicts. Because of the lack of theory-based, empirical research on persuasion in recreation settings, much of what follows must be considered a "best guess" and as testable conjecture.

The effectiveness of persuasion is likely to depend largely on the type of impact, the behavior involved and motives for the behavior. Researchers have suggested two classifications of undesirable park visitor behavior, one dealing with general resource impacts and visitor conflicts (Hendee et al.1978) and the other more specific to depreciative behavior and vandalism (Gramann and Vander Stoep 1987). Both provide guidance as to when persuasive communication might or might not be an effective management tool for reducing impacts. In addition, persuasive information can alter perceptions of crowding and resource impacts in park settings.

Resource Impacts and Visitor Conflicts

Hendee et al. (1990) have identified five types of undesirable visitor actions: illegal, careless, unskilled, uninformed and unavoidable. Table 1 provides examples of each of these problem behaviors and suggests the likely effectiveness of persuasion in resolving each type.

Illegal behaviors are willful violations of park laws and rules, and persuasion is likely to achieve only limited effectiveness. Law enforcement should be the primary management response, but providing information on the rationale for the rules and regulations may assist in lowering violations.

Careless actions involve behaviors such as littering, shouting or playing radios at night, which the recreationist knows is wrong or inconsiderate, but which he or she does without thinking. Persuasion is probably only moderately effective in reducing this sort of problem. Bringing the impacting behavior to the attention of the perpetrators is likely to improve their behavior. For persuasion to be highly effective, however, the reminder must be continual and unless the persuasive cue is frequently changed, it may become dull and screened out.

Persuasive communication seems to have a high potential for reducing impacts and conflicts from unskilled actions. Often the unskilled recreationist wants to do the right thing and may even be able to describe the desirable behavior, but lacks the skill to carry it out. Failure to properly hang a food cache in bear country or to build a low-impact campfire are examples of unskilled behavior. Persuasive programs emphasizing education, demonstration and audience participation would help develop appropriate skills.

Uninformed actions that degrade the environment or cause visitor conflict are common in unfamiliar park settings, and here persuasion has an extremely high potential for reducing problems. For example, some resource managers have developed educational programs to reduce impacts by dispersing camping use in the wilderness; other managers have attempted to concentrate use for the same effect (Washburne and Cole 1983). Wilderness visitors follow both suggestions in their efforts to be sensitive users, but sometimes inadvertently cause more impacts. Both managers and recreationists need to become better informed on whether concentrated or dispersed use is more appropriate.

Unavoidable impacts accompany any use of recreation settings. The mere presence of people is likely to cause changes in wildlife

Table 1
General typology of undesirable visitor behavior and the potential of persuasion for reducing each type.[3]

Type of behavior	Example	Persuasion's potential degree of effectiveness[4]
Illegal	Theft of Indian artifacts	+
	Invasion of wilderness by motorized off-road vehicles	
Careless actions	Littering	++
	Nuisance activity (e.g., shouting)	
Unskilled actions	Selecting improper camping spot	+++
	Building improper campfire	
Uninformed actions	Selecting a lightly used campsite in the wilderness	++++
	Using dead snags for firewood	
	Camping in sight or sound of another party	
Unavoidable actions	Human body waste, loss of ground cover vegetation in the campsite	+

[3] Adapted from Hendee, et al. (1990)
[4] Degree of effectiveness

+	low
++	moderate
+++	high
++++	very high

behavior. People cannot avoid urinating or defecating while in a park, and footsteps do trample ground cover vegetation. For these types of impacts, the potential for benefit of persuasive communication is low. Still, through persuasive messages, recreationists can learn to avoid sensitive wildlife zones or times, dispose of human wastes in a manner causing least impact, select sites with durable vegetation and soil types, wear soft-soled shoes, and select campsites that are already moderately impacted in order to minimize the areal extent of the impact in the park.

Depreciative Behavior

Gramann and Vander Stoep's (1987) typology of normative violations in park settings provides another conceptual approach for predicting the success of persuasive communication in reducing recreational impacts. Their classification is based upon apparent motives for depreciative acts, and includes unintentional, releasor-cue, uninformed, responsibility-denial, status-conforming and willful violations. Table 2 provides examples of each of these deviant behavior types, and suggests the relative effectiveness of persuasion at reducing each type.

Unintentional and uninformed behaviors result from ignorance of the rules, and of the negative consequences of the action in question. Uninformed behaviors are often well-meant but improper. The success of persuasive messages for reducing these types of problem behaviors should be high to very high. Simply informing the recreationist about the rules is likely to induce compliance, unless the individual disagrees with the need for the regulation or the approach taken for its enforcement. Even if recreationists initially oppose the rules, persuasive messages explaining the reason for specific rules and communicating the environmental and social impacts of problem behaviors may alter opinions and gain the necessary compliance.

Responsibility-denial violations occur when people generally believe an action is wrong, but don't assume moral responsibility for the deviant act in a specific circumstance. This may be a frequent reason for undesirable behavior in parks, where common social mores seem to be less operative. Non-payment of the self-administered camping fees in wildland recreation settings is an example. People who fail to pay fees probably would not consider shoplifting or entering a drive-in theater without paying, but somehow don't feel responsible for the public campground fee. Persuasive messages might have a moderate success rate in this case, because the violators are not malicious. By pointing out the costs of campground construction and maintenance, the loss of revenues that could be used for park protection and programming, and the burden of irresponsible actions upon other park users, park managers might be able to substantially increase the level of cooperation.

Releasor-cue violations result from seeing others commit a violation or seeing traces of the violation (e.g., graffiti) in the park setting,

Table 2
Typology of normative violations in park settings and the potential of
persuasion for reducing each type of violation

Type of behavior	Example	Persuasion's potential degree of effectiveness[5]
Unintentional	Violation of quiet hours Entering a wildlife sensitive zone Camping too close to a trail	+++

Releasor-cue	Littering or litter encourages more
	  littering
	Vandalism invites more vandalism
	Noisy group encourages additional noise
	Low maintenance levels encourage
	  damage to public and private property
		+

Uninformed	Hanging lanterns on trees Feeding wildlife Washing dishes and self in stream Building "rock circle" fireplace	++++
Responsibility-denial	Littering Failing to pick up others' litter Failing to pay self-registration camping fee Inadequate disposal of human body wastes	++
Status-conforming	Smoking marijuana Drinking alcohol Exceeding game bag limits Carving initials in trees Graffiti	0
Willful violations	Breaking glass Driving off-road vehicles in wilderness Poaching wildlife	+

[5]Degree of effectivenes

0	none
+	low
++	moderate
+++	high
++++	very high

especially if the violation goes unpunished. Such observations reduce the constraining power of rules and regulations. Recreationists, especially novice recreationists, tend to conclude that the park manager is not serious about the rules. Persuasion can address this type of violation only indirectly by reducing the frequency of occurrence of the releasor-cue.

Willful violations, such as illegal acts in the Hendee et al. (1978) typology, are probably largely impervious to persuasive intervention. However, park managers might have some success through positive or negative persuasive incentives or through fuller explanation of the reasons for park regulations, especially those reasons benefiting the recreationist.

Persuasion by park managers is not likely to reduce status-conforming violations, because individuals committing these depreciative acts do so to affirm membership in a social network. As long as the violator values status in the "deviant" group, park communication, education, and incentive programs will probably not be effective.

Crowding

As described earlier, perceptions of crowding can be predicted by the number of encounters, user motivations and preferences, expectations, attitudes, past experiences, the type of area and the location of an encounter. Table 3 provides some "educated guesses" on whether and to what extent persuasive communication might influence these predictor variables and thus shape crowding perceptions. By informing potential and on-site recreationists about the amount, location and timing of park use, recreation managers should have a high to very high success rate at influencing the number, place and time of encounters among user groups. This prediction is based on the assumption that recreationists are goal-oriented, and that for many recreational experiences, the number of contacts with others is significant. This is especially true for experiences at the primitive or wilderness end of the outdoor recreation spectrum.

We have shown earlier that expectations for encounters have a powerful, consistent and negative correlation with perceived crowding. If recreationists' expectations for the number of encounters with others in a setting increase, then perceived crowding tends to decrease. This is an excellent opportunity for park managers to use persuasive communication to achieve a positive effect. If managers are unable or unwilling

Table 3
The potential of persuasion to shape the predictor variables
of crowding perceptions

Predictors of crowding	Persuasion's potential level of effectiveness[6]
Number of encounters	++++
Motivations for participation	+
Preferences for encounters	+
Expectations for encounters	+++
Attitudes about park	?
Past experience	0
Type of area	0
Location of encounter	+++

[6] Degree of effectiveness
0	none
+	low
++	moderate
+++	high
++++	very high
?	may increase or decrease sensitivity to crowding

to reduce the number of encounters in order to reduce crowding perceptions, then they can use information to develop more realistic expectations.

Motivations for the recreational experience, such as skill development, solitude, and introspection, often influence crowding perceptions, as do preferences for the number, type and location of encounters. Persuasive messages or incentives might have some effect on these variables, but the effect is likely to be low. Driver and Tocher (1970) have classified recreation motives on an "escape from" to "attraction to" spectrum. To the extent that a recreational engagement represents an "escape from" a stressful home or work environment, the recreation manager probably has little influence over motives for the park visit. On the other hand, if the recreationist is "attracted to" the park, then the manager, through persuasive messages, has the potential to shape a desire for "encounter-independent" versus "encounter-dependent" experiences.

Preferences are external expressions of internal need states, and as such are likely to be little influenced by persuasion. Even if the persuasive communicator were able to influence the recreationist's preferences for the number and type of encounters, there are ethical questions about the appropriateness of such interventions. Freedom of choice and expression is a defining characteristic of all leisure, but is an especially important descriptor of recreational engagements at the primitive end of the outdoor recreation opportunity spectrum.

Attitudes about appropriate purposes and uses of recreation areas do influence crowding perceptions at parks. If a recreationist values an area for its wilderness qualities, then encountering a given level of use will engender more feelings of crowding than if a park is defined as an ideal place for meeting and making new friends. Persuasive communication can shift attitudes, and thus has the potential for altering crowding perceptions. We have, however, placed a question mark in Table 3 on the direction and strength of the linkages among persuasion, attitude change and crowding perceptions. We question these linkages because the legal, historical and institutional values and purposes of individual parks determine appropriate attitudes. Park purposes are accepted as givens, and they are not meant to be influenced by persuasive communication. Persuasion can help bring public attitudes in line with park values, but such persuasion might increase or lower perceptions of crowding as well.

Finally, persuasion has no potential influence over the amount of past experience a recreationist has, or on the type or designation of a recreation area. Persuasive communication can influence what type of area people visit, and could help people find an area that meets their recreational needs. However, it would be unethical and illegal to attempt to reduce complaints of crowding by persuading people that an existing wilderness area was really an unclassified piece of public domain land.

Perceptions of Resource Impacts

Park visitors notice resource impacts less frequently than do resource scientists and managers. When recreationists do notice impacts, they tend to notice losses of beauty or cleanliness of the natural environment resulting from behaviors such as littering, rather than the more serious disruptions of natural processes such as erosion or wildlife disturbance. Litter and other aesthetic impacts are strong predictors of crowding perceptions.

Persuasive communication might have a powerful effect on recreational experiences through its potential to educate visitors to "perceive" resource impacts. If persuasion is used to raise park visitors' environmental sensitivity, the short-term effect might be to lower the quality of leisure experiences, resulting in increased complaints about the extent of resource degradation. The long-term effect might be greater political and financial support for park resource protection, greater sensitivity and commitment to resource quality by managers, and a higher-quality resource setting for leisure engagements.

CONCEPTUAL ROUTES TO PERSUASION

Knowingly or unknowingly, recreation managers use one of three distinct conceptual routes to persuasion and learning: applied behavior analysis; the central route to persuasion; and the peripheral route to persuasion.

Each of these approaches has a different foundation in learning psychology, each accomplishes persuasion in a different manner, and each is appropriate or inappropriate for certain recreation settings, audiences and problems.

Applied Behavior Analysis

The applied behavior analysis approach to persuasion focuses on overt behavior rather than beliefs, attitudes, thoughts or values. It seeks to increase the frequency of desired behavior or decrease the frequency of inappropriate behavior, and attempts to accomplish these behavioral changes through behavior prompts, manipulation of the environment, rewarding appropriate behavior or punishing inappropriate behavior (Geller 1987). Rewards and punishments are administered contingent upon overt behavior.

In contrast to common perceptions that behavior change interventions are only administered consequent to the target behavior, the interventions of applied behavioral analysis are frequently applied before the target behaviors are emitted. In a recent taxonomy of behavior change techniques for environmental protection, Geller, Needleman and Randall (1990) noted that 18 of 24 different approaches to change behavior were antecedent procedures. These antecedent activators are all attempts to persuade individuals or groups to give desired responses, and include oral and written messages, demonstrations and modeling, pledges, competitions, incentives and disincentives.

In theory this route to persuasion is simple, straightforward and effective. If a recreation manager has a visitor behavior problem, this approach directly addresses the problem. It doesn't attempt to teach new behavior indirectly through conveying new ideas, beliefs, attitudes and values. As such, the applied behavior analysis approach is more likely to be a quick fix on a specific problem. Its success does not depend on variables that typically intervene in the persuasion process, such as the source of a message, the medium of message transfer, or even the message content.

Perhaps the most important deficiency of the applied behavior analysis approach is that it doesn't often deal with "whys" and therefore is less likely to teach a low-impact ethic effectively. Also, since this route to persuasion does not address attitudes and values, the recreation manager might not expect it to produce long-term behavior change. Generally, if the behavior change is to become permanent, the environmental prompt or manipulation, the reward, or the punishment must continue. However, there is some evidence that elicited behavior change, if continued long enough, does lead to attitude change in tune with the new behavior.

Recreation managers frequently use environmental manipulation to influence public behavior. Putting up or taking down signs at trailheads, changing the size of parking lots at trailheads, placing or not placing garbage cans at trailheads, emptying or not emptying the garbage cans, constructing craters at wilderness trailheads to block off-road vehicles, and routing trails away from high-use zones all change behavior. Such behavior changes could be interpreted to result from persuasion.

Rewarding or punishing behavior is less feasible for park managers, because it is difficult or inappropriate to observe behavior in park settings. However, these reinforcement techniques can be effective if the outcomes (e.g., a clean campsite) of good behavior are rewarded, or the consequences (a littered campsite) of bad behavior are punished. For persuasive learning to occur, park visitors must associate clean campsites—and the subsequent reward—with their appropriate behavior. Managers use punishment as a learning strategy when they levy fines on violators. Again, for fines to have a learning benefit, recipients must connect the fines with inappropriate behavior.

Outcomes such as a clean campsite can be more easily observed than the behavior itself. Thus, a wilderness ranger could note a clean campsite left behind by a horsepacker, and reward that behavior with a letter of commendation, membership in the "Friends of the Wilderness" association, or an increase in the size of the individual's permit allocation.

In summary, the behavior change strategies of applied behavior analysis are important tools of persuasion for the park manager. However, these strategies are much better suited to solving specific behavior problems than to teaching an attitude or ethic.

Central Route to Persuasion

The central route to persuasion is the path to attitude and behavior change that most park managers either knowingly or unknowingly attempt to follow. The defining characteristics of the central route are high attention by the recipient to the persuasive message content, careful thought or elaboration of the message content, and integration of the message content into existing belief systems. Such elaboration and integration result in new beliefs or changes in old beliefs, and this in turn results in behavior change (Manfredo and Bright 1991, Petty and Cacioppo 1986).

According to this approach, the recipient of the message carefully considers the reasons for recommended actions, eventually accepts the advocated action as making good sense, and acts accordingly. This information processing is the ideal kind of persuasive learning for the park visitor and the general public. The learned behavior can be expected to recur in the future because the beliefs and attitudes that support the behavior have been internalized. There is no need for continual promise of reward or punishment as in the applied behavioral analysis approach.

For learning through the information processing or central route of persuasion to occur, the recipient must have high motivation to pay attention to message content, be able to process the information, accept the message arguments, and have the skills to act upon these arguments. Many characteristics of the recipient (e.g., personal involvement with the park, prior experience, prior knowledge and the amount of personal responsibility for actions in the park), of the message (e.g., personal relevance of content, strength of argument, message complexity and message repetition), of the medium or channel of message transfer (e.g., the written word, audio or video presentations), and of the situation (e.g., timing of message transfer and distractions of the communication setting) influence the success of this kind of ideal learning.

Park managers must do everything possible to increase the amount of "teaching" time with recreationists. Managers must know their audience, tailor messages to meet recipients at their interest and knowledge level, develop interesting, understandable, relevant and well-supported messages, use media that permit self-pacing of message processing (usually the written word), and manage the situation so that distractions are few and messages reach recipients on time. Two critically important variables that park managers too often ignore are the strength of message content and the recipient's prior knowledge and experience.

Learning through the central route to persuasion occurs partly through evaluation of message arguments. If arguments are weak, the message will be rejected and pre-existing positions and behavior will be reinforced. Attempts by park managers to redistribute use from a highly used to a lightly used trail by providing information on the amount of use of the two trails have sometimes been unsuccessful. For example, Lucas (1981) found that, when selecting a trail, park visitors use more information than numbers of trail users. The recreationists also did not believe the trail use information provided, and perceived the arguments about use levels, based on trailhead registration data, as weak. Park managers must either develop stronger arguments or use methods of persuasion other than the central or information processing route.

The most consistent finding across all studies on the effectiveness of persuasive information programs, and one finding park managers should always bear in mind, is that a strong relationship exists between recreationists' amount of prior experience and knowledge, and their response to persuasive messages (Manfredo and Bright 1991). The first-time or low-knowledge visitor responds much more readily to persuasive information. Experienced users have established knowledge networks and patterns of behavior, and there is less "room" for incorporating new message content. This may explain why Boy Scout leaders often respond less effectively to wilderness education than do the scouts themselves. Wilderness information specialists must do more to gain the attention of experienced users (e.g., promise rewards for paying attention), and must develop stronger arguments for adopting innovations such as backpack stoves and other low-impact camping techniques in the field. If these actions are not feasible, then an approach to persuasive learning other than the central or information processing route must be used.

Peripheral Route to Persuasion

In contrast to the central route, the peripheral route to persuasion is characterized by a minimum or absence of attention by the recipient to the content of the message, by little thought about the message content, and by little integration of issue-relevant arguments into the recipient's belief and value system. The peripheral route to attitude and behavior change recognizes that when people cannot internally process all the informational stimuli bombarding them, they develop coping methods to respond to persuasive messages. One coping strategy is simply to ignore the message by blocking it out; another is to use simple decision rules, rules largely irrelevant to message content, to respond to the message. These decision rules use environmental and setting cues, including characteristics of the source, message (other than content) and communication channels to guide attitude and behavior change. By knowing something about these decision rules and appropriate message-irrelevant cues, communicators can guide and shape behavior change (Chaiken and Stangor 1987, Petty and Cacioppo 1986).

With the peripheral cue approach to learning, the source of the message becomes important. Message recipients decide what ideas to accept or action to take based on how expert, attractive or powerful the source is. Thus, it is not so much what is said, but who says it that counts. Other simple decision cues used by recipients include: "The consensus is right," "An idea is more likely right if more arguments can be listed in its support," "If I'll be liked, it's right," and "If I get rewarded, I'll do it."

Whether park managers should attempt to use the learning processes of the peripheral route to persuasion depends in part on objectives and the situation. If the learning environment is highly distracting, such as a very noisy and active visitor center, then the peripheral approach is almost a necessity. The peripheral approach can be expected to prompt behavior and reduce or solve specific problems. However, because this approach fails to consider issue-relevant reasons for behavior, it cannot produce a low-impact ethic or long-term behavior change unless the presence of the cue is continued.

APPROPRIATENESS AND FEASIBILITY
OF PERSUASIVE COMMUNICATION

Thus far we have described the nature, extent of, and trends in recreation resource impacts and visitor conflicts; typologies of impact behavior; and educated guesses on the probable success rates of persuasive communication in modifying each behavior type. This discussion suggests that persuasion is a needed and effective management tool in many recreation resource settings. Three questions remain before we can recommend widespread adoption of this management tool: "Is it appropriate?" "Is it feasible?" and "Is there empirical evidence that persuasion is effective?"

Appropriateness of Persuasive Communication

Whether persuasive communication is appropriate in a given recreation situation depends upon the park's legal mandates, its management objectives, and the preferences of clientele groups served. Leisure philosophers, recreation managers, and recreationists have provided strong support for most forms of persuasion, especially the use of information and education.

Leisure philosophers have frequently identified freedom of choice as a defining characteristic of leisure experiences, and recreation researchers and managers generally view persuasive communication as shaping behavior by helping individuals make more rewarding leisure decisions, but not as controlling behavior (Lucas 1982). With most forms of persuasion, the recipient is free to reject the behavioral request; he or she has the freedom to decide where to go, when to go and what to do in recreation settings. This freedom contrasts sharply with more direct and regulatory managerial interventions like assigned travel routes or restrictions on when and where to build a campfire.

Some of the persuasive strategies of applied behavior analysis, such as environmental manipulations and negative reinforcers (e.g., fines), do seem to violate the tenets of freedom of leisure. They may be inappropriate in all but the most serious cases of depreciative behavior in recreation settings, especially in wilderness environments (Lucas 1982). In addition, Burke et al. (1979) have warned that some behavior change strategies of applied behavior analysis might be subtle enough to become insidious. Burke et al. (1979) warn that manipulating people, i.e., influencing people without their being aware of the nature and extent of the influence, is objectionable in general and reprehensible in park settings. Any behavior change strategy should coincide with the goal of maximizing awareness and freedom of choice. Rewarding appropriate behavior (e.g., providing incentives to not litter or to pick up litter) is a behavioral intervention strategy that seems entirely appropriate, and has been successful in recreation settings (Clark et al. 1972a).

Recreation managers have widely adopted one form of persuasion, i.e., the provision of information or education, in a variety of settings, demonstrating that they consider this strategy appropriate. For example, wilderness managers in three different surveys indicated extensive use of persuasive techniques such as advertising patterns of use, educating users to care for the environment, and identifying recreational opportunities in surrounding areas (Fish and Bury 1981, Godin and Leonard 1979, and Washburne and Cole 1983). Forest Service policy statements (USDA 1975, 1976) call for emphasizing lighthanded management strategies such as communicating with the wilderness users. The former chief of the Forest Service (Peterson 1985) defined the wilderness management challenge as being 90 percent education and information and ten percent regulation.

More recently, some recreation researchers have cautioned against going overboard with persuasive information programs, at least in the case of wilderness areas. Lucas (1981) cautioned against compromising the joy of discovery and exploration by providing too much information. Hammitt and Cole (1987) expressed concern that camp visits by wilderness rangers might be viewed more negatively than rules and regulations about camping etiquette. Irwin (1985) expressed doubt that wilderness users consider educational contacts to be as lighthanded as managers think them to be, and called for more research on visitor feelings about the obtrusiveness of educational interventions in the field.

While more research is needed, completed studies indicate pervasive support by recreationists for more information. A large majority of wilderness users favor the availability of maps and information pamphlets and the presence of rangers in the backcountry, and support for these services appears to be growing (Echelberger and Moeller 1977, Hendee et al. 1968, Lime and Lucas 1977, Lucas 1980, 1981, 1985, Stankey 1973, Roggenbuck et al.1982b).

Berrier (1980) and Oliver et al. (1985) provided persuasive messages to recreationists at campsites in the wilderness and at a developed campground, in an effort to reduce resource impacts and visitor conflicts. Participants in the studies valued receiving the information and supported continuation of the programs.

Irwin (1985) examined whether the practice of ranger contacts at trailheads to provide low impact messages impinged on visitors' psychological freedom. He wondered whether recreationists felt a sense of "being watched" after the trailhead message, and whether users really felt free to make their own decisions about camping practices and travel route selection. His results, however, indicated that not only did users find these contacts appropriate, but the vast majority enjoyed the opportunity to talk with an agency representative and to obtain answers to last-minute questions (Roggenbuck and Ham 1986).

Finally, Roggenbuck and Bange (1983) found that more than 70 percent of boaters on the New River Gorge National River in West Virginia favored making available more information on the different kinds of river trips and experiences, providing information about the river environment to prospective river users prior to the trip, and developing maps showing river facilities, features and attractions.

Feasibility of Persuasive Communication

Before recreation managers can decide whether or not to implement a persuasive information program, they must consider its feasibility (Lucas 1981, 1982). Can the target audience be reached? Can the costs be covered? Are the necessary staff and support services available? Programs become feasible and effective when managers are able to identify clientele groups and their characteristics, place information where people can easily receive it, provide information early in the decision-making process, and present the information in an interesting and understandable way (Roggenbuck and Ham 1986). Because recreationists are typically diverse and are often scattered across large areas of relatively undeveloped landscape, it is difficult to develop persuasive messages specifically for a target audience and to get the message to the appropriate audience in a timely fashion. Thus, some informational campaigns have been unsuccessful because the message never reached the intended audience (Lucas 1981). Other programs failed because the information was too late to affect the target decisions (Schomaker 1975). Failures such as these led McAvoy and Dustin (1983) to express doubt that persuasion can be expected to protect wilderness values, and Burke et al. (1979) noted that the many behavior change strategies of applied behavior analysis are often too expensive or don't work for all people.

Two approaches to increase the likelihood of reaching diverse recreationists are identifying key places or times where most recreationists can be reached, and market segmentation to identify those recreationists most in need of persuasive messages. Recognizing that to be effective, informational interventions must reach recreationists early in their decision processes, managers have sometimes used mandatory permits to contact recreationists, sometimes even before the recreationists leave home (Lime and Lucas 1977). A more common contact point is the entrance station, road or trailhead to a recreation area. When the park has multiple entry points, as is often the case, it is common for one or a few of the entrances to receive the most use. Persuasive personnel or recorded or written messages can be placed at the few highest-use entry points to reach the greatest number of recreationists with the least commitment of staff and financial resources (Roggenbuck and Lucas 1987).

Market segmentation provides the recreation manager with both a description of those park visitors most in need of behavior change through persuasive messages, and also with recommendations on how these subgroups can best be reached. For example, Ross and Moeller (1974) found that adolescent, first-time, nonlocal tent campers had the lowest knowledge of campground rules. Matheny (1979) identified 13- to 17-year olds as the group most likely to engage in shortcutting of trails. Robertson (1982) found that the amount of knowledge of low impact behavior was the factor most significantly related to appropriate behavior in the wilderness, and Fazio (1979b) found that day hikers in the backcountry of Rocky Mountain National Park and hunters, day users, pilots and horse campers in the Selway-Bitterroot Wilderness had lower knowledge levels than cross-country hikers, technical climbers, outfitters and group leaders. Financial and staffing resources might be used to target persuasive messages at these low-knowledge groups.

Surveys of park managers indicate that many have adopted information and education programs despite limited budgets. Godin and Leonard (1979) found that wilderness managers considered information and education to be their most effective management strategy, especially in light of budget and manpower constraints. Martin and Taylor (1981) reported that wilderness and backcountry managers frequently used brochures, maps, signs and personnel at agency offices to communicate low impact messages to the recreating public. Less common was the use of articles in newspapers and periodicals; guidebooks; slide shows; backcountry, campground, and trailhead personnel; personnel at major attractions; visitor centers; and public meetings. Personnel-based techniques were judged as the most expensive, but no manager spent more than two percent of his overall budget on persuasive communication. Indeed, informational campaigns usually cost only a fraction of one percent of managers' budgets. Low costs were accomplished through the creative use of volunteers, demonstrating that programs for direct visitor contact are often feasible.

EFFECTIVENESS OF PERSUASIVE COMMUNICATION

Two general approaches have been used to assess the effectiveness of persuasive communication in reducing resource impacts and visitor conflicts in recreation settings. The first and more common approach is to seek the opinions of the recreation managers who implement the programs. Their judgments are typically based on informal observations, the number of complaints received from visitors, and an intuitive feel for how their parks are changing. The second approach is for researchers to conduct systematic evaluations of change in resource quality or visitor conflict level attributable to the persuasive interventions. Sometimes actual observations of resource impacts, behavior and behavior traces have been made, but self reports of behavior or behavioral intentions have been used more often. Cross-sectional survey designs have been used most often, but experimental or quasi-experimental research has also been performed. Longitudinal designs across extended periods of time are rare. In most cases, assessments have been conducted in primitive recreation areas.

Managers' Assessments

Managers have been generally optimistic about the success of their efforts to use lighthanded strategies such as persuasive communication to reduce impacts and conflicts. Most managers believe that problem behaviors on wildlands are unintentional and the result of ignorance (Bradley 1979, Clark et al. 1971, Godin and Leonard 1979, and Hart 1980). Hendee et al. (1990) state that unskilled actions by users constitute the most important kind of problem behaviors in dispersed recreation settings. These kinds of impact behaviors are particularly amenable to reduction through information and education programs (Godin and Leonard 1979).

The majority of wilderness managers believe that their most effective management tool is personal contact with the visitor, leading to increased dispersal of backcountry use and improved low-impact camping behaviors (Washburne and Cole 1983). Martin and Taylor (1981) found generally high manager support for persuasive communication as an effective management strategy, but specific informational techniques were rated differently. Personnel-based techniques such as personal contacts in the backcountry, or at the trailhead, visitor center, or a major attraction were all rated as highly effective. Personal contacts at campgrounds or the agency office, personnel at public meetings, and seminars and school programs were all rated as average in effectiveness, as were brochures, guidebooks, maps, signs, slide shows, television, and articles in newspapers and periodicals.

Bury and Fish (1980), and Fish and Bury (1981) found that while support for persuasive information was high among surveyed managers, opinions on program effectiveness varied by agency and with the nature and severity of the problem behavior. The Fish and Wildlife Service believed their visitor education programs were highly effective, while most Forest Service and Park Service managers rated their programs as moderately effective at best. These differences might be attributable to differences in program objectives or program intensities. For example, the Forest Service attempted to shift use by advertising underused areas and general patterns of use, and by identifying the range of recreational opportunities in surrounding areas. Neither of the other agencies had these objectives (Roggenbuck and Ham 1986). In all three agencies, managers who were attempting to prevent overuse were much more likely to use lighthanded strategies such as persuasive communication than were those responding to existing resource damage; the latter group selected primarily regulatory controls (Fish and Bury 1981).

Systematic Evaluations

Field assessments of the effectiveness of persuasive messages in reducing resource impacts and visitor conflicts have been conducted in a variety of resource settings and with varying degrees of sophistication. These assessments have tended to focus on knowledge and attitudes along with behavior, because it is often easier to assess knowledge than observe behavior in recreation settings. Recreation managers and researchers also widely share the belief that knowledge, attitudes and behavior are highly related, and managers are often interested in attitudes as a measure of visitor support for a particular low-impact behavior. While considerable research shows that knowledge or attitudes are not always related to behavior, some recreation research suggests strong correlations when minimum-impact behavior is the issue (see Brown et al. 1987, Robertson 1981).

Much theoretical and empirical research also suggests that many contextual factors affect the success of persuasive interventions. For example, source, receiver, message, channel and situational factors are all important influences on persuasion (see Ajzen, Chapter 1). Also, Roggenbuck and Watson (1986) noted that the purpose and timing of a persuasive message also affect success in wilderness settings. The following review of studies of persuasion in park settings is organized around each study's effectiveness in improving knowledge, attitudes and behavioral intentions, dispersing visitors to different recreation places, and reducing resouce impacts and conflicts. General findings and the effect of contextual variables will be noted.

Knowledge-Attitude-Behavior Intention Change Resulting from Persuasion
General Findings:

1. Persuasive interventions such as interpretive programs and educational workshops are often effective in increasing knowledge, favorable attitudes and positive behavioral intentions about rules, resource ecology and resource protection in park settings.

2. Personal persuasive interventions (e.g., messages delivered by a park ranger) are often no more effective than many non-personal services in increasing knowledge and favorable attitudes.

3. Findings regarding the relative effectiveness of various non-personal persuasive interventions are mixed, but often brochures, slide programs and cassette tapes are more effective than signs in improving knowledge, attitudes and behavioral attentions.

4. Use of multiple media to convey the persuasive message is generally more effective than a single media in improving knowledge, attitudes and behavioral attentions.

5. Persuasive messages are generally more effective in improving knowledge, attitudes and behavioral intentions of persons with low knowledge or little experience.

Fazio (1974, 1979b) completed one of the first tests of the effectiveness of various education media on increasing learning about and sensitivity to low impact camping practices and propensity to observe park rules. Working in Rocky Mountain National Park, Fazio provided informational messages in a brochure, a trailhead sign, a visitor-activated slide and sound exhibit, a half-hour color television program and a newspaper feature article. So few backpackers in the park saw the newspaper article and the television program that those treatments were dropped. The slide exhibit alone, the slide exhibit plus the brochure, and the slide exhibit plus the trailhead sign were the only treatments that resulted in significant knowledge increases. The trailhead sign and the brochure were not very effective by themselves. Regarding behavior, Fazio found that backpackers who had seen one of several interpretive displays or programs explaining the reasons for park regulations had a significantly higher propensity to observe the rules than those who had not been exposed to the interpretive contact.

Gallup (1981) attempted to increase campers' knowledge of rules and regulations and reduce violations through cartoon brochures that stated reasons for the rules in a non-threatening manner. Knowledge scores increased only slightly from the control group to the treatment group, but this increase was statistically significant. Rule violations remained just as numerous in the treatment group as in the control condition.

Nielsen and Buchanan (1986) compared the learning and attitude change benefits resulting from interpretive programs on fire ecology and fire management among visitors to Grand Teton National Park. The field experiment indicated that both an automated audiovisual slide program about wildfire and a ranger-guided boat tour with a talk about fire while a recent burn was in view increased public knowledge of fire ecology and support for natural fire management (i.e., the "let-burn" policy) significantly over the control situation. However, the two treatments did not differ in effectiveness.

Olson et al. (1984) attempted to raise knowledge levels and favorable attitudes about current policies and practices pertaining to four Ohio state nature preserves. Brochures, a series of on-site signs, and personal services including off-site presentations and on-site guided hikes were developed and implemented to communicate policies about picking wildflowers, burning vegetation, grazing, cutting timber, camping, restricting recreational uses, picnicking, trapping and alcohol use. Over 1,000 visitors were included in the sample, and differences between pre-test and post-test means on knowledge of overall preserve management concepts were greatest for brochures, followed by personal services and signs. Attitude gains were similar. The control group's knowledge actually declined from pre-test to post-test.

Feldman (1978) developed an interpretive message on a tape cassette and in a brochure in an attempt to increase knowledge levels about the environment among recreating motorists. In addition, Feldman attempted to persuade motorists to leave their cars and walk on one of four nature trails in a New York state park. Feldman distributed the interpretive media to recreationists as they began their tour of the park, and measured short-term retention of information after the tour. Using ten multiple-choice items, he found that both the cassette tape and brochure increased learning levels over the control group (i.e., no information condition). Indeed, the group given a brochure scored better than the control group in nine items, and the group exposed to the cassette tape scored better than the control group on all ten items. The brochure group scored higher than the cassette tape group on two of the ten knowledge questions. Only those motorists who received the tape cassette used the nature trails more than those people in the control group who received no information; 39 percent of all parties who received the taped message about the trails and related attractions visited the trails, compared to 21 percent of the control group.

Dowell and McCool (1986) worked with the Forest Service to test the effectiveness of three methods of increasing Boy Scouts' knowledge, favorable attitudes and behavioral intentions about using low impact practices. The three methods included a slide show, a booklet, and a combined booklet and slide show. A knowledge test of wilderness ecology and leave-no-trace practices was administered to a control group and to the targeted Boy Scout groups immediately after they received the educational program and one month after the program. Both the post-test and the retention scores on wilderness ecosystem knowledge were significantly greater than the control group's. The three different media treatments did not differ from each other. Even more significant gains in knowledge of appropriate wilderness use practices were achieved through the educational programs. For knowledge of skills, the slide program appeared better than the booklet condition.

A comparison of the post-training attitude scores among the three treatment groups and the control group showed no difference in scores. However, when mean difference scores between pre-test and post-test were compared across groups, significant differences were found. Children who received the booklet plus slides, and children who received only the booklet developed the most positive attitudes.

All three methods increased behavioral intentions to use appropriate low impact behavior in the wilderness over the control condition, but no one medium was any more effective than any other. Intentions to behave properly had decreased slightly one month after the treatment, but they were still significantly higher than those of the control or no information condition.

The Boundary Waters Canoe Area Wilderness has an outreach program to teach volunteer leaders in communities in the region about wilderness concepts, values and low impact practices. Training workshops typically last from one to four hours. Jones and McAvoy (1988) evaluated knowledge, attitude and intended behavior gains among program participants both immediately after and about three months after the workshops. Knowledge levels among participants were high going into the workshop. Nevertheless, knowledge gains were significant, both immediately following the workshop and after the three-month period. Favorable attitudes also increased significantly from pre-test to post-test, and remained high over the extended period. The behavioral belief scores also increased because of the training workshop. The post-workshop scores on intentions to use appropriate wilderness behavior also showed a significant improvement over intentions before participation in the program.

Sieg et al. (1987) provided a workshop on the natural and cultural history of the New River Gorge National River in West Virginia for whitewater rafting guides. This workshop's goal was to increase the guides' level of interpretation and subsequently, their guests' knowledge levels and intentions to visit the National Park Service's interpretive center. A subjective measure of amount of interpretation provided by guides did increase significantly from before to after the training workshop. Increases in guests' knowledge levels were also significant. During the control condition (before the workshop), passengers averaged 5.44 items correct out of 13 on the river history and ecology test. After the workshop, post-trip scores increased to 8.75. Knowledge gain from the river trip was 1.8 during the control condition; during the treatment condition (after the workshop) knowledge gain averaged 5.2. These scores represent substantial knowledge gains for river guests, likely due to National Park Service-sponsored training of private concessionnaires in a park. However, river rafters did not report stronger behavioral intentions to travel to the Park Service visitor center after the river trip. It may be that the increased on-river interpretation achieved a ceiling effect. Customers felt no need for additional information.

Two recent studies represent possible exceptions to the general trend of positive results from attempts to persuade park visitors to improve their knowledge, attitudes and behavior about resource impacts and conflicts. Burde et al. (1988) completed an evaluation of visitor use and knowledge gained from interpretive materials and contacts at Great Smoky Mountains National Park. Backcountry users who utilized the park's interpretive services were no more knowledgeable about backcountry policies than those who did not use the services. Knowledge levels for both groups were high, with the exception of knowledge of backcountry fire policies.

Similarly, there was no difference in the levels of knowledge about hypothermia and how to treat it between those groups who used and those who had not used park interpretive information. On the other hand, exposure to the Park Service literature on black bear hazards and poisonous snakes did increase knowledge levels about how to react to these dangerous animals. Still, even for those who did get the interpretive materials, knowledge levels about appropriate behaviors were low.

Manfredo and Bright (1991) recently evaluated whether or not a persuasive brochure specifying appropriate human behavior in the bear country of the Boundary Waters Canoe Area Wilderness actually increased proper behavioral intentions and reduced people-bear conflicts. The bear brochure was sent by mail with several other brochures to potential visitors who requested the required wilderness use permit. After the wilderness visit, about three quarters of the study participants remembered the bear brochure. Approximately the same proportion

(74.3 percent) devoted some thought to the brochure's content. However, only 18.2 percent of the respondents received new information from the brochure, only 34.6 percent had some change in beliefs, and only 7.5 percent reported actual or intended change of behavior due to the persuasive brochure. Further analysis indicated that the brochure was quite effective for recipients with low knowledge about bears, and the greater the perceived prior knowledge, the less the change due to the brochure.

Effect of Persuasion on Selection of Different Recreation Places
General Findings:

1. Persuasive messages are often effective in altering the places where recreationists visit, especially within the park.

2. Providing persuasive messages to recreationists early in their trip or route planning process increases the likelihood of change in recreation destination.

3. Recreationists with little previous experience or knowledge of a park are more highly influenced by persuasive messages about route selection or places to visit.

4. Increased credibility assigned to the persuasive message source by recreationists increases the likelihood of selection of the advocated route or place.

5. Persuasive messages with relevant information about multiple attributes of a site or route are more effective than single attribute messages.

6. User-friendly computerized information systems designed to meet individual needs are more effective than other non-personal media in changing route or site selection.

7. A combination of impersonal and personalized channels of persuasive communication is more effective than the impersonal channel alone in changing route or place selection for some groups, especially groups in high risk situations.

A body of forest recreation research has examined the nature, extent and causes of change in recreation site selection attributable to management intervention. Such intervention has usually involved the provision of information to recreationists during their leisure time, and was motivated by a desire to reduce congestion and environmental impacts in leisure settings and increase customer satisfaction.

In an early study, Lime and Lucas (1977) sent a brochure to recreationists visiting high-use zones in the Boundary Waters Canoe Area, informing them about patterns of use and attractions in the area. A follow-up survey after the subsequent summer season demonstrated that one-third of these recreationists had used a new entry point to the BWCA; most had selected a more lightly used canoe route, and three-fourths of them said the brochure was useful in understanding rules and regulations and influenced their choice of a travel route and time of trip. Paddle canoeists were more influenced than motor canoeists and boaters.

Lucas (1981) attempted to change the distribution of trail use at the Selway-Bitterroot Wilderness by distributing informational brochures to area visitors. Lucas's efforts resulted in little behavior change, and subsequent program evaluation suggested that many visitors failed to receive the brochure; most who did get the brochure received it too late in the route planning process; recreationists were using more criteria than just the amount of use to select trail routes; and some recreationists doubted the accuracy of the brochure's information about use.

Roggenbuck and Berrier (1982) followed up the Lucas (1981) study with the use of an informational brochure and ranger contacts encouraging campers to shift away from a heavy-use meadow in the Shining Rock Wilderness of North Carolina. The informational messages, delivered either by trailhead brochures or by the brochure plus ranger contact at the problem meadow, described impact and congestion problems at the meadow and identified the location and characteristics of five alternative, more lightly used campsites within a mile of the spot. Under the control condition, 62 percent of all wilderness user groups camped in the problem meadow; the percentage dropped to 44 percent with the brochure alone, and to 33 percent with the brochure and personal contact. This movement of use to the recommended campsites was highly significant. For certain groups, i.e., groups with no previous experience in the area, groups with children, groups arriving at the meadow by mid-afternoon, and groups of three to six people, the brochure plus personal contact combination was even more effective. Finally, when camper groups arrived at the meadow and found it to have moderate use, in contrast to light or heavy use, they were more likely to disperse to the recommended sites.

Krumpe and Brown (1982) were also successful in changing the behavior of recreationists in a wildland setting. They developed a brochure that used a decision-tree format to describe 28 lightly used trails in the backcountry of Yellowstone National Park. They cited evidence that people process information in a sequential flow when attempting to reach a decision, and thus felt that the decision-tree format would facilitate behavior change. Krumpe and Brown gave the brochure to backpackers when they received their backcountry use permits at ranger stations in the park. During the control condition (no information), only 14 percent of all groups took one of the 28 lightly used trails; this number increased significantly to 37 percent during the brochure's use. Inexperienced hikers were more likely to choose one of the recommended trails. The intervention of an informational brochure without the decision-tree format was not tested, so we do not know the effect of this message format. However, some researchers have suggested that the intervention might have resulted in an even greater amount of behavior change had recreationists been able to choose their own trail selection criteria in their own sequence of relative importance (Roggenbuck and Watson 1986).

Huffman and Williams (1987) followed the Krumpe and Brown study in developing a user-friendly microcomputer program permitting backcountry hikers in Rocky Mountain National Park to gain information on trail attributes in the sequence of their relative importance to individual decision-making. Twenty-nine different trails were included in the decision aid program, and hikers received the information at a park visitor center when they applied for their backcountry use permits. Under the control condition (no information), about 17 percent selected one of the 29 trails. When a brochure describing these trails was distributed to hikers, 38 percent of the groups selected one of the trails. When hiker groups accessed the same information on the microcomputer, 60 percent of all groups selected one of the 29 trails. These findings suggest that information provided by a user-friendly computer program accomplishes substantial behavior change.

Hultsman (1988) tested the effectiveness of microcomputer-based information systems to behavior change among recreationists in the front country of Great Smoky Mountains National Park of North Carolina and Tennessee. There, touch-sensitive computers providing an organized listing of activity opportunities and itineraries in the park were placed in the Sugarlands Visitor Center. Many visitors felt that the computers provided them with new information. Of these visitors, 91 percent said they used the computer-generated itinerary; 93 percent of these individuals felt their itinerary successfully met their activity interests; and 85 percent said the itinerary made their visit more fulfilling. About 91 percent felt that the touch-sensitive computer was appropriate in a visitor center.

Reducing Resource Impacts Through Persuasion
General Findings:

1. Persuasive messages often prompt a reduction of depreciative behaviors such as littering in park settings, at least in the short term.

2. Verbal appeals are sometimes effective in increasing litter pick-up in parks at the primitive end of the spectrum, but for more developed parks, incentives such as a promise of a reward are also needed.

3. Specific and clear persuasive messages are more effective than more generalized messages in reducing littering.

4. Environmental prompts such as the proper placement of attractive trash receptacles can reduce littering.

5. Incentives can reduce the rates of littering and vandalism to park resources, but messages to increase public awareness of consequences of problem behaviors are often just as effective.

6. Role modelling by a park ranger often increases the likelihood that children will pick up litter in a park.

7. Signing a petition indicating support for litter-free parks sometimes reduces littering in the park.

8. Personal requests along with written messages to reduce litter and tree damage in park campgrounds are more often effective than the written message alone.

Surprisingly few published studies have been conducted to determine if persuasive messages actually reduce problem behaviors in wildland recreation settings. Where low impact behaviors have actually been measured, most were studies of littering behavior.

A flurry of studies in the 1970s indicated that persuasion can reduce littering in park settings, but that the effectiveness of persuasion techniques varied widely depending on the type of behavioral intervention used. Applied behavioral analysis attempted to reduce littering and increase voluntary litter clean-up behaviors through written, oral and environmental prompts, incentives such as rewards and punishments, petition signing and role modelling of appropriate behavior.

Marler (1971) evaluated the success of three types of anti-littering messages on campers—a reward-oriented theme, a punishment-oriented theme, and a factual theme—and concluded that a punishment-oriented theme was the most effective. Finnie (1973) reported that anti-littering signs along highways had no effect, but that well-placed litter receptacles reduced littering by 30 percent. Lahart and Bailey (1975) used persuasive appeals and incentives to reduce the amount of littering and to increase the frequency of litter pick-up on a nature trail. The educational message was effective in reducing the amount of litter left on the trail, but only the incentive treatment resulted in litter pick-up.

In contrast, Muth and Clark (1978) found that simple verbal appeals increased the likelihood that wilderness users would pack out other people's litter that had been collected and bagged. Christensen and Clark (1983) reported that appeals to campers to become involved in the management of litter problems resulted in a 22 percent increase in one or more types of involvement. Horsley (1988) compared the effectiveness of specific and positive anti-littering messages with less precise prompts, and found the specific prompts to be more successful in reducing littering.

Ham (1983/1984) also noted the importance of clear messages when park managers attempt to prompt recycling of trash in park campgrounds. In Ham's study, the park manager placed separate garbage receptacles at the campground exit for recycling different materials, with signs indicating what materials should be placed in each can. Only about 55 percent of observed campers actually read the signs, and of these, only about half deposited waste materials as suggested. Of the 81 campers who read the informational signs, only 12 said the instructions were clear. Also, recycling rates would probably have increased if the campers had presorted their trash in appropriate bags prior to leaving their campsites, indicating the need to get persuasive messages to them earlier.

Manipulating cues in the environment has also reduced littering in some cases. For example, Heberlein (1971) found that people litter less in cleaner areas than in littered areas, and Iso-Ahola and Niblock (1981) reconfirmed this finding in a state park campground in Iowa. Burgess et al. (1971) and Clark et al. (1972a, b, c) reported that distributing litterbags to be used at a theater and a national park was not a very effective way to reduce littering. In contrast, Finnie (1973) and Geller et al. (1980) reported much success in reducing littering by proper placement of attractive, innovative trash receptacles.

Clark et al. (1972a, b) found incentives to be the most effective of a variety of tested techniques to reduce littering and increase litter collection in a movie theater, forest campground, and a special hiking area. Powers et al. (1973) offered a small sum of money or a chance for a much larger sum for participation in a litter pick-up program in a national forest. Few visitors participated in the program, but the area was more free of litter under the small payment condition than the chance of a larger sum condition.

Iso-Ahola and Niblock (1981) tested whether or not signing a petition that "every effort should be made to keep our state parks and recreation areas clean and free from litter" resulted in less litter in two comparable campgrounds in an Iowa state park. Signing the petition reduced litter but only in the cleaner of the two campgrounds. Given the design of the study, the authors were unable to determine whether the improved behavior was due to increased cognitive awareness of the social norm against littering, or increased internal commitment because of signing the petition.

Oliver et al. (1985) used informational prompts in a developed campground to help reduce littering and tree damage. Under the control condition, 82 percent of all camper parties left at least one piece of litter at their campsite at their departure; the number of pieces per campsite averaged 3.9. Tree damage was high also, with 38 percent of all groups damaging at least one tree and an average of 1.1 incidents of damage per group. Three interventions were used to change the impact behavior: a brochure with high readability and human interest describing the extent, consequences and costs of the impacts and their management; the same brochure plus a ranger contact at the campsite reinforcing the message; and the brochure, personal contact at the campsite, and a request for camper assistance in reporting impact behaviors to the park ranger. All three treatments reduced impact behaviors. The brochure plus a personal contact was significantly more effective than the brochure alone, reducing the number of groups with littered campsites from 67 percent to 41 percent, and the number of groups causing tree damage from 20 percent to four percent. Interestingly, the request for assistance in rule enforcement did not have any additional positive behavior change effects among study participants. Under this condition, 46 percent of all groups left litter in their campsite; 10 percent damaged trees.

Roggenbuck and Passineau (1986) studied the learning benefits of grade school visits to Indiana Dunes National Lakeshore. The program explained the ways of life, resource utilization and conserva-tion practices, and environmental adaptations of Indians, fur traders and pioneer farmers in the area, and addressed responsible behavior in national parks. The researchers found that children's behavioral intentions not to litter, to recycle materials, and to act in various ways to protect natural and cultural resources increased significantly from before to after their trips. Post-test scores of the control group did not increase over the group's pre-test measures, and the post-test scores of the children who went on the field trip were significantly higher than the comparable scores of the control group.

Actual littering behavior was also observed among field trip participants. When anti-littering messages were given to the children at the start of the field visit, they picked up 66 percent of the litter that had been planted along their trail. When the message was coupled with role modelling of finding and picking up a piece of litter by the park naturalist, 90 percent of all planted litter was retrieved by the children. Approximately three-fourths of the way through the field visit, the children were given a souvenir button in a small envelope. Without the knowledge of the children, observations were made of the extent to which the button envelope was discarded on the ground. Even though more than 350 children received the souvenir button, not one envelope was ever found on the forest floor.

Wagstaff and Wilson (1988) measured the effectiveness of verbal appeals and role modelling by commercial river boatmen in increasing the collection of planted litter on remote river campsites on Idaho's Salmon River. Significantly more of the litter was picked up by guests who had received the persuasive message and observed the boatmen collecting litter, but the experiment covered only the first night's campsite. Thus, this study, like most others reviewed here, can say little about the stability of learned behavior.

Vander Stoep and Gramann (1988) conducted a research program at Shiloh National Military Park in Tennessee to determine whether pro-social behavior prompts, information and incentives would reduce the impacting behavior of youth groups on historical cannons, statues and monuments. Three treatments were tested: an awareness of consequences message (AC); the AC message plus a resource protection message (RP); and the AC message, the RP message and an incentive for being a guardian of the resource. Impacting behaviors were recorded using time lapse photography, and all three interventions resulted in significant behavior improvements. Contrary to study hypotheses, adding the resource protection message and/or the incentive did not have an additional effect on reducing damaging behavior over the simple awareness of consequences message.

SUMMARY

Recreational impacts on soil, vegetation, water and wildlife are common in park settings, and are likely to continue increasing. Many impacts occur under light recreational use conditions, soon after the area is opened to public use. Because of better informed visitors, recreational impacts may be increasing at a slower rate than in the past, at least at recreation areas at the primitive end of the outdoor recreation spectrum. Still, impacts are a problem, in part because the natural healing process of many natural environments is very slow.

As with environmental impacts, visitor conflict is as much a function of behavior and subjective perceptions as it is of density of use or reported encounters. Like environmental impacts, crowding and conflict rates are probably increasing, but not as rapidly as in the 1950s, 1960s and early 1970s. This is because growth rates in the use of many recreation environments have levelled off, because park visitors hold more realistic expectations, and also because behavior, at least at the wilderness end of the spectrum, seems to have improved.

Vandalism and depreciative behavior such as littering are a grave concern for park managers, cost taxpayers millions of dollars each year, and have a greater effect on park visitors' experiences than environmental impacts. While park visitors seem to have a variety of motives for their depreciative acts, many managers and researchers believe that most problem behaviors in park settings are nonmalicious.

Leisure philosophers, recreation managers and recreationists believe persuasion to be a highly effective means of reducing environmental impacts, visitor conflicts and problem behaviors, especially in cases of uninformed, unintentional, unskilled and careless acts. Persuasive messages can reduce perceptions of crowding by informing park visitors of places and times of high and low use, by developing more realistic expectations about encounters, and by teaching appropriate behaviors. On the other hand, developing better informed park visitors through persuasion might raise the awareness of common environmental impacts in park settings, thus increasing perceptions of crowding and conflict.

Attempts of persuasion in park settings have used three conceptual routes: behavior change strategies of applied behavior analysis (i.e., accomplish desired behavior changes through behavior prompts, manipulation of the environment, rewarding appropriate behavior or punishing inappropriate behavior); the central or cognitive route (i.e., high attention by the recipient of the persuasive message to message content, careful thought or elaboration of the message content, and integration of the message content into existing belief systems); and the peripheral route (i.e., belief, attitude and behavior change strategies that place little emphasis upon integration of message arguments into existing cognitive structures, but instead emphasize such peripheral issues as source credibility). Appropriate applications of the three strategies depend on the type of park, the goals of recreationists, and the purposes of the persuasive attempt.

Persuasive communication is generally believed to be a lighthanded or subtle visitor management strategy that protects visitors' freedom and the essence of leisure engagements. This is especially true for information and education programs that are almost universally the first choice of managers of primitive or wilderness areas. While the behavior change strategies of the applied behavior analysts also receive support, some researchers caution that should interventions become so subtle that park visitors do not realize they are being manipulated, visitor awareness and freedom would be lost, defeating the intrinsic value of leisure pursuits.

While persuasion should be a valuable tool in the park administrator's repertoire of management strategies, it is not always feasible to intervene with appropriate persuasive messages. The park manager must consider whether the target audience can be identified and reached, if the costs can be covered, and whether necessary staff and support services are available.

The purpose of the persuasive message, its timing, the message content, recipient characteristics, and source variables all influence the success rates of persuasive communication. Some routes to persuasion are likely to be less appropriate and effective than others for some park management purposes. For example, the central or cognitive route is the only one which seems to be relevant for developing a sensitive and holistic land ethic among park visitors in particular and the public in general. At a more specific level, empirical research has shown that persuasive messages are often very effective in altering travel routes within wilderness areas.

The timing of persuasive messages has been found to be very important in influencing trail route selection and in prompting recycling behavior at park campgrounds. Providing the information at the trailhead or at the trash receptacles at the campground exit point may be too late in the decision-making process for the intervention to have any effect. At a more conceptual level, message timing is critical to the success of behavior modification programs involving reward, negative reinforcement, and punishment, for the recipient must associate the intervention with the appropriate act.

The strength of arguments and the clarity of message contents are critically important to the success of most persuasive communication, especially in the information processing or central route to persuasion. Weak arguments may lead to rejection of the persuasive attempt and reinforce existing beliefs, attitudes or behavior. Poor message clarity has caused some attempts to encourage recycling and lessen littering to fail. Finally, some repetition of message content probably increases the effectiveness of persuasive messages, but too much repetition may cause boredom and rejection of the message.

Recipient characteristics have a powerful influence over the relative success of the various routes to persuasion. For example, some individuals tend to gather, process and integrate information carefully from several sources prior to making a decision. Others make decisions much more spontaneously, especially in leisure situations. The central or cognitive route to persuasion is likely to be very effective for the former personality type, but would probably be ignored by the latter group. Also, past experience is a powerful predictor of response to persuasive messages, with novices much more easily influenced by a message than more experienced users. Finally, an individual's status in the recreation party (i.e., leader or party member) and the size of the recreation user group are likely to influence how persuasive messages are processed, and ultimately, the nature of response.

The source of the message is an important predictor of persuasion's success, especially in the peripheral route to persuasion. In this route the recipient typically pays more attention to "who said it" than to "what was said." The credibility of the source becomes very important, and the recipient's perception of source credibility must be considered.

The channel used to communicate the persuasive message is critically important to its effectiveness. Recreation managers overwhelmingly support personal contact with the visitor by the friendly ranger as the most effective medium. However, recent research suggests that personalized contacts are not always the most effective form of persuasion. For complex messages, the written word, as in a persuasive brochure, is often more effective because the recipient can process information at his or her own pace. Also, the friendly ranger can't always be friendly; sometimes he or she is tired, irritable, or a poor communicator. Finally, the user-friendly microcomputer shows great promise as an effective tool to prompt increased learning and behavior change. If programmed properly and placed at appropriate contact points, the microcomputer can provide up-to-date information, at the desired level of specificity, and in the desired sequence to facilitate and improve decision-making. As such, it is much more adaptable to individual needs than the brochure, and it doesn't get tired like wilderness rangers and contact personnel.

The author acknowledges the assistance of John Morton, Graduate Research Assistant, Department of Fisheries and Wildlife Science, Virginia Polytechnic Institute and State University, for his help on the wildlife literature review.

REFERENCES

Absher, J. D.; Lee, R. G. 1981. Density as an incomplete cause of crowding in backcountry settings. *Leisure Sciences.* 4(3): 231-247.

Anderson, D. W. 1988. Dose-response relationship between human disturbance and brown pelican breeding success. *Wildlife Society Bulletin.* 16: 339-345.

Anderson, D. W.; Keith, J. O. 1980. The human influence on seabird nesting success: Conservation implications. *Biological Conservation. 18*: 65-80.

Auckerman, R.; Springer, W. T. 1976. Effects of recreation on water quality in wildlands. *Eisenhower Consortium Bulletin 2.* Fort Collins, CO: U.S. Department of Agriculture, Forest Service, Rocky Mountain Forest and Range Experiment Station. 25 p.

Bartelt, G. A. 1987. Effects of disturbance and hunting on the behavior of Canada goose family groups in east central Wisconsin. *Journal of Wildlife Management. 51*: 517-522.

Belanger, L.; Bedard, J. 1989. Responses of staging greater snow geese to disturbance. *Journal of Wildlife Management. 53*: 713-719.

Berrier, D. L. 1980. *The effectiveness of information on dispersing wilderness campers.* Blacksburg, VA.: Department of Forestry, Virginia Polytechnic Institute and State Univ., 118 p. M. S. Thesis.

Bradley, J. 1979. A human approach to reducing wildland impacts. In Ittner, R., (ed.) *Recreational impact on wildlands—conference proceedings; No. R-6-001-1979.* Seattle, WA: U.S. Department of Agriculture, Forest Service, Pacific Northwest Region: 222-226.

Brown, P. J.; McCool, S. F.; Manfredo, M. J. 1987. Evolving concepts and tools for recreation user management in wilderness: A state-of-knowledge review. In: Lucas, Robert C., compiler. *Proceedings—National Wilderness Research Conference: Issues, State-of-Knowledge, Future Directions;* 1985 July; Fort Collins, CO. Gen. Tech. Rep. INT-220. Ogden, UT: U.S. Department of Agriculture, Forest Service, Intermountain Research Station: 320-346.

Burde, J. H.; Peine, J. D.; Renfro, J. R.; Curran, K. A. 1988. Communicating with park visitors. Some successes and failures at Great Smoky Mountains National Park. In: Legg, M., (ed.) *National Association of Interpretation 1988 Research Monograph:* 7-12.

Bury, R. L.; Fish, C. B. 1980. Controlling wilderness recreation: What managers think and do. *Journal of Soil and Water Conservation. 35*(2): 90-93.

Burgess, R. L.; Clark, R. N.; Hendee, J. C. 1971. An experimental analysis of anti-litter procedures. *Journal of Applied Behavior Analysis. 4*: 71-75.

Burke, J. F.; Schreyer, R.; Hunt, J. D. 1979. Behavior modification. Trends. 16(4): 33-36.

Chaicken, S.; Stangor, S. 1987. Attitudes and Attitude Change. *Annual Review of Psychology. 38*: 575-630.

Christensen, H. H. 1984. Vandalism: An exploratory assessment of perceived impacts and potential solutions. In: Levy-Leboyer, Claude, (ed.) *Vandalism, behavior and motivations.* Amsterdam: North-Holland Publishing Co.: 269-279.

Christensen, H. H. 1986. Vandalism and depreciative behavior. In: *A literature review, the president's commission on americans outdoors.* Washington, D.C.: Management. 73-87.

Christensen, H. H.; Clark, R. N. 1983. Increasing public involvement to reduce depreciative behavior in recreation settings. *Leisure Sciences. 5*(4): 359-379.

Clark, R. N.; Burgess, R. L.; Hendee, J. C. 1972b. The development of anti-litter behavior in a forest campground. *Journal of Applied Behavior Analysis. 5*: 1-6.

Clark, R. N.; Hendee, J. C.; Burgess, R. L. 1972a. The experimental control of littering. *Journal of Environmental Education. 4*(2): 22-28.

Clark, R. N.; Hendee, J. C.; Campbell, F. L. 1971. Values, behavior, and conflict in modern camping culture. *Journal of Leisure Research. 3*(3): 143-159.

Clark, R. N.; Hendee, J. C.; Washburne, R. F. 1972c. "Litterbags"—An evaluation of their use. *Res. Note PNW-184.* Portland, OR: U.S. Department of Agriculture, Forest Service, Pacific Northwest Forest and Range Experiment Station. 5 p.

Clark, R. N.; Koch, R. W.; Hogans, M. L.; Christensen, H. H.; Hendee, J. C. 1984. The value of roaded, multiple-use areas as recreation sites in three national forests of the Pacific Northwest. *Res. Paper PNW-319*. Portland, OR: U.S. Department of Agriculture, Forest Service, Pacific Northwest Forest and Range Experiment Station. 40 p.

Cole, D. N. 1982. Wilderness campsite impacts: Effect of amount of use. *Res. Paper INT-284*. Ogden, UT: U.S. Department of Agriculture, Forest Service, Intermountain Forest and Range Experiment Station. 32 p.

Cole, D. N. 1983a. Assessing and monitoring backcountry trail conditions. *Res. Paper INT-303*. Ogden, UT: U.S. Department of Agriculture, Forest Service, Intermountain Forest and Range Experiment Station. 10 p.

Cole, D. N. 1983b. Monitoring the condition of wilderness campsites. *Res. Paper INT-302*. Ogden, UT: U.S. Department of Agriculture, Forest Service, Intermountain Forest and Range Experiment Station. 10 p.

Cole, D. N. 1986. Resource impacts caused by recreation. In: *A literature review, the president's commission on americans outdoors*. Washington, D.C.: Management. 1-11.

Cole, D. N.; Benedict, J. 1983. Wilderness campsite selection - what should users be told? *Park Science*. 3(4): 5-7.

Cole, D. N.; Fichtler, R. K. 1983. Campsite impact on three western wilderness areas. *Environmental Management*. 7: 275-288.

Cole, D. N.; Marion, J. L. 1986. Wilderness campsite impacts: Changes over time. In: Lucas, Robert C., compiler. *Proceedings—National Wilderness Research Conference: Current Research*; 1985 July; Fort Collins, CO. *Gen. Tech. Rep. INT-212*. Ogden, UT: U.S. Department of Agriculture, Forest Service, Intermountain Research Station: 144-151.

Cooke, A. S. 1980. Observations on how close certain passerine species will tolerate an approaching human in rural and suburban areas. *Biological Conservation*. 18: 85-88.

Cordell, H. K. 1982. Priorities for recreation research in the southern states. In: Proceedings Southern States recreation research application workshop. *Gen. Tech. Rep. SE-9*. Asheville, NC: U.S. Department of Agriculture, Southeastern Forest Experiment Station: 47-51.

Ditton, R. B.; Fedler, A. J.; Graefe, A. R. 1983. Factors contributing to perceptions of recreational crowding. *Leisure Sciences*. 5(4): 273-288.

Dowell, D. L.; McCool, S. F. 1986. Evaluation of a wilderness information dissemination program. In: Lucas, R. C., compiler. Proceedings—National Wilderness Research Conference: Current Research; 1985 July; Fort Collins, CO. *Gen. Tech. Rep. INT-212*. Ogden, UT: U.S. Department of Agriculture, Forest Service, Intermountain Research Station: 494-500.

Downing, K.; Clark, R. N. 1979. Users' and managers' perceptions of dispersed recreation impacts: A focus on roaded forest lands. In: Ittner, R., (ed.) *Recreational impacts on wildlands—conference proceedings; R-6-001-1979*. Seattle, WA: U.S. Department of Agriculture, Forest Service, Pacific Northwest Regions: 18-23.

Driver, B. L.; Bassett, J. R. 1975. Defining conflicts among river users: A case study of Michigan's Au Sable River. *Naturalist. 26*(2): 19-23.

Driver, B. L.; Knopf, R. C. 1976. Temporary escape: One product of sport fisheries management. *Fisheries. 1*(2): 21-29.

Driver, B. L.; Nash, R.; Haas, G. 1987. Wilderness benefits: A state-of-knowledge review. In: Lucas, R. C., compiler. Proceedings, National Wilderness Research Conference: Issues, State-of-Knowledge, Future Directions. 1985 July; Fort Collins, CO. *Gen. Tech. Rep. INT-220.* Ogden, UT: U.S. Department of Agriculture, Forest Service, Intermountain Research Station: 294-319.

Driver, B. L.; Tocher, R. C. 1970. Toward a behavioral interpretation of recreation engagements, with implications for planning. In: Driver, B.L., (ed.) *Elements of Outdoor Recreation Planning.* Ann Arbor, MI: University Microfilms: 9-13.

Echelberger, H. E.; Moeller, G. H. 1977. Use and users of the Cranberry Backcountry in West Virginia: Insights for eastern backcountry management. *Research Paper NE-363.* Upper Darby, PA: U.S. Department of Agriculture, Forest Service, Northeastern Forest Experiment Station. 8 p.

Erwin, R. M. 1989. Responses to human intruders by birds nesting. *Colonial Waterbirds. 12*: 104-108.

Fazio, J. R. 1974. *A mandatory permit system and interpretation for backcountry user control in Rocky Mountain National Park: An evaluation study.* Fort Collins, CO: Colorado State University. 246 p. Ph.D. dissertation.

Fazio, J. R. 1979a. Information and education techniques to improve minimum impact use knowledge in wilderness areas. In: Ittner, R., (ed.) *Recreational impacts on wildlands conference proceedings*; No. R-6-001-1979. Seattle, WA: U.S. Department of Agriculture, Forest Service, Pacific Northwest Region: 227-233.

Fazio, J. R. 1979b. Communicating with the wilderness user. Moscow, ID: *University of Idaho, College of Forestry, Wildlife, and Range Experiment Station Bulletin No. 28.* 65p.

Feldman, R. L. 1978. Effectiveness of audio-visual media for interpretation to recreating motorists. *Journal of Interpretation. 3*(1): 14-19.

Finnie, W. C. 1973. Field experiments in litter control. *Environment and Behavior. 5*: 123-44.

Fish, L. B.; Bury, R. L. 1981. Wilderness visitor management: Diversity and agency policies. *Journal of Forestry. 79*(9): 608-612.

Fraser, J. D., Frenzel, L. D.; and Mathisen, J. E. 1985. The impact of human activities on breeding bald eagles in north-central Minnesota. *Journal of Wildlife Management. 49*: 585:592.

Freddy, D. J., Bronaugh, W. M.; and Fowler, M. C. 1986. Responses of mule deer to disturbance by persons afoot and snowmobiles. *Wildlife Society Bulletin. 14*: 63-68.

Frissell, S. E.; Duncan, D. P. 1965. Campsite preference and deterioration in the Quetico-Superior canoe country. *Journal of Forestry. 63*: 256-260.

Gallup, T. P. 1981. *The effectiveness of a cartoon illustrated interpretive brochure on the enhancement of campers' knowledge of rules and the decrease in rates of rule violation per campsite.* State College, PA: Pennsylvania State University. 56 p. M.S. thesis.

Geller, E. S. 1987. Applied behavioral analysis and environmental psychology: From strange bedfellows to a productive marriage. In: Stokols, D.; and Altman, I., (eds.) *Handbook of environmental psychology. Vol. 1.* New York: John Wiley and Sons: 361-388.

Geller, E. S.; Brasted, W.; Mann, M. 1980. Waste receptables designs as interventions for litter control. *Journal of Environmental Systems. 9*: 145-160.

Geller, E. S.; Needleman, L. D., Randall, K. 1990. Developing a taxonomy of behavior change techniques for environmental protection. In: *Proceedings of the first conference on muncipal solid waste management.* Washington, D.C.: 25 p.

Godin, V. B.; Leonard, R. E. 1979. Management problems in designated wilderness areas. *Journal of Soil and Water Conservation. 34*(3): 141-143.

Graefe, A. R.; Vaske, J. J.; Kuss, F. R. 1984. Social carrying capacity: An integration and synthesis of twenty years of research. *Leisure Sciences. 6*(4): 395-431.

Gramann, J. H.; Burdge, R. 1981. The effect of recreation goals on conflict perceptions: The case of water skiers and fishermen. *Journal of Leisure Research. 13*(1): 15-27.

Gramann, J. H.; Vander Stoep, G. A. 1987. Prosocial behavior theory and natural resource protection: A conceptual synthesis. *Journal of Environmental Management. 24*: 247-257.

Ham, S. H. 1983/1984. Communication and recycling in park campgrounds. *Journal of Environmental Education. 15*(2): 17-20.

Hammitt, W. E.; Cole, D. N. 1987. *Wildland recreation: Ecology and management.* New York, NY: John Wiley & Sons. 341 p.

Hammitt, W. E.; McDonald, C. D. 1983. Past on-site experience and its relationship to managing river recreation resources. *Forest Science. 29*(2): 262-266.

Hand, J. L. 1980. Human disturbance in western gull *Larus occidentalis livens* colonies and possible amplification by intraspecific predation. *Biological Conservation. 18*: 59-63.

Hansen, E. A. 1975. Does canoeing increase streambank erosion? *Res. Note NC-186*. St. Paul, MN: U.S. Department of Agriculture, Forest Service, North Central Forest Experiment Station. 4 p.

Hart, P. 1980. New backcountry ethic: Leave no trace. *American Forests. 86*: 38-41, 51-54.

Hawes, D. K. 1978. Satisfactions derived from leisure-time pursuits: An exploratory nationwide survey. *Journal of Leisure Research. 10*(4): 247-264.

Heberlein, T. A. 1971. Moral norms, threatened sanctions and littering behavior. Madison, WI.: Univ. of Wisconsin. 253 p. Ph.D. dissertation.

Heberlein, T. A.; Dunwiddie, P. 1979. Systematic observation of use levels, campsite selection and visitor characteristics at a high mountain lake. *Journal of Leisure Research. 11*(4): 307-316.

Helgath, S. F. 1975. Trail deterioration in the Selway-Bitterroot Wilderness. *Res. Note INT-193*. Ogden, UT: U.S. Department of Agriculture, Forest Service, Intermountain Forest and Range Experiment Station. 15 p.

Hendee, J. C.; Catton, W. R., Jr.; Marlow, L. D.; Brockman, C. F. 1968. Wilderness users in the Pacific Northwest: their characteristics, values and management preferences. *Res. Paper PNW-61*. U.S. Department of Agriculture, Forest Service, Pacific Northwest Forest and Range Experiment Station. 92 p.

Hendee, J. C.; Stankey, G. H.; Lucas, R. C. 1990. *Wilderness management. 2nd ed.* Golden, CO: North America Press, An Imprint of Fulcrum Publishing. 546 p.

Horsley, A. D. 1988. The unintended effects of a posted sign on littering attitudes and stated intentions. *Journal of Environmental Education. 19*(3): 10-14.

Huffman, M. G.; Williams, D. R. 1987. The use of microcomputers for park trail information dissemination. *Journal of Park and Recreation Administration. 5*: 34-46.

Hultsman, W. Z. 1988. Applications of a touch-sensitive computer in park settings: Activity alternatives and visitor information. *Journal of Park and Recreation Administration. 6*(1): 1-11.

Irwin, K. M. 1985. *Wilderness visitor response to ranger educational contacts at trailheads.* Blacksburg, VA.: Department of Forestry, Virginia Polytechnic Institute and State University. 125 p. M.S. thesis.

Iso-Ahola, S. E.; Niblock, L. A. 1981. *The effects of signing a petition on the reduction of litter in campgrounds.* Paper presented at the SPRE Leisure Research Symposium, National Recreation and Parks Association Congress, Minneapolis, MN, October 25. 14 p.

Jacob, G. R.; Schreyer, R. 1980. Conflict in outdoor recreation: A theoretical perspective. *Journal of Leisure Research. 12*(4): 368-380.

Jones, P. E.; McAvoy, L. H. 1988. An evaluation of a wilderness user education program: A cognitive and behavioral analysis. In: Legg, M., (ed.) *National Association of Interpretation 1988 Research Monograph*: 13-20.

Kaiser, M. S.; Fritzell, E. K. 1984. Effects of river recreationists on green-backed heron behavior. *Journal of Wildlife Management. 48*: 561-567.

King, J. C.; Mace, A. C., Jr. 1974. Effects of recreation on water quality. *Journal of Water Pollution Control Federation. 46*(11): 2453-2459.

Knight, R. L.; Knight, S. K. 1984. Responses of wintering bald eagles to boating activity. *Journal of Wildlife Management. 48*: 999-1004.

Knight, R. L.; Skagen, S. K. 1986. Effects of recreational disturbance on birds of prey: a review. In: *Proceedings of the Southwest Raptor Management Symposium and Workshop*: 355-359.

Knopp, T.; Tyger, J. 1973. A study of conflict in recreational land use: Snowmobiling vs. ski-touring. *Journal of Leisure Research. 5*: 6-17.

Knudson, D. M.; Curry, E. B. 1981. Campers' perceptions of site deterioration and crowding. *Journal of Forestry. 79*: 92-94.

Krumpe, E. E.; Brown, P. J. 1982. Redistributing backcountry use through information related to recreation experiences. *Journal of Forestry. 80*: 360-362, 364.

Lahart, D.; Bailey, J. 1975. Reducing children's littering on a nature trail. *Journal of Environmental Education. 7*(1): 37-45.

Lee, R. G. 1972. The social definition of outdoor recreation places. In: Burch, W. R.; Cheek, N. H., Jr.; Taylor, L., (eds). *Social behavior, natural resources and the environment.* New York, NY: Harper and Row: 68-84.

Lee, R. G. 1975. *The management of human components in the Yosemite National Park ecosystem: final research report.* Berkeley, CA: University of California.

Lime, D. W.; Lucas, R. C. 1977. Good information improves the wilderness experience. *Naturalist. 28*(4): 18-21.

Lucas, R. C. 1964. The recreational capacity of the Quetico-Superior area. Res. *Paper LS-15.* St. Paul, MN: U.S. Department of Agriculture, Forest Service, Lake Central Forest Experiment Station. 34 p.

Lucas, R. C. 1979. Perceptions of non-motorized recreational impacts: A review of research findings. In: Ittner, R., (ed.) *Recreational impact on wildlands—conference proceedings.* R-6-001-1979, Seattle, WA: U.S. Department of Agriculture, Forest Service, Pacific Northwest Region: 24-31.

Lucas, R. C. 1980. Use patterns and visitor characteristics, attitudes, and preferences in nine wilderness and other roadless areas. *Research Paper INT-253.* Ogden, UT: U.S. Department of Agriculture, Forest Service, Intermountain Forest and Range Experiment Station. 89 p.

Lucas, R. C. 1981. Redistributing wilderness use through information supplied to visitors. *Res. Paper INT-277*. Ogden, UT: U.S. Department of Agriculture, Forest Service, Intermountain Forest and Range Experiment Station. 15 p.

Lucas, R. C. 1982. Recreation regulations—when are they needed? *Journal of Forestry*. *80*(3): 148-151.

Lucas, R. C. 1985. Trends in wilderness use patterns, visitor characteristics, and attitudes in the Bob Marshall Wilderness Complex. *Res. Paper INT-345*. Ogden, UT: U.S. Department of Agriculture, Forest Service, Intermountain Research Station. 32 p.

MacArthur, R. A.; Geist, V.; Johnston, R. H. 1982. Cardiac and behavioral responses of mountain sheep to human disturbance. *Journal of Wildlife Management*. *46*: 351-358.

Manfredo, M. J.; Bright, A. D. 1991. A model for assessing the effects of communication on recreationists. *Journal of Leisure Research*.

Manning, R. E. 1986. *Studies in outdoor recreation—search and research for satisfaction*. Corvallis, OR: Oregon State University Press. 166 p.

Manning R. E.; Ciali, C. P. 1981. Recreation and river type: Social-environmental relationships. *Environmental Management*. *5*(2): 109-120.

Marion, J. L.; Merriam, L. C. 1985. Recreational impacts on well-established campsites in the Boundary Waters Canoe Area Wilderness. St. Paul, MN: Univ. of Minnesota, *Agricultural Experiment Station Bulletin AD-SB-2502*. 16 p.

Marler, L. 1971. A study of anti-litter messages. *Journal of Environmental Education*. *3*(1): 52-53.

Martin, Burnham H.; Taylor, D. T. 1981. *Informing backcountry visitors—A catalog of techniques*. Research Department, Appalachian Mountain Club. 104 p.

Matheny, S. J. 1979. A successful campaign to reduce trail switchback shortcutting. In: Ittner, R., (ed.) *Recreational impacts on wildlands-conference proceedings*; R-6-001-1979. Seattle, WA: U.S. Department of Agriculture, Forest Service, Pacific Northwest Region: 217-221.

McAvoy, L. H.; Dustin, D. L. 1983. Indirect versus direct regulation of recreation behavior. *Journal of Park and Recreation Administration*. *1*(4): 12-17.

McConnell, K. E. 1977. Congestion and willingness to pay: A study of beach use. *Land Economics*. *53* (May): 185-195.

McLellan, B.; Shackleton, D. M. 1989. Immediate reactions of grizzly bears to human activities. *Wildlife Society Bulletin*. *17*: 269-274.

Merriam, L. C., Jr.; Smith, C. K. 1974. Visitor impact on newly developed campsites in the Boundary Waters Canoe Area. *Journal of Forestry*. *72*(10): 627-630.

Morton, J. M.; Kirkpatrick, R. L.; Vaughan, M. R.; Stauffer, D. F. 1989. Habitat use and movement of American black ducks in winter. *Journal of Wildlife Management. 53*: 390-400.

Muth, R. M.; Clark, R. N. 1978. Public participation in wilderness backcountry litter control: A review of research and management experience. *Gen. Tech. Rep. PNW-75*. Portland, OR: U.S. Department of Agriculture, Forest Service, Pacific Northwest Forest and Range Experiment Station. 12 p.

Nelson, D.; Hansen, W. R. 1984. Fecal coliform in the Salt River recreation areas of Arizona. *Journal of Forestry. 82*: 554-555.

Nielsen, C.; Buchanan, T. 1986. A comparison of the effectiveness of two interpretive programs regarding fire ecology and fire management. *Journal of Interpretation. 11*(1): 1-10.

Nixon, C. M.; Hansen, L. P.; Brewer, P.A. 1988. Characteristics of winter habitats used by deer in Illinois. *Journal of Wildlife Management. 52*: 552-555.

Noe, F. P.; Wellman, J. D.; Buhyoff, G. J. 1981. Perceptions of conflict between off-road vehicle users in a leisure setting. *Journal of Environmental Systems. 11*(3): 243-253.

Oliver, S. S.; Roggenbuck, J. W.; Watson, A. E. 1985. Education to reduce impacts in forest campgrounds. *Journal of Forestry. 83*(4): 234-236.

Olson, E. C.; Bowman, M. L.; Roth, R. E. 1984. Interpretation and nonformal education in natural resources management. *Journal of Environmental Education. 15*: 6-10.

Peterson, M. 1985. National forest dimensions and dilemmas. In: Frome, M., (ed.) *Issues in wilderness management: Proceedings of the national wilderness workshop*; 1983 October; Moscow, ID. Boulder, CO: Westview Press: 36-52.

Petty, R. E.; Cacioppo, J. T. 1986. The elaboration likelihood model of persuasion. In: Berkowitz, L., (ed.) *Advances in experimental social psychology*. New York, N.Y.: Academic Press. 19: 123-205.

Pierce, R. C. 1980. Dimensions of Leisure I: Satisfaction. *Journal of Leisure Research. 12*(1): 5-19.

Ponce, S. L.; Gary, H. L. 1979. The effect of lake-based recreation and second home use on surface water quality in the Manitou experimental forest. *Res. Paper RM-211*. Fort Collins, CO: U.S. Department of Agriculture, Forest Service, Rocky Mountain Forest and Range Experiment Station. 10 p.

Powers, R. B.; Osborne, J. G.; Anderson, E. G. 1973. Positive reinforcement of litter removal in the natural environment. *Journal of Applied Behavior Analysis. 6*: 579-586.

Robertson, R. D. 1981. *An investigation of visitor behavior in wilderness areas*. Iowa City, IA: University of Iowa. 174 p. Ph.D. dissertation.

Robertson, R. D. 1982. Visitor knowledge affects behavior. In: Lime, D. W., tech. coord. *Forest and river recreation: Research update.* St. Paul, MN: University of Minnesota, Agriculture Experiment Station, Miscellaneous Publication 18: 49-51.

Roggenbuck, J. W. 1988. Forest Service wilderness management in the south: A review and evaluation. Testimony provided at the Forest Service Wilderness Management Hearing, Subcommittee on National Parks and Public Lands, U.S. House of Representatives, Washington, D.C., July 26,1988.

Roggenbuck, J. W.; Bange, S. P. 1983. *An assessment of the float-trip carrying capacity of the New River Gorge National River.* Final report to the New River Gorge National River, National Park Service. Blacksburg, VA: Department of Forestry, Virginia Polytechnic Institute and State University. 208 p.

Roggenbuck, J. W.; Berrier, B. L. 1982. A comparison of the effectiveness of two communication strategies in dispersing wilderness campers. *Journal of Leisure Research. 14*(1): 77-89.

Roggenbuck, J. W.; Hall, O. F.; Oliver, S. S. 1982. *The effectiveness of interpretation in reducing depreciative behavior in campgrounds.* Report for U.S. Army Corps of Engineers, Waterways Experiment Station. Blacksburg, VA: Department of Forestry, Virginia Polytechnic Institute and State University. 110 p.

Roggenbuck, J. W.; Ham, Sam H. 1986. Use of information and education in recreation management. In: A literature review, *The president's commission on americans outdoors.* Washington, D.C.: Management: 59-71.

Roggenbuck, J. W.; Lucas, R. C. 1987. Wilderness use and user characteristics: A state-of-knowledge review. In: Lucas, Robert C., compiler. *Proceedings—National wilderness research conference: Issues, state-of-knowledge, future directions*; 1985 July; Fort Collins, CO. Gen. Tech. Rep. INT-220. Ogden, UT: U.S. Dept. of Agriculture, Forest Service, Intermountain Research Station: 204-245.

Roggenbuck, J. W.; Passineau, J. 1986. Use of the field experiment to assess the effectiveness of interpretation. In: McDonald, B.; Cordell, H. K. (ed.) *Proceedings, Southeastern recreation research conference.* Athens, GA: Recreation Technical Assistance Office, Institute of Community and Area Development, University of Georgia: 65-86.

Roggenbuck, J. W.; Smith, A. C.; Wellman, J. D. 1982. Canoeists' perceptions of problem behaviors on Virginia rivers. *Journal of Soil and Water Conservation. 37*(2): 122-124.

Roggenbuck, J. W.; Watson, A. E. 1986. Providing information for management purposes. In: Kulhavy, D.L., Conner, R. N.(eds). *Proceedings of the conference on wilderness and natural areas in the east, a management challenge*; 1985 May; Nacogdoches, TX: Stephen F. Austin University: 236-242.

Roggenbuck, J. W.; Watson, Alan E. 1989. Wilderness recreation use: The current situation. In: Watson, A. H. compiler. Outdoor recreation benchmark 1988: Proceedings of the 1988 national outdoor recreation forum. 1988 January; Tampa, FL. *Gen. Tech. Rep. SE-52*. Asheville, N.C.: U.S. Department of Agriculture, Forest Service, Southeastern Forest Experiment Station: 346-356.

Roggenbuck, J. W.; Watson, A. E.; Stankey, G. H. 1982. Wilderness management in the southern Appalachians. *Southern Journal of Applied Forestry*. 6(3): 147-152.

Ross, T. L.; Moeller, G. H. 1974. Communicating rules in recreation areas. *Res. Paper NE-297*. Upper Darby, PA: U.S. Department of Agriculture, Forest Service, Northeastern Forest Experiment Station: 12 p.

Schomaker, J. H. 1975. *Effect of selected information on dispersal of wilderness recreationists*. Fort Collins, CO: Department of Recreation Resources, Colorado State University. 95 p. Ph.D. dissertation.

Schreyer, R.; Roggenbuck, J. W.; McCool, S. F.; Royer, L. E.; Miller, J. 1976. *The Dinosaur National Monument whitewater recreation study*. Logan, UT: Utah State University. 165 p.

Schreyer, R.; Roggenbuck, J. W. 1978. The influence of experience expectations on crowding perceptions and social-psychological carrying capacities. *Leisure Sciences*. 1(4): 373-394.

Sharpe, G. W.; Gensler, D. L. 1978. Interpretation as a management tool. *Journal of Interpretation*. 3(2): 3-9.

Shelby, B. 1980. Crowding models for backcountry recreation. *Land Economics*. 56(1): 43-55.

Shelby, B.; Heberlein, T. A.; Vaske, J. J.; Alfano, G. 1983. Expectations, preferences, and feeling crowded in recreation activities. *Leisure Sciences*. 6(1): 1-14.

Sieg, G. E.; Roggenbuck, J. W.; Bobinski, C. T. 1988. The effectiveness of commercial river guides as interpreters. In: *Proceedings 1987 Southeastern Recreation Research Conference*. 1987 February; Asheville, NC. Athens, GA: Department of Recreation and Leisure Services, University of Georgia: 12-20.

Solomon, M. J.; Hansen, E. A. 1972. Canoeist suggestions for stream management in the Manistee National Forest in Michigan. *Res. Paper NC-77*. St. Paul, MN: U.S. Department of Agriculture, Forest Service, North Central Forest Experiment Station. 10 p.

Stalmaster, M. V.; Newman, J. R. 1978. Behavioral responses of wintering bald eagles to human activity. *Journal of Wildlife Management*. 42: 506-513.

Stankey, G. H. 1973. Visitor perceptions of wilderness carrying capacity. *Res. Paper INT-142*. Ogden UT: U.S. Department of Agriculture, Forest Service, Intermountain Forest and Range Experiment Station. 61 p.

Stankey, G. H. 1980. A comparison of carrying capacity perceptions among visitors to two wildernesses. *Res. Paper INT-242*. Ogden, UT: U.S. Department of Agriculture, Forest Service, Intermountain Forest and Range Experiment Station. 34 p.

Stankey, G. H.; Manning, R.E. 1986. Carrying capacity in recreational settings. In: *A literature review, the president's commission on americans outdoors*. Washington, D.C.: Management. 47-57.

Stankey, G. H.; Schreyer, R. 1987. Attitudes toward wilderness and factors affecting visitor behavior: A state-of-knowledge review. In: Lucas, Robert C., compiler. Proceedings—National wilderness research conference: issues, state-of-knowledge, future directions; 1985 July; Fort Collins, CO. *Gen. Tech. Rep. INT-220*. Ogden, UT: U.S. Department of Agriculture, Forest Service, Intermountain Research Station: 246-293.

Szwak, L. B. 1984. Vandalism: A research priority. *Trends. 21*(1): 43-46.

Taylor, T. P.; Erman, D. C. 1979. The response of benthic plants to past levels of human use in high mountain lakes in Kings Canyon National Park, California, USA. *Journal of Environmental Management. 9*: 271-278.

Tinsley, H. E. A.; Barrett, T. C.; Kass, R. A. 1977. Leisure activities and need satisfaction. *Journal of Leisure Research. 9*(2): 110-120.

Tinsley, H. E. A.; Kass, R. A. 1978. Leisure activities and need satisfaction: A replication and extension. *Journal of Leisure Research. 10*(3): 191-202.

Titre, J.; Mills, A. S. 1982. Effect of encounters on perceived crowding and satisfaction. In: Forest and river recreation: research update. St. Paul, MN: University of Minnesota, Agricultural Experiment Station, *Miscellaneous Publication 18*: 146-153.

U.S. Department of Agriculture. 1975. *11th annual report of the Secretary of Agriculture on the status of national forest units in the National Wilderness Preservation System*, Washington, D.C. 22 p.

U.S. Department of Agriculture. 1976. Wilderness, primitive areas, and wilderness study areas. Forest Service, ch. 2320, *Forest Service Manual, Amendment 73*.

U.S. Department of the Interior. 1981. *A national agenda for recreation research*. Prepared in cooperation with National Recreation and Parks Association. Washington, D.C., U.S. Department of the Interior, National Park Service: 77-84.

Vander Stoep, G. A.; Gramann, J. H. 1987. The effect of verbal appeals and incentives on depreciative behavior among youthful park visitors. *Journal of Leisure Research. 19*(2): 69-83.

Vander Stoep, G. A.; Gramann, J. H. 1988. Use of interpretation as an indirect visitor management tool: An alternative to regulation and enforcement. In: Legg, M. (ed.) *National Association of Interpretation 1988 Research Monograph:* 47-55.

Van Dyke, F. G.; Brocke, R. H.; Shaw, H. G.; Ackerman, B. B.; Hemker, T. P.; Lindsey, F. G. 1986. Reactions of mountain lions to logging and human activity. *Journal of Wildlife Management.* *50*: 95-102.

Vaske, J. J.; Donnelly, M. P.; Heberlein, T. A. 1980. Perceptions of crowding and resource quality by early and more recent visitors. *Leisure Sciences.* *3*: 367-381.

Vaske, J. J.; Graefe, A. R.; Dempster, A. 1982. Social and environmental influences on perceived crowding. In: *Proceedings of the wilderness psychology group conference.* Morgantown, WV: West Virginia University: 211-227.

Vaske, J. J.; Shelby, B.; Graefe, A. R.; Heberlien, T. A. 1986. Backcountry encounter norms: Theory, method, and empirical evidence. *Journal of Leisure Research.* *18*: 137-153.

Wagstaff, M. C.; Wilson, B. E. 1988. The evaluation of litter behavior in a river environment. *Journal of Environmental Education.* *20*(1): 39-44.

Washburne, R. F.; Cole, D. N. 1983. Problems and practices in wilderness management: A survey of managers. *Res. Paper INT-304.* Ogden, UT: U.S. Department of Agriculture, Forest Service, Intermountain Forest and Range Experiment Station. 56 p.

Webb, R. H.; Wilshire, H. G. 1983. *Environmental effects of off-road vehicles: Impacts and management in arid regions.* New York, NY: Springer-Verlag. 4 p.

Werner, R. G.; Leonard, R. E.; Crevelling, J. O. 1985. Impact of backcountry recreationists on the water quality of an Adirondack lake. *Res. Note NE-326.* Broomall, PA: U.S. Department of Agriculture, Forest Service, Northeastern Forest Experiment Station. 4 p.

West, P. C. 1981. Perceived crowding and attitudes toward limiting use in backcountry recreation areas. *Leisure Sciences.* *4*(4): 419-426.

West, P. C. 1982. Effects of user behavior on the perception of crowding in backcountry forest recreation. *Forest Sciences.* *28*(1): 95-105.

Womble, P.; Studebaker, S. 1981. Crowding in a national park campground. *Environment and Behavior.* *13*(5): 557-573.

Yalden, D. W.; Yalden, P. E. 1989. The sensitivity of breeding golden plovers *Pluvialis apricaria* to human intruders. *Bird Study.* *36*: 49-55.

8

A Multidisciplinary Model for Managing Vandalism and Depreciative Behavior in Recreation Settings

Richard C. Knopf
Daniel L. Dustin

INTRODUCTION

Vandalism. The very word stirs emotional heat. And when it happens in our public recreation areas, our anger knows no bounds. Something must be done, we insist. We need to control it, eradicate it; perpetrators of vandalistic acts, or of any kind of depreciative behavior in our public lands, must be held accountable.

At first glance, the issue seems so straightforward. Vandalism in public recreation areas, and the people who cause it, must be stopped. They need to be persuaded—gently or coercively—that their abusive behavior is intolerable. We assert that the answers must lie in persuasion theory, and chapters such as this are born.

But is the issue all that clear-cut? Are those acts we term vandalistic behaviors senseless, without purpose? Is it a given that such behaviors are all bad? Is it really clear what behaviors need to be extinguished? And is it necessarily true that the ultimate culprit is the one committing the behavior?

In this chapter we explore these and other questions that illuminate the difficulties recreation professionals have encountered in reacting consistently and fairly to the problem of vandalism and depreciative behavior. The easy task is to produce insights from other disciplines that relate to the things we are trying to control. The more perplexing challenge is to reach consensus on what it is that needs to be controlled, and why.

We begin by discussing the definitional issues surrounding the concepts of vandalism and depreciative behavior in recreation settings, suggesting that in our haste to resolve the problem, we have hardly taken time to define it. Then we examine possible motives for deviant behaviors, with the implication that these behaviors are not capricious acts, but are calculated and goal-directed forms of transaction with the environment.

Next, we trace lines of inquiry unfolding in several disciplines that carry implications for managing vandalism and depreciative behavior, revealing that such behaviors are precipitated by many things—not just by the persons who commit the acts. We then develop a multi-disciplinary model for managing these behaviors that is constructed with sensitivity to the unique quests of recreation management. One powerful implication of the model is that overt forms of behavioral coercion are not the only option for dealing with deviant behavior. We conclude with a plea to the recreation profession for less judgmentalism and more compassion in the expanding arena of behavioral control.

DISADVANTAGES OF NEGATIVENESS

As a prelude to any conceptional treatment of vandalism and depreciative behavior, it is important to recognize the consequences of assuming that these behaviors are negative and need to be extinguished.

First, a negative conception denies the possibility that such behaviors could result from legitimate motives. It is possible that vandals are attempting to express their needs much the same as any individual attempts to express needs during a recreational outing. Flatly dismissing a category of behaviors as illegitimate is to close the door to understanding them from a scientific—let alone humanistic—perspective.

Second, an overtone of negativeness casts labels upon certain people, defining them as deviant. The body of recreation literature repeatedly asserts that this is a mistake. For one thing, each of us carries some propensity to commit a vandalistic or depreciative act (Wise 1982). For another, demographic analyses have consistently shown that such behaviors are scattered indiscriminately across all social and ethnic groups (Van Vliet 1984). And furthermore, whether or not one is considered deviant can be strictly a function of who holds political power at the time the judgement is made (Cohen 1968).

Third, a negative conception tends to place the origin of an act within the supposedly disturbed mind of an individual. It is quite possible that the responsibility might instead rest in society, the environment, or even within recreation resource managers themselves. By placing the source within the mind of the perpetrator, all other arenas of influence are wrongly absolved of responsibility. And furthermore, the character of the transactions among the purported deviant, society, the environment, and management are ignored.

Finally, a negative disposition implies the futility of remedial action, the pointlessness of scientific investigation, and a desperate need of greater police deterrents and stiffer penalties (Zimbardo 1976). A gentler and perhaps more effective response does not loom as an option.

It is possible to approach the issue of vandalism and depreciative behavior from a more positive and therefore more illuminating perspective. It is possible to approach the issue by understanding that vandalism and depreciative behaviors are need-driven, just like all other behaviors. It is possible to recognize that there are alternatives to dealing with these behaviors other than stiff police sanctions, and to understand that we have an obligation to help all recreationists move toward optimal states of existence—including those states we pass off so quickly as undesirable.

DEFINITIONAL ISSUES

In the recreation literature, the definition of vandalism and depreciative behavior historically has been straightforward. Depreciative behavior has been understood as any act that detracts from the social or physical environment (Clark et al. 1971). More often than not, the term has connoted unintended negative impacts. Vandalism, on the other hand, has been construed as a willful act of damage to the environment (Harrison 1982). Such acts have been understood as intentional. The distinction between depreciative behavior and vandalism turns, then, on the issue of intent. Because vandals know what they are doing and still do it, the argument goes, their infractions are of a fundamentally different nature than the infractions of those who unwittingly engage in depreciative actions. Sharp behavioral controls are needed for the former; gentle and polite education is all that is needed for the latter.

Yet the elegant simplicity of this paradigm wanes when brought into the light of reality. How does it address, for example, the following two situations:

•   On the Bright Angel Trail in Grand Canyon National Park, the murals of Anasazi Indians are cherished as "rock art" and are fervently protected by the National Park Service.

•   In Escondido, California, the murals of teenage gang members are decried as "vandalism" and are hastily removed by local officials.

In both instances, the actions that provoked response were similar—in terms of objective behavioral definition, function and meaning to those who created the actions. In both instances, needs were being expressed. In both instances, murals were created. Yet in the first case, there is regard for cultural value. In the second case, there is not. But for those who committed the acts, the cultural values may have been equally important. The decision to remove the murals in the second case was as much a statement about cultural tolerance, or even of political control, as about aesthetics (Cohen 1968).

The literature makes it clear that the meaning of concepts such as "depreciative behavior" and "vandalism" are fluid and culture-bound (Cohen 1984). Vandalism literature is prolific with tales about acts judged to be wholesomely normative by insiders, yet vandalistic by outsiders. For example, Oscar Newman (1973) in his essay on inner city life writes:

> In certain areas window breaking by small children during the course of a game (usually a competition to see who can break the most windows) is a highly institutionalized form of rule breaking. Derelict houses or houses under construction are usually chosen, and other frequent targets are empty milk bottles and beer bottles. Such activity is usually not regarded as deviant simply because it is part of the local tradition, or because the targets are regarded as fair game.

The literature also makes it clear that judgments about what constitutes depreciative behavior and vandalism can change with the evolving norms of a culture. In ancient Finland, for example, it was considered an act of reverence to shoot arrows into certain sacred trees as frequently as possible (Wise 1982). Today, the act surely would be judged environmentally and aesthetically unsound. It takes no stretch of the imagination to wonder if Mount Rushmore could have been created today on public lands. Certainly many well-intentioned individuals would perceive the act to be an extreme example of environmental vandalism, and would make it difficult for such a project to survive an environmental impact assessment process.

The problem remains: how to define depreciative behavior and vandalism in recreation settings? Clearly, categorizations of such behavior are fluid by nature, constantly changing and conforming to new circumstances.

In his work on the sociology of vandalism, Cohen (1984) suggests that the more illuminating question rests not in the behavioral domain (i.e., why do people do these bad things?) but in the definitional domain (i.e., why are these things construed as bad, deviant or socially problematic in the first place?). Deviance, Cohen maintains, is not a fixed entity to which people respond and around which social control policy is formed. To the contrary, it is through a fusion of tentative social definitions, individual responses and social control policies that particular behaviors acquire their "deviancy." Thus, deviancy is attributed to behavior rather than defined by behavior. Deviancy becomes a matter of degree and is subject to considerable social variability. The process of attribution also becomes political in that (a) not all forms of deviant behavior have rules against them, (b) not all the rules against deviant behavior are equally enforced, (c) not all rule breakers find themselves labeled and processed as deviant, and (d) all of these processes change as those authorities enacting social control policy change.

Cohen's perspective holds important implications for recreation policy-makers. Cohen suggests that we can learn more about the fundamental issues confronting us by studying the process of attribution rather than the process of behavior. However, such a focus has not characterized recreation inquiry. In our field, great detail has been amassed about who is conducting deviant acts, why, and what can be done to curb their behavior (Christensen 1986). Yet there has been very little inquiry on why certain acts are construed as deviant, and or on what the attribution process says about our values and goals as policy-makers.

Without such inquiry, the fundamental questions in depreciative behavior management will remain unsolved. Are we saddling the blame on the recreationists, when we ourselves may be triggering the behavior (Wise 1982)? Are we inadvertently discriminating against certain classes of recreationists because we hold a narrow perspective of what is appropriate (Schur 1980)? Are we unfairly closing out options for free choice because we haven't considered alternatives (Schreyer and Knopf 1984)? Until such questions are answered, we may never know if we are doing an adequate job of defining or managing the problems that confront recreation areas.

While we are waiting for maturation along these fronts within our own literature, there is much we can gain by examining the perspectives unfolding in other disciplines related to the motives and control of vandalism and depreciative behavior. These perspectives can force us to test our notions about the crucial problems of recreation management.

MOTIVATIONS FOR VANDALISM: CONCEPTS AND DIMENSIONS

There is abundant literature on the motives for vandalistic behavior, scattered well beyond recreation management (Alfano and Magill 1976) in such diverse fields as psychology (Zimbardo 1976), environmental psychology (Newman 1972), sociology (Davis 1980), criminology (Martin 1961) and education (Zwier and Vaughan 1984). From this literature, five broad concepts can be extracted that have bearing on our quest to understand the dynamics of vandalism in recreation areas.

First, the propensity to vandalize is more pervasively distributed throughout society than common intuition might suggest. Attempts to establish socioeconomic and ethnic correlates of vandalism behavior have repeatedly failed (Bates and McJunkins 1962, and Van Vliet 1984, Wise 1982). The implication seems to be that no social group is immune to vandalistic tendencies. In fact, numerous self-report surveys of adolescents have revealed that high proportions of purportedly "normal" young people admit to having recently committed at least one act of vandalism (Zimbardo 1976). There is even skepticism about the commonly expressed concern that propensities for vandalism are getting worse. Historical analyses reveal that complaints about vandalism extend back to the beginning of recorded history (Wise 1982).

Second, motives for vandalism are largely goal-directed. The consensus is that vandalistic acts are neither meaningless nor senseless, but are directed, like all other behaviors, toward resolution of needs (Cohen 1984).

Third, motives for vandalism are complex and diverse. In fact, the range and types of motives underlying vandalistic behavior resemble those identified for recreational behavior in general. Themes such as escape (Agnew 1985), control (Zimbardo 1976), achievement (Levy-Leboyer 1984), social affirmation (Brown 1978), exploration (Canter 1984), esteem enhancement (Wade 1967) and arousal (Allen and

Greenberger 1978) are prevalent in the literature. The notion that all vandalism carries a common motivational base has been repeatedly falsified by introspective analyses of vandals themselves (Canter 1984).

Fourth, different people engaging in the same kinds of vandalism can be searching for different kinds of psychological outcomes. Substantiating this concept are the writings of Griffiths and Shapland (1979), who invite us to consider the case of how a window in a deserted home might be broken:

> This may have been done by kids getting in to play; by older children as a game of skill; by adolescents or adults in order to remove the remaining furniture or fittings; by someone with a grudge against the landlord; by a pressure group to advertise the dereliction of empty property; or by an "old lag" to gain attention or to do mischief for the night.

The idea that different people engage in the same form of activity for different reasons is an old one in the recreation literature, yet vandalism has seldom been thought about in these terms (Knopf 1983). And, as would be true with any other form of recreation behavior, the response of management to vandalism necessarily has to vary according to the particular motives that precipitated the behavior (Canter 1984).

Fifth, vandalism is generally directed more toward public property than private property. The attractiveness of public property appears to be linked to: (1) the diffusion of ownership and the consequent diffusion of guilt since clear owners cannot be identified; (2) the lower probability of being apprehended, or being challenged if apprehended; (3) the obvious symbol public property provides as a societal or cultural good—a symbol against which statements can be made; (4) the sense that vandalism of public property is expected, and even built into the budget; and (5) the sense that "someone else" will have to bear the costs of cleanup rather than an immediately recognizable party (Ward 1973, Wilson 1979). The obvious inference here is that proclivity toward vandalizing public spaces can be broken by fostering attitudes of personal involvement, stewardship and ownership. While this implication may seem obvious, it is a notion not normally operationalized by managers of public spaces (Lewis 1973, Newman 1972).

Collectively, these five concepts point to the idea that vandalism is a prevalent aspect of the human condition, that it serves needs, and that the solution to problems related to vandalism may well rest in understanding these needs. But what are the natures of these needs? There appear to be three broad themes that circulate through the literature. These themes relate to people's quest for equity, competence and arousal.

The Need for Equity

The consensus is strong that part of what fuels vandalistic behavior is the desire to react to perceived injustice (Fisher and Baron 1982). Many vandals appear to regard the damage they commit as a form of rightful retaliation against prejudice, discrimination, abuse of power, unfair garnishment of resources, or unfair enforcement of rules and regulations (Wade 1967).

So how does the destruction of an object restore equity? Destruction may offer little more than a vehicle for exchanging rule breaking behaviors (Walster et al. 1978). Vandals respond to one broken set of rules (e.g., violations of fairness in resource distribution) with another (e.g., violations of the sanctity of public recreation resources). In a sense, the vandal is saying, "If they don't give us what we want, they won't get what they want."

Many authors have addressed the depth of the drive for equity among vandals (Adams 1963). They have suggested that the equity drive can account for why the best-intentioned actions aimed at vandalism control have produced the opposite of what was expected—more vandalism. As managers retrofit sites with "hard architecture" to control vandalism, they inadvertently amplify the symbolism of inequitable power arrangements. So, counterintuitive results emerge: attempts to control vandalism fuel the tendencies rather than dissipate them (Sommer 1974).

The Need for Competence

A second theme within the literature on motives for vandalism concerns the insatiable human drive for growth in competency and destiny control. Vandalistic acts are seen as a clear and dramatic statement of effectiveness. Vandalism is a momentary expression of who is in control. It is a way of making a mark, an affirmation that one can indeed make an impact in a world that seems largely beyond control (Zimbardo 1976).

One of the most common understandings is that vandalism is a by-product of chronic goal blockages (Brown 1978, Levey-Leboyer 1984). In fact, one perspective, dubbed the "strain theory" of vandalism, suggests that vandalistic acts are most likely to occur in social groups characterized by two features; first, they have few opportunities for success; second, they are operating in the shadows of others enjoying many opportunities for success (Agnew 1985). Whether the strain theory holds true is debatable (Arnold and Brungardt 1983). However, it seems clear that vandalism is a form of expression emanating from blocked needs. Selosse (1984) suggests that vandalism is a way to make a statement when less deviant ways of doing so have been grossly ineffective:

> Since no one listens to them, adolescents exchange the audible register for the visible. In this way, they leave their mark, create events and have apparent adventures. Young vandals refuse to remain dumb, i.e., with no way of expressing themselves: they seek to communicate at all costs.

The operational relevancy of the need for competence and control is not confined exclusively to those who lead lives of chronic goal suppression. The propensity for vandalism can emerge at any time within any population as perceptions of inadequate control develop (Baron and Fisher 1984). Moser's (1984) "faulty pay telephone" study reveals this propensity. In a study of a "normal" French population, he found acts of vandalism committed by over 50 percent of the people who did not receive proper coin return from a pay telephone.

Vandalistic acts can also be used to gain status within one's social group because others construe the acts as signs of effectiveness and control (Levy-Leboyer 1984). An individual can build social identity and even social prestige by engaging in behavior that is out of the ordinary, unaccountable and unlikely to be performed by others in the same situation (Zimbardo 1976). Or, it may be that certain acts judged as deviant by society at large become institutionalized as positive symbols of effectiveness and control within a smaller social group (Sutherland and Cressey 1982). Even in such cases, there are clear boundaries as to what constitutes acceptable behavior within the group. A normative definition is established of what behaviors are considered as "destructive," what kinds of destructive behaviors are expected as symbols of effectiveness to the group, what the "proper" objects that can be vandalized are, who the "acceptable" victims are, and what the "acceptable" contexts for displaying the behavior are (Wade 1967).

These norms clearly intervene in the expression of "deviant" behavior, and vary widely from group to group.

Once again, the literature is pointing to the premise that vandalism is not a senseless act. We find the vandals yearning for competence and control, and reading their environments for ways to express this yearning. Vandalism is goal-driven behavior, with legitimate needs expressed in ways that have been deemed illegitimate by those external to the world of effective functioning for the vandal.

The Need for Arousal

Much of the anecdotal literature on vandalism motives would lead to the conclusion that the destruction of an object can happen because, quite simply, it is just plain "fun" (Griffiths and Shapland 1979). Of course, the question that must necessarily follow is why the destruction might be "fun." Some investigators have suggested that the importance of "fun" rests not so much in the resolution of unmet needs, but in the sheer enjoyment associated with the act of destruction itself (Allen and Greenberger 1978, Bennett 1969).

The thinking in this regard is that the hedonic value of a vandalistic act can be understood in terms of its arousal-inducing properties (Allen and Greenberger 1978). Here, the suggestion is that all factors that contribute to the enjoyment of art, music, literature and preferred scenic vistas can also contribute to the enjoyment of the destruction of an object. Certain forms of destruction, such as the breaking of glass, generate the complexity, expectation, novelty, intensity and stimulus-structuring that is characteristic of an arousal-inducing stimulus. According to this perspective, people seek out objects in the environment that would break in an enjoyable way. Only norms that sanction against the expression of these desires would stop one from moving forward with the behavior (Wade 1967). Otherwise, the logic goes, people would be fascinated by many forms of destruction, purely for the aesthetics emerging from rearrangement of the stimulus array.

It may be that the power of normative sanctions against these intrinsic propensities dissipates as the levels of baseline boredom escalate. Under such conditions, the arousal-inducing properties of vandalism may increase (Griffiths and Shapland 1979). Numerous authors, relying on case reports of interviews with vandals, speak of the roles of boredom, exploration, curiosity and discovery in motivating the desire to destroy (Canter 1984, Van Dijk et al. 1984). This concept is graphically captured by Cohen's (1973) quote from the introspections of an adolescent vandal from Kansas City:

> The first time we did vandalism, me and my brother and another boy down at the garage, we were smoking and playing cards. They had some old cars in the back and we played around them. We cleaned them out one day. Swept out the broken glass from the busted windshields—rolled down the windows so we couldn't cut ourselves. This one guy threw a whiskey bottle up on the roof; then we threw another. It hit the side of the window. We just started throwing at the windows. When we were through, we'd broken 27 of them; we saw who could break the most. There wasn't anything else to do. We finally got tired and just left.

But arousal-seeking behaviors do not have to emanate from sheer boredom—they could also be motivated by common curiosity. Canter (1984) describes how people might be attracted to vandalize simply to discover how a system or object works. At one level, information is gained about the physical design of a damaged system or object. At another level, information is gained about the dynamics of social organization as one monitors social response to the damage. In the anecdotal literature, this phenomenon is often described as a drive by the vandal to "test the limits" of objects or people or rules (Van Dijk et al. 1984). By so doing, information is revealed to an individual about the way in which an object or society operates.

However tentative these assertions might be, it seems clear that vandalism is valued for its arousal-inducing properties. Several authors have suggested that vandalism can be controlled by offering other outlets for arousal, such as more meaningful employment or greater options for recreational behavior (Canter 1984). The irony here is that in searching for help to solve problems in recreation areas, we happen upon the recommendation to provide for more meaningful recreation opportunities in these areas. In a way, the literature is chastising the recreation field for not doing what it should be doing well—providing more meaningful recreation opportunities. The point of recreation management is to serve human needs, if these needs are served effectively, then the "problem" of vandalism in recreation locales should not emerge.

Typologies of Vandalism

Since the early 1960s, numerous investigators have produced typologies of vandalistic behavior that are intended to capture its motivational richness. The developmental flow of the typological initiatives has been summarized by Levy-Leboyer (1984). Three of the more popular typologies appear below, and they all imply that virtually no form of vandalistic behavior is meaningless. To the contrary, the collective implication is that almost all forms of vandalism provide some rather powerful service function to an individual striving to find a place in the larger social order.

One noteworthy typology is that of John Martin (1961), a scholar of juvenile vandalism. This typology is important historically as one of the first typologies to become broadly incorporated into research designs. The typology carries a tripartite structure:

1. Predatory vandalism—damage created as a means to an end, such as stealing copper from roofs and breaking parking meters to get coins.

2. Vindictive vandalism—damage created to express antagonism and hatred people feel toward specific individuals, groups and institutions.

3. Wanton vandalism—damage created through excitement, achievement or curiosity.

In recent years, the typology carrying the most popular appeal has been that developed by sociologist Stanley Cohen (1973). He expanded Martin's structure into a more effusive six-dimensional array:

1. Acquisitive vandalism—damage created in order to acquire material gain, such as money or goods.

2. Tactical vandalism—damage created in order to achieve some other end, as a means to declare a cause, to draw attention to a grievance, or to force a response.

3. Ideological vandalism—damage that is tactical in nature, but created explicitly to further an ideological cause.

4. Vindictive vandalism—damage created in order to obtain revenge, or to settle some real or imagined grievance.

5. Play vandalism—damage created during the course of a game or play, particularly when the motivations of fun, curiosity or competition are dominant.

6. Malicious vandalism—damage created as part of a general expression of rage or frustration against the perceived subversiveness of public and private institutions or anonymity-producing systems such as schools, subways and automobiles.

Cohen's typology remains definitive, and serves as the foundation for much research and speculation about the requirements of behavioral control mechanisms (Wise 1982). Within the recreation literature, the typing efforts are best represented by Vander Stoep's and

Gramann's (1987) typology. Vander Stoep and Gramann have also developed a six-dimensional structure, but rather than addressing forms of vandalism, they consider forms of behavioral violations that emerge within recreation areas:

1.Unintentional violations—violations created because recreationists are unaware that there are rules prohibiting certain types of behavior.

2.Releasor-cue violations—violations created because cues in the physical environment reduce normal social inhibitions against certain forms of unconventional behavior. In other words, the physical environment can "invite" violations due to non-friendly design elements or due to suggestions that the violations are normative (e.g., presence of picnic table carvings).

3.Uninformed violations—violations created because recreationists are unaware of the damaging consequences of their behavior.

4.Responsibility-denial violations—violations created because recreationists feel they can justifiably deny having a responsibility to conform.

5.Status-informing violations—violations created by normative compliance to a social group with deviant norms.

6. Willful violations—violations created by those pursuing goals in fundamental conflicts with resource protection. These goals may have several motivations, including financial gain, ideological protest, malice or revenge.

While there are many more typologies, these are typical in their noteworthy absence of any behavioral category implying a sense of purposelessness. Thus, activity in the typing arena continues to build the case for understanding vandalism as an integral element of social life rather than as an aberration.

Implications for Recreation Management

For the field of recreation management the implications of research on vandalism motivation are clear. Vandalism must be construed as an intelligent activity. Vandalism is not just a simple product of misguided judgment, but rather, a calculated attempt to express needs generated by the social-environmental-political milieu of an individual. The fault rests not with the deviant, as much as it rests with things gone awry in the environment. Vandalism is not aberrant behavior, but a genuine attempt to reconcile needs.

How the recreation profession responds to this insight will reveal a great deal about the character of our profession and the goals to which the profession ascribes its allegiance. If we continue to view vandals as culprits who need to be controlled, we will miss our quest as conveyors of optimal human experience.

We now turn to the question of what should be appropriate responses to vandalism and other depreciative behavior, given that these are need-reconciling behaviors. We consider appropriate responses by borrowing on insights from other disciplines in general and from persuasion theory in particular. We also raise questions about how the goals of recreation management may differ from the goals of managing behavior in other arenas. In so doing, we suggest that strategies for managing unwanted behaviors in recreation areas might substantially differ from strategies for managing unwanted behaviors in other kinds of environments.

RESPONDING TO THE MOTIVATIONS: DISCIPLINARY PERSPECTIVES

Research on the management and control of vandalism and depreciative behavior is prolific and widespread in many disciplines. This research has been subject to sharp criticism, primarily for its lack of coherent orientation (Richards 1979), the prevalence of ad hoc case studies rich with conjecture (Lesser 1978), and the absence of empirically-based evaluation research capable of directing management response and action (Christensen 1986). Nonetheless, that same body of research offers new perspectives on strategies for dealing with vandalism and depreciative behavior. The literature, in particular, has dispelled many myths about vandalism and about the ability of policymakers to deal with it. Some of the management insights that have emerged from four distinct disciplines are summarized below.

Recreation and Parks Management
Perhaps because of the applied nature of the recreation and parks management discipline, the recreation and parks literature seems to carry more review and synthesis publications on vandalism and depreciative behavior than any other field. Some of the more provocative reviews are offered by Clark (1976), Christensen and Clark (1979) and Gramann and Vander Stoep (1987). In 1976, a major symposium on vandalism and outdoor recreation generated 40 specific strategies for

mitigating vandalistic acts in recreation areas. The proceedings of that symposium (Alfano and Magill 1976) efficiently summarize the prevailing perspectives and practices in the recreation and parks field at that time. In addition to these resources, there are a number of management handbooks, rather exhaustive in scope, outlining strategies for managing vandalism and depreciative behavior. Some of the more comprehensive books include those by Christensen (1983), Dopkeen (1978), and Thayer et al. (1981).

A great deal of insight has been emerging from the rich conglomeration of research reviews, integrative treatises and technical assistance reports. We summarize the research below, framed in terms of ten pervasive themes.

First, there are many points of intervention in the management of vandalism and depreciative behavior. This theme echoes our just-completed review in this chapter of the literature on motives for vandalism, which concluded that the origin of depreciative behavior lies as much in the external environment as within the perpetrator. In a sweeping review of vandalism control strategies, Christensen and Clark (1979) posited nine basic arenas on which controls for vandalism should focus. None of the arenas identified are internal to the perpetrator. Christiansen (1983) identified 24 such external systems, including entities as disparate as the physical environment, the social referent group, the social context of the resource, the surrounding neighborhood, the management environment, the information environment, the legislative environment, the economic environment and the courts. The implication here is that managers and policy-makers need to operate effectively in a multiplicity of environments in order to control, dissipate or deflect depreciative acts. They are dealing not only with individuals, but also with many complex and virtually unbounded systems of influence.

Second, there are a number of behavioral control devices that range from direct forms of influence to indirect forms. Direct forms include coercive acts such as police enforcement and closure of access, while indirect forms include more subtle forms of influence such as user education and site design (Fish and Bury 1981). Across this spectrum, all forms of influence hold a certain level of effectiveness (Peterson and Lime 1979). But, given the quest of recreation management to facilitate freedom of choice, the more indirect forms of control are preferable (Lucas 1982).

Third, one of the most effective means of behavioral control is to simply provide recreationists with information about the consequences of their behavior. Research has repeatedly revealed that many of the depreciative acts transpiring in recreation areas are committed by people unaware of their impacts (Christensen and Clark 1979). Research has also repeatedly demonstrated that when the link between the actions of recreationists and environmental impact is made explicit, depreciative behavior declines (Gramann and Vander Stoep 1987). Perhaps the most frequently cited study in this regard is that of Oliver et al. (1985), who achieved a 50 percent reduction in tree damage and litter at a campground simply by distributing a brochure on low-impact camping to the patrons. While there have been numerous debates about why added information yields less depreciative behavior, the consensus seems to be that making people aware of their negative impacts increases the likelihood that prosocial norms will influence behavior (Gramann and Vander Stoep 1987, Heberlein 1972). Of course, the literature warns, there can be important exceptions: information, in certain cases, can serve to illuminate new targets of sensitivity around which people with vindictive or ideologically-driven depreciative tendencies can focus their behavior (Clark 1976).

Fourth, information transmitted through face-to-face communication tends to be more effective than information transmitted through nonpersonal media (Christensen 1981, Oliver et al. 1985). In the campground study by Oliver et al. (1985), incidents of tree damage and litter decreased an additional 25 percent when face-to-face contact was used in addition to brochures. Face-to-face communication has been judged to be more effective because of its holding power, increased credibility, ability to promote identification with agency goals and management, and ability to reduce the anonymity of visitors as potential helpers (Gramann et al. 1988). All of these elements are effective in promoting information transfer and facilitating helping behavior (Dovidio 1984, McGuire 1969).

Fifth, compliance to desired norms can be encouraged by offering rewards for appropriate behavior. This tenet has been demonstrated most convincingly in the littering arena, where modest awards have resulted in substantial changes in both littering behavior and litter pickup (Clark et al. 1972, Powers et a. 1973).

Sixth, compliance to desired norms can be encouraged by the presence of uniformed enforcement personnel. In an exemplary case study, Samdahl and Christensen (1985) found picnic table carving behavior to be correlated with objective measures of police patrol presence. It has been suggested that this control strategy is particularly effective in recreation areas because it causes people to behave conservatively in what tends to be a normatively ambiguous situation (Gramann and Vander Stoep 1986). However, it has also been suggested that police presence is effective only when potential perpetrators believe they will be detected, indicted and punished for the behavior in question (Clark 1976), which is hardly the case for most recreation areas (Clark et al. 1971). While there is philosophical resistance to the use of police presence in recreation areas (Lucas 1982), police presence does carry an important, and often overlooked, benefit. For many recreationists, police presence can effectively promote the treasured quest for freedom from victimization during the recreation experience (Christensen and Davis 1984).

Seventh, the imposition of rules and regulations as a management technique can fail if the rationale underlying the imposition is not communicated (Clark 1976, Hoots 1976). The failure can emanate from people's resistance to obvious restrictions on behavioral freedom in recreation areas. People attach great value to sensations of autonomy, independence and freedom during recreation experiences (Christensen 1986, Downing and Moutsinas 1978). However, recreationists can be enticed to embrace behavioral restrictions if they are afforded the opportunity to understand the negative consequences of not imposing the restrictions. Often, the costs of not imposing restrictions carry greater threats to freedom than imposing them (Heberlein 1972). There is, however, a potential caveat in this principle. If the recreationists find themselves disagreeing with the rationale, then the propensity to engage in the restricted behavior might actually increase through symbolic statements of disfavor (Christensen and Davis 1984).

Eighth, behavioral controls are more likely to be successful if recreationists are informed of reasonable alternatives to performing the undesired behaviors (Hoots 1976). Without substitutable options, the recreationist is less inclined to see the merit of foregoing a preferred behavior out of moral obligation to an external force (Dovidio 1984, Roggenbuck and Berrier 1982).

Ninth, in recreation areas there appears to be a norm of noninvolvement that impedes the development of social pressures against vandalism and depreciative behavior. In one study, nearly 80 percent of all depreciative acts in a campground area happened in the presence of other recreationists, yet there was no single instance of intervention (Clark et al. 1971). It seems that people value the freedom and positiveness of a recreation experience to such a degree that they are unwilling to set behaviors in motion that direct the experience away from those values. However, research has demonstrated that norms for noninvolvement can be broken through appeals for help (Christensen 1981). As recreationists are informed of the needs and methods for reporting rule infractions of others, they not only are more likely to intervene directly but also are less likely to commit the infractions themselves (Christensen and Clark 1983).

Tenth, it is clear that features of the physical environment profoundly affect the propensity to engage in vandalism or depreciative behavior in recreation settings. Some have speculated that as much as 90 percent of the vandalism in recreation areas can be attributed to improper design of the physical environment (Weinmayer 1973). Field managers are aware of the importance of intervention-based environmental design, and a flurry of technical guides for accomplishing this sort of design have been produced in response to their interests (Christiansen 1983, Dopkeen 1978, Shattuck 1987). But all this activity notwithstanding, there has been a surprising dearth of research on the role of the environment in affecting behavior in recreation areas (Clark 1976). In the meantime, numerous insights have been emerging from the field of environmental psychology that relate to this issue. We now turn to that arena.

Environmental Psychology

The field of environmental psychology bestows us with the perspective that depreciative propensities are better understood by examining the interactions of people with their environment, rather than focusing on characteristics of people themselves. Affirming an intuitive tenet of the recreation and parks field, environmental psychologists who have performed field surveys of property damage estimate that two-thirds to three-fourths of all vandalism can be attributed to characteristics of the physical setting (Wise 1982). Responding to these impressions, many researchers within the field of environmental psychology have developed integrative conceptual perspectives on the character of interactions between people, the environment, and vandalism propensities (Angel 1968, Jacobs 1961, Newman 1972, Perlgut 1983, Sykes 1979, Webb 1984, Wise 1982). Six themes of relevance to the management of vandalism in recreation areas seem to be emerging.

First, it is possible to design and create environments on a human scale that generate respect and a sense of belonging, thus dissipating tendencies toward depreciative acts (Jacobs 1961, Newman 1972). Some of the more vandal-prone settings have been criticized for incivility (Taylor et al. 1980), impersonal meaning (Wise 1982), anonymity (Angel 1968), ill-suitedness for naturally occurring activities (Jacobs 1961), incompleteness (Perlgut 1983) and architectural barrenness (Newman 1972). On the other hand, except in cases of ideological vandalism, vandals seem to avoid property that is attractive, well-maintained and seems to belong to someone who cares about it (Burall 1979). Some of the guidelines for invoking such human-scale settings include the use of natural rather than artificial materials, offering spaces for the expression of social life-styles and personal identities, and designing public spaces around more intimate modules rather than around large, communal, anonymous zones (Newman 1972). While the early advocates of the so-called human-scale design principles have been sharply criticized for the lack of empirical underpinnings for their beliefs, data that affirm the basic tenets of their perspectives are now beginning to emerge (Rubenstein et al. 1980, Sommer 1987).

Second, the propensity for deviant behavior can be reduced by redesigning what has been referred to as the environmental opportunity structure. In the case of vandalism, the opportunity structure is the collection of elements in the environment that allow for the expression of a deviant act (Cloward 1959). At one level, this opportunity structure calls for the removal of unattractive nuisances such as broken water pumps, unsecured construction areas, and closed facilities in secluded areas (Wade 1967). At another level, the opportunity structure concept calls for the development of vandal-resistant facilities and architectural designs, otherwise known as "target hardening" by the environmental planning community (Wise 1982). Scores of detailed guidelines, checklists and other options have been made available to the environmental planner, with boundless strategies for substituting the indestructible for the destructible in facility design (Leather and Matthews 1973, Sykes 1979).

Third, cues or props can be built into the environment to encourage certain forms of use and discourage others. Here, the underlying theme is that creative design can take on a role that accomplishes much more than fortifying the environment to resist attack (Wise 1982). Through behavioral channelling, people can be directed away from environmentally sensitive areas or objects and toward more environmentally enduring ones. Channelling cues can range from direct (traffic-control devices, fences, barrier enshrouded pathways) to subtle (planted flowers to deflect foot traffic, strategically placed benches and water fountains to shape traffic flow).

Fourth, environments that are vandal-prone should have their richness enhanced to allow for increased behavioral options and therefore, behavioral deflection. One of the corollaries of deopportunizing the environment is to offer options for diverting the behavioral expression harmlessly to more acceptable alternatives (Wise 1982). Enhanced richness may take the form of added recreation opportunities, greater complexity in architectural design or enhanced landscape amenities (Burall 1979, Newman 1972). The key is to offer substitute pathways for the expression of otherwise depreciative, need-driven behaviors.

Fifth, it is important to minimize cues in the environment that prompt an individual to regard a deviant act as not serious, or even as normative. Such cues, known as "releasor cues," hold the power of triggering depreciative behavior that otherwise would not have transpired (Marshall 1967). Perhaps the most common releasor cue is evidence of past vandalism. Vandalism seems to trigger even higher levels of vandalism (Samdahl and Christensen 1985). Releasor cues, however, are not confined to physical phenomena. People also search the social environment for cues on how to behave, and these cues can often establish a norm for deviancy. Little is known about the character of releasor cues beyond the fact that they do exist (Gramann and Vander Stoep 1987). But the clear message is that environmental planners need to identify, inventory, and manage these cues as part of any comprehensive program for reducing depreciative tendencies.

Sixth, elements of the physical array must be managed so that defacement, breakage and other forms of impact will provide less enjoyment for the vandals (Allen and Greenberger 1978). This means selecting structures, designs and types of material that provide for the lowest possible levels of complexity, novelty and intensity when they are destroyed. For example, large window panes could be divided into smaller ones (Allen and Greenberger 1978) and metal road signs favored as shooting targets could be replaced with plywood ones (Wise 1982). In concurrence with the findings of research on vandalism motivations, the goal is to minimize the potential for pleasure from the aesthetics of the destruction process itself.

Taken together, these six themes reveal the power of environmental design to affect the propensity for depreciative behaviors. Yet, it is clear that effective environmental design is not the panacea for all depreciative behavior. For perspectives on what other areas of influence might be, we now turn to research within the educational facilities management field.

Educational Research

In the United States alone, local school districts spend at least $200 million annually to replace and repair items damaged by vandalism (Zwier and Vaughan 1984). The result has been a surge of federally-sponsored inquiries and research initiatives on depreciative behavior and vandalism in school settings (Bayh 1978). Some substantive reviews of the voluminous literature on school vandalism are offered by Howard (1978), Tygart (1988), the United States National Institute of Education (1977), and Zwier and Vaughan (1984). While this body of literature has not been spared from concerns about its theoretical and empirical ineptness (Lesser 1978), many meaningful perspectives have emerged that hold clear implications for recreation management.

First, the field of education research has transformed itself with a paradigm shift, away from one paradigm that construes the school vandal as a culprit and toward another that construes the school vandal as a reflection of institutions, norms and community systems gone awry (Tygart 1987). It turned out that the early paradigm that placed blame upon the individual and sought mechanisms for controlling individual behavior was ineffective, because scientists discovered it presumed that systems extended to the individual were working well. In effect, the paradigm was arguing for changing undesired behaviors while emphasizing the importance of preserving the system that created the behaviors in the first place (Zwier and Vaughan 1984). The futility of this quest was not recognized until late inquiry in education research. There is now an imperative for understanding vandalistic acts not so much as aberrant behaviors of maladjusted individuals, but rather as symptoms of sickness inherent in the very systems that must bear the costs of these acts.

Second, management of depreciative behavior is more effective with positively oriented controls than with punitive or coercive controls. It is clear that school vandalism is just like any other form of vandalism in that it is driven largely by feelings of alienation and inadequate control (Mayer et al. 1987). It is also clear that punitive controls can act to intensify these drives rather than dissipate them—often failing to produce the intended outcomes (Lesser 1978). On the other hand, there seems to be no question that positive forms of intervention are profoundly effective. Lower levels of vandalism have been associated with positive acts such as increasing student involvement in governance and decision-making (Olson 1981), instilling a sense of belonging, identification and personal membership in the school (Goldman 1961), instilling positive reinforcers for appropriate behavior (Gold and Mann 1982), increasing participation in after-school activities (Steele 1978) and expanding the diversity of the curriculum (Howard 1978). The aim of all these acts is to arm students with a sense of power to control the outcomes of their education. With that power comes a restored sense of involvement and decreased propensity for depreciative acts (Mayer and Butterworth 1979).

Third, depreciative behavior can be managed in part by enrolling community support. Numerous studies have found that incidences of school vandalism decrease following the creation of community education programs, community advisory boards and other formalized channels of communication between the school and its surrounding community (Howard 1978; Steele 1978). Research shows that community involvement in school problem management and decision-making instills a spirit of common ownership, increased identification with problems and opportunities, and enhanced community vigilance (Danaher and Williamson 1983, Zwier and Vaughan 1984). But community involvement programs will be effective in reducing vandalism only to the extent that the programs are designed to meet the human and social needs of the larger community. The program must do more than solve a problem defined by managers or administrators, it must also be designed to meet a perceived need of the area residents (Ellison 1973).

Fourth, some of the fault for depreciative behavior may lie within aspects of management itself. Violence and vandalism in schools have been strongly correlated with management variables such as teacher apathy (Kiernan 1975), teacher disinterest in pupils (Cardinelli 1974), school administrators not sufficiently concerned with the welfare of staff and students (Goldman 1959), weak and casual administrative practices (Goldman 1961), administrative practices that unnecessarily foster student alienation (Howard 1978), poor communication between staff and within administration (Lesser 1978), low contact levels between maintenance people and clients (Levy-Leboyer 1984), poor informal structures and processes to solidify staff involvement (Lesser 1978), and low levels of social interaction among staff (Cardinelli 1974). The propensity for vandalism seems to be fueled by weak and autocratic administrators who do not fix their vision on the needs of their clientele.

Finally, the importance of effective physical design as a tool for ameliorating depreciative behavior is affirmed. Almost half of the literature on school vandalism concerns the design and protection of school buildings (Zwier and Vaughan 1984). Many detailed accounts on how to upgrade materials, design and construction practices have been written (Hathaway and Edwards 1972, Irwin 1978, Zeisel 1976). Favorite prevention strategies include using enhanced construction materials (Miller 1973), improved illumination (Falk and Colleti 1982), electronic surveillance and alarm systems (Faily and Roundtree 1979), and improved building layout and design (Leather and Matthews 1973). In addition to upgraded designs, maintaining cleanliness and attractiveness are also important. Clean, attractive designs are less subject to damage by vandals, regardless of their age (Howard 1978). Thus, there is convincing evidence from yet another body of literature that the physical setting significantly affects the propensity for depreciative acts.

In sum, the field of education research seems to say that we should find less fault with the vandal in recreation areas and more in the surrounding community, managerial and other social systems. We now turn to yet another set of disciplines that emphasize the importance of the social context—that of criminology and other branches of sociology. An even sharper definition of the role of the social environment in affecting response emerges from these fields.

Criminology and Sociology

Within the field of criminology and its parent discipline of sociology, the presumption is that depreciative behavior, like all other forms of behavior, can be understood only in relation to the larger social matrix in which the behavior occurs. Yet, despite all the research on social deviancy and human aggression within these fields, there has been a surprising absence of activity that focuses directly on depreciative behavior and vandalism (Davis 1980). Nonetheless, there are some important exceptions (e.g., Cohen 1984, Levy-Leboyer 1984, Martin 1961, Wade 1967, Ward 1973) from which emerge four clear themes with a direct bearing on managing depreciative behavior in recreation settings.

First, depreciative behavior is an outgrowth of social organization, so treatment is effective only to the degree that it contributes to social reorganization. Treatment requires reorganizing social structures to strike at the source of motives underlying vandalism, most notably alienation, lack of control, lack of expression and lack of personal identification with objects and spaces prone to vandalism. Some recommended strategies include: (1) increasing the number of programs for leisure behavior and options for community education (Thrasher 1936); (2) creating community spaces that are relevant to the needs of people who live near them (Wilson and Burbridge 1978); (3) creating channels for the expression of opinions and for becoming involved in the crafting of community destiny (Selosse 1984), (4) developing role models for the expression of positive norms as opposed to deviant ones (Korbin 1951); (5) introducing structures for community organization, purposivensss and cohesiveness (Martin 1961); (6) providing means for the expression of territorial behaviors (Taylor et al. 1978); (7) enlisting community leaders to organize preventive forces to serve their neighborhoods (Thrasher 1936); and (8) involving individuals prone to deviancy in programs designed to deal with their needs (Sutherland 1956). The importance of this perspective rests in the promise that much can be gained from instituting preventive efforts within local areas where depreciative behavior occurs, without having to solve personal problems or the deeper ills of society. Put another way, vandalism can be construed as a local problem that communities might be able to solve themselves with guidance and support.

Second, there are mechanisms for moving the behavioral norms of an individual away from depreciative activity and toward more conventional activity (Elliott et al. 1979). Such normative shifts can be accomplished through several routes (Kelman 1961). One route is by instilling within the individual a sense of moral obligation to subscribe to more conventional norms (Schwartz 1977). The tactic is to inform the individual of the negative consequences of not complying to conventional norms, and to shift the focus of responsibility for dealing with the consequences from others to the individual. In addition to appealing to one's interest in self-preservation, the intent is to appeal to the more basic human orientation toward helping behavior. A second route is through promoting identification with referent groups carrying more conventional norms, or with systems or objects likely to bear the results of depreciative behavior (Elliott et al. 1979). A third route is by offering tangible rewards for abandoning deviant norms. While each of these three routes offer lucrative possibilities for producing behavior shifts, the third is the least complex and most widely used. This may be unfortunate, for the changes evoked through the first two routes are more likely to change attitudes as well as behavior, paving the way for more enduring change that is not contingent upon the levying of threat or rewards (Gramann and Vander Stoep 1987).

Third, the administration of detection and punishment programs must reflect local values. In circumstances where law enforcement strategies are perceived as legitimate and effective, they are likely to be successful. In circumstances where such strategies are not viewed favorably, they are likely to be unsuccessful (Christensen 1986). To ensure success, policing programs must be consistent and not capricious, yet they must also reflect local norms and values (Davis 1980). And these programs must be built with a broad range of community representation, including representation by those most likely to commit deviant acts (Sutherland 1956). In sum, law enforcement programs serve as an effective deterrent to depreciative behavior, but are effective only to the degree to which they emerge from within the community as opposed to being imposed upon the community.

These three themes help expand our conception of deviant behavior as an entity remarkably responsive to social influences, and therefore to social control. While the notions seem plausible and the concepts seem rich, the criminology and sociology fields have a sharply limited body of research and empirically-based revelation on depreciative behavior and vandalism. Unfortunately, the study of depreciative behavior and vandalism has been dominated by investigators outside of these fields, carrying a bias toward motivational or dispositional explanations of depreciative behavior as individual actions. Our conception of depreciative behavior as an expression of the workings of the social milieu, rather than as an anomaly of it, remains impoverished (Cohen 1984).

Integration with Persuasion Concepts

We now turn to constructing a model for managing vandalism and depreciative behavior in recreation settings, by synthesizing concepts from the disciplinary initiatives just reviewed with concepts from persuasion theory in social psychology. To be successful, the model must incorporate the following perspectives that have emerged from the review just completed:

1. Vandalism and depreciative behavior is need-driven behavior; it is neither senseless nor meaningless.

2. Such behavior is only in part an emergent property of the individual; it is better understood as a reflection of environmental forces.

3. Important arenas of influence include peer groups, other recreation users, the physical environment, the surrounding community, the legislative and policy-making environment and the recreation management system itself.

4. There is a distinction, for purposes of recreation management, between vandalism and depreciative behavior; the distinction rests on the issue of intent.

5. The distinction implies different forms of treatment from a behavioral management or intervention perspective.

6. For both vandalism and depreciative behavior, these treatments range from subtle and unobtrusive to direct and coercive; in recreation management, the former should be exercised unless the latter is the only viable option.

The model is presented in Figure 1. It is constructed with the need-driven individual as its foundation element. This concept remains salient through the entire model. If a model of recreation management is to be true to the philosophical roots of the recreation field, the focus must rest upon the needs of the individual and not upon the needs of management. Some newer models of recreation management have been criticized for their tendency not to subscribe to this perspective (Schultz et al. 1988)

Influencing Systems

In the model, the need-driven individual acts within an interplay of interacting systems that can extend well beyond the recreation site. Four of the more important systems identified by past research are identified in the model, and include the social community system, the physical environment system, the social policy system and the management system.

Inclusion of the social community system implies that many of the forces giving birth to, shaping or ameliorating the propensity for vandalism and depreciative behavior lie within the bounds of social exchange. The social community is broadly defined, with frames of reference ranging from the individual's immediate recreation group, to other recreationists at the locale of interest, to broader reference groups such as family, friends and significant others, to the surrounding communities, to the individual's home neighborhood and to wider cultural values.

The physical environment system is similarly broad in scope, ranging from the immediate recreation locale of interest to broader

Figure 1
Model for the management of vandalism and depreciative behavior in recreation settings.

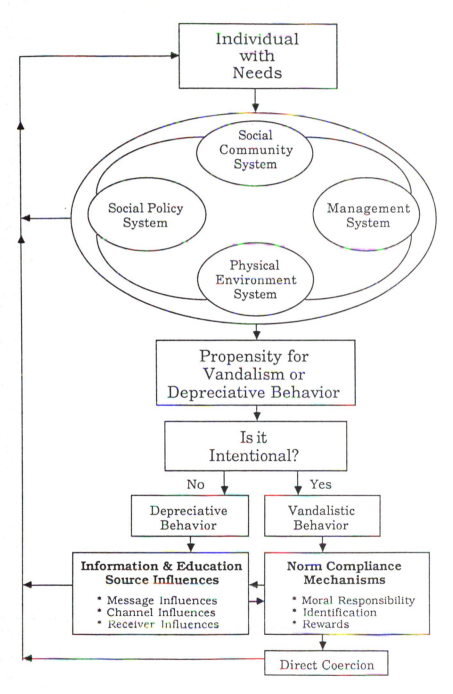

aspects of quality that impinge upon the individual's total life space. With respect to the former, the quest is to understand the role and power of designing the physical setting to deflect the propensity to engage in vandalism and depreciative behavior. With respect to the latter, the quest is to understand how the physical environment can be managed to prevent this propensity.

The social policy system is included in order to recognize the transitory character of what constitutes vandalism and depreciative behavior in recreation settings. Whether any given behavior is to be treated as a transgression is bound by both time and culture. The magnitude of seriousness ascribed to any given transgression is also bound by both time and culture. These perceptions are institutionalized and are often given legal interpretation in the social policy arena. Thus, to appreciate what behaviors are at issue in the model, to question whether they should even be included, and to understand what compliance mechanisms are available for treatment, the social policy arena is included as a primary sphere of influence.

Inclusion of the management system follows from the findings of education research that administrators of service delivery systems hold the capacity not only to dissipate depreciative behavior and vandalism, but to create depreciative behavior and vandalism. And since much of the influence is unintentional, generated by factors such as professional attitude, administrative style and procedural flaws, the management system needs to gain recognition as a salient force in managing vandalism and depreciative behavior in recreation settings.

The four systems in Figure 1 are framed within a circular schema, developed to imply that all the systems are interrelated with no ordered path of influence or linear cause-effect relationships. The schema is also organized to show the individual as working through and within these systems before the propensity for vandalism and depreciative behavior emerges. This is to acknowledge the power of the environment in shaping the propensity for vandalism and depreciative behavior that has been revealed in the literature. Finally, the schema is equipped with an exit arrow with a direct feed back to the foundational element (individual with needs). This loop, which offers a bypass around the propensity to engage in vandalism or depreciative behavior, implies that the systems can be managed so that the tendency to vandalize or engage in depreciative behavior never emerges. The model is arranged to imply that power is available for producing intervention strategies that are preventive, rather than reactive. This perspective echoes persistent calls in the recreation literature for prevention intervention, particularly intervention that extends into environments well beyond recreation spaces themselves (Knopf 1988). To a large degree, however, these calls have not been acted upon in practice.

The Question of Intent

Given the propensity to engage in vandalism or depreciative behavior, the model then suggests that the question of intent be resolved. Resolving this question allows us to distinguish the behavioral propensities into two fundamental classes, one class encompassing depreciative behavior and another encompassing vandalistic behavior. The former class is construed as unintentional, and the latter as intentional.

The question of intent is an important one. If the propensity is unintentional, behavioral interaction might successfully be accomplished through what Petty and Cacioppo (1981) call the central route to persuasion, which emphasizes the provision of information about the behavior and its consequences. The notion is that the provision of information may be all that is necessary when the primary reason for the propensity is a lack of awareness of rules, or the negative consequences of certain behaviors. If this route is successful, the individual will voluntarily shift away from the propensity to engage in depreciative behavior. The decision not to engage in depreciative behavior is then a self-determined behavior. The concept of freedom during the leisure experience is preserved.

However, if the propensity is intentional, the route to persuasion is more likely to be accomplished through what has been called the peripheral route to persuasion, which relies less upon voluntary change induced by information and more upon externally imposed compliance mechanisms, including direct coercion. This route may be successful in invoking the desired change, but it becomes unsuccessful to the extent that the individual perceives that freedom of choice is lost. Furthermore, the peripheral route, while still a viable management option, carries less permanency than the central route. Once the persuasion cues are removed, the propensity for vandalism returns. This is not the case for changes induced through the central route to persuasion (Petty and Cacioppo 1981).

In sum, the model implies that there are two basic categories of behavioral propensities, each with different implications for treatment. Depreciative, unintentional behavior offers the option for treatment through information and education. Vandalistic, intentional behavior suggests that more forced-compliance treatments may be necessary. But the model also suggests that even for vandalism, there is a hierarchy of forced-compliance mechanisms, some of which should be tried first before resorting to direct intervention through law enforcement and punishment. This hierarchy is important because there can be softer alternatives to direct coercion in invoking norm compliance. These softer alternatives also have less impact on perceived freedom for the recreationist. We now draw upon some perspectives from the persuasion literature to gain a better sense of what the various treatment options might be, the relative desirability of these options, and how each option might be executed successfully.

Information and Education

Of all the post-propensity treatments, the information and education option is the most desirable in order to maintain free choice behavior and induce permanent behavioral change. But, as is true for all the post-propensity treatments, the information and education option is less desirable than a treatment operating within the pre-propensity systems of influence.

Much insight has been produced by persuasive communication research on how to create effective programs of information and education to induce behavioral change. Since integrative reviews of the rather complex and unwieldy literature that surrounds persuasive research are already available (McGuire 1969, Petty and Cacioppo 1981), here we concentrate on a sampling of insights that can have a direct bearing on the construction of information and education programs in recreation settings. Our discussion is organized around four classes of variables that are often posited as discrete influencers of persuasive communication effectiveness: source variables, message variables, channel variables and recipient variables.

Source Influences. Research on source effects has made it clear that people can accept or reject a persuasive communication on the basis of source cues rather than on the content of the message itself. In recreation management, the source or originator of a message must be understood as a multidimensional entity. From the perspective of a recreationist, the source may be the person delivering the message, the local management authorities that created the message, or the broader institution or agency that framed the management context for the locale in question. In the latter cases, where the source of the message may not otherwise be obvious, simply identifying the source can have a substantial influence on how the message is received (Kelman 1961). This happens because identifying the source provides the recipient with information above and beyond the revelations of the message (Petty and Cacioppo 1981).

In addressing the issue of inducing voluntary change in recreation behavior through information and education programs, three tenets of the literature on source effects are particularly relevant. First, the source must be perceived by the recreationist as credible (Husek 1965). The source must be trusted for its ability to render expert advice, be informed, carry background evidence to back up the message actually delivered, be capable of representing the interests of a broader consistency, and be recognized by other people or social groups in which the recreationist has confidence. The more credibility the source has, the better. Recreation managers can maximize the effect of credibility by using sources ranking high in socially desirable dimensions such as education, intelligence, social status, age and rank in the professional hierarchy (Hovland et al. 1953). The effect of these variables appears to be so strong that some investigators contend that recipients will accept the conclusions of a persuasive message without paying attention to the arguments presented, as long as the source is highly credible (Anderson 1966).

A second tenet suggests that credibility must be combined with attractiveness if source effects are to be maximized positively (Byrne 1961). While attractiveness can emerge naturally because a recipient likes (Sherwood 1965) or is comfortably familiar (Newcomb 1961) with a source, attractiveness can also be manipulated by making the recipient perceive that the source shares common needs and goals (Burke 1962). In a recreation management context, this tenet suggests that the responsibility is on the source to convince the recreationist that needs and goals of the source and recipient are mutual.

A third tenet is that when the message is delivered face-to-face, sources should be selected on the basis of personal style (Goffman 1959). As a general rule, sources tend to be more effective when they possess such characteristics as good physical appearance (Berscheid and Walster 1974), high self-esteem (McCroskey 1975), dynamism (Ross 1981), high linguistic diversity (Bradac et al. 1976), the ability to analyze audiences (Ross 1981), the ability to invoke varying patterns of verbal emphasis (Ehrensberger 1945), and the tendency to dress conservatively (Mills and Aronson 1965). Selecting information and education specialists based upon these and other attributes identified in the persuasion literature (Goffman 1959, Ross 1981) may be one of the most readily adoptable but underutilized tools in recreation management today.

Message Influences. The impact of an information and education program, as we have seen, depends in part on who or what originates the program. But the program's impact is also influenced by how it is organized, ordered and framed with logic.

The most persuasive messages are those imbedded with high levels of comprehensibility (Bettinghaus 1961), organization (Thislethwaite et al. 1955), coherency (Ross 1981), and clear reasoning and argument (Ross 1981). Messages should be presented when the recipient is least susceptible to distraction (Petty et al. 1976), and more likely to be experiencing positive stimulation at the time the message is received (Rosnow 1966).

To maximize persuasive impact, messages must build on what is known to the recipients; that is, messages must be relevant to recipients' existing attitudes, experience and level of knowledge (Sigall and Helmreich 1969). The communication must also be tailored to an issue that is personally relevant or significant to the recipients (Petty and Cacioppo 1981). More persuasive messages tend to have stronger supporting arguments and a greater number of arguments (Calder et al. 1974). These messages tend to incorporate a certain level of reinforcement for the strongest arguments through review, recapitulation and other forms of repetition (Dietsch and Gurnee 1948). However, such repetition is confined to small doses (Stukat 1958).

The more effective messages must do more than present arguments—they must also converge upon a conclusion (Thistlethwaite et al. 1955). While it is effective for a message to state the conclusion explicitly, there is more persuasive potential if the message can be designed to help the recipients draw their own conclusions based upon the evidence prescribed (Linder and Worchel 1970). However, to accomplish this, recipients must be sufficiently motivated and able to draw their own conclusions (McGuire 1969).

If the recipients are likely to agree with the conclusion, it is probably not necessary or even desirable to address opposing perspectives (Lumsdaine and Janis 1953). To the contrary, if the recipients are open to or partial toward alternate conclusions, then two-sided discussion are more likely to be effective (Faison 1961).

Finally, it is clear that the order in which message contents are presented can influence persuasive impact (McGuire 1966). In general, the message should build from what is known to recipients to what is unknown (Ross 1981), from the least complex concepts to the most complex (Ross 1981), from the concepts that recipients most likely would find agreeable to those that most likely would be disagreeable (Tannenbaum 1966), and from the strongest arguments to the weaker arguments (McGuire 1957). If conclusions are to be made explicit, it is better to present these conclusions at the end of the message than to summarize them at the beginning (McGuire 1969). And if opinions of expert sources are incorporated within the message to endorse the conclusion, it is more effective to incorporate these opinions at the beginning of the message than at the end. If an attractive source is used, there is no such ordering effect (Husek 1965).

These insights are but a sampling of the extensive portfolio of insights related to message effects that have been developed in the persuasion literature. They point to the power of the persuasion literature in addressing issues of message construction in recreation settings. They also point to the necessity for recreation managers to extend their search for problem solutions well beyond the bounds of their own literature.

Channel Influences. Channel effects have to do with the medium through which the persuasive message is communicated. Persuasion theorists have conducted relatively little basic research on these effects, probably because basic theories have not been developed in a way that makes them interesting (McGuire 1969). However, communication practitioners have financial incentive to develop information on channel effectiveness, and have taken it upon themselves to catalyze research in this area.

The general finding is that, given the diversity of target audiences—and given the diversity of messages in terms of inherent appeal, complexity and potential for disagreement—the relative effectiveness of any particular channel is situational (Petty and Cacioppo 1981). However, some recurring themes do appear within that caveat.

Perhaps the most consistent finding is that face-to-face delivery of the message is more effective than delivery in written form (Cantril and Allport 1935). This finding has already proven applicable to recreation settings: Oliver et al. (1985) discovered that campground tree damage and litter decreased by 30 percent as face-to-face message conveyance was added to standard written forms of conveyance. Other things being equal, it appears that face-to-face communication has the edge in persuasive appeal over alternative ways to convey messages, including mass media (Katz and Lazarsfeld 1955). While there is a temptation to rely on mass media devices for their cost-effectiveness, there is also strong evidence that the persuasive impact of mass media is slight (Mendelsohn 1965, Wallack 1981).

In recreation areas, managers often need to weigh the benefits of two of the most heavily employed mediums—written forms of communication and audiovisual forms. From the perspective of persuasive impact, the issues become complex. It seems that complex messages are better comprehended in print than in audiovisual forms (Wright 1981). However, the recipient's tendency to yield to the accrued comprehension is more likely to occur with audiovisual communications than with written ones (Chaiken and Eagley 1976).

For complex issues, the most effective channeling devices seem to be the recipients themselves. When recipients are placed in a position of active participation in the conveyance process (e.g., gathering data, raising questions, generating answers), the potential for persuasive impact increases (Hovland and Mandell 1952).

Receiver Influences. The presumption underlying research on receiver effects is that the impact of a message is modulated by the character of the person receiving the message. Substantial research has been devoted to tracking the effects of variables such as age (Reymert and Kohn 1940), intelligence (Eagley and Warren 1976), gender (Eagley 1978) and self-esteem (Zellner 1970). While such effects have been proven operational, it is clear that they account for only a small portion of variance in persuasion accomplishment. The consensus is that receiver effects generally have less influence on persuasion impact than source, message and channel effects (Petty and Cacioppo 1981). At best, the effects are strongly situational—the relationship between personal variables and susceptibility to influence varies widely from situation to situation (McGuire 1969). Thus, rather than concentrating on the role of personal variables in affecting responses, recreation managers might better spend their energies designing optimal messages and channels that are relevant to the life spaces, attitudes and experiences of the broader social group being served (Petty and Cacioppo 1981, Sigall and Helmreich 1969).

The purpose of this review on information and education strategies is to suggest that the literature on persuasive communication is rich with perspectives that can help recreation managers design effective communications to deter depreciative behavior. The management model summarized in Figure 1 suggests that much of this behavior can be eliminated through these vehicles alone.

However, the model also suggests, with the exit arrow to the right of the information and education box, that not all forms of depreciative behavior will be changed voluntarily after information and education treatments. In such cases, more direct forms of norm compliance mechanisms need to be instituted if the goal is to eliminate all forms of depreciative behavior. It must be recognized, however, that the institution of secondary treatments would generate a new form of intrusion into the recreation experience, plus new financial expenses. Before considering the more direct forms of treatment, the costs of these added impacts must be weighed against the costs of allowing the remaining impacts from depreciative behavior to stand.

Norm Compliance Mechanisms

Our review of the criminology and sociology literature revealed three basic routes to establishing norm compliance: instilling moral obligation, promoting identification with groups possessing more desired norms, and administering rewards and punishment. In the management model in Figure 1, punishment by coercive force is reserved as a treatment of final resort, administered only if the other less direct forms of treatment fail.

Of the three routes, the moral obligation treatment is potentially the most productive, from the perspective of permanent behavior change. This treatment, which delivers appeal for the individual to engage in behavior that is morally responsible or correct from a broader societal view, engages the individual in active thinking about the issue at hand. The other two treatments are more peripheral and do not force such active thinking. Thus, the moral obligation treatment can be construed as a subset of broader forms of information and education treatments. The moral obligation treatment follows the more central route to persuasion by emphasizing the provision of information, and therefore can induce more permanent change (Petty and Cacioppo 1981). Since the moral obligation treatment is a form of information and education, all of the features reviewed earlier for that broader form of intervention are applicable to the moral obligation treatment. Yet the moral obligation treatment carries a subtle but managerially important distinction. Unlike general forms of information and education that are more placid from a direct intervention perspective, the moral obligation treatment seeks to impose a sense of guilt as a motivating force if the simple introduction of awareness is not effective (Kelman 1961).

In the persuasion literature, research on the identification process is not as advanced as that on more conventional message-dominated processes (McGuire 1969). Yet the notion of the potential power of the identification process as a behavioral change agent holds important implications for recreation management. The notion is that most individuals are motivated to establish gratifying relationships with others, and that this motivation can be captured in order to encourage individuals to exhibit behavior that is acceptable to those around them (Sherif and Sherif 1964). It is a well-known finding in social psychology that when individuals encounter opinions or behaviors discrepant from their own, there is considerable pressure to conform to the norms of the group (Festinger 1954). The goal for recreation managers, then, is to maximize a recreationist's exposure to groups with more managerially acceptable norms (Carnevale et al. 1982). This is done by introducing opportunities for identification with people or institutions carrying the more acceptable norms (Kelman 1961).

While the research on identification processes is limited, it points to effective strategies for inducing identification processes. One of the most effective strategies is to encourage identification with the management agency and its implicit creed of desired behavioral norms by playing on people's desire for ego or self-esteem enhancement, and by creating opportunities for enhancement by becoming a partner in management (McGuire 1969). Another strategy is to introduce role models capable of inspiring the expression of more conventional behaviors by individuals (Newcomb 1961). Yet another strategy is through bystander intervention programs, which break down tendencies for nonintervention by vandalism witnesses and encourage the expression of more conventional norms (Latane and Darley 1970). And there are, of course, strategies for designing the environment that encourage the mixing of normative structures to allow the dominance of more conventional norms (Lee 1972). Finally, information and education programs could be used to induce conformity by forcing exposure to the values of those who subscribe to more desired behaviors. The mere exposure to discrepant norms can set forces in motion for shifting normative behavior (Festinger 1954).

Reward and punishment processes are perhaps the most widely employed persuasive devices, and certainly among the simplest to design and administer (McGuire 1969). Given a choice between reward and punishment, the former should be the strategy. Rewards can be in the form of financial gain (Festinger and Carlsmith 1959), social affirmation (Zimbardo et al. 1965), or other opportunities for the gratification of blocked needs (Brown 1978). But as positive as the reward approach may seem, it involves little more than acquiescence to desired behaviors without private commitment to these behaviors. As soon as the reward structure is removed, the individual usually reverts back to the original propensity.

Direct Coercion

Direct coercion or forced compliance is the final intervention-related building block of our model, reserved as a last resort technique to control vandalism. In line with a precept from our review of the criminology literature, coercive efforts must be built with community input and must reflect local norms and values. Coercive efforts must also be judged as legitimate and effective, or they may unleash even greater reactionary levels of vandalism.

The persuasion literature further expands this notion that direct coercion methods have only situational effectiveness, suggesting that five conditions must be met before vandals will be influenced by coercive methods (McGuire 1969). First, it must be clear to potential vandals which behaviors are subject to punishment and which are not. Second, the punishment must be severe enough to make the attractiveness of compliance overshadow the attractiveness of noncompliance. Third, potential vandals must perceive that the administrators of a coercive control program can indeed impose the punishments. Fourth, potential vandals must perceive that program administrators do care about conformity, and care enough to use punishments consistently to bring about compliance. Fifth, potential vandals must believe that the administrators are able to observe them if they commit the unwanted behavior.

While these five conditions are important, they are particularly difficult to maintain in recreation areas. For one thing, control over punishment structures is often off-site and frequently not exercised. Furthermore, many vandal-prone recreation areas suffer from low maintenance and thus convey the impression that there is not much care for the areas. In addition, it is difficult to project an image that recreation areas are under steadfast observation, given the traditional philosophy of minimizing intrusion into the recreation experience, the expansiveness of many recreation sites, and the staffing limitations imposed by restricted budgets.

In conclusion, it is clear that the simple pronouncement of threat is not a sufficient deterrent to vandalism. Deterrence through threat works only when several contingencies are met. In the case of recreation areas, these contingencies often are not met. Yet, it would take little in the way of reconfigured management to meet these contingencies, and to thwart such behavior as a last resort.

An Integrated Model

In summary, our model (Fig. 1) poses an individual with needs acting in several systems of influence before the propensity to engage in depreciative behavior or vandalism in recreation areas even emerges. The model suggests that many propensities for such behaviors could be eliminated through intervention in the social community, in the physical environment, in the social policy arenas and in the recreation management system itself.

For propensities toward vandalism and depreciative behaviors that continue to exist, it is important to discern whether they are intentional. Information and education programs are considered to be the first line of defense against unintended propensities, or depreciative behavior. More direct intervention techniques to induce norm compliance are considered to be the first line of defense against intended propensities, or vandalistic behavior. However, the model implies that a mix of treatments may be necessary before any unwanted propensity is dissipated. Indeed, the recreation manager can resort to more direct and punitive forms of behavioral control through coercion. However, the model makes it clear that such hard intervention strategies are a last resort in the hierarchy of treatments—well beyond prepropensity treatments in the social, physical, policy, and management environments, well beyond information and education programs, and well beyond more subtle forms of norm compliance.

In short, the model provides an understanding of the deviant in recreation settings as an individual with needs—needs that might be serviced with a variety of treatments short of the imposition of punitive controls on his or her behavior.

DIRECTIONS FOR FUTURE RESEARCH

The model we have presented is by its very nature speculative and subject to refinement as further insights accrue in many disciplines. There are many unknowns. For example, we really do not know if more subtle forms of behavioral intervention hold power equal to that of direct coercion. And, we really do not know if all the systems of influence affecting the propensity for vandalism and depreciative behavior have been incorporated into the model. Nor do we know if the causal pathways among the systems have been adequately represented. The answers to some rather basic questions about the scope and content of the model must await empirical testing and theoretical advancements.

As we consider needs for future research, we would be remiss not to echo the perpetual plea of virtually every scholarly review of the literature on vandalism and depreciative behavior: we need greater theoretical development and more evaluation research (Canter 1984, Christensen 1984, Clark 1976, Van Vliet 1984).

In terms of theoretical development, vandalism and depreciative behavior must be understood not as an isolated or bounded activity, but as an aspect of a wider syndrome of needs, attitudes and environmental influences. From this perspective, most of the reviews indicate that existing theoretical structures are impoverished (Canter 1984). The various theoretical expressions, summarized in this chapter and used as a basis for constructing the model in Figure 1, have been built in isolation of each other, separated by disciplinary lines and by the individual philosophical perspectives of those who advocate these structures. The disciplinary boundaries need to be broken and the philosophical perspectives of individual researchers need to be expanded. Vandalism and depreciative behavior research must be situated within a more encompassing theoretical framework than it is at present (Levy-Leboyer 1984, Van Vliet 1984, Wilson 1979).

In terms of evaluation research, most reviewers have expressed dismay at the lack of information on the relative performance of various intervention strategies in different settings (Van Vliet 1984). Recreation managers have expressed concern that there is only minimal empirical guidance for helping them decide which strategies might work and which might not (Christensen 1986). As this review discloses, the literature carries an abundance of recommendations on how to approach and treat vandalism and depreciative behavior. The problem is that few of these recommendations have been translated into implementation, and that fewer still have been assessed with objective measures of their effectiveness. While some rather illuminating evaluation studies have begun to emerge in the recreation literature (eg., Christensen 1981, Clark et al. 1972), managers do not have an organized menu that clearly conveys what intervention strategies would be most effective under what conditions.

But beyond making these standard calls for more theory and evaluation, we would also be remiss not to call attention to needed research on vandalism and depreciative behavior issues unique to the recreation field. The recreation field should be committed to the provision of optimal experiences (Knopf 1983). In this light, the issues that need to be addressed when confronting depreciative behavior and vandalism are much more complex than simply figuring out how to stop those behaviors.

We frame the call for more research around three questions that hint at the complexity of vandalism. These questions echo, for the most part, the questions raised at the beginning of this review. What this suggests is that, after a prolonged and detailed journey through the literature, we are left with many of the same questions that prompted the journey. But these questions are fundamental, and the answers must be forthcoming if we are to effectively execute our roles as facilitators of the quest for optimal recreation.

What behaviors qualify as vandalism and depreciative behavior in recreation areas? At first glance, all that is really needed is a classification scheme, and a subsequent inventory of the degree to which catalogued behaviors appear in the field. But what we have learned is that social consensus on what constitutes such behavior is elusive, and definitions are often concocted for political or discriminatory purposes (Cohen 1968). For example, wilderness purists could attempt to exclude those with less purist philosophies from wilderness areas by decreeing what is normative for the latter group as illegal. Or, those people not sensitive to some of the unique needs of ethnic minority groups could inadvertently bar access by defining the ethnic groups' modes of interacting with the environment as deviant.

The definitional problems in our field are evidenced by the fact that managers frequently do not agree with recreationists about what forms of behavior are appropriate and inappropriate at specific locales (Clark 1976, Driessen 1978), or even about what forms of behavior constitute vandalism (Clark et al. 1972). Many questions remain: What exactly is deviant behavior? Why are there different points of view on what constitutes vandalism and depreciative behavior? Why are certain forms of behavior defined as "bad" and, more importantly, should they be? Is there potential for discrimination against certain classes of people with certain classes of needs? Is the very process of labeling behaviors and individuals obscuring our understanding of all recreationists as people with legitimate needs that require attention (Cohen 1968)?

The fundamental question that needs to be addressed is whether our desire to intervene and control in recreation areas is founded in our own perceptions and self-interests or in the perceptions and interests of the people we are trying to serve. While this question may never be fully answered, some empirical information would significantly advance our ability to answer this question.

What are the systems of influence on vandalism and depreciative behavior in recreation areas? Already, the broader literature on vandalism and depreciative behavior offers some direction. The literature has posited a number of influential factors such as the physical environment, the social community, the social policy arena and the management system. It has also specified a number of treatments for behavioral change, ranging from unobtrusive to coercive treatments. But we now need to advance beyond these generalities and specify the forces that are most germane in preventing or changing these behaviors in recreation areas.

Precisely what forms of information and education, what forms of more direct norm compliance mechanisms, and what forms of direct coercion are most effective? What specific dimensions of the social community are most relevant, and under what conditions? What are the relative roles of social influence and physical environmental influence upon the propensity to engage in vandalism and depreciative behavior? How adequately does the social policy arena represent the will of the social community? Which specific operations within this arena are effectively reducing the propensity to engage in vandalism and depreciative behavior, and which are failing? In what ways are management environments inadvertently creating greater propensities for vandalism and depreciative behavior? What are the relative contributions of the diverse sources of influence? What patterns of causality exist? Finally, and perhaps most importantly, what systems of influence are missing from our present models because of our own limitations in our disciplinary or philosophical perspectives?

Addressing such questions will equip us with an awareness that those people engaging in vandalism and depreciative behavior in recreation areas have needs that are no more or less legitimate than those of other recreationists. And, the answers will also equip us with a strategy for dissipating the propensity to engage in depreciative behavior and vandalism well before the individual arrives at the recreation site.

What is the role of perceived freedom in mediating response to vandalism and depreciative behavior? This question brings us to the heart of why the treatment of undesirable behavior in recreation areas may be a fundamentally different problem than the treatment of undesirable behaviors in other areas. Philosophically, the quest of recreation is not to control, but to unleash (Knopf 1990). But implicit in our models for managing vandalism and depreciative behavior is the understanding that without a certain level of behavior control, many other forms of freedom would be lost, such as the freedom to experience an environment unmarred by vandalism or depreciative behavior.

The question then becomes, how does perceived freedom operate as a variable in managing recreation experiences? To what degree is it possible to maximize perceived freedom, given that perfect freedom for one recreationist can generate imperfect freedom for another? Can we measure the impact of one person's behavior upon the perceived freedom of another? Can we develop models to help us understand the trade-offs between intervention and nonintervention in terms of maximizing overall perceived freedom within a recreation locale? Can we identify intervention strategies that maximize behavioral control, yet minimize disruption of perceived freedom? In the way we tend to intervene, are we limiting the options for free choice because we haven't considered alternatives?

To date, there is no instrumentation available to help a manager monitor the real impacts of vandalism and depreciative behavior upon other recreationists. Conversely, there is no instrumentation available to assess the total impact of an intervention strategy upon the person one seeks to control. Without such data, the trade-offs between the consequences of intervention and the consequences of nonintervention can never be fully assessed.

There is another compelling reason to understand the operational effects of the quest for freedom beyond that of maximizing satisfaction levels for the recreationist. Recreationists clearly treasure their freedom

(Christensen and Davis 1984). Thus, when they encounter intervention strategies that they construe to be threats to their freedom, they may attempt to reassert their freedom by resisting change or even by exhibiting behavior overtly opposed to the intentions of the intervention (Worchel and Brehm 1970). As we have stated in this review, this has often been the case in arenas that have been target-hardened or have experienced new forms of behavioral restrictions (Wise 1982). In sum, research is needed not only on the impact of intervention upon perceived freedom, but also on how individuals will behave in response to intervention. Without such information, managers run the risk of generating secondary effects that run counter to the goal of intervention.

CONCLUSION

In this chapter we have provided a perspective that tests prevailing notions about the fundamental problems of recreation management. Rather than promote strategies to extinguish vandalistic and depreciative behavior, we have prompted recreation professionals to understand deviant behavior, to discern the forces that give it substance, to examine the human needs that fuel it, and to meet those needs in ways that minimize impacts on the environment and other people.

Research on school vandalism shows that if the school is damaged, there must be something wrong with the school and the school's community (Cohen 1968); the highest rates of vandalism tend to occur in schools with obsolete facilities and equipment, low staff morale, and high dissatisfaction and boredom among pupils. The same concepts may apply to recreation areas, where we see that vandalistic and depreciative behaviors are need-driven, rather than capricious acts. As recreation managers, we need to spend more time identifying the sources of those needs, and engineering ways to address them.

Our review has affirmed that coercive force will sometimes be necessary, particularly when its absence would result in the erosion of positive experiences for those who comply with desired norms. However, we have also made it clear that alternatives to coercive force exist, and that these alternatives have not been fully exercised in recreation settings. Perhaps this is true because we, as recreation managers, have not entirely come to grips wiht the reality that those who exhibit deviant behaviors have needs that, in many ways, differ little from the needs of other recreationists.

As we come to understand deviants as individuals with unique needs, we are more likely to discover alternatives to punishment for managing behavior. Perhaps what our review offers most explicitly is an emergent imperative for change; that the recreation profession should carry less judgmentalism and more compassion as it sweeps with increasing force into the arena of behavioral control.

REFERENCES

Adams, J.S. 1963. Toward an understanding of inequity. *Journal of Abnormal and Social Psychology.* *67*: 422-436.

Agnew, R. 1985. A revised strained theory of delinquency. *Social Forces.* *64*: 151-671.

Alfano, S.; Magill, A. (eds.). 1976. Vandalism and outdoor recreation: symposium proceedings. *USDA Forest Service General Technical Report PSW-17.* Berkeley, CA: Pacific Southwest Forest and Range Experiment Station. 72 p.

Allen, V.L. 1984. Toward an understanding of the hedonic component in vandalism. In: Levy-Leboyer, C., (ed.) *Vandalism:behavior and motivation.* New York, NY: Elsevier Science Publishing Company: 77-89.

Allen, V.L.; Greenberger, D.B. 1978. An aesthetic theory of vandalism. *Crime and Delinquency.* *24*: 309-321.

Angel, S. 1968. Discouraging crime through city planning. *Institute of Urban and Regional Development Working Paper No. 75.* Berkeley, CA: University of California. 75 p.

Anderson, L.R. 1966. Discrediting sources as a means of belief defense of cultural truisms. *American Psychologist.* *21*: 708.

Arnold, W.R.; Brungardt, T.M. 1983. *Juvenile misconduct and delinquency.* Boston, MA: Houghton-Mifflin Company. 482 p.

Baron, R.M.; Fisher, J.D. 1984. The equity-control model of vandalism: a refinement. In: Levy-Leboyer, C., (ed.) *Vandalism: behavior and motivation.* New York, NY: 63-75.

Bates, W.; McJunkins, T. 1962. Vandalism and status differences. *Pacific Sociological Review.* *5* (2): 89-92.

Bayh, B. 1978. School violence and vandalism: problems and solutions. *Journal of Research and Development in Education.* *11* (2): 3-7.

Bennett, J.W. 1969. *Vandals Wild.* Portland, OR: Bennett-Publishing House Company. 236 p.

Berscheid, E.; Walster, E. 1974. Physical attractiveness. In: Berkowitz, L., (ed.) *Advances in Experimental Social Psychology, Volume 7.* New York, NY: Academic Press: 174-189.

Bettinghaus, E.P. 1961. Operation of congruity in an oral communication setting. *Speech Monographs.* *28*: 131-142.

Bradac, J.J.; Konsky, C.W.; Davies, R.A. 1976. Two studies of the effects of linguistic diversity upon judgements of communicator attributes and message effectiveness. *Communication Monographs*. *43*: 70-79.

Brown, W.K. 1978. Graffiti, identity and the delinquent gang. *International Journal of Offender Therapy and Comparative Criminology*. *22* (1): 46-48.

Burall, P. 1979. Introduction to designing against vandalism. In: Sykes, J., (ed.) *Designing against vandalism*. London: Heinemann Educational Books: 7-10.

Burke, K. 1962. *A grammar of motives and a rhetoric of motives*. Cleveland, OH. World Publishing. 272 p.

Byrne, D. 1961. International attraction and attitude similarity. *Journal of Abnormal Social Psychology*. *62*: 713-715.

Calder, B.J.; Insko, C.A.; Yandell, B. 1974. The relation of cognitive and memorial processes to persuasion in a simulated jury trial. *Journal of Applied Social Psychology*. *4*: 62-93.

Canter, D. 1984. Vandalism: overview and prospect. In: Levy-Leboyer, C., (ed.) *Vandalism: behavior and motivation*. New York, NY: Elsevier Science Publishing Company: 345-356.

Cantril, H.; Allport, G.W. 1935. *The psychology of radio*. New York, NY: Harper. 276 p.

Cardinelli, C.F. 1974. Another view: Let's get at the causes of youthful vandalism. *The American School Board Journal*. *61* (1): 68-69.

Carnevale, P.J.: Pruitt, D.G.; Carrington, P.I. 1982. Effects of future dependence, liking and repeated requests for help or helping behavior. *Social Psychology Quarterly*. *45*: 1-9.

Chaiken, S.; Eagley, A.H. 1976. Communication modality as a determinant of message persuasiveness and message comprehensibility. *Journal of Personality and Social Psychology*. *34*: 605-614.

Christensen, H.H. 1981. Bystander intervention and litter control: evaluation of an appeal-to-help program. *USDA Forest Service Research Paper PNW-287*. Portland, OR: Pacific Northwest Forest and Range Experiment Station. 25 p.

Christensen, H.H. 1986. Vandalism and depreciative behavior. In: *President's Commission on Americans Outdoors: literature review*. Washington, DC: U.S. Government Printing Office: 73-85.

Christensen, H.H.; Clark, R.N. 1979. Understanding and controlling vandalism and other rule violations in urban areas. In: Proceedings, national urban forestry conference. *Environmental Sciences and Forestry Publication 80-003*. Syracuse, NY: State University of New York, College of Environmental Sciences and Forestry: 63-84.

Christensen, H.H.; Clark, R.N. 1983. Increasing public involvement to reduce depreciative behavior in recreation settings. *Leisure Sciences. 5* (4): 359-379.

Christensen, H.H.; Davis, N.J. 1984. Evaluating user impacts and management controls: implications for recreation choice behavior. In: Proceedings-symposium on recreation choice behavior. *USDA Forest Service General Technical Report INT-184.* Ogden, UT: Intermountain Forest and Range Experiment Station: 71-77.

Christiansen, M.L. 1983. *Vandalism control management for parks and recreation.* State College, PA: Venture Publications. 123 p.

Clark, R.N. 1976. Control of vandalism in recreation areas—fact, fiction, or folklore? In: Alfano, S.S. and Magill, A.W., (eds.) Vandalism and outdoor recreation: symposium proceedings. *USDA Forest Service General Technical Report PSW-17.* Berkeley, CA: Pacific Southwest Forest and Range Experiment Station: 62-72.

Clark, R.N.; Burgess, R.L.; Hendee, J.C. 1972. The development of anti-litter behavior in a forest campground. *Journal of Applied Behavioral Analysis. 5* (1): 1-5.

Clark, R.N.; Hendee, J.C.; Campbell, F.L. 1971. values, behavior and conflict in modern camping culture. *Journal of Leisure Research. 3* (3): 143-159.

Cloward, R.A. 1959. Illegitimate means, anomie and deviant behavior. *American Sociological Review. 24*: 168-175.

Cohen, S. 1968. The politics of vandalism. *The Nation.* 207 (16): 497-500.

Cohen, S. 1973. Property destruction: motives and meanings. In: Ward, C., (ed.) *Vandalism.* London: Architectural Press: 23-53.

Cohen, S. 1984. Sociological approaches to vandalism. In: Levy-Leboyer, C., (ed.) *Vandalism: behavior and motivation.* New York, NY: Elsevier Science Publishing Company: 51-61.

Danaher, D.; Williamson, J.D. 1983. Newtown blues: planning versus mutual co-operation. *International Journal of Social Psychiatry. 29*: 147-152.

Davis, N.J. 1980. *Sociological constructions of deviance: perspectives and issues in the field.* Dubuque, IA: William C. Brown Publishers. 264 p.

Dietsch, R.W.; Gurnee H. 1948. Cumulative effects of a series of campaign leaflets. *Journal of Applied Psychology. 32*: 189-194.

Driessen, J. 1978. *Problems in managing forest recreation facilities: a survey of field personnel.* Missoula, MT: USDA Forest Service, Equipment Development Center. 106 p.

Dopkeen, J.C. 1978. *Managing vandalism: a guide to reducing damage in parks and recreation areas.* Boston, MA: Parkman Center for Urban Affairs, City of Boston. 157 p.

Dovidio, J.F. 1984. Helping behavior and altruism: an empirical and conceptual overview. In: Berkowitz, C., (ed.) *Advances in Experimental Social Psychology*, Volume 17. New York, NY: Academic Press: 361-427.

Downing, K.B.; Moutsinas, C.M. 1978. Managers' views of dispersed recreation along forest roads. *Journal of Forestry. 76* (9): 583-585.

Eagley, A.H.; Warren, R. 1976. Intelligence, comprehension, and opinion change. *Journal of Personality. 44*: 226-242.

Eagley, A.H. 1978. Sex differences in influenceability. *Psychological Bulletin. 85*: 86-116.

Ehrensberger, R. 1945. An experimental study of the relative effectiveness of certain forms of emphasis in public speaking. *Speech Monographs. 12* (2): 94-111.

Elliott, D.S.; Ageton, S.S.; Canter, R.J. 1979. An integrated theoretical perspective on delinquent behavior. *Journal of Research in Crime and Delinquency. 9*: 3-27.

Ellison, W.S. 1973. School vandalism: one hundred million dollar challenge. *Community Education Journal. 3*(1): 27-33, 50-52.

Faily, A.; Roundtree, G.A. 1979. Combatting violence and vandalism in schools. *National Association of Secondary School Principals Bulletin. 58* (384): 44-49.

Faison, E.W. 1961. Effectiveness of one-sided and two-sided mass communications and advertising. *Public Opinion Quarterly. 25*: 468-469.

Falk, N.; Coletti, R.F. 1982. Better vandalism protection at less cost. *American School and University. 54* (6): 52-54.

Festinger, L. 1954. A theory of social comparison processes. *Human Relations. 7*: 117-140.

Fistinger, L.; Carlsmith, J.M. 1959. Cognitive consequences of forced compliance. *Journal of Abnormal Social Psychology. 58*: 203-210.

Fish, C.B.; Bury, R.L. 1981. Wilderness visitor management: diversity and agency policies. *Journal of Forestry. 79* (9): 608-612.

Fisher, J.D.; Baron, R.M. 1982. An equity-based model of vandalism. *Population and Environment. 5* (3): 182-200.

Goffman, E. 1959. *The presentation of self in everyday life.* Garden City, NY: Doubleday. 327 p.

Gold, M.; Mann, D.W. 1982. Alternative schools for troublesome secondary students. *The Urban Review. 14*: 305-316.

Goldman, N. 1959. *A sociopsychological study of school vandalism.* Syracuse, NY: Syracuse University, New York Research Institute. (ERIC Document No. ED 002 807). 37 p.

Goldman, N. 1961. A sociopsychological study of school vandalism. *Crime and Delinquency. 7* (3): 221-230.

Gramann, J.; Christensen, H.H.; Vander Stoep, G.A. 1988. Indirect management to protect cultural and natural resources: research, ethics and social policy. Paper presented at the International Symposium on Vandalism: Research, Prevention and Social Policy, April 20-22. Seattle, Washington. 41 p.

Gramann, J.; Vander Stoep, G.A. 1986. *Reducing depreciative behavior at Shiloh National Military Park.* College Station, TX: Texas A&M University, Department of Recreation Resources. 136 p.

Gramann, J.; Vander Stoep, G.A. 1987. Prosocial behavior theory and natural resource protection: a conceptual synthesis. *Journal of Environment Management. 24*: 247-257.

Griffiths, R., Shapland, J.M. 1979. The vandal's perspective: meanings and motives. In: Burall, P., (ed.) *Designing against vandalism.* London: Heinemann Educational Books, Ltd.: 11-18.

Harrison, A. 1982. Problems: vandalism and depreciative behavior. In: Sharpe, G.W., (ed.) *Interpreting the environment, 2nd edition.* New York, NY: John Wiley and Sons: 473-495.

Hathaway, J.A.; Edwards, L.F. 1972. How to (just about) vandal-proof every school in your district. *American School Board Journal. 159* (7): 27-31.

Heberlein, T.A. 1972. The land ethnic realized: some psychological explanations for changing environmental attitudes. *Journal of Social Issues. 28*: 79-87.

Hoots, T.A. 1976. Vandalism and law enforcement in national forest lands. In: Alfano, S.; Magill, A., (eds). Vandalism and outdoor recreation symposium proceedings. *USDA Forest Service General Technical Report PSW-17.* Berkeley,CA: Pacific Southwest Forest and Range Experiment Station: 20-22.

Hovland, C.I.; Janis, I.L.; Kelley, H.H. 1953. *Communication and persuasion.* New Haven, CT: Yale University Press. 437 p.

Hovland, C.I.; Mandell, W. 1952. An experimental comparison of conclusion-drawing by the communicator and by the audience. *Journal of Abnormal and Social Psychology. 47*: 581-588.

Howard, J.L. 1978. Factors in school vandalism. Journal of Research and *Development in Education. 11* (2): 53-63.

Husek, T.R. 1965. Persuasive impacts on early, late or no mention of a negative source. *Journal of Personality and Social Psychology. 2*: 125-128.

Irwin, G. 1978. Planning vandalism-resistant educational facilities. *Journal of Research and Development in Education. 11* (2): 42-52.

Jacobs, J. 1961. *Death and life of great american cities.* Harmondsworth, NY: Penguin. 458 p.

Katz, E.; Lazarsfeld, P. 1955. *Personal influence.* Glencoe, IL: Free Press. 523 p.

Kelman, H.C. 1961. Processes of opinion change. *Public Opinion Quarterly. 25*: 57-78.

Kiernan, O.B. 1975. *School violence and vandalism*. Washington, DC: National Association of Secondary School Principals. (ERIC Document No. ED 106987). 15 p.

Knopf, R.C. 1983. Recreational needs and behavior in natural settings. In: Altman, I.I.; Wohlwill, J.F., (eds). *Behavior and the natural environment*. New York, NY: Plenum: 204-233.

Knopf, R.C. 1988. *Human experience and wildlands: a review of needs and policy*. Western Wildlands. 14 (3): 2-7.

Knopf, R.C. 1990. Marketing public lands: is it the right thing to do? *Parks and Recreation*. March: 56-61.

Korbin, S. 1951. The conflict of values in delinquency areas. *American Sociological Review*. *16*: 653-661.

Latane, B.; Darley, J.M. 1970. *The unresponsive bystander: why doesn't he help?* New York, NY: Appleton-Century-Crofts. 242 p.

Leather, A.; Matthews, A. 1973. What the architect can do: a series of design guidelines. In: Ward, C., (ed.) *Vandalism*. New York, NY: Van Nostrand Reinhold: 117-172.

Lee, R.G. 1972. The social definition of outdoor recreation places. In: Burch, W.R.; Cheek, N.H.; Taylor, L., (eds). *Social behavior, natural resources and the environment*. New York, NY: Harper and Row: 68-84.

Lesser, P. 1978. Social science and educational policy: the case of school violence. *Urban Education*. *12* (4): 389-411.

Levy-Leboyer, C. 1984. Vandalism and the social sciences. In: Levy-Leboyer, C., (ed.) *Vandalism: behavior and motivation*. New York, NY: Elsevier Science Publishing Company: 1-11.

Lewis, C.A. 1973. People-plant interaction: a new horticultural perspective. *American Horticulturalist*. *(52)*: 18-25.

Lucas, R.C. 1982. Recreation regulations—when are they needed? *Journal of Forestry*. *80*: 148-151.

Lumsdaine, A.A.; Janis, I.L. 1953. Resistance to "counterpropaganda" produced by one-sided and two-sided "propaganda" presentations. *Public Opinion Quarterly*. *17*: 311-318.

Marshall, T. 1967. Vandalism: the seeds of destruction. *New Society*. (June 17): 625-627.

Martin, J.M. 1961. *Juvenile vandalism: a study of its nature and prevention*. Springfield, IL: Charles C. Thomas Publishing. 189 p.

Mayer, G.R.; Butterworth, T.W. 1979. A preventive approach to school violence and vandalism: an experimental study. *The Personnel and Guidance Journal*. *57*: 436-441.

Mayer, G.R.; Nafpaktitis, M.; Butterworth, T.; Hollingsworth, P. 1987. A search for the elusive setting effects of school vandalism: a correlational study. *Education and Treatment of Children*. *10* (3): 259-270.

McCroskey, J. 1975. The effects of communication apprehension on interpersonal attraction. *Human Communication Research*. *2* (1): 51-65.

McGuire, W.J. 1957. Order of presentation as a factor in 'conditioning' persuasiveness. In: Hovland, C.I., (ed.) *Order of presentation in persuasiveness.* New Haven, CT: Yale University Press: 98-414.

McGuire, W.J. 1966. Attitudes and opinions. *Annual Review of Psychology. 17:* 475-514.

McGuire, W.J. 1969. The nature of attitudes and attitude change. In: Linzey, G.; Aronson, E., (eds.) *The handbook of social psychology.* Reading, MA: Addison-Wesley Publishing Company: 136-314.

Mendelsohn, H. 1965. Ballots and broadcasts, exposure to election broadcasts and terminal voting decisions. *Public Opinion Quarterly. 29:* 445-446.

Miller, A. 1973. Vandalism and the architect. In: Ward, C., (ed.) *Vandalism.* New York, NY: Van Nostrand Reinhold: 96-111.

Mills, J.; Aronson, E. 1965. Opinion change as a function of communicator's attractiveness and desire to influence. *Journal of Personality and Social Psychology. 1:* 173-177.

Moser, G. 1984. Everyday vandalism. In: Levy-Leboyer, C., (ed.) *Vandalism: behavior and motivation.* New York, NY: Elsevier Science Publishing Company: 167-174.

Newcomb, T.M. 1961. *The acquaintance process.* New York, NY: Holt, Rinehart and Winston. 432 p.

Newman, O. 1972. *Defensible space.* London: The Architectural Press. 264 p.

Oliver, S.S.; Roggenbuck, J.W.; Watson, A.E. 1985. Education to reduce impacts in forest campgrounds. *Journal of Forestry. 83* (4): 234-236.

Olson, J.R. 1981. Curbing vandalism and theft. *Educational Horizons. 59* (4): 195-197.

Perlgut, D. 1983. Vandalism: the environmental crime. *Australian Journal of Social Issues. 18* (3): 209-216.

Peterson, G.L.; Lime, D.W. 1979. People and their behavior: a challenge for recreation management. *Journal of Forestry. 80:* 343-346.

Petty, R.E.; Cacioppo, J.T. 1981. *Attitudes and persuasion: classic and contemporary approaches.* Dubuque, IA: William C. Brown Company. 314 p.

Petty, R.E.; Wells, G.L.; Brock, T.C. 1976. Distraction can enhance or reduce yielding to propaganda: tough disruption versus effort justification. *Journal of Personality and Social Psychology. 34:* 874-884.

Powers, R.B.; Osborne, J.G.; Anderson, E.G. 1973. Positive reinforcement of litter removal in the natural environment. *Journal of Applied Behavior Analysis. 6:* 579-586.

Reymert, M.L. Kohn, H.A. 1940. An objective investigation of suggestibility. *Character and Personality. 9:* 44-48.

Richards, P. 1979. Middle-class vandalism and age-status conflict. *Social Problems. 26:* 482-497.

Roggenbuck, J.W.; Berrier, D. 1982. A comparison of the effectiveness of two communication strategies in dispersing wilderness campers. *Journal of Leisure Research. 14*: 77-89.

Rosnow, R.L. 1966. 'Conditioning' the direction of opinion change in persuasive communication. *Journal of Social Psychology. 69:* 291-303.

Ross, R.S. 1981. *Understanding persuasion: foundations and practice.* Englewood Cliffs, NJ: Prentice-Hall. 236 p.

Rubenstein, H.; Murray, C.; Motoyama, R.; Rouse, W.V. 1980. *The link between crime and the built environment. Vol. 1.* Washington, DC: U.S. Department of Justice. 43 p.

Samdahl, D.M.; Christensen, H.H. 1985. Environmental cues and vandalism: an exploratory study of picnic table carving. *Environment and Behavior. 17* (4): 445-458.

Schreyer, R.; Knopf, R.C. 1984. The dynamics of change in outdoor recreation environments—some equity issues. *Journal of Park and Recreation Administration. 2* (1): 9-19.

Schultz, J.H.; McAvoy, L.H.; Dustin, D.L. 1988. What are we in business for? *Parks and Recreation.* (January): 52-54.

Schur, E. 1980. *The politics of deviance: stigman contests and the uses of power.* Englewood Cliffs, NJ: Prentice-Hall. 217 p.

Schwartz, S.H. 1977. Normative influences on altruism. In: Berkowitz, L., (ed). *Advances in experimental psychology, Volume 10.* New York, NY: Academic Press: 221-279.

Selosse, J. 1984. Vandalism: speech acts. In: Levy-Leboyer, C., (Ed.) *Vandalism: behavior and motivation.* New York, NY: Elsevier Science Publishing Company: 39-49.

Shattuck, J.B. 1987. *Vandalism in public park facilities.* Columbus, OH: Publishing Horizons. 58 p.

Sherif, M.; Sherif, C.W. 1964. *Reference groups.* New York, NY: Harper. 420 p.

Sherwood, J.J. 1965. Social identity and referent others. *Sociometry. 28:* 66-81.

Sigall, H.; Helmreich, R. 1969. Opinion damage as a function of stress and communicator credibility. *Journal of Experimental Social Psychology. 5:* 70-78.

Sommer, R. 1974. *Tight spaces: hard architecture and how to humanize it.* Englewood Cliffs, NJ: Prentice-Hall. 255 p.

Sommer, R. 1987. Crime and vandalism in university residence halls: a confirmation of defensible space theory. *Journal of Environmental Psychology. 7:* 1-12.

Steele, M. 1978. Enrolling community support. *Journal of Research and Development in Education. 11* (2): 84-94.

Stukat, K.G. 1958. *Suggestibility: a factorial and experimental study.* Stockholm: Almquist and Wiksell. 248 p.

Sutherland, E.H.; Cressey, D.R. 1982. Theory of differential association. In: Giallombardo, R., (ed.) *Juvenile delinquency: a book of readings*. New York, NY: John Wiley and Sons, Inc.: 105-108.

Sykes, J. 1979. Vandal-resistant equipment and detail design. In: Sykes, J., (ed.) *Designing against vandalism*. London: Heinemann Educational Books Ltd.: 69-89.

Tannenbaum, P.H. 1966. Mediated generalization of attitude change via the principle of congruity. *Journal of Personality and Social Psychology*. *3*: 493-499.

Taylor, R.B.; Gottfredson, S.D.; Brower, S. 1978. Urban territoriality and crime in residential settings. *Environmental Psychology and Nonverbal Behavior*. *3*: 121-122.

Thayer, R.E.; Wagner, F.W.; Coleman, R. 1981. *Vandalism: the menace to leisure resources in the 1980s*. Arlington, VA: The National Recreation Park Association. 65 p.

Thrasher, F.M. 1936. *The gang*. Chicago, IL: The University of Chicago Press. 388 p.

Tygart, C. 1987. Public school vandalism—some revised strain theory perspectives. *Urban Education*. *22* (2): 154-171.

Tygart, C. 1988. Public school vandalism: toward a synthesis of theories and transition to paradigm analysis. *Adolescence*. *13* (89): 187-200.

United States National Institute of Education. 1977. *Violent schools—safe schools; the safe school study report to congress. Volume 1*. Washington, DC: United States Government Printing Office. (ERIC No. ED 149 466). 73 p.

Vander Stoep, G.; Gramann, J. 1987. The effect of verbal appeals and incentives on depreciative behavior among youthful park visitors. *Journal of Leisure Research*. *19* (2): 69-83.

Van Dijk, B.; Van Soomeran, P.; Walop, P. 1984. Vandalism in Amsterdam. In: Levy-Leboyer, C., (ed.) *Vandalism: behavior and motivation*. New York, NY: Elsevier Science Publishing Company: 319-324.

Van Vliet, W. 1984. Vandalism: an assessment and agenda. In: Levy-Leboyer, C., (ed.) *Vandalism behaviour and motivation*. Amsterdam: North-Holland Publishing Company: 13-36.

Wade, A.L. 1967. Social processes in the act of juvenile vandalism. In: Clinard, M.B.; Quinney, K., (eds). *Criminal behavior systems*. New York, NY: Holt, Rinehart and Winston: 94-109.

Wallack, L.M. 1981. Mass media campaigns: the odds against finding behavior change. *Health Education Quarterly*. *8* (3): 209-259.

Walster, E.; Walster, G.W.; Berscheid, E. 1978. *Equity: theory and research*. Boston, MA: Allyn and Bacon. 312 p.

Ward, C. 1973. *Vandalism*. London: The Architectural Press. 320 p.

Webb, B. 1984. Is there a place for vandalism? In: Levy-Leboyer, C., (ed.) *Vandalism: behavior and motivation.* New York, NY: Elsevier Science Publishing Company: 175-188.

Weinmayer, M. 1973. Vandalism by design—a critique. In: Gray, D. (ed.) *Reflections on the recreation and park movement.* New York, NY: William C. Brown Company 47-59.

Wilson, S. 1979. Observations on the nature of vandalism. In: Burall, P., (ed.) *Designing against vandalism.* London: Heinemann Education Books, Ltd.: 19-29.

Wilson, S.; Burbridge, M. 1978. An investigation of difficult-to-let housing. *Housing Review.* (July): 100-104.

Wise, J. 1982. A gentle deterrent to vandalism. *Psychology Today.* (Sept): 31-36.

Worchel, S.; Brehm, J.W. 1970. Effects of threats to attitudinal freedom as a function of agreement with the communicator. *Journal of Personality and Social Psychology. 14*: 18-22.

Wright, P. 1981. Cognitive responses to mass media advocacy. In: Petty, R.E.; Ostrom, T.M.; Brock, T.C., (eds). *Cognitive responses in persuasion.* Hillsdale, NJ: Erlbaum: 376-397.

Zeisel, J. 1976. *Stopping school property damage: design and administrative guidelines to reduce school vandalism.* Washington, DC: American Association of School Administrators. (ERIC Document No. ED 136 447). 194 p.

Zellner, M. 1970. Self-esteem, reception and influenceability. *Journal of Personality and Social Psychology. 15*: 310-320.

Zimbardo, P.G. 1976. A social psychological analysis of vandalism: making sense of senseless violence. In: Hollander, P. and Hunt, R., (eds.) *Current perspectives in social psychology.* Condor: Oxford University Press: 129-134.

Zimbardo, P.G.; Weisenberg, M.; Firestone, I.; Levey, B. 1965. Communicator effectiveness in producing public conformity and private attitude change. *Journal of Personality. 33*: 233-255.

Zwier, G.; Vaughan, G.M. 1984. Three ideological orientations in school vandalism research. *Review of Educational Research. 54* (2): 263-292.

9

Persuasive Communication and the Pricing of Public Leisure Services

Ronald E. McCarville
B. L. Driver
John L. Crompton

INTRODUCTION

Seldom does an issue generate such ambivalence in the minds of users and providers alike as do prices for public recreation services. The user is both attracted by high fees that suggest quality and exclusivity, and repelled by the idea of paying those fees. The public agency providing recreation services needs the revenues, yet hesitates because charging fees may discourage participation. It is little wonder that our perceptions of and attitudes toward the prices of recreation services are not well understood. This chapter considers how these attitudes and the behaviors they prompt have been influenced by systematic persuasion efforts, and recommends future research on this subject.

The chapter has four sections. The first section reviews the traditional role of price in the provision of public recreation services. The second section offers an integrative, general model of persuasion which we have interpreted from earlier chapters in this volume. This model suggests directions for future research efforts on pricing and persuasion. We believe the model can be of considerable utility, because existing pricing literature incorporates little of the current thinking on persuasive communication. What exists is an array of studies that do suggest considerable potential for future applications of the integrative model of persuasion to the pricing of public leisure services.

These past studies are reviewed in the third section of the chapter so that the reader can relate those designs to the integrative model offered. The literature has generally considered price in terms of patterns of use, notions of equity or fairness, and persuasive communication. This chapter considers persuasive communication applications to the pricing of public leisure services in order to gain support for price increases and/or prevent adverse responses.

The fourth section offers recommendations for promoting more research on our topic within the most recent theory.

Traditional Role of Price for Public Leisure Services

In the hypothetical pure market economy, prices are used to guide what is produced and for whom those services are produced (Monroe 1979). Through their willingness to purchase one product or service over another, individuals "control" production; those goods or services that receive sufficient consumer support continue to be produced, while those that do not disappear.

In the private sector, producers are more likely to focus on price than any other short-term marketing element because of the immediate improvement in profitability that can be achieved through price manipulation (Monroe 1979). Price is the only marketing element that directly generates monetary income.

Consumers also concentrate on price information. Jacoby et al. (1976) have estimated that up to 40 percent of all the information consumers seek before purchasing a product relates to price. Thus, price is one of the most important pieces of information processed in the purchase decision (Berning and Jacoby 1974). Jacoby et al. (1976) found that 71 percent of the study subjects acquired price information before making a purchase decision, and such information was likely to be the first rather than the last piece of information gathered. For these reasons, pricing decisions are among the most vital decisions made by management in the private sector (Monroe 1979).

Contrastingly, price has traditionally been viewed with some ambivalence in the public sector, where resources are typically allocated according to priorities established through the political process rather than by market forces. Social notions of equity rather than price frequently determine how public resources are allocated. Equity relates to what is fair or "what ought to be (Rawls 1971)." Public leisure services are a good case in point because equity, rather than price, has been the primary concern. For example, the first public playgrounds were provided free of charge to furnish leisure opportunities for the poor (Kelly 1982). As the public sector became more involved in the provision of leisure services, the expectation of free or nominal pricing has remained.

Budget deficits have grown at all levels of government, and more people now accept the argument that it is only fair for recreationists to pay a larger portion of the costs, especially operating costs, of providing public leisure opportunities. Consequently, more public leisure service agencies have implemented increased price/fee structures. But those who advocate such increases are still confronted with strong sentiments and heated emotional arguments.

Fees for public leisure services are controversial because there are compelling arguments both for and against price increases. For example, Driver and Koch (1986), studied trends in user fees charged by federal (national) agencies in eleven countries for outdoor recreation opportunities. In this study, Driver and Koch identified and reported nine arguments for and eleven arguments against recreation fees commonly used in each country. Some of the more pertinent and persuasive arguments are reviewed briefly below.

Recreation is often considered to be an essential part of a happy, healthy existence, and the implementation of a fee implies that the opportunity could be denied to those who cannot pay (Ellerbrock 1982). When recreation is placed in this context, decision-makers have sometimes refused to impose or raise prices. The potential denial of this component of a healthy, meaningful lifestyle to certain segments of the population for economic reasons has been repugnant to both the general public and to many public decision-makers. One member of the United States Congress stated this opinion of admission fees in the National Parks:

> It is my sincere opinion that the placing of any type of entrance admission or any other kind of fee would do violence and damage to this great system of parks and forests and lands and would impose a burden upon the people of this great country, which is wholly unjustified . . . (cited in Macintosh 1983: 12).

Thus, some public leisure service administrators have resisted imposing or raising prices because of their belief that the benefits provided through recreation should not be denied to anyone unable to pay (Klar and Rodman 1984, Manning et al. 1984). The related "merit-good" argument against fees postulates that since there are spill-over benefits beyond the users to society at large, society should pay through general taxation for these meritorious impacts of the use of public leisure services. Both arguments extol the "good" of recreation.

In some contexts, prices are perceived to be antithetical to the philosophy of equity underlying the provision of public services (Manning et al. 1984.) But equity is a two-edged sword, and many people who support the implementation of pricing policies also do so from an equity or fairness perspective. They believe that since those people who use leisure programs are the principal beneficiaries of the services, they should pay a higher proportion of the related costs (Economic Research Associates 1976).

In addition to the argument that recreational users should pay their fair share of the costs, there has also been a need to generate public revenue at all levels of government. For example, the recent tax limitation movement created a crisis for many public administrators. The passage of Proposition 2.5 in Massachusetts resulted in perceived reductions in the morale of public leisure service employees, and in fewer perceived service opportunities for low income residents (Klar and Rodman 1984). In Massachusetts and elsewhere public leisure service administrators have responded by broadening their funding base in an effort to become less dependent on tax dollars. Traditional tax-based budgets have been supplemented with income raised from pricing services and a variety of other self-generated revenues, so that one in five dollars expended on public leisure services in the United States at the local level is now self-generated (McCarville and Crompton 1988).

Economic Research Associates (1976) suggested that fee revenues are an attractive alternative for raising funds because they offer specific benefits. Fees can provide a minimum base of revenue, thereby assuring continuity in the services provided, and fees can supplement other funds for improving services and facilities. Ellerbrock (1982:59) suggested that the absence of realistic prices reduces the ability of administrators to offer quality programs and services:

> If we have a goal of providing free recreation to all citizens, then we will be destined for failure and frustration. Charging those who can

afford recreation allows subsidization of a greater number of people who cannot. Striving to subsidize everyone hinders the opportunities for people who are poor.

Proponents of pricing further suggest that fees not only generate revenue for the sponsoring agency but also encourage more efficient use of existing resources. Given a fee structure, administrators can use the purchase patterns of participants to allocate scarce resources more efficiently (Binkley and Mendelsohn 1987, Monroe 1979). Prices can be considered a possible means through which the use of limited public resources might be rationed (Rosenthal et al. 1984) and conserved (Harris and Driver 1987). It has also been suggested that, because only those who benefit from a service actually pay the associated prices, such prices may be more fair than taxation which requires both those who do and those who do not benefit from a service to fiscally support it (Kotler and Andreasen 1987).

Pricing recreational opportunities may facilitate the development of a wider range of program opportunities. Program restrictions resulting from financial restraints may be eased if new and existing programs can be self financed (Binkley and Mendelsohn 1987). In addition, there may be wider public support for capital expenditures if proposed facilities are to be supported through self-generated revenues rather than through tax subsidies (Crompton and Lamb 1986).

The Problem

Although the pricing of public leisure services is becoming more pervasive, strong opposition still exists. This opposition may occur because new pricing strategies violate long held expectations regarding public sector prices, because there is resistance to "paying the government" through taxes or user charges, or simply because users would prefer to allocate personal financial resources in other ways.

If a public leisure service agency decides to increase its fees, the agency will probably desire to minimize the opposition to this policy decision. This opposition to fees can be expressed by the publics served—and not just by the on-site users—in several ways.

1. Articulation of unfavorable attitudes or opinions about the fee program, the public officials responsible for the program, branches of the agency, or the agency itself. This articulation can include protests and litigations.

2. Refusal to pay fees and decreasing use, or continued use in violation of the agency fee policy.

3. Non-use by groups whom the agency hoped to attract as new users.

4. Depreciative behaviors as a form of protest.

5. Reduced motivation or willingness of users to engage in special programs (i.e., volunteering as workers for the agency, or participating fully in on-site educational programs).

6. Reduced general public support for the agency.

7. Thwarting of fee-program goals, such as the use of differential pricing to distribute use over time or space.

8. A less happy and less satisfied group of users and customers.

From an agency's viewpoint, these problems can be resolved to the extent that client groups understand and believe the need for the increased fees, and accept and support the fees both in attitude and behavior. Even when these attitudes and behaviors are not negative, the agency might desire that they became more positive and supportive.

Ajzen (Chapter 1) points out that there are several ways for a public agency to effect attitude and behavior change, including coercion, conditioning, subterfuge, and persuasion through appeals to reason. Persuasive appeal to reason is the preferred method in a society that values freedom of choice.

A SUMMARY INTEGRATED MODEL OF CURRENT THEORIES OF PERSUASION

This volume includes several theoretical chapters by leading theorists and methodologists (Ajzen, Fazio, Fishbein, and Petty) in the general area of attitude and behavioral change, and in the specific area of persuasive communication. These chapters facilitate our integration of a general model of persuasion that combines the current thinking in the field of persuasive communication. This model should serve as a useful conceptual scaffolding within which other leisure scientists can frame their research, or at least help those who are not versed in persuasion theory get a conceptual start on the literature.

Although there was much debate in the 1960s and 1970s about relationships between attitudes and behavior, predictive relationships among beliefs, attitudes, and behavior have since been documented empirically and persuasive communication is known to influence all three under specified conditions.

By "persuasion" we mean the use of messages to influence beliefs, attitudes, and behavior. Those messages are usually verbal but can also be visual or behavioral (body language), or a combination of these and other stimuli.

A persuasive situation consists of five components: a message source, the message, the channel, the recipient, and the context (sometimes called the situation). Characteristics of each component can affect the persuasion process. Since Ajzen (Chapter 1) describes each of these components, they will only be touched upon here. The message source reflects observed or inferred characteristics of the person communicating the message, including attractiveness, likability, credibility, age, and sex. The message itself has three parts: an advocated position, a set of general arguments in support of the advocated position, and specific factual evidence to bolster the general arguments. The channel depicts the characteristics of the means used to communicate the message, such as video, personal appearance, or print media. The recipient component reflects certain characteristics of the receiver or the audience. The context (or situation) covers factors such as background noise and distractions, forewarning of the receiver of an impending message, and other features of the situation.

Historically, research on persuasion has primarily addressed the effects of these situational variables. Contemporary efforts focus more on understanding the overall persuasion process.

Figure 1 shows the integrative model of the persuasion process we have interpreted from the chapters in this volume authored or coauthored by Ajzen, Fazio, Fishbein, and Petty.

Persuasion or Nonpersuasion

The persuasive communication process starts at the top of Figure 1 with the Transmission of a Message, or an attempt at communication. That attempt can result in persuasion or nonpersuasion. A message is persuasive when it effects changes in beliefs, attitudes, and/or behaviors. Persuasion occurs when existing attitudes toward the message object are strengthened, weakened, and/or new favorable or unfavorable attitudes are articulated and integrated into the recipient's belief structure. Changes in behavior may then follow.

The first box in the Persuasive Route defines whether or not the recipient of the message is Motivated and has the Ability to Process the message and its associated information. This is a key point in determin-

Figure 1
A Summary, Integrative Model of Persuasive Communication

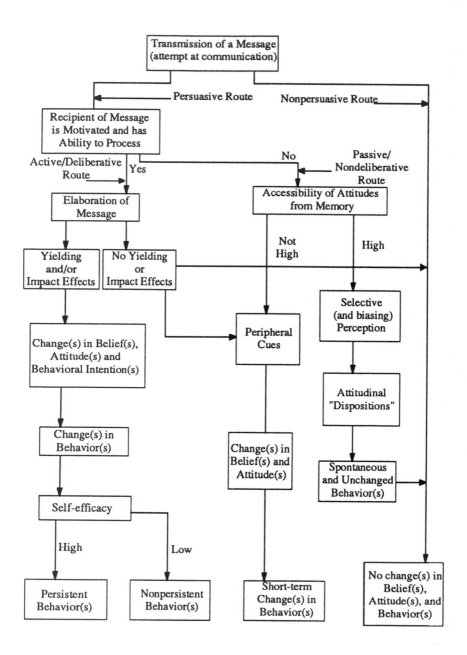

ing whether what we label an Active/Deliberative processing of the message, or a more Passive/Nondeliberative process will occur. The model can best be understood if the reader notices that it uses a "decision-tree" approach to define both the requirements for persuasion to take place and the alternative responses that will be elicited under different conditions.

For an Active/Deliberative process to occur, the recipient of the message must be motivated and have the ability to process the communicated message. This route is what Petty and Cacioppo (1986a, 1986b) and Petty et al. (Chapter 4) call the central route to persuasion, or what Chaiken and her associates (Chaiken et al. 1989) refer to as systematic information processing. This route also reflects the reasoned actions explicit to Ajzen and Fishbein's (1980), and Fishbein and Manfredo's, (Chapter 2) model of attitude and behavior change, and Ajzen's (1985) more recent theory of planned behavior (see Ajzen, Chapter 1). Put simply, in the Active/Deliberative route, the recipient cognitively evaluates the merits of the arguments presented in the message.

The Passive/Nondeliberative route is taken when the recipient of the message is not motivated and/or does not have the cognitive ability to process the communicated message. This route explicitly reflects the peripheral route of Petty and Cacioppo (1986a, 1986b, see also Petty et al. Chapter 4), the heuristic processing of Chaiken and her associates (Chaiken et. al. 1989), and the attitude-to-behavior process model of Fazio (1989) and his associates (see Vincent and Fazio, Chapter 3) that addresses spontaneous attitude retrieval and behavior.

The Active/Deliberative Route

Ajzen, Vincent and Fazio, and Petty et al. (this volume), as well as other recent reviews on attitudes and behavior (cf. Chaiken et al. 1989, McGuire 1985, Tesser and Shaffer 1990), show that a great number of variables can influence a recipient's motivation and ability to process a message. These authors tend to discuss motivation and ability separately, but we consider these variables together for simplicity.

These variables include: the perceived personal relevance of the message and its implications (i.e., perceived consequences); prior knowledge about and experience with the message object; the complexity of the message or its understandability, reflecting such things as the speed and length of the message, the number of arguments made, and whether there is repeated exposure to or expression of the message, which among other things influences how accessible beliefs and attitudes about the attitude object are from memory; the credibility of the source of the message; the attractiveness/likability of the source; social norms and the influence of significant others; whether questions are asked by the message; the novelty of the message; its use of humor; the mood of the recipient; the strength of the argument; any internal or external distractions for the recipient; the way the message is framed; involvement in and commitment to the message object by the recipient; expectations of the recipient regarding the message object; and personality traits of the recipient such as need for cognition and tolerance of ambiguity.

While each of these many variables has been shown to influence a recipient's motivation and ability to process a communicated message, they can also affect the recipient's response later in the Active/ Deliberative and Passive/Nondeliberative routes shown in Figure 1. Petty et al. (Chapter 4) emphasize this point as one of the central characteristics of the Elaboration Likelihood Model of persuasion. For example, they point out that motivational factors, especially attractiveness and credibility of the source of the message, can serve as cues that might effect attitude and behavioral change by the peripheral route to persuasion. Also, many motivational variables such as mood, self-acceptance, need for cognition, intolerance of ambiguity, and distraction, can serve as intervening variables through which the messages are processed at various stages along the route shown in Figure 1.

If there is motivation and ability to process information, the recipient will then Elaborate the Message through active thought processes. This concept of elaboration is central to the model of persuasion developed by Petty and Cacioppo (1986). During this elaboration process, the recipient reflects on the arguments in the message, develops counterarguments, forms new beliefs, or alters old beliefs. This is a very active process during which new thoughts are generated and belief structures are changed, which is why it is called the elaboration element of the persuasive process. One way to determine the effects of elaboration is to examine shifts in salient beliefs toward the message object prior to and after communication (cf. Ajzen and Fishbein 1980).

The elaboration process may or may not result in Yielding and Impact Effects. Yielding is acceptance of the arguments, and impact effects occur when beliefs secondary to the central message of the argument are changed through inference and judgment of consequences that might result from adopting the argument. For example, a person being encouraged to pay a fee for a public leisure program might assess the other things they would have to give up if they paid that fee, and then form beliefs and attitudes about the fee because of those related impacts.

If there are yielding or impact effects, Changes in the Beliefs, Attitudes, and Behavioral Intentions toward the message object will follow. Because the relationships between these three variables and behavioral change are central to Ajzen and Fishbein's well known work, they will not be elaborated here (Ajzen and Fishbein, and Manfredo, this volume). The main point, however, is that the attitude changes will reflect alterations in the recipient's favorable or unfavorable dispositions toward the message object that are caused by the elaboration process. Attitudes that are well articulated and integrated into the recipient's belief structure will result from this attitude change process. Changes in Attitudes will lead to Changes in Behavior.

If there are no Yielding or perceived Impact Effects, no changes in beliefs, attitudes, behavioral intentions, or behaviors will result from the elaboration process. In this case the person will either enter the Passive/Nondeliberative route or the Nonpersuasive route, as shown in Figure 1.

When the recipient has high self-efficacy, or perceived self-competence in the skills necessary to continue the changed behavior, there is a higher likelihood that the persuasive process will result in relatively persistent behavioral change as indicated by the bottom box to the left side of Figure 1. If there is low self-efficacy, the changed behavior is not as likely to persist over time as it would be with higher self-efficacy (Petty et al., this volume). Bandura (1986) argues that for persistent behavioral change to occur as a result of high self-efficacy, the person might need to learn new skills or a new sequence of already acquired skills.

The works in this volume and elsewhere by Ajzen, Fazio, Fishbein, and Petty agree closely in their conclusions about the Active/Deliberative route to persuasion. However, we speculate about how Fazio's (1989) process model meshes with Petty's and Cacioppo's (1986a, 1986b) and Chaiken's (1987) interpretation of the Passive/Nondeliberative route.

Fazio (this volume with Vincent) argues that much human behavior is spontaneous and does not involve systematic information processing as required by the Active/Deliberative route on the left hand side of

Figure 1. Fazio maintains that Passive/Nondeliberative processing occurs when the recipient's motivation or ability to process the message is low. As mentioned earlier, this idea is also supported by Petty and Cacioppo (1986a, 1986b) and Chaiken (1987) in their concepts of peripheral and heuristic information processing, respectively. Following the Passive/Nondeliberative route, the recipient is not actively engaged in reasoned actions, but beliefs, attitudes, and behavior might be changed with respect to the transmitted message more or less spontaneously or voluntarily, especially by peripheral cues (see Petty et al., Chapter 4).

Fazio (with Vincent, Chapter 3) argues that if there is high accessibility of attitudes from memory, there will be a relatively strong bond between those attitudes and the evaluations of the object triggered by the message. This bond is particularly strengthened by repeated expression of the message and by prior experience with the message object. Fazio believes that selective perceptions triggered by the message will "color" the recipient's attitudes with respect to the message object, and these favorable or unfavorable attitude dispositions will trigger some type of spontaneous behavior with respect to the message object.

Furthermore, Vincent and Fazio (Chapter 3) state that "accessible attitudes...[are] likely to persist over time." We interpret this to mean that attempts at persuasive communication within the Passive/ Nondeliberative route (i.e., when there is low motivation and ability to process) are not likely to result in attitude or behavioral change if the message triggers a highly accessible attitude about the message object from memory. We indicate such in Figure 1.

Petty and Cacioppo (1986a, 1986b) in their Elaboration Likelihood Model of persuasion do not discuss the accessibility of the attitude from memory as Fazio does. Instead, they refer to peripheral cues that can influence attitude and behavior change during the peripheral route, which we have labeled the Passive/Nondeliberative route, and which Chaiken (1987) calls heuristic processing. Chaiken and Stangor 1987: differentiate the peripheral and heuristic approaches:

> The heuristic model asserts that persuasion is often mediated by simple decision rules (e.g. "length implies strength") that associate certain persuasion cues (e.g. message length) with message validity (Chaiken 1980, 1986). In contrast, the peripheral route refers to a family of attitude change theories that specify factors or motives that

produce attitude change without engendering active message and issue-relevant thinking (Petty and Cacioppo 1981, 1986[a]). These peripheral routes include cognitive perspectives such as heuristic processing (Chaiken 1980) and attributional reasoning (e.g. Kelly 1967, Berning 1972, Eagly et al. 1981). However, the peripheral label is also used to refer to models which specify simple affective mechanisms in attitude change (e.g. classical and operant conditioning; also see Batra and Ray 1985, and Lutz 1985), perceptual models such as social judgment theory (Sherif and Sherif 1967), and social-role perspectives which assert that people often agree (or disagree) with messages for reasons that (presumably) would not necessitate thinking about message content [e.g. to identify with or promote a social relationship with liked communicators or comply with powerful ones (Kelman 1961); to manage a favorable social identity (Schlenker 1980).

The differences in the perspectives offered by Petty and Cacioppo, and Chaiken appear to be that a wider array of variables are permitted to affect peripheral cues in the Elaboration Likelihood Model. The essential point from our summary perspective is: if message-relevant attitudes are not readily accessible from memory (and, per Fazio, will lead to spontaneous behavior that is unchanged by the message), persuasion can occur "passively" because "... simple cues in the persuasion context influence attitudes" (Petty et al., Chapter 4). These cue-induced changes in beliefs and attitudes cause Short-term Changes in Behavior as indicated in Figure 1. Particularly important as cues are the attractiveness/likability of the person communicating the message, the credibility of the message source, the number of arguments in the message, the length of the arguments used, and the number and influence of other people thought to endorse the argument (see Petty et al., Chapter 4).

The extreme right hand side of Figure 1 shows that the message may have no persuasive effects whatsoever, meaning that it causes no changes in existing beliefs, attitudes, or behaviors—even if the message is understood completely, a point not adequately understood by many leisure researchers and managers who believe that if the message is learned it will be accepted. Figure 1 also shows nonpersuasion if there are no yielding or impact effects or no effects of peripheral cues following elaboration of the message when the Active/Deliberative route is followed. According to Fazio (Chapter 3), if there is low motivation and ability to process the message and high accessibility of attitudes from memory, there will be no persuasive impacts. This is indicated in Figure 1.

The Figure 1 model, which reflects the current state of theory about the persuasive process, explains why some messages can be understood but still not result in changes in beliefs, attitudes, or behaviors. This model explains why some recipients will engage in Active/Deliberative processing and others in Passive/Nondeliberative processing. It also emphasizes that for persistent behavioral change to occur, the recipient of the message must be actively involved in information processing and that many characteristics of the source, the message, the channel, the recipient, and the context must be considered for effective persuasive communication. Therefore people who are interested in changing beliefs, attitudes, and behavior about increased fees for leisure services must be attentive to variables such as the credibility of the message, the complexity of the message, the motivation and ability of the receiver to process the message, the recipient's salient beliefs about the message object (fees), and the change in skills necessary to behave consistently with the intent of the message.

The chapters in this volume by Ajzen, Fishbein and Manfredo, Petty et al., and Vincent and Fazio provide more details about how these variables operate to influence persuasion. The readers are encouraged to read those chapters for additional information.

REVIEW OF PAST EMPIRICAL STUDIES

Empirical Studies of Reactions to Prices of Public Leisure Services

Past research efforts have considered price and persuasive communication in one of two ways. The first relates to how price itself effects changes in beliefs, attitudes, and behavior, such as altering patterns of use. The concern in these studies is with price-caused changes in leisure behavior, and we examine it here because it suggests both the degree to which price itself can be persuasive and the varied responses that might be elicited by a single persuasive message or tool. This topic is important because managers frequently need to distribute use over time or space to reduce user congestion or protect a resource.

The second approach considers price as the object of persuasive communication with emphasis not on how price causes changes in leisure behavior but on changes in beliefs and attitudes toward price.

This represents a more recent trend in the leisure pricing literature that is devoted to altering consumers' assessments of given price levels. This second research is more closely aligned with existing persuasion literature.

Price as a Tool of Persuasion

The use of price as a persuasive tool represents a prevalent theme in the study of pricing in the delivery of leisure services. Related studies have considered reaction to price in terms of use patterns. For example, Bamford et al. (1988) considered variations in campsite occupancy levels with differential campsite fees. Campers were given a campground map indicating prime and non-prime campsites with associated fee differentials information. Price levels generally ranged from $1.00 to $5.00, with prime sites demanding higher prices. Prime sites tended to be adjacent to water and had shown high occupancy rates during the year preceding the study. The investigators found: (1) "In water-based parks, increasing the price of prime campsites did not decrease demand enough to prevent an increase in total revenue (pg. 333);" and (2) "Demand for prime campsites in non-water based parks was much more price responsive than in water-based parks (pp. 337-338)." A view across water or direct access to water was probably a strong factor in the strength of prime campsite preference. Patrons seemed unwilling to lose access to preferred water-based sites even when they could save money by doing so. In the case of water-based parks, at least, differential prices were not persuasive in altering use patterns. In addition, low income campers were only slightly more likely to choose lower-priced campsites than were high income campers.

In a different study, Manning et al. (1984) found that differential prices were moderately persuasive in altering use patterns. Visitors to three Vermont state parks ". . . were given a campground map with available unoccupied campsites circled. Using this map, campers inspected the available sites and register[ed] for the sites of their choice....In this way, campers had full knowledge of the differential costs associated with each campsite (pg. 26-27)." The investigators found a slight decline in the occupancy rates of the higher priced sites and a corresponding rise in occupancy rates for lower priced sites. This trend was not consistent in all three parks, however. Again, occupancy rates for sites adjacent to water did not decline as fee levels increased. Though low income visitors tended to consider price as an important variable in site selection, level of income was not related to the type of site eventually chosen. It seems that although price can be persuasive when a camper is making site selection decisions, site characteristics may override fee considerations.

Other studies support this contention. Leuschner et al. (1987:101) suggest that fees may not influence backcountry trip patterns: "Responses indicated that users would rather not pay fees than pay them, but that behavior and use patterns would not be drastically altered if fees were implemented." Another study found that fees had little effect on overall visitation levels (Becker et al. 1985). The study by Becker et al. considered the response to entrance fees implemented in South Carolina State Parks. Although park visitation declined following the institution of these fees, the authors concluded that the decreased demand was not associated with the new fees. It may be that the relatively low fee levels cited in all these studies were insufficient to encourage campers to reassess current use patterns. Higher fees may be more likely to encourage elaboration and active assessments of fees and related recreation behavior.

Related research efforts have addressed the notion of price as either inhibiting or enhancing participation. This research has suggested that price may not be the major obstacle to participation, as opponents to pricing believe. In a study of three United States cities, Howard and Crompton (1984) found that low income residents were the least frequent users of eight selected facilities, but the reasons behind the low use were primarily related to personal preference and low levels of personal commitment. Price did not adversely affect more than eight percent of the respondents in any of the three cities.

Shelby et al. (1982) reported that river running and backpacking enthusiasts actually reacted favorably to pricing if it assisted in allocating scarce natural resources. Avid users felt that prices would discourage other potential users, thereby easing demand and enhancing their own recreational experiences.

These studies suggest that, although price can be a determinant of leisure behavior, other variables may render price unimportant. One explanation for discrepant findings is advanced by Kerr and Manfredo (1991), who propose that it is important to distinguish between attitudes toward price and attitudes toward using a specific facility or area. Beliefs about price may or may not have an impact on facility or area decision. When price-related beliefs play an important role in affecting attitudes toward facilities or areas, it is more likely these beliefs will affect *behavior*. The literature suggests that emphasis on price as the message object may prove inappropriate in some instances.

Price As The Object of Persuasion

The second approach to price and persuasion has considered price as the object of persuasive communication. These studies have considered reactions to price by both users and nonusers of recreation services, with the object being to reduce negative beliefs, attitudes and responses caused by the price or fee.

We could find only one study that considered price as the object of persuasion that explicitly adopted the conceptual orientation described by the Figure 1 model. Building from Fishbein and Ajzen's theory of measured action (Ajzen and Fishbein 1980), Kerr and Manfredo (1991) propose an attitude-based model of recreation service pricing. Kerr and Manfredo argue that increased price is new information that affects purchase behavior by first affecting a person's attitude toward paying. Price would then be information that affects the structure of salient beliefs about the attitude toward paying. Prior experience in paying and elaboration of the issue of fees are seen as important influences on how price information is processed. Empirical tests by Kerr and Manfredo (1991) generally supported this model. The results suggest that by targeting beliefs about fees, attitudes toward paying can be changed, in turn affecting attitudes and behaviors regarding facilities.

Several studies have considered price levels that individuals think are fair or which they are willing to tolerate. While these studies were not designed explicitly within the Figure 1 model we offered to guide future research, they are helpful in many ways. They suggest conditions under which persuasion might be considered appropriate, identify variables consumers consider as important when assessing price levels, and assess the degree of tolerance that might exist toward different price strategies—each of which can be relevant if persuasive communication is contemplated to gain support for price changes.

Howard and Selin (1987) considered price tolerance levels for different public recreation programs. They proposed that when such tolerance levels were breached through price increases, resistance resulted. They found that, for some services, prices could be raised to a specified level without resistance, and concluded that tolerance levels did exist. Howard and Selin discovered, however, that tolerance levels varied from one program to another. Perhaps, as our integrative model proposes, prior knowledge and experience with each program influenced these assessments; participants may have expected to pay more for some programs than for others as a result of knowledge regarding program characteristics or past pricing practices. Tolerance levels regarding fair prices may have varied as a result.

Prices that are considered fair may relate to more than actual price levels. Residents may consider any monetary price as inappropriate under some conditions, and social norms can influence the recipient's motivation to process a message. Such beliefs may influence public receptivity to messages designed to alter attitudes and expectations. For example, there was considerable adverse reaction to a proposed one dollar admission fee to be imposed for visits to the Statue of Liberty. The outcry was no less vehement when it was pointed out that "this modest charge [was] far less than fees charged by tour boat operators and parking lot managers for their services (Noble, 1987:13)." The fees associated with visiting the Statue of Liberty apparently violated existing norms, and price information related to boat rides and parking rates failed to address the violation of such norms. As a result, provision of such unrelated comparative price information proved ineffective in gaining acceptance for the fees.

Such norms may apply to the recipient of a program as well to a specific program or site. Wicks and Crompton (1986) found Texas residents favored public subsidization of leisure programs for the very young and the elderly but were unwilling to offer such support for similar programs offered to adults. As suggested above, communication is most likely to be persuasive if it is consistent with existing norms and expectations. In the Texas example, an appeal to norms related to prices for adults registered in public programs could be persuasive because this appeal is consistent with existing norms.

Clearly, the context in which persuasive communication is assessed will influence the nature and degree of the recipient's assessment. This context may determine whether or not the message is persuasive. No one message is likely to be effective under all conditions. As the context changes, so too will the norms and expectations of the message recipient. To be persuasive, the message must address the prevailing concerns found within that setting or context.

Other variables describing individual differences have been found to influence the individual's motivation to process a price-related message. Certain segments of the population, such as the elderly and low income residents, may be most in favor of the implementation of user fees to support some recreation programs. They may be unwilling to pay taxes that are used to support programs in which they have no interest and from which they derive no personal benefits. On the other hand, young, high-income, and college-educated groups who exhibit higher levels of participation (Economic Research Associates, 1976), and users of public leisure services (Manning and Baker, 1981), have been found least likely to support user fees presumably because they perceive direct personal costs from higher fee levels. Such groups represent a fundamental pricing dilemma. They are the most likely candidates for persuasive efforts because of their relative affluence and current levels of use. Yet, they are least likely to be motivated to process messages that suggest that higher fees are justified.

Recent studies have found that several persuasive communications may be used to successfully influence attitudes toward prices for public leisure services. These communications may facilitate both deliberative and nondeliberative message processing. Issue-relevant messages that encourage active/deliberative processes may relate to cost-of-service provisions and/or cost-of-service alternatives (Reiling et al. 1988), and disposition of revenues obtained from the fees (Driver 1984, Miles and Fedler 1986).

For example, Reiling et al. (1988) considered attitudes toward prices for public campground facilities. The authors thought persuasive communication was critical to the success of new public campground prices: "Implementation of new fees requires new users to pay for a service that was available to them at no cost prior to the policy change. Hence, the change may be more controversial than the amount of the fee itself (Reiling et al. 1988:209)." Here, the existing norms and expectations were important determinants of reactions to price. A random sample of campground users were given information about substitute camping fees and about costs related to campground provisions. Though these messages were unable to influence all respondents, both types of information altered attitudes toward price levels. For many participants this information proved persuasive even though the prices suggested were inconsistent with past experience.

Other studies suggest that the potential for personal benefits can influence reactions to the payment of fees. Miles and Fedler (1986) provided park visitors with information outlining the eventual allocation of fees. Information that suggested that fees were to be returned to the actual park at which they were gathered was most effective in elevating visitors' willingness to pay. Messages suggesting that fees would be placed in a general treasury created much lower levels of willingness to pay.

Driver's (1984) review of past studies showed less negative reactions to entrance fees when visitors were told that such fees could improve levels of service (see especially Economic Research Associates 1976 and Market Opinion Research 1986). These studies suggest that users are more willing to pay fees for leisure opportunities if they believe that their leisure opportunities will be enhanced. The likelihood of personal benefit may act as a motivational incentive that facilitates elaboration and subsequent yielding behavior. Related studies that have enabled users to review park site alternatives—thereby facilitating evaluation of the relative merits of each site—have found that consumers are willing to pay higher prices for those sites they believe offer the greatest benefits. This suggests that benefits that are either described or displayed can be persuasive in facilitating the acceptance of prices.

Much of the pricing research conducted in the context of public leisure services has assumed that those people confronted with price-related messages will undertake active/deliberative thought processes. As suggested, emphasis is often placed on the provision of messages that outline specific costs and benefits, and resulting changes in attitudes or willingness to pay have been monitored.

The role of the Passive/Nondeliberative route has remained largely ignored in the leisure literature, yet this route offers considerable potential for understanding responses to price of public leisure services. As described in the Figure 1 model, this route is taken when the recipient's use of peripheral cues and/or memories causes changes in behavior. Studies in the consumer psychology literature suggest that reference price may provide such a cue to the individual who is faced with price information.

Reference price has been operationally defined as "expected price" (Nwokoye 1975) which "will be some average of the range of prices for similar products; it need not correspond with any actual price (Monroe and Petroshius 1981:50)." For example, Zeithaml and Graham (1983) compared consumers' reference prices and actual prices for selected professional services. As a result of infrequent use, inadequate pre-purchase information, and nonstandarized pricing policies, consumers were found to hold generally inaccurate reference prices for professional services. In other words, given even minimal information or experience, consumers will develop reference price expectations. This expectation may or may not represent an accurate assessment of actual price levels.

Reference price seems to provide a point of comparison for new price information (Helgeson and Beatty 1985, Monroe and Della 1984, Monroe and Petroshius 1981). As the consumer is exposed to new price information or to potentially persuasive communications, the new information is evaluated in terms of the reference point stored in memory. If prices fall within the region of indifference around the reference price, a neutral evaluation may occur (Emery 1970). It is unclear how large this region of indifference around the reference price might be. Uhl (1970) found that deviations in price greater than 15 percent were detected more frequently than were five percent deviations, so consumers seem to be aware of prices that fall outside a given threshold.

Prices which fall below a given threshold may be evaluated positively, while those perceived as existing above the region may receive a negative evaluation (Anderson 1973). In this way, reference price may act as a heuristic point of reference. During peripheral information processing, the reference price stored in memory may influence subsequent reactions to the message and message object.

If, as Jacoby and Olson (1977) suggest, the actual price-reference price comparison serves an accept/reject threshold function, consideration should be given to providing potential users of leisure services with information that encourages formation of reference prices consistent with actual price levels. Peripheral cues may be helpful in this regard. Nwokoye (1975) notes that information about comparative prices may provide such cues. For example, information suggesting that current prices are less than those charged by competitors (Sewall and Goldstein 1979) or less than "regular" price levels (Urbany et al. 1988) may increase the acceptability of the price level. Blair and Landon (1981) found that consumers' estimates of "regular" price levels could be elevated by introducing comparative price information. It seems that just as internal price standards stored in memory can influence price evaluations, new price information can encourage reevaluation of the internal standard.

Such comparative information can be effective even when it is obviously exaggerated. Urbany et al. (1988) found that consumers' assessments of value increased as comparative prices rose, despite a corresponding decline in message believability. "The exaggerated price improved even skeptical subjects' perceptions of the advertised offer (pg. 106)." Two variables could compromise the influence exerted by the provision of such exaggerated messages. First of all, if existing price memories are salient and accessible, it is unlikely that such an extreme message would prove effective. Also, if the message became sufficiently extreme so as to encourage elaboration and more active information processing, then the message may be discounted or ignored.

Few studies have investigated the manner in which reference price for public leisure services might be influenced. However, the type of messages found to alter attitudes to prices levels (Reiling et al. 1988) may also influence price expectations. McCarville and Crompton (1987) found that comparative information raised price expectations among both users and nonusers of public swimming pools. Subjects were randomly assigned to treatment groups that were exposed to messages about cost-of-service provision, prices charged by a commercial alternative, and a combination of both types of information. Though the level of use moderated subjects' reactions to these messages, the treatment information exerted considerable influence over users' price expectations. Such information may have been persuasive because it provided a cue with which price expectations could be established. Unfortunately, no follow-up studies have been conducted to determine if changes in reference price levels influence subsequent changes in belief, attitude or behavior.

DIRECTIONS FOR FUTURE RESEARCH

The previous section documents much useful research that has examined price increases for public leisure services. Variables that have increased favorable dispositions and behaviors toward fees include:

1. Communicating a reference price.

2. Providing information in the message about beneficial consequences of the price structures. Such influential messages in past studies have included information on likely improved quality of opportunities following increased prices—e.g., more solitude, less congestion, and more or better services/facilities—as well as ability to maintain existing opportunities rather then reduce service provision because of budget constraints.

3. Informing users of costs of providing the opportunities, and of the costs of commercial alternatives.

4. Arguments pointing out the social justness of users bearing a

more equitable portion of the costs, especially for operation and maintenance.

5. Incremental rather than lump-sum increases in fees.

6. Differential pricing to relate price to the quality of service provided and/or to relate price to high- versus low-use periods (weekend versus weekday and night versus day rates for downhill skiing).

7. Identifying fee-related attitudes of different market segments, defined by age, type of activity used, type of setting used, and so on.

The results of these past studies have helped administrators and managers of public leisure services improve fee programs at all levels of government. However, these studies have not contributed greatly to a unified body of empirically supported theory about the role of persuasive communication in affecting benefits, attitudes, and behaviors as related to increased prices for public leisure services. This is explained by three major reasons: first, there has been relatively little research done in this area; second, probably 95 percent of this research has been done since 1980; and third, the currently accepted theories of persuasion are quite recent, so integrative summaries of those theories, such as the one provided in Figure 1, have not been available as a unifying conceptual scaffold for leisure scientists. Instead, these scientists have tended to work either without a theoretical structure or with a "fragment" of the current theories, such as social judgment theory, adaptation level theory, social learning theory, attribution theory, and so on.

We see the following points as promising and needed in the future:

- More research on pricing is needed.
- We do not believe there are any theories of persuasion unique to the pricing of leisure behavior. Thus, the current theories integrated in Figure 1 are relevant to this topic. They should be applied to future research to avoid remaking the wheel, and so we can build on empirically supported theory and achieve a more united body of knowledge on this subject within the leisure professions.
- The theoretical structure in Figure 1 explicitly shows many variables that should be considered more carefully and added to future persuasion research on the pricing of leisure services.
- These variables and considerations include giving greater or new attention to the vast array of factors that influence motivation and ability to process a message, especially the credibility of the message and its source, its understandability, its relevance (are

benefits of fee increases pointed out clearly?), the strength of the arguments (are costs of services and the justness/fairness of paying a fair price explained?), the involvement and commitment of the recipients, and the appeal of the message (attractiveness, use of humor, use of rhetorical questions).

- In addition, the targeted audience's salient beliefs about fees should be determined by focus group inquiries and other qualitative studies. Are new skills needed to maintain self-efficacy so the persistence of desirable attitudes and willingness to pay will be maintained? How accessible are beliefs and attitudes about the message object? How are reference prices developed and affected? What are the peripheral cues, such as reference prices, that affect desired changes? Do these cues effect changes in attitudes and behavior, and for how long? How do difficult market segments respond?
- Replications of the same design are needed over time and space to test for consistency in response patterns.
- Leisure scientists should team up with recognized experts in persuasion theory and methodology to tap their skills.

The "price" of following these recommendations is low, given that the theories and methods are well established.

REFERENCES

Ajzen, I. 1985. From intentions to actions: A theory of planned behavior. In: Kuhl, J.; Beckmann, J., (eds.), *Action-control: From cognition to behavior*. Heidelberg-Springer. 11-39.

Ajzen, I.; Fishbein, M. 1980. *Understanding attitudes and predicting social behavior*. Englewood Cliffs, NJ: Prentice-Hall. 278 p.

Anderson, R. E. 1973. Consumer dissatisfaction: The effect of disconfirmed expectancy on perceived product performance. *Journal of Marketing*. 10 (Feb): 38-44.

Bamford, T.; Koenemann, E.; Manning, R.; Forcier, L. 1988. Differential campsite pricing: An experiment. *Journal of Leisure Research*. 20(4): 324-342.

Bandura, A. 1986. *Social foundations of thought and action*. Englewood Cliffs, NJ: Prentice-Hall.

Batra, R.; Ray, M. L. 1985. How advertising works at contact. In: Alwitt, L. F.; Mitchell, A. A., (eds.) *Psychological processes and advertising effects*. Hillsdale, N.J. Erbaum: 13-43.

Becker, R.; Berrier, D.; Barker, G. 1985. Entrance fees and visitation levels. *Journal of Park and Recreation Administration*. 3(1): 28-32.

Berm, D.J. 1972. Self-perception theory. *Advances in Experimental Social Psychology.* 6: 1-62.

Berning, C. A.; Jacoby, J. 1974. Patterns of information acquisition in new product purchases. *Journal of Consumer Research.* 1: 18-22.

Binkley, C. S.; Mendelsohn, R.O. 1987. Recreation user fees: An economic analysis. *Journal of Forestry. May:* 31-35.

Blair, E. A.; Landon, E.A. 1981 . The effects of reference prices in retail advertisements. *Journal of Marketing.* Spring: 61-69.

Buchanan, T. 1985. Commitment and leisure behavior: A theoretical perspective. *Leisure Sciences.* 7(4): 401-420.

Chaiken, S.; Liberman, A.; Eagly, A. H. 1989. Heuristic and systematic information processing within and beyond the persuasion context. In: Uleman, J. S; Bargh, J. A., (eds.) *Unintended thought: Limits of awareness, intention, and control.* New York: Guilford. In Press. 212-252.

Chaiken, S.; Stangor, C. 1987. Attitudes and attitude change. *Annual Review of Psychology.* 38: 575-630.

Chaiken, S. 1987. The heuristic model of persuasion. In: Zanna, M. P.; Olson, J. M.; Herman, C. P., (eds.) *Social influence: The Ontario symposium.* Vol. 5. Hillsdale, NJ: Erbaum.

Chaiken, S. 1980. Heuristic versus systematic information processing and the use of source versus message cues in persuasion. *Journal Pers. Social Psychology.* 39: 752-66.

Cicchetti, Smith; Smith, K. 1981. Congestion, quality deterioration, and optimal use: Wilderness recreation in the Spanish Peaks primitive area. *Social Science Research,* 2(1): 15-30.

Crompton, J.; Lamb, C. 1986. *Marketing government and social services.* New York: John Wiley and Sons. 485 p.

Driver, B. L.; Koch, N. E. 1986. Cross-cultural trends in user fees charged at national outdoor recreation areas. In: *Proceedings, 18th IUFRO World Congress. Division 6. IUFRO Secretariat.* Schbrunn-Tirolergarten. A-1131 Vienna, Austria. p. 370-385.

Driver, B.L. 1984. Public responses to user fees at public recreation areas. *Proceedings: Fees for outdoor recreation on lands open to public conference.* Research Department Appalachian Mountain Club. p. 45-52.

Eagly, A. H.; Chaiken, S. 1984. Cognitive theories of persuasion. *Advances in Experimental Social Psychology.* 17: 268-359.

Eagly, A. H.; Chaiken, S.; Wood, W. 1981. An attribution analysis of persuasion. In: Harvey, J. H.; Ickes, W. J.; Kidd, R. F., (eds.) *New directions in attribution research.* Hillsdale, NJ: Erlbaum. 3: 37-62.

Economic Research Associates. 1976. *Evaluation of public willingness to pay user charges for use of outdoor recreation areas and facilities.* Washington, D.C.: Heritage Conservation and Recreation Service. U.S. Superintendent of Documents.

Ellerbrock, M. 1982. Some straight talk on user fees. *Parks and Recreation.* January: 59-62.

Emery, F. 1970. Some psychological aspects of price. In: Taylor, B.; Willis, G., (eds.) *Pricing strategy.* Princeton: Brandon/Systems Press. p. 132-151.

Fazio, R. H. 1989. Multiple processes by which attitudes guide behavior: The MODE model as an integrative framework. *Advances in Experimental Social Psychology.* In press.

Funkhouser, R. 1984. Using consumer expectations as an input to pricing decisions. *Journal of Consumer Marketing. 6*(3): 35-41.

Harris, C.; Driver, B. L. 1987. User fees pros and cons. *Journal of Forestry. 85*(5): 25-29.

Helgeson, J.; Beatty, S. 1985. An information processing perspective in the internalization of price stimuli. In: Henselmann, E.; Holbrook, M., (eds.) *Advances in consumer research.* Provo, UT: Association for Consumer Behavior. 91-96.

Howard, D.; Crompton, J. 1984. Who are the consumers? *Journal of Park and Recreation Administration. 2*(3): 35-47.

Howard, D.; Selin, S. 1987. A method for establishing consumer price tolerance levels for public recreation services. *Journal of Park and Recreation Administration. 5*(3): 48-59.

Jacoby, J.; Chestnut, R.; Weigl, K.; Fisher, W. 1976. Pre-purchase information acquisition: Description of a process methodology. In: Anderson, B., (ed.) *Advances in consumer research.* Cincinnati, OH: Association for Consumer Research. p. 306-314.

Jacoby, J.; Olson, J. 1977. Consumer response to price: An attitudinal information processing perspective. In: Wind, Y.; Greenberg, M., (eds.) *Moving ahead with attitude research.* Chicago: American Marketing Association. p. 73-86.

Kahneman, D.; Tversky, A. 1979. Prospect theory: An analysis of decision under risk. *Econometrica. 47*(2): 263-291.

Kamen, J.; Toman, R. 1970. Psychographics of prices. *Journal of Marketing Research. 7*: 27-35.

Kelly, H. H. 1967. *Attribution theory in social psychology.* Nebraska Symposium on Motivation. 15: 192-241.

Kelly, J. 1982. *Leisure.* Englewood Cliffs, N.J.: Prentice Hall. 426 p.

Kelman, H. C. 1961. Processes of opinion change. *Public Opinion Quarterly. 25*: 57-78.

Kerr, G. N.; Manfredo, M.J. 1991. An attitudinal based model of pricing for recreation services. *Journal of Leisure Research. 23*(1): 37-50.

Klar, L.; Rodman, C. 1984. Budgetary and administrative impacts of tax-limiting legislation on municipal recreation and parks departments. *Journal of Park and Recreation Administration. 2*(4): 31-44.

Kotler, P.; Andreasen, A. 1987. *Strategic marketing for nonprofit organizations*. Englewood Cliffs, NJ: Prentice Hall. 670 p.

Leuschner, W.; Cook, P.; Roggenbuck, J.; Oderwald, R. 1987. A comparative analysis for wilderness user fee policy. *Journal of Leisure Research.* *19*(2): 101-114.

Lutz, R. 1985. Affective and cognitive antecedents of attitude toward the ad: A conceptual framework. In Alwitt, L. F.; Mitchell, A. A., (eds.) *Psychological Processes and Advertising Effects*. Hilsdale, NJ: Erlbaum. p. 45-63.

Mackintosh, Barry. 1983. *Visitor fees in the national park system, a legislative and administrative history*. Washington, DC: National Park Service.

Manning, R.; Baker, S. 1981. Discrimination through user fees: Fact or fiction? *Parks and Recreation.* *16*(9): 70-74.

Manning, R.; Callinan, E.; Echelberger, E.; Koemann, E.; McEwen, D. 1984. Differential fees: Raising revenue, distributing demand. *Journal of Recreation and Park Administration.* *2*(1): 20-38.

Market Opinion Research. 1986. *Participation in outdoor recreation among American adults and motivations which drive participation*. For the President's Commission on Americans Outdoors. Washington, DC: Market Opinion Research.

McCarville, R.; Crompton, J. 1987. An empirical investigation of the influence of information on reference prices for public swimming pools. *Journal of Leisure Research.* *19*(3): 223-235.

McCarville, R.; Crompton, J. 1988. A review of selected local park and recreation financial indicators in the first half of the 1980s: A challenge to conventional wisdom. *Journal of Park and Recreation Administration.* *6*(3): 43-54.

McConnell, K. 1982. Some problems in estimating the demand for outdoor recreation. *American Journal of Agricultural Economics.* *57*: 330-340.

McGuire, W.J. 1985. Attitudes and attitude change. In: Lindzey, G.; Aronson, E., (eds.) *Handbook of social psychology*. New York: Random House. 2: 233-346.

Menz, F.; Mullen, J. 1981. Expected encounters and willingness to pay for outdoor recreation. *Land Economics.* *57*(1): 33-40.

Miles, A.; Fedler, T. 1986. *Paying for backcountry recreation experiences: Understanding the acceptability of user fees*. Presentation at the First National Symposium on Social Science in Resource Management, Oregon State University, Corvallis, OR.

Monroe, K. 1979. *Pricing: Making profitable decisions*. New York: McGraw-Hill Company.

Monroe, K.; Della B. A. 1984. The effect of anchoring stimuli on price judgments. In: Kinnear, T. C., (ed.), *Proceedings: Advances in consumer research*. Ann Arbor: Association for Consumer Research. p. 85-91.

Monroe, K.; Petroshius, S. 1981. Buyers perception of price: An update of the evidence. In: Kassarjian, H.; Robertson, T., (eds.) *Perspectives in consumer behavior*, 3rd Edition. Dallas: Scott, Foresman and Co. p. 43-55.

Noble, K. 1987. Congress votes to bar $1.00 admission fee at Statue of Liberty. *New York Times.* 6(13): 13.

Nwokoye, N. G. 1975. Subjective judgments in price: The effects of price parameters on adaptation levels. *Proceedings: American Marketing Association Fall Conference.* p. 545-548.

Olander, F. 1970. The influence of price on the consumer's evaluation of products and purchases. In: Taylor, B.; Walls, G., (eds.) *Pricing strategy*, Princeton: Brandon Systems Press. p. 50-69.

Petty, R. E.; Cacioppo, J. 1981. *Attitudes and persuasion: Classic and contemporary approaches.* Dubuque: William C. Brown Company. 314 p.

Petty, R. E.; Cacioppo, J.T. 1986a. The elaboration likelihood model of persuasion. *Advances in Experimental Social Psychology. 19*:123-205.

Petty, R. E.; Cacioppo, J.T. 1986b. The elaboration likelihood model of persuasion. In: Berkowitz, L., (ed.) *Advances in experimental social psychology.* New York: Academic Press. 19: 123-205.

Petty, R. E.; Cacioppo, J.T. 1989. Involvement and persuasion: Tradition versus integration. *Psychology Bulletin.* In press.

Raman, K. 1985. The effects of advertising and promotions on reference prices: A varying parameters approach. Unpublished doctoral dissertation. University of Texas at Dallas, TX.

Rawls, J. 1971. *A theory of justice.* Cambridge: Bilknop Press. 605 p.

Reiling, S.; Criner, G.; Oltmanns, S. 1988. The influence of information on users' attitudes toward campground user fees. *Journal of Leisure Research. 20*(3): 19-24.

Rinne, H. 1981. An empirical investigation of the effects of reference price on sales. Unpublished doctoral dissertation. Purdue University, West Lafayette, IL.

Rosenthal, D.; Loomis, J.; Peterson, G. 1984. The travel cost model: Concepts and applications. *Gen. Tech. Report RM 109.* Fort Collins, CO. Rocky Mountain Forest and Range Experiment Station, Forest Service, U.S. Department of Agriculture.

Schlenker, B. R. 1980. *Impression management: The self-concept, social identity, and interpersonal relations.* Monterey, CA. Brooks/Cole.

Sewall, M.; Goldstein, M. 1979. The comparative price advertising controversy: Consumer perceptions of catalogue showroom reference prices. *Journal of Marketing. 43*: 85-92.

Shelby, B.; Danley, K.; Peterson, M. 1982. Preferences of backpackers and river runners for allocation techniques. Journal of Forestry. 80(7): p. 416-419.

Sherif, J. M.; Sherif, C. W. 1967. Attitude as the individual's own categories: The social judgment-involvement approach to attitude and attitude change. In: Sherif, C. W.; Sherif, M., (eds.) *Attitude, ego evolvement, and change.* NY: Wiley.

Tesser, A.; Shaffer, D. R. 1990. Attitudes and attitude change. *Annual Review of Psychology. 41*: 479-523.

Tversky, A.; Kahneman, D. 1986. Rational choice and the framing of decisions. *Journal of Business. 59*(4): 251-278.

Uhl, J. 1970. *Consumer perception of retail food price changes.* Paper presented at the first annual meeting of the Association for Consumer Research, Amherst, MA.

Urbany, J.; Beardon, W; Weilbaker, D. 1988. The effect of plausible and exaggerated reference prices on consumer perceptions and price search. *Journal of Consumer Research. 15*: 95-110.

Wicks, B.; Crompton, J. 1986. Citizen and administrator perceptions of equity in the delivery of park services. *Leisure Sciences. 8*(4): 341-365.

Zaichkowsky, J. 1985. Measuring the involvement construct. *Journal of Consumer Research. 12*: 341-352.

Ziethaml, V.; Graham, K. 1983. The accuracy of reported reference prices for professional services. In: Bagozzi, R.P.; Tybout, A.M. (eds.) *Proceedings: Advances in Consumer Research.* Ann Arbor: Association for Consumer Research. p. 83-92.

10

Persuasive Messages and Safety Hazards in Dispersed and Natural Recreation Settings

Stephen F. McCool
Amy M. Braithwaite

INTRODUCTION

Dispersed and natural areas are recreational settings character-ized by widely scattered use and dominated by substantially unmodified environments. Visitors to such environments typically encounter a wide variety of hazards, and because they may be unprepared to deal effectively with unfamiliar hazards, such encounters may result in discomfort, anguish, injury, or even death.

Our objectives in this chapter are to outline the nature of hazards in dispersed recreational settings, and differentiate between the con-cepts of hazard and risk; to briefly review research on hazards and risk from other fields; and to examine research on persuasive messages intending to reduce hazards in recreational settings.

Webster's Dictionary defines "hazard" in terms of chance, dan-ger, and lack of control over events. In this chapter we consider hazards to be those uncontrollable components and processes encountered in natural environments that may lead to the injury or death of recreationists. To qualify as hazards, components must be perceived by recreationists as obstacles to achieving particular goals, and must be either subject to random processes or beyond the control of the recreationists.

Recreationists may have prior knowledge that a setting attribute constitutes a hazard, or may be unaware that the hazard exists. If recreationists are aware of a hazardous attribute, they tend to avoid it. They may also perceive a hazard as an unpredictable or uncontrollable threat to their health and safety (Houston 1968). For example, backpackers in Glacier National Park may perceive grizzly bears as a hazard because bears are unpredictable and constitute an obstacle to a secure backcountry experience. While they may understand the potential for bear encounters, recreationists may also believe that they can do little to significantly reduce such potential.

Risk may be understood as exposure to hazards. We differentiate between hazards confronting recreationists, and voluntary recreational activities such as mountain climbing that entail some risk. In risk-taking recreation, the participant seeks or manipulates the hazardous attribute as a means of achieving a desired experience. The cliff a climber challenges is part and parcel of the experience, and the risk-taking recreationist carefully chooses the routes and manipulates various setting attributes, such as type of equipment, to optimize the experience. The risk-taking recreationist is aware of the potential of injury, and of the actions needed to control factors contributing to exposure to hazards (Allen 1980).

To non-risk-seeking visitors, hazards are impediments to an optimal experience. These visitors prepare themselves and manipulate their behavior to reduce or modify their exposure to the hazard. For example, flash floods may be perceived as a hazard when hiking in a deeply entrenched canyon. Hikers can limit risk associated with this hazard by manipulating certain behaviors — camping in safe locations, being alert to weather, and minimizing time spent in hazardous situations. While the hazard itself is not controllable, the recreationists' response - and thus, the amount of risk - is controllable.

Other types of hazards include stream crossings, high water, falling trees and rocks, severe storms and lightning, avalanches, wildlife, insects, and underwater dropoffs and currents. Inappropriate or reckless behavior by other recreationists may also constitute a hazard, as can heat exhaustion, hypothermia, or frostbite. Informed, experienced recreationists may view these hazards as controllable factors, while inexperienced or uninformed recreationists would seek to avoid them, or be unaware of appropriate behavioral responses.

Although the definitions of hazard and risk are similar, it is important to distinguish between the two. A hazard is a "set of circumstances which may cause harmful consequences" (British Medical Association Guide 1987). Risk, on the other hand, is the likelihood of being harmed by a hazard. A cliff is a hazard; there is a risk that people may be injured by rocks falling off the cliff, or by falling off the cliff themselves. In dispersed recreation settings, managers cannot control hazards (e.g., the cliff cannot be removed) but, by managing people's behavior around the hazard, they can often reduce risks.

REASONS FOR CONCERN

Land management agencies have important reasons to be concerned about hazards in dispersed, natural environmental settings. First is the generally accepted view that people have a moral responsibility to other people, and should attempt to inform others of hazards. Most people would agree that recreationists should be rescued from hazardous predicaments, regardless of proximate cause, although there is no general legal responsibility to do so (Rankin 1989). For example, even though a mountain climber may be injured because of personal negligence, our societal values would support a rescue operation. If a sudden snowstorm strands a climber, few people would contend that the climber should be left to his own devices.

More than a few scholars and recreationists have proposed and debated the notion of "no-rescue" wildernesses (Allen 1981, McAvoy and Dustin 1981). Once recreationists cross the boundary of a no-rescue wilderness, society would be free of its moral and legal obligation to rescue them from whatever peril — including risk of death — they may encounter.

Second, agencies have a legal duty to protect people recreating on public lands from hazards known to the agencies. The level of responsibility varies according to each state and according to actions taken on the part of agencies and recreationists, and is affected by the type of recreational setting (Rankin 1989). For example, agencies have minimal responsibility to warn trespassers of hazards unknown to the agencies, but have a greater duty when recreationists are invited (through designation and signs) to visit agency-administered land. In cases of known hazards, agencies usually must take action to correct the hazards. For example, in national parks, recreationists must be warned of the presence of grizzly bears and informed about actions they can take to reduce confrontations. Troublesome bears must also be removed.

Generally, the duty to protect recreationists from hazards is greater in developed settings than in undeveloped ones. In developed settings, agencies have usually adopted the policy of removing hazards or protecting recreationists, while in undeveloped settings the policy is to warn recreationists of the hazards.

CONSEQUENCES OF HAZARDS

Hazards pose a number of adverse consequences for managers, visitors and the natural resource. Obviously, hazards may result in injury or death to recreationists. Unfortunately, it is difficult to determine the extent of actual human injury and death in recreational settings, particularly natural ones, because land management agencies do not maintain and consistently report statistics on accidents caused by natural hazards.

National accident statistics, however, indicate that the number of deaths attributable to natural events may be significant in some recreational activities and settings. It is difficult to determine from these data how many deaths are caused by hazards. About 150,000 recreationists sustained injuries in wildland-related activities during 1987 (National Safety Council 1988). Lightning causes about 70 deaths per year (National Safety Council 1988), many occurring in recreational settings. More than 2,100 people drown annually while swimming and about 1,400 people are killed while bicycling. Statistics collected by the American Alpine Club (1987) indicate steady growth in the number of mountaineering accidents reported from 1981 to 1986. However, mountaineering accident reporting tends to be somewhat anecdotal and is subject to individual efforts to identify or illustrate incidents more comprehensively.

While the popular press often reports wildlife hazards, particularly those pertaining to grizzly bears, statistics on confrontations with bears suggest that this type of hazard is relatively infrequent. In Glacier National Park, the confrontation rate with grizzly bears has averaged about one per 1.3 million visitors the last several years (Table 1), although this rate is increasing.

Incidentally, there is also a significant question as to what base statistic accurately reflects the rate of hazard-caused injuries in natural environments. Is the number of incidents most appropriate? Injury rate per thousand visitors entering the park? Injuries per thousand backcountry campers?

Beyond the immediate human effects, injuries and deaths in recreational settings have significant monetary consequences. These include monetary and productivity loss from people unable to work during recovery, permanent income loss because of a death, and the suffering, anguish and trauma associated with caring for an injured relative or friend. However, the actual monetary losses from hazards in recreational settings are unknown.

Table 1
Human/bear confrontations that resulted in human injury or death, visitation levels, and confrontation rates for Glacier National Park

Period	Number of Confrontations	Visits	Confrontation[1] Rate
1961-1965	3	3,629,000	.83
1966-1970	4	4,006,000	1.00
1971-1975	6	5,049,000	1.20
1976-1980	9	11,161,000	.82
1981-1985	8	9,185,000	.89
1986-1989	9	6,862,000	1.30

[1]Confrontations per million visits.
Source: National Park Service files

Hazard concerns also cause impacts on wildlife populations, because problem bears, alligators, snakes, skunks, and mountain lions may require relocation or destruction. While incidents with these animals receive widespread publicity, wildlife hazard reduction in backcountry recreation areas is more often directed at changing visitor behavior. Inappropriate behavior by recreationists usually causes the animal habituation that leads to wildlife hazards. Thus, removing the problem animals may deal with an immediate problem but does not remedy the cause. When problem animals such as grizzly bears are listed as threatened or endangered, removals may have significant implications for population enhancement objectives.

Hazards also cause adverse impacts on site vegetation. Vegetation hazards may result from ground plants such as poison ivy or stinging nettle, or from dead and rotting trees that could fall on recreationists. While many such hazards mainly cause discomfort, a few, such as falling trees, can cause injury and death. Removing this sort of hazard, which usually occurs only in developed settings, normally has only minor consequences for the setting and for the resource itself.

Hazards can result in significant costs to some agencies, such as the National Park Service, which take direct financial responsibility for search and rescue operations. Many other operations are directed by local volunteer organizations such as a Search and Rescue group. However, their loss of work time can have a significant monetary impact on the volunteers. The number of search and rescue operations initiated by federal, state and local agencies and groups to save recreationists in dispersed settings is not summarized at any level for easy retrieval. Regardless of what agency bears the cost of a particular search and rescue effort, a major debate centers on whether injured recreationists should reimburse the rescue cost.

Other costs incurred by an agency include those associated with hazard removal, programs to educate visitors about hazards, personnel time and travel costs to develop hazard control programs, and costs to defend and resolve litigation resulting from hazards. Again, national statistics measuring these costs are not available.

A final consequence of hazards concerns their impact on the visitor's level of satisfaction with the recreational experience. By definition, the presence of hazards would seem likely to lead to dissatisfaction for visitors. However, how visitors perceive hazards and the relationship of hazards to reported satisfaction levels has not been systematically researched.

Significant debate exists among recreation management professionals and users about the extent of needed protections from hazards, and the impact of those protections on recreational experiences. Many people support Joseph Sax's (1980) view that visitors should not be overprotected from the environment when they visit a park. Beck et al. (1989) argue, for example, that "... emphasis on visitor safety carries hidden costs, represented by the opportunities foregone by protecting recreationists from themselves." While these authors are deeply concerned about potential loss of opportunities because of too much protection, agencies are confronted with potential liability from not doing enough.

METHODS FOR DEALING WITH HAZARDS

Hazard management involves several components. The hazard must first be identified and described. Then a method for controlling, reducing, or eliminating the hazard is identified by agency managers, and a specific method or combination of methods is implemented. The specific control method used will vary with the nature of the hazard and the setting, the level of skill and knowledge held by recreationists, and the management objectives for the area. After the method is implemented, the effectiveness of management actions directed at controlling exposure to hazards is monitored.

Once managers identify and describe the hazard, they can select from four methods of hazard control. One method is to reduce or eliminate the hazard - for example, removal of poison ivy and dead trees in developed settings. This action results in immediate hazard reduction, but has no long term consequences for visitor education or behavior changes. In backcountry areas, removal of vegetation hazards may be viewed as an unacceptable manipulation of the natural environment.

A second method is to impose a barrier between stationary hazards and visitors. For example, a hazardous cliff could be fenced to reduce the probability of visitors falling. Or, a campground could be physically closed off to protect campers from falling trees. These first two methods are usually appropriate in developed settings, but would not be acceptable in backcountry settings where manipulation of the environment may be inconsistent with management objectives. In addition, hazards such as lightning or wildlife would not be susceptible to these actions.

A third approach is to regulate visitor behavior. For example, the Virgin River Narrows in Zion National Park contains a significant flash flood hazard. During the summer recreational use season, thunderstorms above the river's upper watershed may result in rapidly rising water levels while unaware recreationists hike through the deeply entrenched and narrow canyon below. Obviously, there is no practical way of controlling thunderstorms and resulting flash floods, or to notify endangered hikers already within the Narrows.

The Park Service can reduce this sort of hazard by regulating visitor use of the Narrows during periods of thunderstorm activity. Closing the Narrows is an effective tool if visitors comply with the closure. The rate of compliance with closures in recreational settings, however, needs further research. For example, Cole and Ranz (1983) found that 84 percent of backcountry campers complied with a campsite closure in the Selway-Bitterroot Wilderness.

While often viewed as necessary by managers, regulations on recreation behavior are frequently regarded by recreationists as intrusions into the recreational experience, particularly in wilderness settings where regulations conflict with expectations of autonomy (Brown and Haas 1980). Regulations interfere with the feeling of freedom or internal locus of control that is an essential component of recreational experiences. Levy (1978) defines internal locus of control as "the degree to which individuals perceive that they are in control of their actions and outcomes." Lucas (1983) notes that the "appropriateness of recreation regulations depends largely on the balance between the benefits and costs of a specific regulation and alternative nonregulatory management actions ..."

The fourth method of hazard management is the use of persuasive messages. Land management agencies commonly use written information and verbal warnings to notify recreationists about hazards in order to meet the legal duties imposed upon the agency. For example, to reduce the level of exposure to flash flooding in the Virgin River Narrows, the National Park Service advises hikers that thunderstorms may occur, and recommends appropriate behavior to guard against the flash flood hazard if a storm occurs while the hiker is in the Narrows. The National Park Service can also inform hikers of what to look for in selecting campsites that are not vulnerable to flash floods.

The Forest Service commonly warns winter backcountry travelers of snow avalanche hazard conditions, and attempts to educate recreationists to recognize and avoid avalanche areas. Agencies also inform travelers about what to do if they are caught in an avalanche.

Such persuasive messages are often built on passive models of the communication process that assume that, if a message is transmitted, it is received, accepted, and acted upon by the recreationist. However, many managers are concerned about the effectiveness of these warnings in influencing and modifying visitor behavior, implicitly recognizing that communicating persuasive messages to their clients is more complex than it may initially appear.

HAZARD RESEARCH IN OTHER DISCIPLINES

Information is frequently used as a management tool for reducing visitor-induced impacts, particularly in the areas of campsite selection, appropriate disposal of human wastes, dishwashing, trash, and encounters with other types of recreationists. Information is also used as a means for reducing the probability of confronting various hazards (Haydock and McCool 1976). For example, land management agencies in the northern Rockies have several programs for informing backcountry visitors of the appropriate behavior for reducing confrontations with grizzly bears.

While there is a generally accepted philosophy in dispersed and natural recreational settings that favors education and information over regulation and enforcement (McCool and Lucas 1989), little effort has been devoted to evaluating the effectiveness of message campaigns (Brown et al. 1987). Much of the research concerning message effectiveness in recreation settings has dealt with minimum impact behavior (see Roggenbuck, this volume). Although many recreation managers consider information an effective and preferred method of addressing human induced impacts and conflicts, very little research has analyzed how recreationists perceive, evaluate and respond to recreation setting hazards, let alone the role of information in influencing behavioral responses. To increase understanding of the effectiveness of persuasive messages in informing recreationists of hazards, we first briefly review research on hazards and human behavior conducted in other disciplines.

Many fields and disciplines other than recreation management have examined human perceptions of and responses to hazards and risks. For example, borrowing concepts from psychology and sociology, geographers, marketing researchers and health professionals have had some success in explaining the perceptions and behaviors of individuals exposed to hazards or risks. Two major theories that have directed much of the hazard and risk perception research in consumer behavior, geography and other disciplines are the cognitive dissonance and locus of control theories.

Festinger's (1957) theory of cognitive dissonance is one of the most widely discussed theories in social psychology. Derived from consistency theory, cognitive dissonance theory states that when dissonance is present, tension or stress are produced pressuring the individual to change behavior to reduce the dissonance. In addition, the individual will tend to avoid situations that may produce dissonance in the future. As a tool for understanding risk perceptions, this theory carries many implications. For example, an individual residing in an area frequented by tornadoes may feel some tension or stress, a state of dissonance, during the tornado season. For some individuals, their habitation in a tornado zone is inconsistent with their beliefs that a significant risk of injury or death exists in such regions. The theory of cognitive dissonance states that to reduce this sense of discord, these people will seek various alternatives (i.e., leaving the area during tornado season or constructing a tornado proof shelter) in order to return to a state of balance or homeostasis.

Other researchers have used locus of control theory to explain hazard perceptions and subsequent behavior. Basically, two types of locus of control exist, internal and external. Individuals with an internal locus of control feel they can influence their future through appropriate behavior; people with an external locus disposition believe their future is predominantly determined by forces (i.e., fate, luck, chance, other people) beyond their control. In risk or hazard situations, researchers hypothesize that these latter individuals will usually fail to make proper adjustments. For example, some may fail to engage in recommended techniques for reducing the risk associated with living in tornado areas. Their failure to adopt risk-reduction procedures may stem from a conviction that the forces of nature determine the path of a destructive tornado. Therefore, they may believe that the element of risk associated with tornadoes is controlled by fate, luck or chance, rendering them powerless and risk-reduction behaviors useless.

On the other hand, internal locus of control individuals who believe their personal actions largely control the outcomes of events in their lives are more likely to make necessary adjustments to reduce potential risks or hazards. In the case of tornadoes, internal locus individuals would engage in risk-reduction behaviors more frequently than external locus individuals. The perception of being in control of their fate motivates them to manipulate specific situations and circumstances to increase their likelihood of surviving tornadoes.

Geography

The geography and health fields define hazards as a set of circumstances that may lead to harmful consequences (British Medical Association Guide 1987) - for example, earthquakes and air pollution. Risk is defined as the likelihood of the hazard actually resulting in injury, illness or death: the risk of being injured or killed during an earthquake is much greater in a poorly constructed building than in a structurally-reinforced building.

Hazard perception studies were introduced by Kates (1962), who examined why people chose to live in floodplains where the probability of a flood is high. Kates found that different people encountering similar exposure to risks in floodplains responded to these risks differently. Some individuals had no knowledge of the hazard or risk, others cognitively reduced the severity of the hazard, and others actively planned measures for reducing their risk.

White (1974) stated that human responses to risks and hazards are a function of several components. Attitudes and beliefs toward a particular hazard can influence individual responses to the risk of encountering that hazard. Similarly, researchers have found that people's perceptions of their environments, as well as some demographic variables, may explain actual behavior (e.g., Anderson 1980, Cockrell 1981, Fedler 1981, and Robertson 1981). As outlined in the locus of control discussion, an individual's perception of a hazard can influence the behaviors selected to reduce the potential effects of that hazard. Mitchell (1984), however, stated that populations at risk and public hazard managers often perceive hazards to be significantly different from the actual characteristics of the hazard. Thus, inaccurate perceptions about a serious hazard could result in inappropriate behavioral responses. Factors that influence an individual's perception of a hazard include the magnitude and frequency of the hazard, the recency of personal experience with the hazard, and the importance of the hazard to the person's income. Other factors influencing hazard perception involve personality factors, such as risk-taking propensity, perceptions of who controls one's fate, and attitudes toward nature.

White (1974) states that behavior may be influenced by an individual's perception of the alternatives available for reducing or adjusting to a potential hazard. Fishbein and Ajzen (1975) contend that an individual's attitude toward a particular behavior directly affects behavior. Therefore, an individual's perception of a hazard-reducing behavior as either beneficial or useless may determine whether the individual engages in that behavior. An individual's command of technological advances for adjusting to hazards may also influence behavior in the event of a disaster. For example, an individual living in a structurally-reinforced building in an earthquake zone may be less likely to engage in appropriate behaviors (i.e., leaving the building, standing in doorway, or getting under a table or desk) for reducing the probability of injury or death.

The relative economic efficiency of the alternatives available to an individual may affect behavior. If an individual perceives the risk of a potential hazard as minimal, the individual may be unwilling to pay for hazard reduction products (disaster insurance, structural reinforcements, water purifiers, raingear, etc.). In addition, the expectations of significant others may influence an individual's behavior prior to or during a disaster. An individual may behave in a particular manner to reduce the likelihood of injury to himself or others in order to meet the behavioral expectations of family, friends, co-workers, or public service personnel.

One of the difficulties in understanding the conclusions of the hazard perception literature is the variety of applications of the term "perception." Mitchell (1984) examined hazard perception research and indicated that the term "perception" has been equated to such concepts as: (1) potential victim's risk assessment, (2) attitudes toward the environment, (3) reported information about hazards, (4) awareness of physical processes contributing to hazards, and (5) identification of adjustments to hazards. "Perception" appears to be the generic term for many sociological and psychological concepts being applied to investigate the human element of hazard research. In essence, the term has come to represent such widely varying concepts as cognition, knowledge, decision-making and choice behavior. Scientists definitely need to develop sound conceptual and methodological strategies for examining how risk perception affects human behavior.

Consumer Behavior

Consumer behavior research defines hazard as either a product (i.e., automobile, chain saw, toilet cleaner) or an activity which involves the use of a product (i.e., driving a sports car fast, pruning trees), and the distinction between risk and hazard is not explicit in some of the research. However, risk appears to be the more important concept in the study of consumer behavior, and involves more than just the extent to which an individual may be harmed by buying a product or engaging in an activity using a product. The risk of harm is directly linked to the hazards intrinsically associated with the product (even those deemed safe by the government), environmental factors, and individual impairment or disability (British Medical Association Guide 1987). For example, the elderly, the very young, individuals under the influence of drugs or alcohol, and ailing individuals are at the greatest risk of being injured by products. Viscusi et al. (1986) determined that providing product-hazard information greatly reduced the risks associated with certain products and is an effective alternative to more direct regulation of safety risks.

Besides the physical risks associated with bodily harm, consumer behavior involves other forms of risk. Social and economic risks also exist when purchasing and using products. For example, a product closely related to a consumer's public image (i.e., clothes, car, etc.) could present high social risk. Other products, due to their price or technical complexity (i.e., computers) represent high economic risks (Hawkins et al. 1983). In consumer behavior research, "perceived risk" has also been used to refer to those beliefs about the risks associated with product purchase (Engel et al. 1986).

Bennett and Kassarjian (1972) state that risk may be perceived by the consumer as a result of several factors. Individuals may be uncertain of their buying goals - for example, whether to buy a new outfit or a new household appliance. If this person chooses the outfit, should it be a formal outfit for a classy affair, or should it be a more practical everyday outfit? Consumers may also be uncertain as to other purchase needs: should the new outfit be bought at Macy's, Sears or a local discount house? Would a fashionable outfit provide more satisfaction than a conservative one? A consumer may also perceive that a purchase may result in adverse consequences. For example, a lower middle class individual who buys a new BMW rather than a used car may have to cut back on other purchases for a long period of time. Additionally, the purchaser's family and friends may scorn the individual for buying a product associated with higher social stratum.

Bennett and Kassarjian (1972) state that a perceived risk exists if one or more of the above conditions (uncertainty about buying goals, uncertainty about product selection, and uncertainty about adverse consequences) is present within the buyer's cognitions. They view risk as a function of uncertainty and the possibility of negative consequences. Perceived risks may stimulate the consumer to search for information to learn more about other alternatives. King (1975) states that the greater a person's level of uncertainty is in a given social situation, the higher the probability of being influenced by information provided by others. Therefore, the natural response to ambiguity is to seek informational sources to clarify any uncertainty that may exist.

In cases where the perceived risk is too great, consumers may postpone or drop their intentions to purchase a product. Even if a consumer does make a purchase, risk can influence decision-making factors. An individual may select the alternative that minimizes the amount of perceived risk, even though it may not have been the preferred alternative.

The above review raises implications for managing exposure to hazards in risk situations. Recreation managers need to understand that the objective exposure to risk may be different from recreationists' subjective perceptions of risk. These perceptions, however, can be influenced by information managers provide about the hazard. However, too much emphasis on recreation setting hazards may cause people to stay away from the setting. For example, high fear-arousing messages about grizzly bears in Glacier National Park may discourage some people from hiking in the backcountry even though they would like to do so.

Furthermore, visitor perceptions of uncertainties in the setting, including hazards, may motivate them to seek additional information in order to reduce those uncertainties. Uncertainty could be a function of experience. It is highly probable that inexperienced visitors in some settings may have no knowledge about hazards, and thus would not be motivated by feelings of uncertainty to obtain information. More experienced recreationists who perceive that hazards may exist, but may be uncertain about the risk of the hazards or how to deal with the risks, would seek additional information. An implication of this process is that recreationists will have needs for different types of information from the managing agency.

Health

A health hazard is a set of circumstances that may lead an individual to contract an illness or disease, or incur an injury. A health risk is the likelihood of an individual's contracting a disease or illness, or incurring an injury (British Medical Association Guide 1987).

Health risks can often be greatly reduced by the adoption of preventive health practices, even though the hazard remains. For example, certain groups of individuals (i.e., homosexuals, intravenous drug-users, individuals with multiple sexual partners) have a much higher likelihood of contracting AIDS than other groups of people. However, the risk of an individual's contracting AIDS, regardless of being in a high or low risk group, can be greatly reduced through the adoption of safe sexual practices. Dissemination of information to increase the adoption of preventive behaviors or practices is a technique used extensively by health professionals.

A widely accepted conceptual framework for explaining the adoption of preventive health practices is the Health Belief Model (Bauman and Siegel 1987). This model identifies several dimensions that may influence the adoption of health practices. The first dimension is individuals' perceptions of their vulnerability to developing a health problem. The greater the perception of personal vulnerability to a disease or illness, the more likely individuals will engage in preventive health behaviors. However, most people tend to consistently underestimate the degree to which they are at risk (e.g., Harris and Guten 1979, Larwood 1978, Robertson 1977, Weinstein 1984).

Individual perceptions of the severity of a particular illness influence the adoption of preventive health practices. Since AIDS is considered a terminal disease, most people would likely engage in those behaviors that will greatly reduce the possibility of contracting the disease. Individuals may be less likely to engage in preventive behaviors for less severe illnesses, such as influenza or the common cold. Another factor influencing the adoption of preventive health practices is the perception of benefits that may result from modifying health behavior. Will engaging in recommended health behaviors result in a longer life span, decreased medical bills, reduced susceptibility to disease and better quality of life? If individuals believe that certain benefits may derive from particular behaviors, they will be more likely to adopt preventive health behaviors.

Individual perceptions of barriers or possible negative effects associated with change can influence the extent to which people will adopt preventive health behaviors. For example, an individual who smokes may be unwilling to suffer the agony of nicotine withdrawal in order to reduce the likelihood of contracting lung cancer. The individual may perceive the benefits of engaging in a behavior as being worth less than the risks associated with not engaging in the behavior (Ajzen and Fishbein 1980).

Various cues or stimuli directed at change, such as a symptom or a health communication, may also influence the adoption of preventive health behaviors. Similar to the theory of cognitive dissonance, experiencing a symptom of an illness may cause an individual cognitive as well as physical discomfort. This dissonance should motivate the individual to take action so the condition does not worsen. Additionally, health communications may inculcate a sense of fear or concern, motivating an individual to engage in preventive health actions to reduce the cognitive discomfort associated with the fear and concern. However, under some circumstances fear communications may be ineffective in achieving desired behavioral change (Job 1988). When the fear resulting from a message is high, it may cause feelings of hopelessness within the message receiver, decreasing the likelihood that the individual will engage in the suggested behaviors. Since many health communications have the potential to arouse fear and concern, they must be designed to evoke sufficient threat to motivate behavioral change without causing despair.

This research on hazard perceptions and behavioral decisions of individuals exposed to hazards or risks presents several implications for future research on hazard situations in recreation settings. Researchers need to identify recreationists' perceptions of hazards and the alternatives available for reducing the risk of potential hazards. If perceptions of hazards are accurate, and if available alternatives for reducing the risks of hazards are perceived as beneficial, recreationists may be more likely to engage in risk-reducing behaviors. However, if perceptions are inaccurate and alternatives are viewed as useless in reducing risks, recreationists may not engage in risk-reducing behaviors. Therefore, perceptions concerning hazards need to be adjusted so that individuals are more inclined to engage in risk-reducing behaviors. An intensive, persuasive communication program aimed at altering misperceptions may be an effective means for changing inappropriate behavior.

Researchers also need to determine whether technological advances in outdoor equipment affect recreationists' perceptions of hazards and risks. Do individuals possessing the most technologically safe equipment perceive risk to be lower than do individuals possessing outdated equipment? Researchers may also want to investigate how social pressure from peer groups such as family, friends, or management staff may influence individuals' behavior when exposed to hazards and risks. Future research should also examine the extent to which recreationists seek out hazardous or risky situations as a component of their recreation experience. Do individuals choose to ignore recommended behaviors in hazardous situations in order to enhance recreational experiences?

RESEARCH ON THE EFFECTIVENESS OF PERSUASIVE MESSAGES ABOUT HAZARDS IN DISPERSED RECREATION SETTINGS

Within this useful context of theoretical models from other fields we now turn to recreation management research on visitor behavior and hazards. Few researchers have addressed the issues of visitors' perceptions of and responses to hazards, or hazard warning effectiveness, in recreational settings. However, the problem of effectively communicating appropriate behavior to recreational visitors in order to minimize impacts upon the biophysical setting is increasing in importance. There is now a small but growing literature on message effectiveness for minimum impact behavior. And in response to the amount of attention the press gives to confrontations between grizzly bears and humans, a literature is developing in this area.

The problem of message effectiveness with respect to confrontations with bears is most graphically illustrated by Cella's and Keay's (1979) study of visitor behavior in the Yosemite National Park backcountry. These researchers reported that 95 percent of the visitors contacted received a brochure on proper food storage techniques. While 92 percent of the visitors queried believed they were properly storing their food, checks by the researchers indicated that only 3 percent were actually doing so. Clearly, researchers need to examine fundamental questions about the nature of communications, message design, and factors associated with message reception and acceptance. Researchers also need to scrutinize the variables influencing the message receiver's ability or motivation to engage in the recommended behaviors.

Fishbein and Ajzen (1975) state that behavioral intentions predict actual behavior. Two variables, attitudes about the behavior and its consequences, and social normative influences on message receivers, affect behavioral intentions. Figure 1 shows how this approach is incorporated into the study of the effectiveness of persuasive messages. We will use this model to discuss research about hazard messages in recreational settings, but before explaining the persuasive communication model, we must recall the purpose and definition of persuasive messages. Persuasive messages contain a set of arguments supporting a particular position and one or more recommended actions. Their primary goal is to change or produce certain behaviors in the message recipient (Ajzen and Fishbein 1980).

The persuasive communication model demonstrates that information affects behavior only indirectly. Once an individual receives and accepts a particular piece of information, certain changes in beliefs and attitudes may occur. These changes may, in turn, affect the recipient's intentions to perform the suggested behavior, therefore potentially influencing actual behavior in any given situation. The large number of variables intervening between transmission of information and actual behavior suggests that wildland managers need to better understand the processes of belief and attitude formation and how these influence actual behavior. Without such understanding, managers will probably continue to base persuasive communication efforts on inappropriate models of behavioral change.

The model shows that in the first phases of the persuasive process, information about appropriate behavior can be received from several sources, including friends and significant others, agency brochures and literature, books, magazine articles and even films. Previous recreation experiences may also play an important role at this stage in determining appropriate behavior. Such sources help establish and influence broad

Figure 1
Model of Persuasive Communication Process
(after Fishbein and Ajzen 1975)

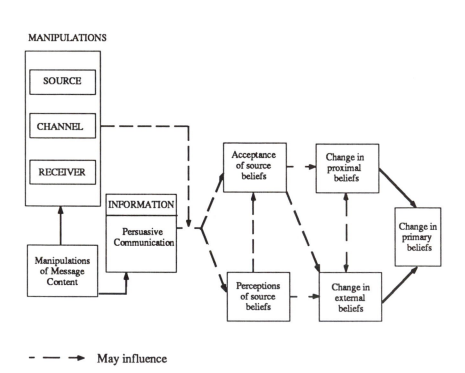

(termed "external" by Ajzen and Fishbein 1980) beliefs about hazards that in turn may affect more direct beliefs about appropriate behaviors required to deal with particular hazards. For example, some people hold beliefs that the grizzly bear is an essential component of a naturally functioning and "healthy" ecosystem. These beliefs may in turn influence a more direct belief that food should be carefully stored to deter a dependency by bears on unnatural food sources, thus reducing the probability of confrontations. These types of existing, broad (external) beliefs, or more direct (primary) ones may support or contradict agency communications concerning appropriate behavior.

Another model that focuses upon how individuals receive and respond to persuasive messages is the Elaboration Likelihood Model (Petty and Cacioppo 1986). This model specifies how persuasive communication can result in enduring attitude shifts rather than temporary shifts. The model proposes two basic routes to attitude change, the central route and the peripheral route. Persuasion occurs via the central route when the receiver of the message expends much energy processing the issues or arguments under consideration. On the other hand, persuasion resulting from non-issue-relevant thinking, such as the receiver's impressions of the message, source or channel, occur by way of the peripheral route. Petty and Cacioppo argue that attitude change is more likely to be enduring with the central route. When the peripheral route is taken, attitude adjustments usually exist only as long as the persuasion cues remain salient. Therefore, the more cognitive activity (elaboration) a message receiver engages in, the more likely that attitude change will endure.

Petty and Cacioppo prefer the central route for constructing messages and effecting behavioral changes. However, much of the published research on persuasive communication in recreation settings focuses predominantly on situations where a communicator prepares and delivers a peripheral message designed to produce attitudinal and/or behavioral change in message receivers. Burgoon and Miller (1985) have labelled this focus the "passive message reception paradigm" of persuasive communication research. For example, the current persuasive communication efforts of state and federal land management agencies that are responsible for managing occupied grizzly bear habitat would be categorized as part of this paradigm.

The models of communication discussed earlier (Fishbein and Ajzen 1975; Petty and Cacioppo 1986) allow managers to ask a number of questions about their persuasive campaigns: What message contents are most effective in correcting inappropriate backcountry visitor behavior? What sources are perceived as most credible by message receivers, and thus most effective in altering inappropriate behaviors? What channel methods are most effective for the acceptance of messages for altering backpackers' beliefs and attitudes? Many studies in the larger field of persuasive communications have examined these types of questions in a multitude of situations. However, the pertinent literature indicates mixed results from specific manipulations of source, message, channel and receiver factors to influence behavioral change.

Research on Manipulations of Message Content

Because attitudes and behaviors can be greatly influenced by the content of a persuasive message, message content is a major concern of backcountry managers. For example, recent mandates within the federal court system require Glacier National Park to provide both verbal and written warnings concerning the inherent risks associated with hiking in Glacier's backcountry. Therefore, persuasive messages must be developed to adjust backcountry users' attitudes, so that every individual is aware of and accepts these risks as a basic element of their backcountry experience. Once backcountry users accept this risk, they may be more likely to engage in behaviors that should minimize the risk of injury or death. But what message content, structure and style is the best for conveying risk and proper behavior information to backcountry visitors?

Message manipulation can reflect the strength of the source's belief and have a direct influence on the nature of persuasive communication. Not only can manipulating message content influence communication effectiveness, but also the characteristics of the source, channel and receiver are important considerations. For example, a message that has a clear, concise and logical argument may enhance the perceived credibility of the source. Adding new information via a variety of techniques (audio-visual, personal contact) manipulates channel characteristics. Message manipulation may also affect the emotional state of the receiver by creating anxiety or fear.

Fear arousal has been frequently used as a message content area for hazard warnings, has been studied at length for its influence on attitude and behavioral change, and is a constant source of debate in persuasive communication research. The original hypothesis in fear appeals research was that a message containing high amounts of fear-arousing information will be more persuasive than a weaker fear-arousing message. This hypothesis is largely based on the theory of cognitive dissonance, assuming that once fear or emotional tension is aroused, the audience will become motivated to accept the recommendations advocated by the communicator to reduce anxiety or dissonance.

In a study of the effects of threat appeal in messages concerning hazards in grizzly bear habitat, Hodgson (1974) attempted to determine how fear or threat is associated with backcountry users' attitudes toward bears and appropriate behaviors. He determined that strong threat appeals were significantly less persuasive than mild threat appeals. Hodgson states that the use of explicit, gruesome details in messages may result in increased aggression towards the grizzly bear. Fear appeals may increase negative attitudes toward the bear and lead to reduced public support for the protection of the species and the habitat it needs for survival.

Research on Source Influences

The source of a message exerts powerful influence on message acceptance and on resulting behavior. A major factor affecting attitudinal and behavioral change is communicator or source credibility - "... a set of perceptions held by the message receiver pertaining to the source of a message" (King 1975). High credibility sources tend to be more persuasive than low credibility sources (e.g., Bannister 1986, Clark and Maass 1988, and McNeill and Stoltenberg 1988).

Initial research on the attitudinal effects of communicator credibility focused primarily on the receiver's perceptions of the message source. Various characteristics of source credibility that may contribute to a receiver's perceptions are expertise, trustworthiness and attractiveness (Smith 1982). In an examination of individuals' perceptions of trustworthiness, Petty and Cacioppo (1981) state that a source who intends to persuade another is presumed to be less trustworthy than a person who simply wants to communicate some message to the audience. Petty and Cacioppo further their argument by reporting that source attractiveness and expertise appear to facilitate persuasion.

Another area of research in source influences has focused on the multiple source effect. Harkins and Petty (1987) indicate that information presented by multiple sources receives more cognitive examination than information presented by a single source. However, the strength of these messages also plays an important role in influencing receiver attention and creating agreement with the message. Their research indicated that weak arguments presented by a single source result in greater receiver agreement than weak arguments presented by multiple sources.

Source credibility has not been an important variable in research on persuasive messages in recreational settings. Only a few studies can be found. For example, Cockrell et al. (1984) studied the amount of influence held by definers (people who verbally expressed expectations of others) and models (those who served as examples) on recreationists' behavior during a river trip outing. These found that models (guides, family members and others present on the trip) were significantly more influential than definers (managers, family, friends, and other recreationists not present on the trip). Braithwaite and McCool (1989), however, reported that rangers contacted during the process of receiving a backcountry permit were perceived as the most reliable of 17 sources of information about grizzly bears. Dowell and McCool (1986) reported no differences in effectiveness of the same message (about minimum impact camping behavior) delivered by a uniformed male agency employee and a non-uniformed female to Boy Scouts.

While it is difficult to generate applications to recreation settings from such little research, it does appear that visitor perception of source credibility is an important factor in effectively communicating messages about hazards. Personal contact with agency staff may be the most effective way of communicating these messages. An important factor implied, but not directly studied in these investigations is the visitor's perception of the source's knowledge. We would expect that this is a major factor in explaining the results found above.

Research on Channel Influences

Messages come in a variety of forms and use numerous channels. Persuasive messages are usually aimed at stimulating a receiver's senses, particularly sight and sound. In recreation settings, the channels most frequently used by managing agencies include brochures and paper handouts, talks by ranger-naturalists, signs, park newspapers, and personal contact by agency staff. In many dispersed recreation settings, however, relatively few visitors may learn about an area and its hazards from agency communications. For example, Lucas (1985) found that only about 20 percent of the visitors to the Bob Marshall Wilderness used agency information to plan their trips. Thus, it is important for managers to understand where and how visitors receive information about hazards.

Trahan (1987) reports that the most important sources of information for Yellowstone backcountry hikers about bear dangers were printed materials handed out at the park entrance, and signs and bulletin boards. In Glacier National Park, McCool and Braithwaite (1989) reported that most visitors prefer verbal communication with backcountry rangers over other forms of communication. Sundstrom's (1985) study of efforts at Denali National Park to educate visitors about the behaviors appropriate in the backcountry found that most park visitors believed written information to be the most effective interpretive method for communicating knowledge about bears. However, backcountry users indicated that information delivered verbally was the most effective.

However, excessive noise or distraction can severely hinder effective communication of these messages. For example, abundant auditory and visual stimuli compete for visitors' attention as they are receiving backcountry permits. Most permits are obtained in crowded park visitor centers during the summer months. A backcountry permit office located in a quiet room with no background noise or other distractions would be ideal. The less competition for an individual's attention during the communication process, the greater the probability of reception and acceptance of the persuasive message.

Research on Receiver Characteristics

All forms of communication are transactional in nature. People's cognitive responses may be as important in facilitating attitude and behavior change as message characteristics (Smith 1982). Therefore, an understanding of specific audience characteristics should give communicators some insight into the potential cognitive responses to particular messages. Receiver characteristics include not only previous experience and social- demographic variables, but also normative group influences and cognitive processing.

Cacioppo et al. (1986) suggest that individuals who engage in extensive issue-relevant thinking when forming a position on an issue tend to display an enduring attitude change, and also exhibit stronger attitude-behavior correspondence. Individuals must be motivated and have the ability to process information cognitively in order for attitude change to occur.

For example, researchers need to investigate whether backpackers have both the motivation and the ability to process thought-provoking messages concerning appropriate behavior. If backpackers do not, messages demanding little cognitive processing may be a more effective strategy for attitude and behavior change. Considerable research (Roggenbuck and Lucas 1981) demonstrates that backcountry users are highly educated, many with college or advanced degrees. This suggests that backcountry users are able to receive and process messages that have some level of complexity, and then combine past experiences with newly acquired knowledge to make judgements about behavior in problematic situations.

As wilderness managers know, however, a wide variety of individuals use backcountry settings. This audience variability is a source of frustration to many designers of persuasive communication programs because to most effectively persuade recreationists, managers must identify and tailor messages to particular audiences. One audience may respond positively to a specific message while another may react neutrally or negatively. Audience characteristics that may facilitate the persuasion process in one type of communication may detract from the effectiveness of another. Audience characteristics other than educational attainment include previous experience, the type of recreational group, and degree of recreation activity specialization.

Individuals' previous backcountry experience and degree of activity specialization affect the reception and acceptance rates of relevant agency messages. For example, Huffman and Williams (1986) found that experienced visitors were less likely to use trail information, while highly specialized recreationists tended to seek out additional information. A study of backpackers at Glacier National Park indicated that individuals who typically travel with family members tended to be more susceptible to influence from others than individuals who backpack alone (Braithwaite 1989). In addition, inexperienced backpackers were more susceptible to social influence than experienced backpackers. These findings indicate that family groups and inexperienced backpackers are prime audiences for persuasive messages containing strong social normative factors.

Social normative factors or reference group norms can be powerful influences on the reception and acceptance of agency persuasive communications. Fishbein and Ajzen (1975) argue that, ultimately, perceptions of significant others' expectations concerning appropriate behavior, and individual motivations to comply with those expectations, are important influences. These factors may influence behavior as much as changes in beliefs brought about by a persuasive communications program, a hypothesis which has not been addressed in the literature concerning effectiveness of agency communications.

One can easily visualize how the normative expectations of camping companions could outweigh anonymous advice about appropriate behavior contained in an agency brochure. Braithwaite and McCool (1989), however, reported little evidence supporting the influence of reference groups on backcountry camper behaviors to reduce confrontations with grizzly bears. Additional research needs to address these issues in depth. Since people attend to messages and information on their own volition, persuasive messages may maximize an audience's attention, reception, comprehension, retention and yielding if the message is directed toward specific needs and characteristics of that audience. Future research must identify not only the specific needs and characteristics of recreationist audiences, but also the type of persuasive messages they prefer. Do audiences prefer cognitively stimulating messages or simple messages focusing on a single issue? Are messages containing social normative factors more persuasive than messages without? The effectiveness of future persuasive communication programs should increase as message producers attain greater understanding of how their audiences receive and process information.

Visitor Beliefs and Knowledge

In their study of interactions between hikers and grizzly bears, Jope and Shelby (1984) stated that visitor attitudes toward bears are difficult to change and may not be directly related to the behaviors that actually cause or avert confrontations. Attitudes are affected by how a person perceives a risk and deals with danger or uncertainty, and by potential behavioral responses when a hazard is present. In a survey of visitors to Glacier National Park, Mihalic (1974) found that 65 percent had positive attitudes toward bears. Reading outdoor literature or past knowledge had little effect on these attitudes. When given a hypothetical bear encounter most respondents chose the "correct" course of action. However, the behavioral intentions of the respondents were unrelated to attitude intensity.

Trahan (1987) studied overnight and day visitors in one section of Yellowstone's backcountry, and most respondents felt that grizzly bears did not represent a significant danger for backcountry hikers. Over 20 percent of the day-hikers and 30 percent of the overnight users indicated that they would like to get close enough to a grizzly bear for a "good look," a behavior contradictory to minimizing confrontations with bears. On the other hand, Maw's (1987) study of visitors to Waterton Lakes National Park in Canada determined that 80 percent of the respondents considered bears to be somewhat dangerous. It was further determined that individuals with high levels of knowledge about bears exhibited more positive attitudes toward bears than visitors with low knowledge levels.

Linking Messages, Attitudes, and Risk Reducing Behavior

Because visitors to dispersed recreation settings frequently expose themselves to a variety of hazards, and even the slightest exposure to a hazard constitutes a risk, land management agencies must persuade recreationists to engage in behaviors that will minimize the risk associated with particular recreational activities or settings. As previously discussed, Fishbein and Ajzen (1975) state that understanding human behavior requires linking beliefs and attitudes with behavioral intentions. A persuasive message can cause receivers to question their initial attitudes, evaluate the recommended adoption of a new attitude, and provide incentives for yielding to and retaining new attitudes.

Studies by Chester (1977), Sundstrom (1985), Trahan (1987) and Maw (1987) have examined linkages among sources of information, attitudes and participation in recommended appropriate behaviors. Chester's study of human-bear interactions in Yellowstone revealed that a considerable number of backcountry users engaged in activities such as not securing food properly, cooking highly odorous foods, and not carrying out garbage that could increase the number of detrimental encounters with grizzly bears.

Sundstrom evaluated Denali National Park's efforts to educate visitors about appropriate behaviors for bear country. Consistent with Chester's findings, Sundstrom found that visitors to Denali were also engaging in behaviors that would increase the likelihood of an incident with a bear. Sundstrom's evaluation of the relationship between knowledge of grizzly bears and behavior indicated that knowledge levels provided little help in predicting visitor behavior.

Similarly, although Maw (1987) found that individuals with high knowledge levels concerning the biology of bears were more likely to exhibit positive attitudes toward bears, he also found that visitor perceptions of bears as hazards apparently are not linked to behavior. For example, while over 80 percent of survey respondents considered bears to be dangerous, 55 percent indicated that they took no precautions to prevent an encounter with a bear. Therefore, the message "bears are dangerous" is being transferred to the visitor, but the portion of the message indicating the need to adopt specific behaviors to reduce the amount of danger associated with travelling in grizzly habitat is not being universally accepted.

McCool and Braithwaite's (1989) study of backcountry user behavior in Glacier National Park also reported confusing linkages among beliefs, information and behavior. In this study, the strength of ecologistic beliefs (i.e., the bear is an essential component of a naturally functioning ecosystem) was positively correlated with knowledge about grizzly bear biology, knowledge of appropriate behavior, and understanding the consequences of appropriate behavior (in terms of reducing confrontations). Negativistic beliefs (bears should be avoided) were negatively or not associated with these variables. Participation in appropriate behaviors was positively correlated with ecologistic beliefs with the exception of the distance some respondents would wish to be from a bear: individuals scoring higher on ecologistic beliefs wanted to get closer to bears than individuals scoring lower on this scale. The message to be careful at campsites and along trails seems to be accepted and applied, but the message about keeping away from bears altogether may be counterbalanced in highly ecologistic individuals by their motivation to actually see a bear in the wild. This research indicates that even though backcountry visitors are receiving persuasive messages, the information may not always influence behavior in a positive manner. Most past research has assumed a direct link between belief change and behavioral change. Since in many recreation settings it is often easier to measure overt behavioral change than belief change, researchers have assumed that if behavioral change occurred, belief change also occurred. Very little research on behavioral change in hazardous recreation settings has investigated the entire belief change process as described by Fishbein and Ajzen (1975). Is the lack of behavioral change a direct result of the lack of belief change? Future research in dispersed recreation areas needs to address belief change and its relationship to message reception and behavioral change.

REMAINING QUESTIONS

Message effectiveness with respect to hazards in dispersed and natural recreation settings remains a largely ignored area of inquiry. Present research focuses primarily on the issue of wildlife hazards, particularly confrontations with bears. This lack of broader hazard/risk research is unfortunate because the consequences of ineffective messages can be significant in terms of injury or death to visitors as well as financial loss to recreationists and to managing agencies. We propose that recreation research address the following issues:

What are we telling visitors about hazards? We need to simply compile an inventory (data base) of messages agencies are sending through their brochures, newspapers, rangers, and campfire programs. Are these messages technically correct? Are messages from different agencies and personnel consistent with each other?

What messages channels seem to be most effective for the different users of recreation areas? We know there is great diversity in client backgrounds; how can we use this knowledge to design message channels that will more effectively communicate agency intentions and needs to visitors? What channels do different visitor types perceive as credible or reliable? What levels of educational attainment do we target among different users? How do visitor motivations affect their perceptions of message sources?

What seems to be the most effective medium for facilitating message reception about hazards? Fear arousal? Humor? Science? Religion? How do these facilitating contacts relate to visitor background, motivations, beliefs and experience?

Social group contexts may affect message acceptance and performance of appropriate behavior. People rarely visit dispersed and natural recreation areas alone. Therefore, most messages will be received within the context of social group norms and expectations of appropriate behavior. How do social norms affect message acceptance rates, and the eventual performance of appropriate behavior? What social norms facilitate this process, and which norms hamper it? How can messages be designed to build upon social-normative influences?

How do visitor beliefs affect message acceptance? People bring a variety of beliefs about hazards to recreational settings. Some of these beliefs may be ill-formed, others may derive from careful thought and analysis. Which visitor beliefs are important in message acceptance and in performance of appropriate behavior? How can message design take advantage of existing beliefs for increased effectiveness? What factually incorrect beliefs do visitors hold and what message design is most effective in countering them?

We suspect that many of these questions plague researchers in other disciplines as well. Research traditions from the fields of communication and social psychology provide legitimate theoretical frameworks from which to expand everyone's knowledge in this area.

In our review of the literature of research on message effectiveness in recreation settings, we were struck by the obvious lack of well-constructed and theoretically-based studies. Much of the research we have seen appears to be well-motivated but lacking in the conceptual foundations needed to make significant and continuing contributions to the knowledge of message effectiveness. Given the great importance managers of natural settings have placed on information as a major management tool, this is a puzzling situation. If agencies are to rely on information to accomplish their objectives in protecting resources and enhancing recreational experiences, a well developed and continuous research program on information is essential.

We are also surprised at not finding more research literature on the effectiveness of hazard communications in recreational settings. While we can learn much from research in the health disciplines, it seems important, given the consequences of exposure to hazards, to develop a research program specifically aimed at hazard message effectiveness in recreational settings. We suggest that researchers and managers join in cooperative projects that will help advance our understanding of message effectiveness. In particular, we recommend further examination of the two models of the persuasive communications process that we briefly reviewed here: Fishbein and Ajzen's (1975) approach to attitude and behavioral change and Cacioppo and Petty's (1986) theory on central and peripheral message construction. These two approaches — more explicitly presented in Chapters 2 and 4 of this volume — have much to offer both researchers and managers.

REFERENCES

Ajzen, Icek; Fishbein, Martin. 1980. *Understanding attitudes and predicting social behavior*. Englewood Cliffs, NJ: Prentice Hall, Inc. 278 p.

Allen, Stewart. 1980. Risk recreation: a literature review and conceptual model. In: Meier, J., Morash, T., Welton, G. (eds.) *Readings in high adventure outdoor activities*. Salt Lake City, UT: Brighton Press. 52-81.

Allen, Stewart. 1981. Comment: No-rescue wilderness—a risky proposition. *Journal of Forestry*. 79(3): 153-154.

American Alpine Club. 1987. *Accidents in North American Mountaineering: 1987*. New York, N.Y. 95 p.

Anderson, Dorothy H. 1980. Displacement of visitors within the Boundary Waters Canoe Area Wilderness. Fort Collins, CO: Colorado State University. Unpublished Ph.D. dissertation. 138 p.

Bannister, Brendan D. 1986. Performance outcome feedback and attributional feedback: interactive effects on recipient responses. *Journal of Applied Psychology. 71*: 203-210.

Bauman, Laurie J.; Siegel, Karolynn. 1987. Misperception among gay men of their risk for AIDS associated with their sexual behavior. *Journal of Applied Social Psychology. 17*: 329-350.

Beck, Lawrence A.; McAvoy, Leo H.; Dustin, Daniel L. 1989. Limits to growth: institutional barriers to recreationist self-sufficiency. *Western Wildlands. 15*(1): 28-33.

Bennett, Peter D.; Kassarjian, Harold H. 1972. *Consumer behavior*. Englewood Cliffs, NJ: Prentice-Hall Inc. 184 p.

Braithwaite, Amy M. 1989. Effects of normative and informational social influence on visitor behavior in occupied grizzly bear habitat. Missoula, MT: University of Montana. Unpublished Master's thesis. 139 p.

Braithwaite, Amy M.; McCool, Stephen F. 1989. Social influences and backcountry visitor behavior in occupied grizzly bear habitat. *Society and Natural Resources. 2*: 273-283.

British Medical Association Guide. 1987. *Living with risk*. New York, NY: John Wiley and Sons. 179 p.

Brown, Perry J.; Haas, Glen. 1980. Wilderness recreation experiences: the Rawah case. *Journal of Leisure Research. 12*: 229-241.

Brown, Perry J.; McCool, Stephen F.; Manfredo, Michael J. 1987. Evolving concepts and tools for recreation user management in wilderness: a state-of-knowledge review. In: Proceedings—National Wilderness Research Conference: Issues, State of Knowledge, Future Directions. *Gen. Tech. Report INT-220, Ogden, UT*. USDA Forest Service. Intermountain Forest and Range Experiment Station: 320-346.

Burgoon, Michael; Miller, Gerald R. 1985. An expectancy interpretation of language and persuasion. In: H. Giles and St. Clair, R. N. (eds.) *Recent advances in language, communication, and social psychology*. London: Lawrence Erlbaum Associates Ltd. 199-229.

Cacioppo, John T.; Petty, Richard E.; Dao, Chuan Feng; Rodriguez, Regina. 1986. Central and peripheral routes to persuasion: an individual difference perspective. *Journal of Personality and Social Psychology. 51*: 1032-1043.

Cella, W. B.; Keay, J. 1979. Annual bear management and incident report, Yosemite National Park: survey of bear incidents, including survey of reasons and amounts of damage done; also a survey of bear information visitors received from the Park Service. National Park Service, El Portal, CA. 23 p.

Chester, James M. 1977. Factors influencing human-grizzly interactions in a backcountry setting. In: *Bears—their biology and management: Selections from the 4th International Conference on Bear Research and Management*. The Bear Biology Association Conference Series Number 3. pp. 351-357.

Clark, Russell D.; Maass, Anne. 1988. The role of social categorization and perceived source credibility in minority influence. *European Journal of Social Psychology. 18*: 381-394.

Cockrell, David E. 1981. Motivation, satisfaction, and social influence in wild river recreation. Moscow, ID: University of Idaho. Unpublished Ph.D. dissertation. 302 p.

Cockrell, David; Bange, Steve; Roggenbuck, Joseph. 1984. Persuasion and normative influence in commercial river recreation. *Journal of Environmental Education. 15*(4): 20-26.

Cole, David N.; Ranz, Beth. 1983. Temporary campsite closures in the Selway-Betterroot Wilderness. *Journal of Forestry. 81*: 729-732.

Dowell, D. L.; McCool, Stephen F. 1986. Evaluation of a wilderness information dissemination program. In: Proceedings—National Wilderness Research Conference - *Current Research Gen. Tech. Report INT-212, Ogden, UT.* USDA Forest Service. Intermountain Forest and Range Experiment Station: 494-500.

Engel, James F.; Blackwell, Roger D.; Miniard, Paul W. 1986. *Consumer behavior*. Chicago: Dryden Press. 633 p.

Fedler, Anthony J. 1981. Attitudes, social norms and behavioral intentions as inputs for understanding recreation. College Station, TX: Texas A&M University. Unpublished Ph.D. dissertation. 161 p.

Festinger, Leon. 1957. *A theory of cognitive dissonance*. Stanford: Stanford University Press. 291 p.

Fishbein, Martin; Ajzen, Icek. 1975. *Belief, attitude, and intention and behavior: an introduction to theory and research.* Reading, MA: Addison-Wesley Publishing Co. 572 p.

Harkins, Stephen G.; Petty, Richard E. 1987. Information utility and the multiple source effect. *Journal of Personality and Social Pyschology. 52*: 260-268.

Harris, Daniel M.; Guten, Sharon. 1979. Health-protective behavior: an exploratory study. *Journal of Health and Social Behavior. 20*: 17-29.

Hawkins, Del. I.; Best, Roger J.; Coney, Kenneth A. 1983. *Consumer behavior: implications for marketing strategy.* Plano, TX: Business Publications, Inc. 645 p.

Haydock S.; McCool, S. F. 1976. *Hikers of the Virgin River Narrows*. Institute for the Study of Outdoor Recreation and Tourism. Logan, UT: Utah State University. 80 p.

Hodgson, Ronald W. 1974. Some effects of threat appeal in messages about hazards of grizzly bears in national parks: an experiment. Lansing, MI: Michigan State University. Unpublished Ph.D. dissertation. 138 p.

Houston, C. 1968. The last blue mountain. In: S. Z. Klausner (ed.) *Why man takes chances.* Garden City, NY: Doubleday and Co. 49-58.

Huffman, Michael G.; Williams, Daniel R. 1986. Computer versus brochure information dissemination as a backcountry management tool. In: Proceedings—National Wilderness Research Conference-Current Research. *Gen. Tech. Report INT-212, Ogden, UT.* USDA Forest Service. Intermountain Forest and Range Experiment Station: 501-508.

Job, R. F. Soames. 1988. Effective and ineffective use of fear in health promotion campaigns. *American Journal of Public Health. 78*: 163-167.

Jope, Katherine; Shelby, Bo. 1984. Hiker behavior and the outcome of interactions with grizzly bears. *Leisure Sciences. 6*: 257-270.

Kates, Robert W. 1962. *Hazard and choice perception in flood plain management.* Chicago: University of Chicago, Department of Geography Research Paper No. 78. 157 p.

King, Stephen W. 1975. *Communication and social influence.* Reading, MA: Addison-Wesley Publishing Co., Inc. 169 p.

Larwood, L. 1978. Swine flu: a field study of self-serving biases. *Journal of Applied Social Psychology. 8*: 283-289.

Levy, J. 1978. *Play behavior.* New York, NY: John Wiley and Sons. 232 p.

Lucas, Robert C. 1983. The role of regulations in recreation management. *Western Wildlands. 9*(2): 6-10.

Lucas, Robert C. 1985. Visitor characteristics, attitudes, and use patterns in the Bob Marshall Wilderness Complex, 1970-1982. *Research Paper INT-345, Ogden, UT.* USDA Forest Service. Intermountain Forest and Range Experiment Station: 32 p.

Maw, Roland R. 1987. Visitor attitudes, perceptions, and knowledge concerning bears and bear management practices, Waterton Lakes National Park, Canada. Edmonton, Alberta. University of Alberta. Unpublished Ph.D. dissertation. 187 p.

McAvoy, Leo H.; Dustin, Daniel L. 1981. The right to risk in wilderness. *Journal of Forestry. 79*(3): 150-152.

McCool, Stephen F.; Braithwaite, Amy M. 1989. Beliefs and behaviors of backcountry campers in Montana toward grizzly bears. *Wildlife Society Bulletin. 17*: 514-519.

McCool, Stephen F.; Lucas, Robert C. 1989. *Managing resources and people within wilderness: accomplishments and challenges. Managing America's Enduring Wilderness Resource: A Conference.* Paper presented at Minneapolis, MN: September 11-14. 64-75.

McNeill, Brian W.; Stoltenberg, Cal D. 1988. A test of the elaboration likelihood model for therapy. *Cognitive Therapy and Research. 12*: 69-80.

Mihalic, D. A. 1974. Visitor attitudes toward grizzly bears in Glacier National Park, Montana. Lansing, MI: Michigan State University. Unpublished Master's Thesis. 131 p.

Mitchell, James. 1984. Hazard perception studies: convergent concerns and divergent approaches during the past decade. In: Saarinen, Thomas F.; Seamon, David; Sell, James L. (eds.) *Environmental perception and behavior: an inventory and prospect.* Chicago: University of Chicago, Department of Geography Research Paper Number 209. 33-59.

National Safety Council. 1988. *Accident facts.* Chicago, IL. 104 p.

Petty, Richard E.; Cacioppo, John T. 1981. *Attitudes and persuasion: classic and contemporary approaches.* Dubuque, IA: Wm. C. Brown Company Publishers, Inc. 314 p.

Petty, Richard E.; Cacioppo, John T. 1986. The elaboration likelihood model of persuasion. *Advances in Experimental Social Psychology. 19*: 123-205.

Rankin, Janna S. 1989. The rescue doctrine: a reinterpretation of the common law. *Western Wildlands. 15*(1): 24-27.

Robertson, L. S. 1977. Car crashes: perceived vulnerability and willingness to pay for crash protection. *Journal of Community Health. 3*: 136-141.

Robertson, Rachel D. 1981. An investigation of visitor behavior in wilderness areas. Iowa City, IA: University of Iowa. Unpublished Ph.D. dissertation. 184 p.

Roggenbuck, Joseph W.; Lucas, Robert C. 1987. Wilderness use and user characteristics: a state-of-knowledge review. In: Proceedings—National Wilderness Research Conference: Issues, State of Knowledge, Future Directions. *Gen. Tech. Report INT-220. Ogden, UT.* USDA Forest Service. Intermountain Forest and Range Experiment Station: 204-245.

Sax, Joseph. 1980. *Mountains without handrails: reflections on the national parks.* Ann Arbor, MI: University of Michigan Press. 152 p.

Smith, Mary J. 1982. *Persuasion and human actions: a review and critique of social influence theories.* Belmont, CA: Wadsworth Publishing Co. 383 p.

Sundstrom, Thord C. 1985. An analysis of Denali National Park and Preserve's management program to educate visitors regarding proper behavior while in bear country. Laramie, WY: University of Wyoming. Unpublished Master's thesis. 291 p.

Trahan, Richard G. 1987. *Wilderness user's attitudes, information use and behaviors in relation to grizzly bear dangers in the backcountry: a survey of backcountry users in the Northeastern section of Yellowstone National Park.* Greeley, CO. University of Northern Colorado. 35 p.

Viscusi, W. Kip; Magat, Wesley A.; and Huber, Joel. 1986. Informational regulation of consumer health risks: an empirical evaluation of health hazards. *Rand Journal of Economics. 17*(3): 351-365.

Weinstein, N. D. 1984. Why it won't happen to me: perceptions of risk factors and susceptibility. *Health Psychology.* *3:* 431-457.

White, Gilbert F. 1974. *Natural hazards: local, national, global.* New York, NY: Oxford University Press. 288 p.

11

Research in Tourism Advertising

Michael J. Manfredo

Alan D. Bright

Glenn E. Haas

INTRODUCTION

J. D. Hunt has suggested (1986) that tourism has "come of age in the 1980s." The attention devoted to tourism in presidential speeches and by the mass media, its promotion by international committees and state and local tourism bureaus, and the explosive growth in tourism curricula at colleges and universities all lend ample support to Hunt's contention. Rightly or wrongly, tourism is increasingly perceived as the answer to a variety of socioeconomic, political, and environmental challenges. Statistics attest to the magnitude of tourism's economic impact: in 1988 travelers spent more than $337 billion on travel and tourism. Those dollars generated more than 5.5 million jobs with aggregate earnings exceeding $70 billion (National Travel and Tourism Awareness Council 1989).

Clearly, advertising is playing an increasingly significant role in the tourism industry, yet the dollar amount of tourism advertising is unknown. State tourism promotion budgets provide a clue: the United States Travel Data Center projected the total 1987-1988 budget for the 50 state tourism agencies to reach an all-time high of $283 million (Hunt 1986), with allocations for advertising ranging from 26 percent to 54 percent of agency budgets (Table 1). Among the top ten states, the average allocation for advertising topped 44 percent of budget.

Table 1
Summary of selected state tourism budget information for the top ten states for fiscal year 1987-1988 proposed budgets

Top Ten States by largest Tourism Budgets	Overall Budget	Advertising Budgets (percent of overall budget)	Research Budgets (percent of overall budget)
New York	$21,543,300	$11,400,000 (53%)	N/A*
Illinois	20,543,300	10,000,000 (49%)	N/A*
Hawaii	13,665,000	4,266,000 (31%)	$318,000 (2%)
Pennsylvania	12,130,400	5,729,400 (47%)	145,000 (1%)
Texas	11,969,000	5,250,000 (44%)	50,000 (.4%)
Michigan	10,889,400	4,900,000 (45%)	178,800 (2%)
Florida	10,723,551	4,790,176 (45%)	262,352 (2%)
Massachusetts	10,173,972	5,000,000 (49%)	2,228,524 (22%)
Tennessee	9,390,400	2,450,750 (26%)	150,000 (2%)
Alaska	9,346,800	5,066,900 (54%)	164,000 (2%)

*Indicates data are not available
Source: United States Travel Data Center, *Survey of State Travel Offices 1987-1988* (Washington, DC: United States Travel Data Center, 1988), pp.5, 10, 48-52.

If tourism came of age in the 1980s, we would propose that the 1990s will be the decade of dramatic advances in technological capabilities. As researchers, we also predict tourism's maturing in intellectual substance. Specifically, with marketing seen as the best answer to increasing competition for the tourist dollar among private enterprises and public agencies, tourism advertising promises to enjoy a quantum leap in sophistication. Travel and tourism professionals will achieve the competitive advantage partly through advances in quality research to guide their advertising efforts.

The purpose of this chapter is to provide an overview of available tourism advertising research and to suggest future directions that will increase research and advertising effectiveness. In the first of the chapter's two major sections, we review what we found to be a paucity of available tourism advertising research, noting that much of it is applied in nature. In the second part of the chapter, we review the broader research field of consumer psychology and its applications to advertising, concluding that tourism professionals have much to gain from the integration of consumer psychology research with future tourism advertising research.

PAST RESEARCH IN TOURISM ADVERTISING

Concurrent with growth within the tourism industry, recent research on various aspects of the tourism industry has increased significantly. Much of this research has focused on the social, political, economic and cultural impacts of tourism, and areas such as tourism planning and policy and tourist characteristics and motivations have also been examined. However, the area of tourism advertising has received relatively limited attention. In reviewing four journals in the tourism and recreation field, *Annals of Tourism Research*, *Journal of Travel Research*, *Journal of Leisure Research* and *Leisure Sciences*, we found that, since 1980, only about five percent of the articles pertain directly to tourism advertising. Furthermore, research also shows that journals in marketing, advertising and general business rarely address tourism, and all but ignore tourism advertising (Rovelstad and Blazer 1983).

Two basic types of available research relate to advertising. The first "indirect" type does not examine aspects of tourism advertising directly but carries tangential advertising implications. Specific topics that fall into this category include market segmentation, perception/image of tourist areas, and traveler destination choice. We have omitted these "indirect" articles in our review.

The second type of research directly relates to tourism advertising. Areas examined in this category include: (1) conversion studies, (2) information seeking, (3) comparison of advertising content and media and (4) validation of conceptual issues. We will address each of these four areas in turn.

Conversion Studies

Much of the existing research related to tourism advertising is evaluative and uses conversion study methodology. Advertising conversion research measures the number of inquiries that are "converted" into actual visitation, and also measures the resulting costs and revenues. Typically, this involves a promotional campaign in which readers of advertisements can mail in a coupon or call a telephone number and in return, receive a package of brochures and travel information on the advertised destination. Subsequently, a questionnaire concerning visitation and spending is sent to persons who requested the information. Conversion studies are usually conducted to evaluate advertising campaigns and to compare the effectiveness of various media vehicles (Woodside and Ronkainen 1982; Yochum 1985), or one ad campaign with another (Woodside 1981). Advantages of this methodology include the high precision of visitation and expenditure estimates that can be achieved and the low costs of collecting data (Schweiger and Hruschka 1980).

Despite the widespread use of conversion study methodology in the travel and tourism area, researchers have raised questions concerning the validity and reliability of traditional coupon conversion studies. The first problem involves whether advertisements actually produce visitation. Conversion studies generally do not ascertain whether tourists decided to visit the area based on the information received or whether tourists wrote for more information *after* deciding to visit an area. Yet studies generally imply that exposure to an advertisement generates a certain number of inquiries, leading to a certain number of visits and, in turn, resulting in "X" dollars being spent at the tourist destination.

In reality, conversion studies may be limited to making descriptive statements about the relationship between the advertisement and the search for information rather than identifying a specific causal relationship. Ballman, Burke, Blank and Korte (1984: 28) point out: "Just exactly what caused [trip] decisions to be made and how much can be credited to the advertising campaign are separate and highly complex issues." As suggested by Woodside (1981), determining whether or not the advertising and the literature influenced visitation to a destination requires the use of true experiment methodologies. However, we were unable to find any studies in the available literature that employed this type of methodology, and Woodside (1990) has noted this should be a priority for future research.

A second problem inherent in the use of the conversion study methodology relates to the effects attributable to those who observe the initial advertisement but do not request further information. Perhaps upon seeing the initial ad, peoples' awareness and interest are aroused, thus leading to purchase. Those nonrespondents omitted from the group receiving a conversion survey might include people with high familiarity with a destination, those who have adequate access to information, or those who are simply not information seekers.

A third problem involves the influence of non-response bias on the results of the conversion study. Studies suggest that respondents from second and third mailings have a lower tendency to visit an area than those respondents to the first mailing (Woodside and Ronkainen 1984). Hunt and Dalton (1983) used two questionnaire mailings to estimate the conversion rate of a Utah Travel Council ski advertising program. The first mailing produced a conversion rate of 38 percent, whereas the second mailing produced a 26 percent conversion rate. The combined mailings resulted in a conversion rate of 33.2 percent with a response rate of 68.4 percent. If the results from the first mailing had been used alone, rather than an average of the first two mailings, Utah would have grossly overestimated the number of skiers responding to the advertising campaign. This would have led to a significant overestimation of total visitor expenditures.

Assuming a similar difference between a second and third mailing, as suggested by Ellerbrock (1981), the overestimation of response would be even greater. Hunt and Dalton (1983) concluded that mail-questionnaire conversion studies require a response rate of at least 80 percent to overcome inflated results due to non-response bias. They also concluded that three or more mailings are required to reach an 80 percent response rate.

A fourth problem with conversion study methodology involves the presence of recall bias in the estimation of trip expenditures. Mak, Moncur and Yonamine (1977), in a 1974 study for the Hawaii Visitor Bureau, found that reported expenditures of visitors filling out a mail questionnaire subsequent to their trips were nearly 15 percent lower than expenditures reported by visitors who filled out a diary as their expenditures took place. This difference implied a deviation of about $140 million in total visitor expenditures for 1974. These researchers concluded that survey respondents attempting to recall spending after returning home tend to underestimate their expenditures.

Finally, identification of the sponsor of the study is problematic in many conversion studies—for two reasons. First, this may lead to positive bias in answering the questions. Second, identifying several travel destinations in the study, as opposed to identifying only the sponsor, provides the additional benefit of learning about travel behavior in terms of several competing destinations. The sponsor of a conversion study should not be identified; rather, an independent research agency should be identified as the sponsor of the study (Woodside 1981).

Alternatives to conversion study methodology. In light of the problems inherent in conversion studies, alternatives to this methodology have been introduced. Studies introducing possible alternatives compare the use of visitor surveys and conversion studies as substitute methods of data collection, and examine an econometric model that predicts visitation rates to a recreation area.

In a study involving nonresident automobile visitors to Nebraska, Perdue and Botkin (1988) examined the differences and similarities between an inquiry conversion study and a survey of a sample of state visitors. Their purpose was to determine if it is appropriate to use two methods of data collection simultaneously. They found that the two methodologies produced different estimates of virtually every travel behavior and visitor characteristic tested. For example, respondents to the conversion study tended to live in the Great Lakes region, the area originally targeted by the Nebraska Division of Travel and Tourism. Conversely, a higher proportion of those in the visitor survey traveled from the far west and states adjacent to Nebraska. Significant differences were also found between the two methodologies in the magnitude, distribution and probability of making each type of expenditure.

Based on these results, it was concluded that estimating visitation rates and expenditures using either method interchangeably appears to be inappropriate. Perdue and Botkin suggested that a conversion study should be limited to an evaluation of advertising campaigns, whereas a visitor survey should be used to describe visitors to an area during a specified time period.

Another alternative to conversion studies has been proposed in the form of an econometric model that considers several factors influencing the level of visitation to a particular recreation area. Silberman and Klock (1986) developed a travel cost model in order to estimate the effects that aggregate advertising, destination substitutability, visitor income levels, and travel costs may have on aggregate sales. Aggregate sales were measured as the number of individuals from a particular origin zone visiting a particular recreation area as a proportion of the total population of the origin zone. The model is estimated using multiple regression and is as follows:

$$V_{ij} / P_i = (C_{ij}, Y_{ij}, S_{ij}, A_{ij}) \text{ where}$$

$V_{ij} =$ the number of individuals from the ith origin zone visiting the jth recreation area;

$P_i =$ population of the ith origin zone;

$C_{ij} =$ travel cost per party of visitors from the ith origin zone to the jth recreation area;

$Y_{ij} =$ median income level of visitors from the ith origin zone to the jth recreation area;

$S_{ij} =$ an index of the degree of substitutability of alternative recreation sites to an individual from origin i visiting site j;

$A_{ij} =$ a measure of the amount of advertising for recreation area j in origin zone i.

Silberman and Klock recognized several limitations of this model, such as omitted variables and linear specification of nonlinear relationships. In addition, whereas conversion studies employ individual data, the travel cost model uses origin zones as observations, potentially leading to aggregation bias.

In summary, conversion studies have attained wide use because they obtain managerially useful information at a reasonable cost. Perhaps their greatest advantage is in providing relative measures useful for examining trends or comparing different methods of advertising. Because of various methodological problems, conversion studies, as they are currently employed appear to have serious shortcomings when used to estimate total visitation rates and expenditures attributable to advertisements.

Information Seeking

Since the use of conversion studies is grounded in certain assumptions about consumer information seeking, it is not surprising that the search for information has been the object of a number of tourism advertising studies. Information seekers are of interest because they are presumably ready to act (i.e., make a purchase or visit a given area), and because they may be susceptible to persuasive appeals. Since information campaigns are frequently only effective with small segments of their audiences, there may be advantages to placing greater emphasis on reaching the information seeker directly (Manfredo 1989a).

Although external search for information has been found to be minimal when consumer products are involved (Newman and Staelin 1972), information seeking is generally believed to be quite high for tourism services. Gitelson and Crompton (1983) identified three reasons that external searches for information may be used to a greater extent in the tourism field:

1. A vacation involves a high risk purchase, requiring considerable investments of time and money. The greater the perceived risk of the purchase, the greater the tendency toward an external search for information.

2. As opposed to the typical retail shopper, vacationers have less opportunity to view what they are purchasing in advance, causing the search for information to involve more time and energy.

3. Vacationers often visit new destinations during each vacation. Unfamiliarity with a destination may persuade individuals to spend more time and effort searching for new information.

Research on information search in the area of tourism has focused on descriptive aspects of search behaviors and identifying the determinants of information seeking.

Research on the descriptive aspects of search behaviors has traditionally focused on the vehicle by which information is obtained. For example, in a study of state welcome centers in North Carolina, Gitelson and Perdue (1987) found that 62 percent of the surveyed visitors to welcome centers stopped specifically for a state highway map that included descriptions of North Carolina attractions. Also, 25 percent of the respondents stopped for information about routes, 22 percent about the attractions, and 20 percent about lodging information.

In support of a convergency of findings in similar studies, Gitelson and Crompton (1983) found that the primary sources of information for travelers were friends and relatives (71 percent). However, nearly three-fourths of the subjects were exposed to at least one additional source of information such as the print media (26 percent), broadcast media (20 percent), travel consultants (31 percent) and destination-specific travel literature (50 percent). Destination-specific travel literature was also found to be a significant source of information by Etzel and Wahlers (1985), who reported that nearly 45 percent of vacation travelers used this type of literature.

Less descriptive research has sought to explain the determinants of information seeking. Gitelson and Crompton (1983) examined information search differences as a function of trip motivations and planning horizons. Those subjects whose primary trip goal was to experience excitement were the most likely to use more sources of information. There was also a significant, direct relationship between travelers with longer planning horizons and the number of outside information sources used.

Psychographic factors such as cultural interest, comfort, familiarity/convenience, activity, opinion leadership and knowledge-seeking, and sociodemographic variables such as age, sex, and education level have been hypothesized as potential determinants of the level of external information search. Schul and Crompton (1983) examined the ability of travel-specific psychographic factors and sociodemographic variables to (1) predict and explain external search behavior, and (2) differentiate between respondents engaging in active versus passive external search behavior. These researchers found that search behavior is better explained by travel-specific psychographics than by sociodemographics. Although various travel-specific psychographics were significant in explaining the length of planning horizons during which external information search occurred, these psychographics did not explain differences in the levels to which travelers used multiple sources of travel information while planning their vacations.

Finally, those vacationers who engaged in active information search showed a significantly greater tendency to desire many activities, have an interest in cultural attractions, require comfortable accommodations, and prefer guided tours and prearranged schedules than did passive information seekers.

In his study of the determinants of information search, Manfredo (1989a) proposed that many advertising strategies assume the constraint reduction model of information seeking. Manfredo examined the proposal that persons seeking information regarding recreation experiences exhibit positive interests, attitudes and intentions toward participation, but may be constrained by inadequate knowledge. Four groups of people with various levels of experience in information search were compared regarding their interests, attitudes and intentions of participation in an ocean charterboat trip along the Oregon coast. Information seeking was defined as whether or not the individuals requested a free brochure on charterboating when given the opportunity to do so. This research found that inexperienced boaters who sought information had positive attitudes, interest and intentions to participate, but showed significantly less prior knowledge of boating than experienced boaters. Experienced seekers and experienced nonseekers of information both had positive attitudes, a high interest in and a high level of knowledge of charterboating; however, the experienced information seekers showed significantly higher intentions to participate than any other group. Manfredo (1989a) concluded that while constraint reduction may be the basis for information search among inexperienced information seekers, experienced seekers may be seeking information to reassure their existing knowledge or to add small increments of knowledge that are difficult to measure in standard survey methodologies.

Manfredo (1989a) suggested that an alternative explanation for information seeking other than to acquire information might be sought by examining the recreational motives for information seeking. This explanation suggests that some people seek information not to lessen constraints but as a recreational end in itself. Evidence for this recreational motive may be found in Bloch, Sherrel and Ridgeway (1986), whose research suggested that many consumers obtain product information with two objectives: to increase product knowledge and to experience pleasure. Although both objectives may be satisfied simultaneously, these researchers found that the recreational benefits were more prevalent than knowledge acquisition.

Comparison of Advertising Content and Media

At the core of the advertiser's task is the actual development of the advertisement, which involves answering a host of questions related to the message to be conveyed, the ad format and design, and the media to be used. Research related to this task, excluding research attempting to gain better focus on target audiences, has examined the effects of advertising across several advertising media and the visual effects of advertising.

Comparison of advertising media. One of the most basic choices for the advertiser is which media vehicles to use. The seemingly endless options include brochures, catalogs and flyers, print media such as travel magazines and newspapers, television and radio, or any combination of the above. In addition to variability in potential media vehicles, other variables such as geographic location, services or attributes analyzed, messages, and advertising formats make generalizations very difficult. Some research has provided isolated descriptive studies that indicate the utility of a particular approach in a given situation. For example, Bass, Manfredo, Lee and Allen (1989) concluded that brochures are ineffective for directly increasing participation in charter angling, but may influence awareness levels and intentions to take future trips.

A greater concentration of research, however, has focused on comparing the effectiveness of various media types when these media are employed with the more conventional conversion methodology. Woodside and Ronkainen (1982) examined the 1979/1980 advertising campaign of North Carolina's tourism promotion program in order to evaluate the differences in effectiveness of black-and-white versus color advertisements in magazines and newspapers. Black-and-white advertisements in newspapers had the highest conversion rate of 61 percent, followed by black-and-white magazine ads (50 percent), color newspaper ads (44 percent) and color magazine ads (43 percent). These researchers also questioned the efficacy of measuring the economic value of advertising campaigns using only a CPM (cost-per-thousand readers) criterion. Woodside and Ronkainen indicated that there is a significant level of uncertainty in economic data using this criterion only. Instead, they measured the average revenue-per-inquiry (RPI) and the average cost-per-inquiry (CPI). RPI and CPI are calculated for each type of media campaign as follows:

RPI = estimated revenue generated by advertising/total inquiries
CPI =total advertising costs/total inquiries

Results indicated that while the CPI for black-and-white magazine advertisements ($5.36) is lower than that of black-and-white newspaper ads ($7.27), the RPI is also significantly lower ($123 vs $192). Overall, the black-and-white newspaper ads slightly outperformed the black-and-white magazine ads in terms of the CPI/RPI ratio (3.4 percent vs. 4.3 percent). Newspaper advertisements again exhibited a better CPI/RPI ratio for color than did magazine advertisements (16.3 percent vs. 24.7 percent).

Yochum (1985) conducted a similar study of tourism advertising at the city of Virginia Beach, Virginia. In addition to a comparison of newspaper and magazine advertising, the conversion rate and economic performance of a radio ad campaign were evaluated. Again, the conversion rate for newspapers (31 percent) was greater than that for magazines (19 percent), as was the rate for radio advertisements (26 percent). In terms of the CPI/RPI ratio, newspaper advertisements again outperformed magazine advertisements (3.0 percent versus 3.3 percent). For the radio campaign, however, this ratio (66.4 percent) was more than 20 times higher (less favorable) than both newspaper and magazine advertisements.

Visual effects of advertising. Another emerging area of research considers the effects of the pictorial content of advertising copy. Oleson, McAlexander and Roberts (1986) examined the impact of the visual content of advertisements on perceived vacation experiences. The purpose of their study was to (1) identify the relevant dimensions of a vacation location portrayed in advertisements, and (2) investigate the effect that different pictorial themes have upon evaluations of tourist locations made by potential travelers. Specifically, these researchers looked at the effect that familiarity with a destination, and the advertising format (e.g., locations that are stimulating, frightening, relaxing and so on) as portrayed by the pictorial theme of the advertisement, had in influencing vacationers' evaluations of a vacation experience. Oleson et al. found that familiar landmarks were seen as less stimulating, more beautiful, and more romantic destinations, suggesting that pictorial themes of advertisements do in fact have an effect on tourists' evaluations of vacation destinations.

Weaver and McCleary (1984) studied the pictorial content of an advertising plan by examining the reaction of different market segments, based on age or gender, to nine different advertising formats. The formats differed in the use of female and male models, couples and single models, and various stages of undress. These researchers found that the format of the advertisement did have an effect on the evaluations of the company presenting the advertisements. It was further noted that age of the respondent appeared to be a significant segmentation variable in assessing the perceived reputability of a travel advertiser.

Validation of Conceptual Bases

A fourth major area of research deals with conceptual bases of tourism advertising. Two lines of inquiry have attempted to validate concepts for advertising related to (1) the response of separate market segments to advertising, and to (2) multiattribute theory.

Response of separate market segments to advertising. Although much of the marketing-related research in the area of tourism and recreation involves the identification of specific travel segments, little of this research has been directed toward its specific application to tourism advertising. In general, researchers believe that market segments may differ in their sensitivities to certain types of advertising (Calantone, Schewe and Allen 1980). These differences will affect measures of, and price elasticities inherent in, various types of advertising, ultimately affecting the return on advertising investment.

Tourism advertising research that validates the use of market segmentation focuses on the use and effects of advertising on individual market segments. Woodside and Motes (1981) developed five different advertising strategies using different creative approaches, media schedules, and direct mail literature. Their goal was to determine the effect of varying advertising on five market segments in a South Carolina tourism promotion program. The market segments were preidentified by demographic, lifestyle and travel behavior profiles, and a distinct advertising program was developed for each segment. These researchers found that the conversion rates of inquiries into visits differed significantly across advertisements. Specifically, segment conversion rates were: 47 percent for the "beach vacationer," 49 percent for the "colonial sightseer," 52 percent for the "fisherman," 47 percent for the "highlands vacationer," and 58 percent for the "second home vacationer." They also found that the actual profiles of market segments responding to the specific advertisements matched well with the preidentified profiles.

Finally, this research found significant differences in the total revenues and costs produced by each market segment and advertising strategy. The CPI/RPI ratio was 9.3 percent for the "highlands vacationer," 4.6 percent for the "colonial sightseer," 3.8 percent for the "beach vacationer" and the "second home vacationer," and 3.3 percent for the "fisherman" (Woodside and Motes 1981).

Future research should focus on the development of more complex experimental designs for comparing different advertisements for different segments. In the Woodside and Motes (1981) study, each segment ad appeared in magazines deemed to be suitable for reaching the preidentified segment. To avoid confounding effects from separate advertisements and schedules of media vehicles, segment advertisements should be placed in the same media vehicle in several different time periods. This would allow more definitive conclusions about what ad performs best in what media vehicle (Woodside and Motes 1981).

Multiattribute theory. Another area of research in tourism advertising effectiveness concerns the efficacy of attribute-specific advertisements, i.e. ads that emphasize specific product attributes desired by a consumer group. Several market segmentation studies have focused on identifying trip attributes preferred by a specific market segment. These studies suggest that advertising effectiveness may be increased by using ads that focus on highly desired trip attributes. For example, Scott, Schewe and Frederick (1978) concluded that attributes that determined visitation rates to Massachusetts differed between travelers visiting the state from within 200 miles and those visiting from further than 200 miles. Scott et al. suggested that promotions targeted to those visitors from within 200 miles should concentrate on the friendliness of the local people, whereas promotions geared toward those travelers from more than 200 miles away should focus on attributes such as a clean environment, relaxing atmosphere, quality of highways, and the availability of enjoyable cold weather activities.

Manfredo (1989b) conducted a three-phased study to test the validity of this type of inference. The first phase was a survey to determine the desired attributes of a charter trip. In the second phase, color postcard ads were developed representing the highest and lowest ranked (in terms of salience) attributes of a certain trip, followed by a mass mailing of each type of post card. Phase three recorded response to postcard types and conducted a follow-up survey of recipients. The response for information was 33 percent greater with the high salience attribute, and those responding to the highly salient attribute rated that attribute higher than other attributes and exhibited intentions to purchase trips focusing on that attribute. Respondents to the low salience attribute rated that attribute highly along with other important attributes. This low salience group also showed stronger intentions to engage in a trip that featured the high salience attribute.

To summarize this section of the chapter, advertising research has not attained a prominent place in tourism related literature. Most tourism advertising research has concentrated on conversion studies and has revealed conceptual and methodological weaknesses in these studies. Other research has compared the effectiveness of different advertising media and content, has explored information-seeking behavior and, to a lesser extent, has cited basic conceptual issues regarding response rates to advertisements.

Given the incomplete picture of tourism advertising sketched by this array of studies, we now consider insights on this topic from the fields of social and consumer psychology.

Integrating Tourism Advertising Research with Consumer Psychology

In the broader context of social psychology and consumer psychology, two weaknesses of tourism advertising research become immediately apparent. One weakness is that many studies are limited by focusing on characteristics of a persuasion event that are highly situational. This might include, for example, studies that focus on media characteristics (newspaper vs. radio vs. television), audience characteristics (age, gender), sender characteristics (source credibility) and message content (humor, fear). While tourism research of this nature might be highly valuable to its partisan sponsor, its ability to generalize may be low. As noted by Petty and Cacioppo (1986), previous attempts in psychology to conceptualize these types of characteristics as acting in a simple and uniform manner across persuasion situations have been frustrating and ineffective. Instead of attempting to identify lists of factors that directly influence persuasion, the current research emphasis in psychology and consumer behavior is on understanding the basic processes that occur in persuasion and the factors that mediate this process (Bettman 1986).

The second weakness of tourism advertising research is that many studies focus solely on behavioral outcomes of advertising, such as purchase of advertising inquiries. This limited focus is unfortunate because it offers little understanding of the reasons why advertising is effective or ineffective, and it does not address nonobservable changes that over the long term, might influence purchase behaviors or interpretations of experiences with a product or service.

These weaknesses reflect the approaches to persuasion of an earlier era. While researchers in the 1970s concluded that ". . . after several decades of research . . . few simple and direct empirical generalizations can be made. . ." (Himmelfarb and Eagly 1974, p. 594), the 1980s have been ". . . a time of increased interest and theoretical refinement in the persuasion area" (Cooper and Croyle 1984).

In fact, the past two decades have seen important advancements in persuasion and consumer psychology, and in the remainder of this chapter we shall highlight some of the key developments. Our selective overview is guided by our interest in topics that seem relevant to tourism research.[1] We address three major areas: (1) high versus low levels of processing advertised information, and factors affecting processing; (2) the effects of nonverbal stimuli in advertisements; and (3) the role of affect in persuasion.

High Versus Low Information Processing of Advertised Information

Recent reviews acknowledge two broad approaches to persuasion that currently prevail in the literature (Chaiken and Stangor 1987; Tesser and Shafer 1990). One approach emphasizes detailed information processing (high processing levels), and the other (low processing levels) de-emphasizes detailed information processing (Chaiken and Stangor 1987). Interestingly, the high-low dichotomy was introduced in advertising (but not developed) as early as 1965 by Krugman.

Approaches involving high processing levels assume that purchase of a product is based on an individual's thorough evaluation of known information about each purchase alternative. Advertising is persuasive because it provides information that is integrated with and weighed against other available information. Advertisements are also persuasive to the extent that they stimulate thought and influence the evaluation process resulting in changed beliefs, attitudes and purchase intentions. One of the most widely recognized theories that assumes high levels of processing is Fishbein's and Ajzen's Theory of Reasoned Action (see Chapters 1 and 2 of this volume).

Prominent persuasion theories suggest that people will engage in detailed information processing when they are motivated and possess the ability to engage in message-relevant thinking (Chaiken and Stangor 1987; Petty and Cacioppo 1981). As theorized by Petty and Cacioppo, enduring attitude change occurs only when there is a high level of information processing, known in their theory as the *central route to persuasion* (see Chapter 4 of this volume).

Low processing explanations recognize that, frequently, people do not engage in a thorough evaluation of alternatives. Chaiken (1980;

---

1. [For a broader treatment of these topics, see Chapters 1-7 this volume, Cafferata and Tybout 1989, Chaiken and Stangor 1987, McGuire 1981, Pechman and Stewart 1989, and Petty and Cacioppo 1981]

Chaiken, Liberman and Eagly, 1989s) suggests that people use heuristics or simple decision rules in making choices. The heuristic model suggests that persuasion is often mediated by cues in the persuasive message that give it validity. For example, in selecting an airline, people might be influenced by the choices made by a well-known person who travels frequently. In selecting tourist destinations, people might base their choices on the locations featured by a specific travel magazine.

In a broader conceptualization of low information processing, Petty and Cacioppo (1981) propose the *peripheral route to persuasion*. This route suggests that persuasion can occur based on factors tangential to the message itself (e.g., message or source attractiveness). Peripheral processing encompasses a wide variety of explanations. Ads might be effective because they associate a product with positive moods or emotional states, because the product is perceived to promote social relationships with liked or powerful communicators, or because ads project a favorable social identity. Peripheral processing can affect behavior but is unlikely to produce enduring attitude change.

Although in some cases it is possible to classify theories as proposing either low or high levels of information processing, the leading theories of persuasion account for *both* high and low processing situations. For example, Petty and Cacioppo's Elaboration Likelihood Model describes both central (high processing) and peripheral (low processing) routes to persuasion (see Chapter 3 of this volume), and Chaiken's Heuristic and Systematic Processing Theory describes systematic (high) information processing and heuristic (low) information processing (Chaiken, 1980; Chaiken et al. 1989). The contrast between high and low information processing in persuasion seems to be particularly relevant to tourism advertising research. One argument is that most tourism decisions involve high information processing. Most people planning tourist ventures are investing high amounts of time and money for a tourist experience and are likely to engage in some thoughtful deliberation of information about destinations. However, the selection of individual components of the experience pertinent to tourism advertising research—such as lodging, restaurants, and recreation activities—might be more susceptible to peripheral types of decisions.

Useful directions for tourism advertising research might include examining (1) the extent of message-relevant (or elaboration) thinking that occurs in tourism choice situations, (2) the extent to which tourism ads evoke message-relevant thinking and the extent to which this thinking influences attitude, intention and behavior change, and (3) factors relevant to tourism advertising that influence message-relevant thinking.

On the latter point, researchers have examined a variety of situational and individual characteristics that theoretically affect persuasion (e.g., McGuire 1981; Chaiken and Stangor 1987; Petty and Cacioppo 1986). The following section discusses specific individual and situational factors that theoretically determine the mode of processing (message-relevant thinking) and mediate the persuasion process: message comprehension, topic involvement, prior knowledge, message repetition, source credibility, and attitude toward the ad.

Comprehension of the advertisement. An important determinant of message-relevant thinking relates to one's actual comprehension of an advertisement. Without the ability to comprehend (because of, e.g., distraction or misunderstanding), elaboration is limited (Petty and Cacioppo 1986).

Significantly, research suggests that lack of comprehension may be an obstacle to effective advertising. Russo, Metcalf and Stephens (1981) found that miscomprehension of magazine ads occurred at a rate of 50 percent. Similarly, Jacoby, Nelson and Hoyer (1982) tested the comprehension of Federal Trade Commission statements accompanying analgesic ads. They found that comprehension was completely inaccurate for 35 percent of people tested, and partially inaccurate for 40 percent. Finally, Jacoby and Hoyer (1989) examined the comprehension of 54 advertisements and determined that miscomprehension occurred at a rate of 19.3 percent and "don't know" responses occurred with 15.3 percent of subjects.

The tourism literature has directed some attention to the ability of people to comprehend tourist information. Results suggest that in many cases, printed information is written at a level beyond the comprehension of a significant number of the people for whom the information is targeted. For example, Hunt and Brown (1971) used Flesch's (1949) techniques for rating the readability and human interest levels of information in a sample of publications distributed by the U.S. Forest Service, the National Park Service, and the Bureau of Land Management. Most publications tested were "difficult" to read, were written at "the college level," would be classified as "academic" types of magazines, and had a human interest rating of "dull."

Similarly, Wolff, Kossack and Fried (1989), using the Fry Readability Formula, evaluated the level of education required to read visitor information distributed by 48 state tourism departments. These researchers found that the introductory materials of 64 percent of the states were rated above the level normally associated with mass market adult reading material.

Both of these studies suggest potential problems with the comprehension of tourist materials; however, neither actually examines the effects of more complex reading material. A valuable task for future research would be to vary the levels of readability and assess the effects on the persuasion process.

Effects of prior knowledge. Recent reviews (Bettman 1986; Cohen and Chakravarti 1990) have noted that the relationship between prior knowledge and current information processing is a major concern in the area of consumer research. Several questions about prior knowledge are directly applicable to tourism advertising. To what extent does prior knowledge (about an advertised tourism product or service) influence the attention or amount of thought given to an advertised tourism message? How does prior knowledge about a topic relate to resistance to attitude change? Does the amount of prior knowledge influence the extent to which people actively search for tourist information? To what extent does advertising contribute, overall, to consumer knowledge? Does advertising provide knowledge that actually influences the interpretation of one's experience?

Research suggests that the amount of prior knowledge held by an individual may be a particularly important influence on the acceptance of new information. In general, increased levels of knowledge appear to allow increased processing but have less effect on the message recipient. Studies show that greater amounts of prior information are associated with a higher likelihood of integration of persuasive information (Tybout and Scott 1983), the ease with which information is processed (Johnson and Russo 1984; Sujan 1985), and greater attitude-behavior consistency (Davidson, Yantis, Norwood and Montano 1985). Prior knowledge also has been associated with greater resistance to attitude change (Wood 1982); that is, the more knowledge people have about an issue, the greater their ability to argue against messages that are counter to their initial position, and the greater their ability to support arguments congruent with their initial positions (Lord, Ross, and

Lepper 1979). Furthermore, researchers have noted a "decelerating set-size effect" in which pieces of information added to an evaluation of an object become incrementally less important in influencing overall attitude (Davidson et al. 1985).

Direct knowledge experience. Apparently, the way that information is acquired has an important effect on how new information is processed. In particular, research suggests that prior information obtained through direct experience, as opposed to reading or being told about a topic, will result in higher attitude-behavior consistency (Fazio and Zanna 1981; Sample and Warland 1973) and will result in attitudes held with greater certainty (Fazio, Powell and Herr 1983). Direct experience attitudes result in more favorable responses to persuasive appeals that have a content consistent with such attitudes. Similarly, direct experience attitudes produce more resistant responses to appeals that have a content inconsistent with such attitudes (Wu and Shaffer 1987).

Research directly in the tourism and recreation areas provides further evidence that the amount of subjects' direct experience has a crucial effect on their reaction to persuasive appeals. For example, Krumpe and Brown (1982) and Roggenbuck and Berrier (1982) found that inexperienced backcountry users are more easily influenced than experienced users.

Manfredo and Bright (1991) also show support for direct experience effects in a study examining the effects of Forest Service information packets on Boundary Waters Canoe Area visitors. Causal modeling, however, shows that direct experience affected message elaboration indirectly through the level of prior knowledge. These researchers found prior knowledge to be the only *direct* effect on message elaboration, and found that prior knowledge also mediated the effects of perceived source credibility, topic involvement and status in social groups.

Past knowledge and information search. Although information search is typically discussed as a phenomenon separate from persuasion, the topic is particularly relevant when discussing past knowledge. As noted earlier, information seekers are of interest because there is greater likelihood that those seeking information are predisposed toward purchase, will elaborate upon advertised messages and are more susceptible to persuasive appeals (Manfredo 1989a).

Research concerning the effects of prior knowledge on information search has been mixed. Three explanations offer contrasting views: (1) information search decreases with increases in knowledge, because at higher levels of knowledge there is less need for new information (Kiel and Layton 1981; Reilly and Conover 1983); (2) information search increases with increases in knowledge because, as people acquire information, they can formulate new questions more easily (Jacoby, Chestnut, and Fischer 1978); and (3) the relationship between prior knowledge and information search takes on an inverted "U" shape. This occurs where information search increases until an individual acquires moderate amounts of knowledge, after which the search decreases because the need for information no longer exists (Bettman and Parks 1980; Brucks 1985; Johnson and Russo 1984).

While these explanations each have their own intuitive appeal and empirical support, the relationship between past knowledge and information search defies easy description. In this regard, research on information-seeking in tourism is not atypical. Manfredo (1989a) found no relationship between past knowledge and information seeking when examining information-seeking response to advertising for recreational charterboats. Certainly past knowledge is important in determining information seeking; however, it is likely that the effects of past knowledge are partially dependent upon other factors, such as the level of involvement, motives for information-seeking (recreational versus constraint reduction), and direct versus indirect knowledge.

Effects of ads in forming knowledge. How do advertisements affect tourists' levels of knowledge about a destination or recreation experience? Based on reports about information sources used in making tourist decisions, advertisements appear to provide only small portions of new knowledge to consumers. However, the information acquired through advertising might have effects that are not readily apparent, particularly when consumers are asked to recall these effects (Nesbitt and Wilson 1977).

Deighton (1986; Deighton and Shindler 1988) proposed that advertisements not only stimulate preferences or provide new knowledge that is processed objectively, but also influence consumers' interpretations of their experiences. These researchers proposed a model in which advertising makes salient a claim about the outcome of a product's performance which results in a causal association of the outcome and product in memory. Aspects of the consumption experience trigger recall and subsequent validation of the claim. Positive confirmations unduly influence the assessment of the validity of a claim, so that belief in the claim increases with experience. This model suggests that, in part, people form beliefs about tourist destinations and services based on a confirmation of the advertised claims. Tourists' descriptions and interpretations of their experiences will be influenced by advertised claims, as would their future preferences for taking trips to those destinations.

This explanation of advertising effects seems particularly relevant for tourism research and is an important area for further investigation. There are apparent implications for expanding markets or building new markets, directing people away from over utilized resources, and creating or changing popular images of tourist destinations.

Involvement. Although conceptual orientations differ, it is generally recognized that effective persuasion is facilitated by the recipient's interest or personal involvment in the message topic (Petty and Cacioppo 1979, 1984). For example, Leippe and Elkin (1987) found that when subjects were led to believe that information was personally relevant outside the lab setting, the subjects were more likely to think about a message. The researchers also found that when the message is personally relevant, there is a positive relationship between message quality or strength and message acceptance. In another study, Celsi and Olson (1988) introduced the topic of "felt involvement," defined as a motivational state determined by the self-relevance of the goals and values activated in a situation and the strength of the association with salient objects and actions in that situation. Celsi and Olson suggest that involvement is a function of situational sources from the immediate environment and intrinsic sources (past knowledge), and they provide evidence that "felt involvement" affects attention and comprehension of communication.

It is interesting to note that although people who are highly involved are more likely to process a message, these people are also more biased in how they process information. Studies show that highly involved people tend to process new information in a way that is biased towards their initial attitudes (Howard-Pitney, Borgida and Omoto 1986; Petty and Cacioppo 1986).

A pervasive concern in conceptualizing the topic of involvement is that of dealing with the variety of types of involvement that have been identified (Chaiken and Stangor 1987). For example, "response involvement" refers to involvement because a person will be asked to respond on a given topic; "position involvement" refers to the extent that people have a vested interest in one side of an issue; "accuracy involvement" refers to the need for information in order to make objective and fair judgments; and "self-identity involvement" deals with the importance that one attaches to favorable social impressions. The use of involvement is further confused because in some cases it is used to describe stages in information processing (e.g., Greenwald and Leavitt 1984).

A topic somewhat related to involvement is brand loyalty. Although there is no widely accepted definition of this concept, studies have focused on its behavioral component, which includes repeat purchases of the same brand over time, and its attitudinal component, an expressed intention and preference over alternatives (Jacoby and Chestnut 1978). While McCann (1974) found no differences between loyal and nonloyal customers in response to advertising, Raj (1982) suggests that loyalty mediates the effects of advertisement repetition. Raj's study examined a frequently purchased product, and found that purchase rates increased with increased repetitions of an advertisement among those people with high loyalty to particular brands. At low loyalty levels there was little brand switching as a result of the advertisements.

A topic related to involvement that has emerged in the recreation/ tourism literature is recreation specialization. This concept, introduced by Bryan (1977), refers to a continuum of behavior from the general to the specific, and is reflected in equipment, skills used, and recreation setting preferences. Using anglers as a case study, Bryan found that with increased specialization, there are changes in philosophy on specific types of resources. Other research has explored specialization as a means of identifying boater types (Donneley, Vaske and Gracfe 1986), in evaluating user conflict (Devall and Harry 1981), and as a mediator of perceived crowding (Graefe, Donnelley, and Vaske 1987). The specialization topic may be particularly useful in evaluating peoples' response to tourism advertisements.

Source credibility. Two aspects of source credibility, expertise and trustworthiness, have been identified in the literature (Cooper and Croyle 1984). On the topic of expertise, findings support the view that a communicator perceived to be an expert is more persuasive than a communicator who lacks expertise. Similar findings are less consistent when examining the effects of the trustworthiness of the communicator. Overall, both effects have been found to be more effective when subjects have low motivation to process the information (Chaiken 1980; Petty et al. 1981).

For example, Petty, Cacioppo and Schumann (1983) examined responses to disposable razor ads in terms of high versus low personal relevance, high (well known and liked celebrities) versus low (middle aged Californians) source credibility, and high (specific) versus low (vague) message quality. Results indicated that the credibility of the source had no effect on those in the high relevance group, but that message quality did (higher quality statements had greater effects). However, for those in the low relevance group, the more credible source enhanced the effects of both high and low quality messages. Eagly, Chaiken and Wood (1981) have suggested that people's view of the credibility of a source are based on the inferences they make about the cause of the communicator's advocacy. Applying attribution theory, Eagly et al. suggest that the inferences people make about credibility are based on whether people infer the cause to be situational (e.g., someone says the product or service is good because he is being paid to say so) or dispositional (someone says the product or service is good because he truly believes this). Attribution theory is related to people's knowledge of the situational constraints, and to inferred knowledge about the communicator's true attitudes. Findings in this area suggest that persuasion is magnified when communicators express attitudes contrary to what they might be expected to express (Eagly, Wood and Chaiken 1978; Wood and Eagly 1981).

Source credibility seems to be relevant to tourism advertising, particularly that conducted by state tourism departments. To what extent are these states seen as nonpartisan or as facilitators acting on behalf of both the recreationist and the provider? What effects does this view have on how people respond to state advertisements? What types of advertisements might affect perceptions of credibility?

Message repetition. A number of econometric studies have examined the purchase response to advertising repetition and have generally found that purchase rates increase with advertising (Haley 1978; Little 1979). The relationship between increased advertising and sales, however, is unlikely to be perfectly linear. For example, Rao and Miller (1975) determined that purchases follows an "S" shaped response to advertising expenditures.

Research concerning the psychological processes involved in responses to repetition has been less conclusive. Studies have been conducted to evaluate the effects of repetition on attention (Grass and Wallace 1969), recall (Appel 1971), brand evaluation (Batra and Ray 1986; Ray and Sawyer 1971), and attitude toward the ad (Cox and Cox 1988), and these studies have produced mixed results. For example, Calder and Sternthal (1980) found that increased exposure resulted in a decreased liking of advertisements for some products, while liking remained unchanged for other advertisements. Burke and Edell (1986) found that consumers who reported higher levels of exposure to an advertisement had more negative attitudes toward the ad, but the effect varied from advertisement to advertisement. Finally, Rethans, Swasy, and Marks (1986) found no relationship between advertisement exposure and advertisement liking.

These findings suggest that the effects of repetition appear to depend upon the type of advertisement being evaluated. For example, Ray and Sawyer (1971) found that repetition had less effect on "grabber" advertisements (those that are distinctive or different) than on nongrabber advertisements. Also, Silk and Vavara (1974) found that a soothing, pleasant advertisement had better response with repetition than did an irritating advertisement. Similarly, Cox and Cox (1988) provided evidence that the variability in findings may be related to the complexity of advertisements, concluding that evaluations of more complex advertisements become more positive with exposure, while those of simple advertisements do not.

Research in psychology seems to support the notion that the repetition of a persuasive message first increases agreement with the message and then decreases agreement (Cacioppo and Petty 1979; Calder and Sternthal 1980; Gorn and Goldberg 1980). Cacioppo and Petty (1979) propose that repetition affects attitude in a two stage process. In the first stage, repeated communications allow the recipient a greater opportunity to evaluate the claims being made. To support this finding, Cacioppo and Petty conducted two separate studies (1980, 1985) that showed that, with increased repetition, strong messages had a greater effect and weak messages had a weaker effect on attitude.

The second stage occurs after the person has considered and evaluated the communication. In this stage, tedium and reactance are elicited by excessive exposures, both of which lead to decreased message acceptance. Petty and Cacioppo (1986) suggest that tedium and reactance will result in decreased message effectiveness by creating negative affect or by biasing the nature of information processing in a negative direction.

Most research on repetition deals with multiple repetitions of the same message via the same mode. Little research has examined the effects of varying advertisement types, however, available research suggests that type variation may be quite important. For example, in the study by Calder and Sternthal (1980), advertisement liking decreased or was unchanged with increased repetition; however, when advertisement executions were varied, advertisement liking increased with repetition. Similarly, Harkins and Petty (1987) suggest that multiple sources of information will be more effective in the persuasion process than single sources.

Attitude toward the ad. Attitude toward the ad is a measure of a person's liking or disliking of the advertiser's attempt (i.e., the advertisement) to persuade as distinguished from attitude toward the product or service being advertised. Growing amounts of attention are being given to understanding the relationship between a person's attitude toward an ad and the evaluation of the product or service being advertised. In a study by Mitchell and Olson (1981), subjects were shown four different advertisements for facial tissues. The advertisements varied in their affective content and in the amount of product information conveyed. Results showed that subjects formed significantly different beliefs about the advertisements, but that product attribute beliefs did not explain all of the differences in attitudes toward the tissue brands. Attitude toward the ad was also found to be a significant covariate. In a later study, Mitchell (1986) provides further evidence of the distinction between attitude toward the ad and attitude toward the brand.

It has generally been determined that if people have a positive attitude toward the ad, they are more likely to have a positive attitude toward what is being advertised and will be more likely to buy it. Mackenzie and Lutz (1983) found support for a model that proposes that attitude toward the ad leads to attitude toward the brand which leads to behavioral intention. Moore and Hutchinson (1983) found that attitude toward the ad can have an enduring effect on attitude toward the brand, if the attitudes toward the ad are either positive or negative but not neutral. Furthermore, Shimp (1981) provided evidence that attitude toward the ad affects purchasing behavior.

In tourism research, attitude toward the ad could take on a unique application. In some cases, states are in fact advertising themselves. Since the "product" is the state's resources, its people, and the services they provide, it is reasonable to expect one's attitudes toward advertisements to affect one's attitudes toward a given state and its people. This suggests that when states plan their tourism advertisement campaigns, it is important to not only consider the specific beliefs or images people have about the state, but also what attitudes different advertisements will evoke that will ultimately affect these beliefs.

Non-verbal communications

A preponderance of modern advertisements include at least two of the following: a visual component (photo, video, film), a nonverbal audio component (music, environmental sounds) and a verbal component (characters speaking or voice-over text). Even though the nonverbal effects of an advertisement can be important, there has been little research in this area. This is, however, an area of growing attention (Bettman 1986; Hecker and Stewart 1988).

One aspect of nonverbal communication relates to visual effects. In an early study, Starch (1966) determined that when a print advertisement contained a picture, people were more likely to recall the advertisement than if it did not contain a picture. Also, Shepard (1967) found that people more easily recognized previously seen photographs than previously seen written sentences.

More recently, researchers have explored the relationship between verbal and visual components of an ad. Edell and Staelin (1983) compared the effects of framed photographs (photographs are accompanied by verbal information that reinforces the photograph) and unframed photographs (photograph and verbal information are unrelated). Framed photos evoked greater recall and more brand-evaluative thoughts in a shorter response time. Lutz and Lutz (1977) provided evidence that pictorial advertisements are more effective when they explicitly show the association between brand and product categories. Kisielius and Sternthal (1984) determined that people could recall more brand information when sentences and drawings were used, rather than just drawings. This finding supports the notion that visual effects operate by stimulating elaboration and result in more storage locations and pathways in memory.

Another area of investigation is the differences in effectiveness among different types of visuals in advertisements. For example,

Rossiter and Percy (1978) found that subjects rated brands more positively when photos were large rather than small. Schindler (1986) found that when color advertisements have high contrast, the ads will be more effective; he also found that a substantial proportion of existing advertisements do not employ the contrast strategy.

In the area of audio effects, studies are inconclusive concerning the role of music in advertising. Gorn (1982) found that product choice is associated with a like or dislike of the music accompanying the advertisement for the product. Furthermore, when background music was presented, its emotional appeal had a greater effect than did the attribute preference statements. Other studies suggest that music can have an effect on affective or attitudinal responses to a product. Park and Young (1986) found that under conditions of low involvement, music facilitated more favorable brand attitudes and purchase intentions, but if consumers were highly involved, music produced a distracting effect. Conversely, Stout and Rust (1986) found no differences between two commercials—one with music and one without—on cognitive and emotional responses to advertising. Furthermore, Kellaris and Cox (1989) were unable to replicate Gorn's (1982) findings.

Stout and Leckenby (1989) examined the cognitive, emotional, and purchase intent responses to 50 professionally produced television commercials, 10 without music and 40 with music. No differences were found between the emotional responses to advertisements with and without music. Minor differences were found on cognitive and purchase intent measures: commercials without music were more informative, and there was greater intent to purchase for commercials with music. Additional factors distinguished the responses among those advertisements using music. For example, slow tempo and low volume produced more emotional responses, and commercials in major modes produced more positive responses.

Part of the problem in studying the nonverbal effects of advertising is related to conceptual and methodological inadequacies. For example, cognitive approaches suggest that nonverbal stimuli produce effects in a manner similar to verbal stimuli—by affecting existing beliefs. In the case of verbal stimuli, people infer beliefs based on what is observed, which then affects their beliefs about what is advertised. This approach is exemplified by Middlestadt and Fishbein (1987), who evaluated the effect of an orange juice advertisement with only visuals and music. They found that the advertisement created certain beliefs about the naturalness of the orange juice. A variation of this approach was proposed by Mitchell (1986), who provides empirical evidence for a dual component model. This model suggests that the visual component of an advertisement can affect brand attitudes by affecting attitudes toward the advertisement or by affecting product attribute beliefs.

Some researchers have noted that there is a need to go beyond the use of the cognitive approach in studying the effects of nonverbal stimuli. This need is justified, given the multitude of forms of nonverbal communication (e.g., photographs, music, drawings and paintings, product symbols, body movements, facial expressions, spacing and touch) and the belief that nonverbal communication can elicit responses that respondents do not consciously recognize (Stewart and Hecker 1988). There is a need for research to investigate the applicability of alternative conceptual approaches (e.g., operant conditioning and modeling—see Hecker and Stewart [1988] for more on this topic). There is also a need to explore alternative methods (to self-report) for investigating nonverbal effects.

Regarding the latter point, Stewart and Hecker (1988) identified two priorities for future research. First, research methodologies must place considerable emphasis on observational technologies. Traditional self-report methods may be inadequate since, in some cases, subjects are unaware of how or why they are affected. Second, these methods must focus on studying the communication stimuli as well as the consumer's response. It seems highly probable that the disparity in findings regarding the effects of visual and musical stimuli is due to variability in stimuli. Without a greater understanding of the stimuli, it is unlikely that we will be able to reveal a consistent pattern of responses to nonverbal stimuli.

One approach to this problem has been proposed by Pechman and Stewart (1989), who suggested that advertisements and responses to these advertisements should be classified along two dimensions, one cognitively based (a systematic-heuristic dimension) and one affectively based (an emotional-nonemotional dimension). Pechman and Stewart use a procedure of having subjects classify advertisements in order to place them empirically on these dimensions.

Clearly, it is important to explore the effects of visual and musical stimuli in tourism advertising. Tourism advertisements typically convey subject matter that is difficult to effectively describe verbally, such as pleasant scenery, people engaged in action-oriented activities, or attractive living accommodations. How do visual images portrayed in such advertisements affect the beliefs and images held about destinations? This is an important area for future research.

Affective Responses to Advertisements

Another important area of debate regards the distinction between cognition and affect. A significant proportion of advertisements are not intended to convey factual information. Coulson (1989) suggests that most advertisements can be arrayed along a continuum ranging from mood-targeted advertising to rational advertising. Rational advertising provides specific product information which the advertiser assumes people will process in making their decisions. Cognitive models would presumably be best suited for explaining the effects of these types of ads.

Mood advertising says little about the product itself but evokes emotional responses, affective states or feelings that the viewer associates with the product. Cognitive theories suggest that mood advertisements create beliefs about a product, conscious or unconscious, that precede an emotional response (Anand, Holbrook and Stephens 1988). Within this view, affect is a variable like source, message, recipient and context variables that are important primarily in the way they influence cognitive processes (Cacioppo and Petty 1989). However, Zajonc (1980) has suggested that affect and cognition are independent systems, and that affect is often predominant. Zajonc also suggested that in some situations affective preferences precede cognitive appraisals. Janiszewski (1988) supported this in finding that attitude formation might occur in a preconscious processing period.

There are two noncognitive, alternative, theoretical approaches that explain the role of affect in persuasion (Pechman and Stewart 1989). One of these approaches is classical conditioning. Using this approach, advertisements that have attractive or gratifying stimuli evoke pleasant affective responses. If consumers are repeatedly exposed to the advertisement, the product advertised should evoke the same pleasant feelings. In this way, consumers acquire favorable attitudes toward a product or service even though their original beliefs may not have changed. Studies by Plummer and Hecker (1984) and Gorn (1982) suggest that more favorable attitudes can be formed through classical conditioning.

Interestingly, according to the classical conditioning paradigm, the advertising stimuli that evoke a response need not be logically related to the advertised brand in order for the emotion to be transfered to the brand. For example, a tourist advertisement depicting family togetherness in the Midwest (perhaps a coming home scene) might evoke a security feeling that a person may come to associate with that area, even though that person may not have relatives in the Midwest.

The second conceptual approach is through vicarious learning or modeling (Bandura 1969; Knouse 1986; Nord and Peter 1980). This approach proposes that people are persuaded because they vicariously experience the actions and consequences of a model. In this case, the advertisement portrays a model's reward or punishment (e.g., someone losing money on his vacation); the viewer identifies with the model and experiences an emotional reaction like the model's (anguish over loss, but relieved to know the money was in travelers checks), and the brand then acquires the capacity to evoke these responses.

A variety of criticisms have been directed toward these noncognitive approaches to understanding the role of affect (e.g., Kellaris and Cox 1989; Lazarus 1981) and recent research is divided in offering support for the cognitive model (Anand, Holbrook and Stephens 1988; Liu and Stout 1987) or for a model suggesting a separate affective system (Janiszewski 1988). However, there is general agreement as to the considerable need for research on the relationship between cognition and affect (Cafferata and Tybout 1989).

Several studies have explored various approaches for examining the emotional aspects of advertisements. Holbrook and Westwood (1989) have suggested that unidimensional evaluations (e.g., good-bad) are inadequate for dealing with the "... full sweep of rich, variegated and multifarious emotional reactions that pervade the consumption experience (p.353)." These researchers provide empirical support for use of a typology that includes eight emotional types, including acceptance, disgust, fear, anger, joy, sadness and surprise.

Aaker and Stayman (1989) propose the importance of conducting an in-depth analysis of just one emotion and examining the factors that mediate that emotion. They focus on the emotion of "warmth" and, after a review of applicable literature, suggest a variety of hypotheses regarding this emotion. For example, they propose that warmth responses are more likely when the subject is an emotional female who is interested in the subject of the commercial, and has had a similar experience to that shown in the commercial.

A related area of inquiry deals with the "feeling" states of viewers. "Subjective feeling states" refers to the mood of the viewer when experiencing an advertisement. The mood might be created by the environment in which the advertisement is viewed (e.g., a positive feeling state because one has been watching a comedy prior to the advertisement), or an ad might induce the emotional state (Mitchell 1988).

Research by Srull (1984) determined that when subjects were in a positive feeling state, they were more likely to form favorable evaluations of advertised brands. Similarly, Mitchell (1988) determined that (1) moods induced before and during an advertisement have strong effects on attitude formation, (2) moods induced during an advertisement will affect the encoding of information presented in the advertisement, and (3) changes in mood seem to have no effect on cognitive responses to the advertisement or attitude toward the ad. In support of this finding, Stayman and Aaker (1988) determined that the effects of feeling states were not totally mediated by an attitude toward the ad.

These results suggest that mood states can significantly influence how advertisements are processed. For the tourism researcher, mood states represent another important area for investigation. Questions for future research should address what types of mood states are induced by tourism advertisements; what mood states relate to positive attitudes toward advertised services, and what sorts of contexts (types of music, television programs, magazines) produce desired mood states.

Recapping, we have examined three broad areas where future tourism research could be fruitful: high versus low processing, and factors that mediate processing; effects of nonverbal stimuli; and emotional responses to advertisements. Research in consumer psychology offers the basis for this research, and serves to guide its direction.

SUMMARY AND CONCLUSIONS

This chapter's review of tourism advertising research reveals that, while tourism research has been increasing over the past decade, few studies have focused on advertising. The sparse research available provides these general findings:

—Tourism advertising research has focused on conversion studies as the primary means by which practitioners evaluate their advertising. Although conversion studies can be useful, research indicates that they typically suffer from design problems which prohibit statements of causality, omit assessments of initial advertising effects, and are affected by nonresponse and recall bias.

—The predominant sources of information consumers use to make tourism destination decisions are family and friends; however, at least half do use destination-specific travel literature. Information seeking seems to be a function of planning horizons and psychographic factors; it also seems, at least for the inexperienced tourist, to follow a constraint reduction model (i.e., the tourist has a positive interest, attitude, and intention but is constrained by inadequate knowledge). The recreational motive for information seeking may also be significant.

—Research demonstrates that newspaper ads generate both greater revenue and lower costs per inquiry than other media vehicles, and that black and white ads have greater conversion rates than color ads. Furthermore, the visual component affects evaluation of a tourist destination.

—Research suggests that directing advertisements to specific market segments is productive, and can be accomplished by identifying and promoting in the advertisements the attributes of a desired experience.

We propose that future tourism advertising research would benefit from becoming more fully integrated into the area of consumer psychology. Research indicates that attempts to generalize more conventional variables across persuasion situations have not been fruitful. The trend in this area is to examine variables basic to the persuasion process that offer better explanations and generalizations.

Three areas of study merit the attention of tourism research:

1. The examination of tourism in the context of high versus low involvement processing. What types of ads evoke these types of processing, what factors mediate processing of these advertisements, and how does the level of processing affect the purchase decision?

2. The effects of nonverbal stimuli in advertising. Some attention has been given to visual stimuli, but considerable work needs to be done. For example, what are the effects of music, natural sounds, motion, and other variables on the persuasion process?

3. The affective reactions to advertisements, and how these emotional responses affect purchase decisions. Much of the work in both tourism and consumer psychology has applied cognitive models, yet these approaches appear inadequate in assessing the response to

various types of advertisements, many of which intend to evoke an emotional response. We need improved conceptual designs and methodologies for investigating this problem.

Clearly, the types of improvements we advocate in tourism research are theoretical in nature. That is not to suggest that tourism researchers ignore the applied problems inherent in conversion studies or abandon examination of the variables specific to advertising situations. These can be very useful in evaluating the efforts of partisan sponsors. We do suggest that, in addition to these efforts, our research contributes to and draws upon generalizations from the broader field of consumer psychology. Doing so will strengthen and broaden the credibility of tourism and recreation research, and eventually improve the contributions tourism researchers make to the challenge of improving the effectiveness of tourism advertising.

REFERENCES

Aaker, D.A.; Stayman, D.M. 1989. What mediates the emotional responses to advertising? The case of warmth. In: Cafferata, P.; Tybout A.M., (eds.) *Cognitive and affective responses to advertising*; Lexington, MA: Lexington Books: p.287-303.

Anand, P; Holbrook, M.B.; Stephens, D. 1988. The formation of affective judgments: The cognitive-affective model versus the independence hypothesis. *Journal of Consumer Research. 15* (December): 386-391.

Appel, V. 1971. On advertising wearout. *Journal of Advertising Research. 1*(February): 11-13.

Ballman, G.; Burke, J.; Blank, U.; Korte, D. 1984. Toward higher quality conversion studies: redefining the numbers game. *Journal of Travel Research. 22* (Spring): 28-33.

Bandura, A. 1969. *Principles of behavior modification.* New York: Holt Rinehart and Winston.

Baas, J.M.; Manfredo, M.J.; Lee, M.E.; Allen, D.J. 1989. Evaluation of an informational brochure for promoting charterboat trip opportunities along the Oregon coast. *Journal of Travel Research. 27* (Winter): 35-37.

Batra, R.; Ray, M. 1986. Situational effects of advertising repetition: the moderating influence of motivation, ability, and opportunity to respond. *Journal of Consumer Research. 12* (March): 432-445.

Bettman, J.R. 1986. Consumer psychology. *Annual Review of Psychology. 37*: 257-89.

Bettman, J.R.; Parks, C.W. 1980. Effects of prior knowledge and experience and phase of choice on consumer decision processes. *Journal of Consumer Research. 7* (December): 234-248.

Bloch, P.H.; Sherrell, D.L.; Ridgeway, N.M. 1986. Consumer search: an extended framework. *Journal of Consumer Research. 13* (June): 119-126.

Brucks, J. 1985. The effects of product class knowledge on information search behavior. *Journal of Consumer Research. 12* (June): 1-16.

Bryan, H. 1977. Leisure value systems and recreation specialization: the case of trout fishermen. *Journal of Leisure Research. 9*(3): 174-187.

Burke, M.; Edel, J. 1986. Ad reactions over time: capturing changes in the real world. *Journal of Consumer Research. 13* (June): 114-118.

Cacioppo, J.T.; Petty, R.E. 1979. Effects of message repetition and position on cognitive responses, recall and persuasion. *Journal of Personality and Social Psychology. 37*: 97-109.

———. 1980. Persuasiveness of communications is affected by exposure frequency and message quality: a theoretical and empirical analysis of persisting attitude change:.In: Leigh, J.H.; Martin, C.R., (eds.) *Current issues and research in advertising.* Ann Arbor, MI: University of Michigan Graduate School of Business Administration.

———. 1985. Central and peripheral routes to persuasion: the role of message repetition. In: Mitchell, A.; and Alwitt, L. (eds.) *Psychological processes and advertising effects.* Hiilsdale, NJ: Erlbaum. p. 91-111.

———. 1989. The elaboration likelihood model: the role of affect and affect-laden information processing in persuasion. In: Cafferata, P.; Tybout A.M., (eds.) *Cognitive and affective responses to advertising*; Lexington, MA: Lexington Books; p.69-89.

Cafferata, P.; Tybout, A.M., (eds.) 1989. *Cognitive and affective responses to advertising.* Lexington, MA: Lexington Books. 414 p.

Calantone, R.J., Schewe, R.; Allen, C.T. 1980. Targeting specific advertising messages at tourist segments. *Tourism Marketing and Management Issues.* Washington DC: Geo. Washington University. p. 149-160.

Calder, B.J.; Sternthal, B. 1980. Television commercial wearout: An information processing view. *Journal of Marketing Research. 17* (May): 173-186.

Celsi, R.L; Olson, J.C. 1988. The role of involvement in attention and comprehension processes. *Journal of Consumer Research, 15*:2 (September): 210-224.

Chaiken, S. 1980. Heuristic versus sytematic information processing and the use of source versus message cues in persuasion. *Journal of Personality and Social Psychology. 39*: 752-766.

Chaiken, S.; Stangor, C. 1987. Attitudes and attitude change. *Annual Review of Psychology. 38*: 575-630.

Chaiken, S.; Liberman, A.; Eagly, A.H. 1989. Heuristic and systematic processing within and beyond the persuasion context. In: Uleman, J.S.; Bargh, J.A., (eds.) *Unintended thought: limits of awareness, intention and control.* New York, NY: Guilford.

Cohen, J.B; and Chakravarti, D. 1990. Consumer psychology. *Annual Review of Psychology. 41*: 243-288.

Cooper, J.; Croyle, R.T. 1984. Attitudes and attitude change. *Annual Review of Psychology. 35*: 395-426.

Coulson, J.S. 1989. An investigation of mood commercials. In: Cafferata, P.; Tybout A.M., (eds.) *Cognitive and affective responses to advertising.* Lexington, MA: Lexington Books. p. 21-30.

Cox, D.S.; Cox, A.D. 1988. What does familiarity breed? Complexity as a moderator of repetition effects in advertisement evaluation. *Journal of Consumer Research. 15* (June): 111-116.

Davidson, A.R.; Yantis, S.; Norwood, M.; Montano, D.E. 1985. Amount of information about the attitude object and attitude-behavior consistency. *Journal of Personality and Social Psychology. 49*: 5: 1184-1198.

Deighton, J. 1986. Advertising as influence on inference. *Advances in Consumer Research, 13*: 558-561.

Deighton, J.; Schindler, R.M. 1988. Can advertising influence experience? *Psychology and Marketing. 5*:2 (Summer): 103-115.

Devall, B.; Harry J. 1981. Who hates whom in the great outdoors: The impact of recreation specialization and technologies of play. *Leisure Sciences. 4*:4; 399-418.

Donneley, M.P.; Vaske, J.J.; Graefe, A.R. 1986. Degree and range of recreation specialization: toward a typology of boating-related activities. *Journal of Leisure Research. 18*:2: 81-95.

Eagly, A.H.; Wood, W.; Chaiken, S. 1978. Causal inferenes about communicators and their effect on opinion change. *Journal of Personality and Social Psychology. 36*: 424-435.

Eagly, A.H.; Chaiken, S.; Wood, W. 1981. An attribution analysis of persuasion. In: Harvey, J.H.; Ickes, W.J.; Kidd, R.F., (eds.) *New directions in attribution research.* Hillsdale, NJ: Erlbaum. 3: 37-62.

Edell, J.A.; Staelin, R. 1983. The information processing of pictures in print advertisements. *Journal of Consumer Research. 10* (June): 45-60.

Ellerbrock, M.J. 1981. Improving coupon conversion studies. *Journal of Travel Research. 19* (Spring): 37-38.

Etzel, M.J.; Wahlers, R.G. 1985. The use of requested promotional material by pleasure travelers. *Journal of Travel Research. 23* (Spring): 2-6.

Fazio, R.H.; Zanna, M.P. 1981. Direct experience and attitude-behavior consistency. In: Berkowitz, L. (ed.) *Advances in experimental social psychology.* New York, NY: Academic Press. 14:161-202.

Fazio, R.H.; Powell, M.C.; Herr, M.P. 1983. Toward a process model of the attitude-behavior relation: accessing one's attitude upon mere observation of the attitude object. *Journal of Personality and Social Psychology; 44*; 723-735.

Flesch, R. 1949. *The Art of Readable Writing.* Harper and Row, New York, NY. 237 pp.

Gitelson, R.J.; Crompton J.L. 1983. The planning horizons and sources of information used by pleasure vacationers. *Journal of Travel Research. 21* (Winter): 2-7.

Gitelson, R.J.; Perdue, R.R. 1987. Evaluating the role of state welcome centers in disseminating travel related information in North Carolina. *Journal of Travel Research. 24* (spring): 15-19.

Gorn, G.J. 1982. The effects of music on choice behavior: A classical conditioning approach. *Journal of Marketing 46*: (March): 421-424.

Gorn, G.J.; Goldberg, M. 1980. Children's responses to repetitive TV commercials. *Journal of Consumer Research. 6* (March): 421-424.

Graefe, A.R.; Donnelley, M.P.; Vaske, J.J. 1987. *Crowding and specialization: A reexamination of the crowding model.* Paper presented at the National Wilderness Conference. Fort Collins Co. July 23-26, 1985.

Grass, R.; Wallace, W.H. 1969. Satiation effects of television commercials. *Journal of Adveritisng Research. 9* (September): 3-8.

Greenwald, A.G.; Leavitt, C. 1984. Audience involvement in advertising: four levels. *Journal of Consumer Research. 11*: 581-592.

Haley, R. H. 1978. Sales effects of media weight. *Journal of Advertising Research; 18*(3): 9-18.

Harkins, S.G.; Petty R.E. 1987. Information utility and the multiple source effect. *Journal of Personality and Social Psychology. 52*(2); 260-268.

Hecker, S.; Stewart, D.W., (eds.) 1988. *Nonverbal communication in advertising.* Lexington, MA: Lexington Books. 296 pp.

Himmelfarb, S.; Eagly, A.H., (eds.) 1974. *Readings in attitude change.* New York, NY: Wiley. 665 pp.

Holbrook, M.B.; Westwood, R.A. 1989. The role of emtoion in advertising revisited: testing a typology of emotional responses. In: Cafferata, P.; Tybout A.M., (eds.) *Cogntive and affective responses to advertising*; Lexington, MA: Lexington Books. p. 353-371.

Howard-Pitney, B.; Borgida, E.; Omoto, A.M. 1986. Personal involvement: An examination of processing differences. *Social Cognition. 4*: 39-57.

Hunt, J.D. 1986. Tourism comes of age in the 1980s. *Journal of Park and Recreation.* October: 30-36, 66.

Hunt, J.D.; Brown, P.J. 1971. Who can read our writing? *Journal of Environmental Education. 2*:4 (Summer): 27-29.

Hunt, J.D.; Dalton, M. 1983. Comparing mail and telephone for conducting coupon conversion studies. *Journal of Travel Research. 21*: 3: 16-18.

Jacoby, J.; Chestnut, R.W.; Fischer, W. 1978. A behavioral approach in nondurable purchasing. *Journal of Marketing Research. 15* (November): 532-544.

Jacoby, J.; Chestnut, R.W. 1978. *Brand loyalty measurement and management.* New York: NY: Wiley.

Jacoby, J.; Nelson, M.C.; Hoyer, W.D. 1982. Corrective advertising and affirmation disclosure statements: their potential for confusing and misleading the consumer. *Journal of Marketing Research 46*: 61-72.

Jacoby, J.; Hoyer, W.D. 1989. The comprehension/miscomprehension of print communication: selected findings. *Journal of Consumer Research. 15* (March): 434-443.

Janiszewski, C. 1988. Preconscious processing effects: the independence of attitude formation and conscious thought. *Journal of Consumer Research. 11* (June): 542-550.

Johnson, E.J.; Russo, J.E. 1984. Product familiarity and learning new information. *Journal of Consumer Research. 11* (June): 542-550.

Kellaris, J.J.; Cox, A.D. 1989. The effects of background music in advertising: a reassessment. *Journal of Consumer Reseach, 16*:1 (June): 113-18.

Kiel, G.C.; Layton, R.A. 1981. Dimensions of consumer information seeking behavior. *Journal of Marketing Research. 18*: 233-39.

Kisielius, J.; Sternthal, B. 1984. Detecting and explaining vividness effects in attitudinal judgments. *Journal of Marketing Research 21*: 54-64.

Knouse, S.B. 1986. Brand loyalty and sequential learning theory. *Psychology and Marketing. 3*(Summer): 87-98.

Krugman, H.E. 1965. The impact of television advertising: learning without involvement. *Public Opinion Quarterly. 29* (Fall): 249-356.

Krumpe, E.; Brown, P.J. 1982. Redistributing backcountry use through information related to recreation experiences. *Journal of Forestry. June*: 360-362, 364.

Lazarus, R.S. 1981. A cognitivists reply to Zajonc on emotion and cognition. *American Psychologist. 36*; 222-223.

Leippe, M.R.; Elkin, R.A. 1987. When motives clash: issue involvement and response involvement as determinants of persuasion. *Journal of Personality and Social Psychology. 52*(2): 269-278.

Little, J.D. C. 1979. Aggregate advertising models: the state of the art. *Operations Research, 27*: 629-667.

Liu, S.S.; Stout, P.A. 1987. Effects of message modality and appeal on advertising acceptance. *Psychology and Marketing. 4*:3 (Fall): 167-187.

Lord, C.G.; Ross, L.; Lepper, M.R. 1979. Biased assimilation and attitude polarization: the effects of prior theories on subsequently considered evidence. *Journal of Personality and Social Psychology. 37*:2089-2109.

Lutz, K.A.; Lutz, R.J. 1977. Effects of interactive imagery on learning: applications to advertising. *Journal of Applied Psychology. 62*: 493-498.

MacKenzie, S.B.; Lutz, R.J. 1983. Testing competing theories of effectiveness via structural equation models. *Proceedings of the Winter Conference, American Marketing Association.* p. 70-75.

Mak, J.; Moncur, J.; Yonamine, D. 1977. How or how not to measure visitor expenditures. *Journal of Travel Research 16*(1): 1-4.

Manfredo, M.J. 1989a. An investigation of the basis for external information search in recreation and tourism. *Leisure Science. 11*(1): 29-45.

———. 1989b. A test of assumptions inherent in attribute-specific advertising. *Journal of Travel Research. 27*(Winter): 8-13.

Manfredo, M.J.; Bright, A.D. 1991. A model for evaluating the effects of recreation communication campaigns. *Journal of Leisure Research. 23*: 1:1-20.

McCann, J.M. 1974. Market segment response to market decision variables. *Journal of Marketing Research. 11*: 399-412.

McGuire, W.J. 1981. Theoretical foundations of campaigns. In: Rice, R.E.; Paisley, W.J., (eds.) *Public Communication Campaigns*. Beverly Hills, CA: Sage Publications. p. 41-70.

Middlestadt, S.; Fishbein, M. 1987. *Non-cognitive effects on attitude formation and change: fact or artifact?* Paper presented to the sixth annual advertising and consumer psychology conference, Chicago IL.

Mitchell, A.A. 1986. The effect of verbal and visual components of advertisements on brand attitudes and attitude toward advertisement. *Journal of Consumer Research. 13*: 12-24.

———. 1988. Current perspectives and issues concerning the explanation of "feeling" advertising effects. In: Hecker, S. Stewart, D.W., (eds.) *Nonverbal communication in advertising*. Lexington, MA: Lexington Books. p. 127-143.

Mitchell, A.A.; Olson, J.C. 1981. Are product attribute beliefs the only mediator of advertising effects on brand attitude? *Journal of Marketing Research; 18*: 318-332.

Moore, D.L.; Hutchinson, J.W. 1983. The effects of ad affect on advertising effectiveness. *Advances in Consumer Research. 10*: 526-531.

National Travel and Tourism Awarenes Council. 1989. (1988 estimates of tourism's impact on the U.S. economy). Unpublished raw data.

Nesbitt, R.E.; Wilson, T.D. 1977. Telling more than we can know: verbal reports on mental processes. *Psychological Review. 84*(30): 231-59.

Newman, J.W.; Staelin, R. 1972. Pre-purchase information seeking for new cars and major household appliances. *Journal of Marketing Research. 9* (August): 249-257.

Nord, W.R.; Peter, P.J. 1980. A behavior modification perspective on marketing. *Journal of Marketing. 44*: 36-47.

Oleson, J.E.; McAlexander, J.H.; Roberts, S.D. 1986. The impact of the visual context of advertisments upon the perceived vacation experience. *Tourism Services Marketing: Advances in Theory and Practice*. Volume II. p. 260-269.

Park, C.W.; Young, S.M. 1986. Consumer response to television commercials: The impact of involvement and background music on brand attitude formation. *Journal of Marketing Research. 23* (February): 11-24.

Pechman, C.; Stewart, D.W. 1989. The multidimensionality of persuasive communications: theoretical and empirical foundations. In: Cafferata, P.; Tybout A.M., (eds.), *Cognitive and affective responses to advertising*, Lexington, MA: Lexington Books. p. 31-65.

Perdue, R.R.; Botkin, M.R. 1988. Visitor survey versus conversion study. *Annals of Tourism Research. 15*: 76-87.

Petty, R.E.; Cacioppo, J.T. 1979. Issue involvement can increase or decrease persuasion by enhancing message-relevant cognitive responses. *Journal of Personality and Social Psychology. 37*:1915-1926.

_____. 1981. *Attitudes and persuasion: Classic and contemporary approaches*. Dubuque, IA: WM. C. Brown. 314 pp.

_____. 1984. The effects of involvement on responses to argument quantity and quality: central and peripheral routes to persuasion. *Journal of Personality and Social Psychology. 46*: 69-81.

_____. 1986. The elaboration likelihood model of persuasion. In: Berkowitz L. (ed.) *Advances in Experimental Social Psychology*. New York, NY: Academic Press. 19:123-205.

_____; Cacioppo, J.T.; Heesacker, M. 1981. The use of rhetorical questions in persuasion: a cognitive response analysis. *Journal of Personality and Social Psychology. 40*: 432-440.

_____; Cacioppo, J.T.; Schumann D. 1983. Central and peripheral routes to advertising effectiveness: The moderating roles of involvement. *Journal of Consumer Research. 10*:2(September): 135-146.

Plummer, J.T.; Hecker, S. 1984. Consumer empathy and advertising. In: Sewart, D.W., (ed.) *Proceedings of the Division of Consumer Psychology, APA 1984 Annual Convention*, Toronto, Canada. p.3-4.

Raj. S.P. 1982. The effects of advertising on high and low loyalty consumer segments. *Journal of Consumer Research. 9*: 77-89.

Rao, A.G.; Miller, P.B. 1975. Advertising/sales response functions. *Journal of Advertising Research. 15*(2): 7-15.

Ray, M.L.; Sawyer, A.G. 1971. Repetition in media models: a laboratory technique. *Journal of Marketing Research, 8*: (February): 20-29.

Reilly, M.D.; Conover, J.N. 1983. Meta-analysis: integrating results from consumer research studies. *Advances in Consumer Research 10*: 510-513.

Rethans, A.; Swasy, J; Marks, L. 1986. Effects of television commercial repetition, receiver knowledge and commercial length: a test of the two factor model. *Journal of Marketing Research. 23* (February): 20-29.

Roggenbuck, J.W.; Berrier, D.L. 1982. A comparison of the effectiveness of two communication strategies in dispersing wilderness campers. *Journal of Leisure Research. 14*:1:77-89.

Rossiter, J.R.; Percy, L. 1978. Visual imaging ability as a mediator of advertising response. *Advances in Consumer Research. 5*: 621-629.

Rovelstad, J.M.; Blazer, S.R. 1983. Research and strategic marketing in tourism: a status report. *Journal of Travel Research. 22*(Fall): 2-7.

Russo, J.E.; Metcalf, B.L.; Stephens, D. 1981. Identifying misleading advertising. *Journal of Consumer Research. 8* (September): 119-131.

Sample, J.; Warland, R. 1973. Attitude and prediction of behavior. *Social Forces. 51*: 292-304.

Schindler, P.S. 1986. Color and contrast in magazine advertising. *Psychology and Marketing. 3*:69-78.

Schul, P.; Crompton, J.L. 1983. Search behavior of international vacationers: travel-specific lifestyle and sociodemographic variables. *Journal of Travel Research 22*(Fall): 25-30.

Schweiger, G.C.; Hruschka, H. 1980. Analysis of advertising imquiries. *Journal of Advertising Research. 20* (5): 37-39.

Scott, D.; Schewe C.D.; Frederick, D.G. 1978. A multi-attribute brand/multi-attribute model of tourist state choice. *Journal of Travel Research. 17*: 23-29.

Shepard, R.N. 1967. Recognition memory for words, sentences, and pictures. *Journal of Verbal Learning and Verbal Behavior. 6*:156-163.

Shimp, T.A. 1981. Attitude toward the ad as a mediator of brand choice. *Journal of Advertising Research. 10*: 9-15.

Silberman, J.; Klock, M. 1986. An alternative to conversion studies for measuring the impact of travel ads. *Journal of Travel Research* (Spring): 12-16.

Silk, A.J.; Vavara, T.G. 1974. The influence of advertisings' affective qualities on consumer response. In: Hughes, G. D.; Ray, M.L., (eds.) *Buyer/ Consumer Information Processing*. Chapel Hill NC: University of North Carolina Press.

Srull, T.K. 1984. Effects of subjective affect states on memory and judgment. In; Kinnear, T.C. (ed.) *Advances in Consumer Research*. Volume 11. Provo, UT: Association for Consumer Research.

Starch, D. 1966. How does the shape of ads affect readership? *Media/Scope. 10*: 83-85.

Stayman, D.M.; Aaker, D.A. 1988. Are all the effects of ad-induced feelings mediated by ads? *Journal of Consumer Research 15*:3 (December): 368-373.

Stewart, D.W.; Hecker, S. 1988. The future of research on nonverbal communication in advertising. In: Hecker, S.; Stewart, D.W., (eds.) *Nonverbal communication in advertising*. Lexington, MA: Lexington Books. p. 255-264.

Stout, P.A.; Rust, R.T. 1986. The effect of music on emotional response to advertising. In: Larkin, E., (ed.) *Proceedings of the 1986 Convention of the American Academy of Advertising*, Norman, OK: University of Oklahoma.

Stout, P.A.; Leckenby, J.D. 1989. Let the music play: music as a nonverbal element in television commercials. in: Hecker, S.; Stewart, D.W., (eds.) *Nonverbal communication in advertising.* Lexington, MA: Lexington Books. p. 207-223.

Sujan, M. 1985. Consumer knowledge: effects on evaluation strategies mediating consumer judgments. *Journal of Consumer Research. 12*: 31-46.

Tesser, A.; Schaffer, D. 1990. Attitudes and attitude change. *Annual Review of Psychology. 41*: 479-523.

Tybout, A.M.; Scott, C.A. 1983. Availability of well-defined internal knowledge and the attitude formation process: information integration versus self perception. *Journal of Personality and Social Psychology. 44*: 474-491.

Weaver, P.A.; McLeary, K.W. 1984. A market segment study to determine the appropriate ad/model format for travel advertising. *Journal of Travel Research. 23*: 12-16.

Wolff, R.; Kossack, S.; Fried, L. 1989. State tourism literature: how understandable are the messages? In: Henderson, K.A.; McAvoy, L.H. (eds.) *Abstracts of the Proceedings of the 1988 NRPA Leisure Research Symposium.* National Recreation and Parks Association, Alexandria, VA. p. 67.

Wood, W. 1982. Retrieval of attitude-relevant information from memory: effects on susceptability to persuasion and on intrinsic motivation. *Journal of Personality and Social Psychology. 42*:798-810.

Wood, W.; Eagly, A.M. 1981. Stages in the analysis of persuasive messages: the role of causal attributions and message comprehension. *Journal of Personaltiy and Social Psychology. 40*:246-259.

Woodside, A.G. 1981. Measuring the conversion of advertising coupon inquirers into visitors. *Journal of Travel Research. 19*(Spring): 38-41.

_____; 1990. Measuirng advertising effectiveness in destination marketing strategies. *Journal of Travel Research. 29* (Fall): 3-8.

Woodside, A.G.; Motes, W.H. 1981. Sensitivities of market segments to separate advertising strategies. *Journal of Marketing 45*(1): 63-73.

Woodside, A.G.; Ronkainen, I.A. 1982. Travel advertising: newspapers versus magazines. *Journal of Advertising Research. 22*(3): 39-43.

_____. 1984. How serious is nonresponse bias in advertising conversion research? *Journal of Travel Research. 23*(Spring): 34-37.

Wu, C.; Shaffer, D.R. 1987. Susceptability to persuasive appeals as a function of source credibility and prior experience with the attitude object. *Journal of Personality and Social Psychology. 52*(4) 677-688.

Yochum, G.R. 1985. The economics of travel advertising revisited. *Journal of Travel Research. 24*(Fall); 9-12.

Zajonc, R.B. 1980. Feeling and thinking: preferences need no inferences. *American Psychologist. 35* (February): 151-175.

Index

A

Active/deliberative/processing 270, 271, 272, 273, 275, 276, 281, 282
Advertisements 127
Advertising content 329, 336
Affect transfer 4
Agenda-setting 129, 130
Applied behavior analysis 170, 171, 172, 175, 176, 178, 193
Appropriateness of persuasion 149, 169, 175
Arousal 214, 216, 218, 219
Attitude change 77, 78, 79, 80, 92, 95, 97
Attitude toward the ad 344, 351, 352, 353, 358
Attitude-behavior link 92
Attitude-behavior relationship 52, 53, 54, 70
Audience segmentation 138
Audience selectivity 136
Audiences 128, 129, 135, 126, 137, 138, 140, 141, 143, 144, 144
Awareness 130, 135, 138, 139, 140

B

Behavioral criterion 31
Behavioral intentions 179, 181, 182, 183, 184, 185, 192
Behavioral management 103, 126
Behavioral modeling 106, 111, 115
Behavioral systems 108, 109, 110, 116, 119, 122

C

Central route to persuasion 16, 17, 22, 81, 82, 84, 86, 93, 94, 95, 170, 172, 173, 195, 244, 250, 271, 342
Channel selection 128, 138

Channels 135, 140, 142, 145, 149, 173, 174, 181, 186, 195
Classical conditioning 4, 356
Coercive Persuasion 3
Cognitive dissonance 301, 307, 313
Cognitive structure 31, 38, 41, 46
Competence 216, 217, 218
Conflicts 149, 151, 154, 158, 161, 167, 169, 170, 193
Constraint reduction model, 335, 336, 347, 359
Consumer behavior 301, 304, 305
Consumer psychology 329, 341, 342, 358, 364
Convergence models 137
Conversion studies 329, 330, 331, 332, 333, 340, 358, 360
Criminology 214, 231, 233, 243, 252
Crowding 154, 155, 157, 160, 167, 169, 170, 193
Cultivation theory 130

D

Demographics 136, 141
Depreciative behavior 150, 161, 162, 165, 176, 189, 193, 209, 212, 214, 222, 225, 230, 233, 236, 247, 249, 250, 251
Diffusion 126, 134, 135
Diffusion theory 111
Direct coercion 237, 238, 245, 247, 249
Direct experience 62, 71

E

Econometric models 332, 350
Economic risk 304, 305
Editors 131
Effectiveness of persuasion 162, 163, 165, 189

Elaboration likelihood model 16, 17, 77, 80, 82, 86, 272, 274, 275, 311, 343
Environmental Psychology 214, 226
Equity 216

F
Feasibility of persuasion 149, 175, 177
Fire safety 143
Formative evaluation 141
Formative research 143
Frames of reference 137

G
Gatekeeping 131
Geodemographics 141
Geography 301, 302
Goal intentions 34

H
Hazards 293, 294, 295, 296 298, 300, 304, 308, 311, 313, 318, 320, 321
Health hazard 306,
Health-belief model 306
Heuristic and systematic processing theory 343
Heuristic processing 271, 274, 275
Heuristics 5, 14
Hierarchy of effects 138, 139, 140
Hunting 144
Hypnosis 3, 4

I
Impacts 149, 150, 153, 159, 163, 170, 179, 181, 187, 188, 193, 194, 195
Information processing 53, 59, 65, 66, 67, 68, 70, 139
Information seeking 127, 329, 333, 334, 335, 336, 347, 359
Interpersonal influence 134
Intervention 108, 110, 111, 112, 114, 126
Involvement 83, 90, 138, 139, 140, 143, 144, 344, 346, 347, 348, 349, 354, 359

K
Knowledge 161, 173, 178, 181, 182, 184, 185 192, 196
Knowledge gap 135, 136

L
Lifestyle segmentation 141
Littering 143
Locus of control theory 302

M
Management System 234, 236, 246, 249
Market segmentation 329, 339, 340
Media coverage 130
Message content 171, 172, 173, 174, 194, 195
Message design 128, 138, 140
Message exposure 145
Messages 133, 136, 137, 138, 139, 140, 143, 144, 145
Modeling 346, 355, 357
Mood 90, 91, 92, 97
Mood advertising 356
Motivation 143, 214, 220, 221, 222, 228
Motivation and opportunity as determinants model 70
Multi-attribute theory 338, 340
Multiple source effect 313

N
News hole 131
Nonresponse bias 359
Nonverbal communications 353, 355
Norm compliance 238, 243, 246, 249
Normative beliefs 30, 38, 39, 40, 41, 48
Normative guidelines 56, 57

P
Passive message reception paradigm 311
Passive/nondeliberative/processing 271, 272, 273, 274, 276, 282
Peripheral route to persuasion 14, 15,

16, 82, 86, 93, 95, 97, 170, 174, 195, 237, 271, 272, 274, 275, 343
Persuasion message factors 88
Persuasion recipient factors 90
Persuasion source factors 87, 88
Persuasive communication 263, 264, 268, 269, 274, 276, 279, 280, 281, 183, 285,
Physical environment system 234
Press releases 127, 131
Pricing 263, 264, 267, 277, 279, 280, 281, 282, 285
Priming 63, 65, 66
Producers 131
Propaganda 127
Psychographics 141
Public opinion 128, 129, 130
Public service announcements 127
Publics 130, 139, 140, 141, 142

R
Rational advertising 356
Reactance 85
Recipient characteristics 194, 195
Repeated expression 60, 62, 63, 66, 67, 68, 71
Reporter 133
Revenue per inquiry 359
Risk 293, 294, 302, 303, 304, 306, 308, 312, 318
Routes to persuasion 80, 82, 92
Rule of correspondence 41

S
Salience 40
Self-efficacy 94, 95, 270, 273, 286
Self-monitoring 88, 96
Self-perception theory 62
Semiotics 133
Situational theory 139, 140
Social cognitive theory 110, 111, 112, 115, 126
Social community system 234
Social policy system 234, 236
Social psychology 341
Social risk 305

Social-cognitive learning model 93
Sociology 213, 214, 231, 233, 243
Source credibility 313, 314, 341, 344, 346, 349, 350
Source of message 171, 174, 186, 195
Subjective norm 21, 22, 30, 35, 36, 37, 38, 41, 42, 46, 48
Subliminal perception 3, 4
Subterfuge 5
Systematic information processing 271, 273

T
Target beliefs 40
The process model 54, 57, 64, 65, 69, 70, 71
Theory of planned behavior 271
Theory of reasoned action 21, 22, 30, 33, 34, 35, 38, 40, 42, 43, 47, 48, 69, 92, 93, 94, 342
Timing 149, 173, 181, 194, 195
Tourism advertising 327, 329, 333, 337, 339, 341, 343, 345, 350, 355, 358, 360
Tourism promotion 142
Travel cost model 332, 333
Trends 149, 153, 154, 160, 161, 175
Two-step flow 134, 135
Typologies 219, 220, 221

U
User fees 265, 281

V
Vicarious learning 357
Visitor surveys 332

W
Waste disposal 144
Weak-effects model 107, 126

Y
Yielding 17, 18, 23